Siren Songs

PRINCETON STUDIES IN OPERA

Carolyn Abbate and Roger Parker
SERIES EDITORS

Siren Songs

REPRESENTATIONS OF GENDER
AND SEXUALITY IN OPERA

Edited by
Mary Ann Smart

PRINCETON UNIVERSITY PRESS   PRINCETON AND OXFORD

Library of Congress Cataloging-in-Publication Data

Siren songs : representations of gender and sexuality in opera / edited by Mary Ann Smart.
p.   cm. — (Princeton studies in opera)
Selected papers from Representations of Gender and Sexuality in Opera, a conference held
Sept. 1995 at the State University of New York, Stony Brook.
Includes bibliographical references and index.
ISBN 0-691-05814-8 (alk. paper) — ISBN 0-691-05813-X (pbk. : alk. paper)
1. Women in opera—Congresses.   2. Sex in opera—Congresses.   3. Feminism and
music—Congresses.   I. Smart, Mary Ann.   II. Representations of Gender and Sexuality
in Opera (1995 : Stony Brook, N.Y.)   III. Series.
ML2100 .S52   2000
782.1—dc21   00-038500

This book has been composed in Galliard

The paper used in this publication meets the minimum
requirements of ANSI/NISO Z39.48-1992
(R1997) (*Permanence of Paper*)

www.pup.princeton.edu

Printed in the United States of America

1   3   5   7   9   10   8   6   4   2

1   3   5   7   9   10   8   6   4   2
(Pbk.)

Contents

Acknowledgments

THIS BOOK BEGAN LIFE as a conference on "Representations of Gender and Sexuality in Opera" held at the State University of New York, Stony Brook in September 1995. The conference could not have taken place without the generous support of the National Endowment for the Humanities, and its success was equally indebted to many friends and colleagues at Stony Brook. Sarah Fuller, then chair of the music department, greeted the idea of the conference with enthusiasm and brought her unique vision to most aspects of the planning. The Stony Brook Humanities Center funded Catherine Clément's participation, and the center's director, E. Ann Kaplan, helped to connect us to an interdisciplinary audience. The high energy level of the conference also owed much to a number of speakers whose articles could not be published here—Susan Cook, Paula Higgins, Elizabeth Hudson, Jeffrey Kallberg, Susan McClary, Peter Rabinowitz, Ruth Solie, Gary Tomlinson, and Gilles de Van—and to my Stony Brook colleagues Joseph Auner, Richard Kramer, David Lawton, Judy Lochead, Jane Sugarman, and many others. The organization of the event was eased and enlivened by my wonderful assistants Jennifer Bain and Kirsten Yri.

The transformation of the conference papers into this book went on mostly in Berkeley, and here again I am grateful to colleagues and students for intellectual support and practical help. Benjamin Walton did heroic service preparing the manuscript for publication, Christina Schiffner prepared the index, and Gee Gee Lang helped with computer problems. On a less practical plane, Wendy Allanbrook and Katherine Bergeron were always ready with encouragement and lively conversation. Interrupted by a cross-country move, the book was slow to come together, and I owe a huge debt to all the contributors for their patience and good humor through many phases of correspondence and revision. Malcolm Litchfield, then music editor for Princeton University Press, continued to believe in the project at times when many editors would surely have lost patience. Finally, this book would certainly not exist without the contributions of Elizabeth Hudson: as co-organizer of the Stony Brook conference she was indispensable, inspiring, and fun to work with. Her rigorous intelligence and thoughtful feminism have been shaping forces from beginning to end of the project.

Siren Songs

Introduction

MARY ANN SMART

ONE SATURDAY BEFORE EASTER a few years ago, I turned on the Metropolitan Opera broadcast to catch the tail end of the quiz. The performance was *Salome* and, as if in penance for the gender politics the audience was about to be subjected to, the quiz was devoted to the topic of women in opera, the panelists all female. Most of the questions were of the usual type: five recordings of a fragment of the Habañera were played, and the contestants had some difficulty identifying the singers; this wasn't one of those quizzes where the participants elbowed each other out of the way to be the first to answer or twisted the questions into clever jokes. Just before time ran out, quizmaster Peter Allen read a question written (unusually enough) by a musicologist. It went something like this: "Women can sing opera, write about opera, even compose opera, but apparently they can't talk about it, at least judging by the Met Opera quiz panels. Why do you suppose this is?"[1] The question initially made me bristle a bit, but at least some of the panelists seemed to grasp its feminist spirit and replied that the Met and its broadcasts had long been controlled by men and that women might perhaps have found it difficult to gain a foothold.

No doubt this is true. But as any reader of Kristeva or Cixous knows, patriarchal power structures are rooted at least partly in language, so the listener's query also raised more interesting questions: of whether the discourse of opera fandom *is* indeed marked as male, and why even the quiz on that particular day, populated by lively, intelligent women, should have turned out to be so cautious and dutiful. Surely part of the reason lies not in old-boy networks or in the particular questions posed, but in the very structure of the quiz, which is underpinned by the notion that opera can be experienced as lists and facts, to be delivered to a mass audience (courtesy of a multinational oil company) in the form of witty aperçus and reminiscences of unforgettable performances from the distant past. Listening to the participants labeling the various Carmens—even when Carolyn Abbate injected a bit of resistance by insisting on dividing the singers according to those who "did the laugh" and those who did not—one had to wonder whether part of the appeal of the quiz was the possibility for *control* it promised: a way of organizing an unruly phenomenon into manageable bits of information, perhaps thus countering the threatening performative power of all those seductive Carmens. If the quiz stands for positivistic command, Abbate's flippant remark about "doing the laugh" points the way toward a more rhapsodic approach, an ear for vocal *jouissance*.

1

The quiz may invite us to construe factual control and feminine performative power as opposites, but a contradiction arises as soon as these qualities are transposed to a scholarly context: facts and lists may be dry or stifling, but systematic ways of organizing knowledge are crucial to interpretation, and perhaps particularly so when the objective is to ground music's slippery charms in a social context. For those seeking to uncover the attitudes to gender and sexuality encoded in opera, such grounding begins with an originary opposition that can itself be parsed in terms of systems versus rhapsody, or even as masculine versus feminine: that between words and music. As Susan McClary observed in her foreword to the 1988 English translation of Catherine Clément's *Opera, or the Undoing of Women*, it is no accident that feminist criticism of music began with opera, where gender relationships and sexual conflict are usually at center stage, and where the very presence of words provides a quick riposte to those skeptics who wonder how music can have anything to do with gender. The lessons of post-structuralism notwithstanding, words can convey clear meanings, at least compared to music's more elusive patterns of signification. However, McClary was also quick to caution against the illusion of comfort and clarity offered by interpretations that deal only with words:

> [t]he strategy of relying on texted music . . . is always vulnerable to the charge that one is finally dealing only with words (which we already knew were socially contaminated) and that music itself—in particular the "Absolute Music" of the classical symphonic repertory—remains essentially pure, ineffable, and emphatically not concerned with such mundane issues.[2]

While Clément's approach in *Opera, or the Undoing of Women* did little to challenge music's status as "pure" or "ineffable," she did reinterpret this tendency toward transcendence as a purely negative feature. Indeed, Clément might be seen as elevating the scrutiny of plot to the status of doctrine, making disregard for the music into the cornerstone of her approach. In her quest to reveal the darkly misogynistic aspects of opera's plots, she depicts music as a sort of siren song that lures us to wallow in the operatic experience while forgetting the violence done to women. Despite the obfuscating spell cast by the music, we are ultimately affected by these fatal messages:

The music makes one forget the plot, but the plot sets traps for the imaginary. The plot works quietly, plainly visible to all, but outside the code of the pleasures of opera. It is totally dull . . . ; it is all familiar and forgettable. But beyond the romantic ideology, lines are being woven, tying up the characters and leading them to death for transgression—for transgressions of familial rules, political rules, the things at stake in sexual and authoritarian power. That is what it is all about.[3]

In other words, the very predictability and absurdity of opera's plots allows them to exert sinister force on the unconscious: music facilitates a state of identification, and once the spectator is sedated by this immediacy (and by the apparent irrelevance of the story), plot creeps up and gently does its cultural work. The sinister cooperation extends even further, in that music is not only capable of smoothing over the awful fates of female characters: the wish to experience musical intensity can even make us *desire* their sacrifices.

What might be described as a "first wave" of feminist opera criticism responded to Clément by way of the problem identified so forcefullly by McClary: how to draw operatic *music* into feminist interpretation. Strategies for dislodging music from the pedestal of the transcendent, for uncovering its social meanings, have been impressively varied, but in direct contrast to Clément's free-form Gallic rhapsodies, all veer closer to the more "quiz-like" method of Anglo-American analytic systems and equations with social context.[4] Many of the pioneering texts linked music to the social world by identifying a set of practices, techniques, or assumptions that represented a societally approved norm and interpreting departures from these conventions as traces of resistance and trangression. These conventional/trangressive pairs map easily onto contrasts of musical style (tonic/dominant, loud/soft, diatonic/chromatic) and they can in turn spin out to implicate much broader social and emotive realms. In her analysis of the discourse of the Monteverdi-Artusi controversy, Suzanne Cusick has traced a chain of binaries that proceeds from the basic oppositions masculine/feminine and active/passive to stretch as far afield as "substance/ornament," "stable/changeable," and "dry/wet."[5] And while such an opposition-oriented approach risks reductiveness, flattening out the distinctions between different kinds of "difference," it at least offers a clear conduit to social meaning and (often) a political conviction to show how operatic strategies of representation relate to women's lived experience. The quest for *jouissance,* on the other hand, the ear that thrills to the isolated laugh or cry, is rich in texture, but can easily slip loose from history, pursuing vocal and erotic pleasure into a subjective echo chamber.[6]

Partly as a result of her strong (and remarkably successful) commitment to changing the ways we hear and write about music, Susan McClary has approached the gendered meanings of opera with something closer to the first of these orientations. Thus she hears formal structures such as the Italianate double aria (in *Lucia di Lammermoor*) as analogies for societal or patriarchal control, while digressions into chromaticism or vocal ornament represent a (usually temporary) escape from that control; conventional musical language—and by extension society's rules—invariably reassert themselves to "frame" rebellious discourse. Almost anyone writing about music and gender since the 1991 publication of McClary's *Feminine Endings* must count as a daughter (or son) of McClary; and like many a child's reaction to an impressive parent, these relationships tend to be equal parts idolizing and rebellious.[7] These recent studies rely heavily on McClary's analytical paradigms—indeed most are unimaginable without her example—but they often differ by choosing to focus on narrower repertories and by rooting their interpretation more acquiescently in musical convention, dispensing with her suspicion of discourse that would normalize music's seductive patriarchal rhetoric.[8]

Despite the scope of these recent studies, one can gain a surprisingly clear sense of the evolution of gender studies in opera by reading analyses of a single opera, Bizet's *Carmen*. *Carmen* has been a favorite object of feminist study, not only because of the overt sexual politics—and sexual violence—of its plot, but because its heroine can be understood to bring death upon herself, willfully and knowingly, by her persistent pleasure in singing, dancing, and loving where and as she pleases—all of which daring pursuits amount to pretty much the same thing within the universe of nineteenth-century opera. Pessimistic, as always, Clément's account concentrates on Carmen's death, in part through the haunting anecdote of the old woman too poor to buy opera tickets who made a habit of arriving just in time for the last act night after night, saying "I come for the death."[9]

If Clément's view of *Carmen* could be telegraphically summed up as "Carmen dies," McClary's extensive discussion of the opera focuses on the seductive rhetoric of Carmen's songs and the way her death is necessitated by the workings of operatic convention.[10] And while the musical specificity of McClary's interpretations has been both liberating and instructive, more and more (feminist) listeners now seem to prefer telling stories with the moral: "Carmen sings." Paul Robinson famously complained that Clément's negative verdict on opera was skewed by her inability to hear the voices of the sopranos who so often sing the most compelling and pyrotechnically impressive music in any opera, even as they are being oppressed and murdered by plot.[11] More recently, many have taken up and embellished this basic objection, so that the idea of "voice" in all its manifestations has become a central and controversial issue. Michel Poizat has merged the opposing forces in a Lacan-inspired theory that sees the entire history of opera as a quest to recapture the pure primal cry uttered before the infant is imprinted with language and with specific desires. For Poizat, the impulse toward the soprano's death in nineteenth- and twentieth-century operas is really an impulse toward the inarticulate cry often uttered by these heroines at the moment of death.[12] As Gary Tomlinson and others have pointed out, however, Poizat's embrace of Lacan tends toward the ahistorical, toward an undifferentiated glorification of the cry, a vocal utterance that bears so little musical patterning that it can sound very similar whether "composed" by Mozart, Wagner, or Berg.[13]

But such accounts are attractive because they make room for what is *different* about opera—the centrality of performers to the experience, the tenor who may or may not hit that high Bb. This view has been refined by Carolyn Abbate, who has argued that the reality of opera lies as much in its tangible performed voices as in the printed (or even the recorded) text.[14] By listening carefully to what the characters *sing* (rather than what they say, or what is done to them), Abbate suggests that we can restore a sense of opera's physicality and counter the controlling voice of the composer with multiple voices—some of them female:

> far from being a revenge-tragedy that Catherine Clément calls "the undoing of women," [opera might be seen as] a genre that so displaces the authorial musical voice onto female characters and female singers that it largely reverses the conventional opposition of male (speaking) subject and female (observed) subject.[15]

Some of the most interesting consequences of this approach emerge in connection with the most maniacally controlling composer of all: Wagner. Musicology has traditionally heard Wagner's operas as driven above all by plot, by way of an omniscient and male authorial voice that dominates our experience through the elaborate apparatus of leitmotifs. So when Brünnhilde "does the laugh" in the last act of *Götterdämmerung,* she can be heard as commandeering the opera's "voice" and overturning the usual hierarchy of words and music, modeling a way we might teach ourselves to hear music as more than merely an elaboration of patriarchal plot.[16]

2

The space between Carmen's laugh and Brünnhilde's encompasses a wide array of approaches to musical discourse and social meaning, but all share a tendency to pose their questions in terms of a basic opposition between male and female, whether they do so by setting Carmen's style of singing against that of José or by imagining a struggle for authorial primacy between female singer and male composer. The male/female opposition can of course simply be reconfigured as one between straight and queer, but the very intellectual and political imprecision of this mapping points to the methodological problems with contructing such chains of binaries as if each term occupied the same discursive position. One founding text cuts flamboyantly across the gender/sexuality opposition, positing a singing body without gender. Although Roland Barthes's *S/Z* predates musicological interest in gender issues by nearly two decades and has only episodically had any influence on writing about opera, Barthes's multifaceted reading of Balzac's story "Sarrasine" marks out an attractive theoretical ground by showing how exploding the fundamental opposition male/female can lead to the collapse of other epistemological categories, including that between systematic analysis and operatic *jouissance*.

The allure of Barthes's approach originates partly in Balzac: not only in his compelling depiction of the Roman opera house where the sculptor Sarrasine first sees the castrato La Zambinella as a place of intense, secret pleasures, but also in the story's resonances with recent attitudes to gender, especially its eerie (if imprecise) anticipation of Judith Butler's influential notion of "gender as performance."[17] La Zambinella's physical appearance, her mannerisms, and even the grammatical formulations used to describe her all finally emerge as divorced from her "real" gender, a disjunction that lies at the heart of Barthes's text. Moreover, it is Balzac more than Barthes who seems to demolish the idea of essentialism—very much *avant la lettre*—when he assures us that

> This was woman herself, with her sudden fears, her irrational values, her instinctive worries, her impetuous boldness, her fussings, and her delicious sensibility.

For Barthes, La Zambinella's perfect—and perfectly deceptive—female beauty and soprano voice not only call into question the reliability of information gained through the senses; the instability of vision and hearing demonstrated by Sarrasine's error ultimately undermines all fixed categories, binary oppositions, and critical certainties. In this sense, the undecidability of the singer's gender is responsible for one of the strangest features of *S/Z*, its eclectic combination of structuralist segmentation of the text (the famous "codes" and "lexias") and more postmodern interludes that, often spurred by an individual word or phrase, weave florid meditations around a single critical insight. This exhilarating layering of poststructuralist riffs over a structuralist framework is arguably a consequence of the collapse of the male/female opposition, an implicit acknowledgment of the inadequacy of closed analytical systems.

For musicologists, Barthes's combination of strict segmentation and free-associative rhapsody feels both familiar and liberating, a resemblance to our established modes of analysis that perhaps holds the promise of transdisciplinary interpretation based on a shared semiotic system. At one point Barthes even uses musical notation as a metaphor, hinting that music's structures are so clear that they can serve as an aid for deciphering the more elusive meanings of the verbal text.[18] The analogy cannot help but provoke skepticism, and indeed, in the larger scope of *S/Z*, Barthes shows himself to be interested in music mainly as an abstract idea. Musical *notation* may reveal clear structures, but Barthes describes La Zambinella's *voice* in nearly opposite terms, as invading and "lubricating" Sarrasine's being, arousing an erotic ecstasy that the sculptor will forever seek to recapture:

> Voice is diffusion, insinuation, it passes through the whole extent of the body, the skin; insofar as it is passage, abolition of limits, of classifications, of names, . . . it possesses a particular power of hallucination.[19]

Just as music and voice do away with systems and classifications, overflowing into sheer expression, the castrato's enigmatic body eliminates the possibility of meaning by negating the binary oppositions on which all language is based.

> in copying woman, in assuming her position on the other side of the sexual barrier, the castrato will transgress morphology, grammar, discourse, and because of this abolition of meaning Sarrasine will die.[20]

Certain aspects of Barthes's love affair with music will sound very familiar to feminists and musicologists, recalling the formulations of the French feminists with whom he shared an intellectual lineage and, more surprisingly, the discourse of romanticism.[21] This idea of music as a free flow exceeding cognitive grasp turns out to be amazingly resilient, the romantic doctrine of transcendence and spirituality translated with surprising ease to the psychoanalytic notion of music as an outpouring or immersion that recalls union with the mother's body, of voice as singing "from a time before law."[22]

But even if Barthes sometimes lapses into an uncharacteristic passivity when confronted with music, *S/Z* can be a rich source of inspiration and innovation for opera studies.[23] Besides the book's intriguing split between structuralism and passionate outpouring, the analysis of "Sarrasine" shows a way beyond binary oppositions, beyond the idea that all gendered meaning is arranged around a confrontation between male and female. And, perhaps most important, Barthes provides models for writing about the body on stage, an aspect of opera so thoroughly ignored until recently that both staging and the mechanics of vocal performance were relegated to the margins of critical discourse, as if the actual presence of either body or voice could overwhelm analysis with an ungraspable excess of materiality.

One corrective has come from the direction of queer theory, where the body is constantly an object of contention and is seen as instrumental in the formation of identity.[24] Writers such as Wayne Koestenbaum and Terry Castle have extended the limits of operatic gender studies, to focus on such "extratextual" material as the experience of the fan, cults of diva worship, the role of opera in the formation of identity.[25] Much of this writing partakes of Barthes's relationship to opera as a place of escape: autobiographically, offering freedom from socially defined gender roles and compulsory heterosexuality, and intellectually, as a liberation from theory, from the responsibility to study a text systematically, to amass historical context, to be exhaustive.[26] Koestenbaum's desire to fuse with the diva's body recalls Barthes's description of La Zambinella's voice, but proposes a radically different view of how a body can mean and consequently of how one might write about opera:

> Her voice enters me, makes me a "me," an interior, by virtue of the fact that I have been entered. The singer, through osmosis, passes through the self's porous membrane, and discredits the fiction that bodies are separate, boundaried packages. The singer destroys the division between her body and our own, for her sound enters our system. I am sitting at the Met at Leontyne Price's recital in 1985 and Price's vibrations are *inside my body,* dressing it up with the accoutrements of interiority. Am I listening to Leontyne Price or am I incorporating her, swallowing her, memorizing her?[27]

The closeted gay listener gains both a voice and an authentic body through the diva's presence, as the pulse, the vital organs vibrate with every turn of her phrase. And if the idea of the singer's voice resonating through the listener's body sounds almost universal, relevant beyond the psyche of the queer fan, perhaps this is the point: the experiences Koestenbaum describes can be felt by almost anyone, but his concern with same-sex desire and the queer body has made it possible to transcend the fundamental male/female opposition, to gain access to writing styles that eschew limits and classifications, and to integrate the body (the fan's, the singer's, the character's) into opera studies.

3

In some ways Koestenbaum brings us full circle, back to that Metropolitan opera quiz, with its extremes of hard facts and listening to Carmen laugh. Even if his fantasy of swallowing Leontyne Price might seem to occupy exactly the opposite end of the spectrum from McClary's insistence on reclaiming music from the realm of the ineffable through analysis and social context, Koestenbaum too consumes opera by way of lists. He keeps an opera journal that merely lists performances attended, its purpose "not to refine or browbeat, but to include."[28] This is a radically different view of the drive to name and categorize, not so much a controlling grasp at threatening excess, but a way of filling the gap left when words fail:

> And so the opera queen keeps lists. Experiences are accreted, because none can be exhaustively explained. If once you could describe the summons a voice sends out, maybe you could stop listening, stop looking to opera for satisfaction and consummation.[29]

If these approaches have traditionally been employed as implicit opposites—using analysis to uncover music's misogyny compared to wallowing uncritically in sensuous texture and individual experience—the essays in this volume move toward merging the two tendencies, letting them enrich (and at times undermine or deconstruct) each other. There is plenty of musical analysis in *Siren Songs*—quite a bit more than there is of the confessional mode or the language of the opera fan. But much of it is analysis of a particular type, similar to what Naomi Schor has called "reading in detail," focusing on a single aria or even on a single motive or detail from an aria.[30] The contributors seem refreshingly free from a need to demonstrate unity or coherence in the texts they analyze, and this willingness to draw meaning from isolated moments frees their readings from the yoke of the systematic while allowing the telling detail to prompt alternative analytical narratives.

It also seems significant that many of the authors included here arrive at this interpretive middle ground by way of immersion in historical documents. Some essays (Feldman, Auner, the Hutcheons, Brett) turn to facts and principles of political history as a foundation for their readings of gendered meaning; others (Parker, Hadlock, Smart, and the Hutcheons again) locate a sense of history in documents that lie closer to the musical text: literary sources, a composer's letters, staging manuals. Yet another group (Brooks, Bergeron, Kramer) aims to interpret operatic texts of the later nineteenth century through the specific filter of psychoanalysis. But whatever the nature of the texts and contexts, the cumulative effect is of a view of opera as embedded in history—not so much in the sweeping political history that gives rise to mottoes like "Verdi and the Risorgimento," but in a personal, often anecdotal, setting that might best be desribed as New Historical. What this return to a reliance on documentary evidence offers, perhaps, is a way to replace personal testimony with a vivid sense of other, past experiences of making and hearing opera; and, equally important, to displace attention from the composer's text to a broad fabric of collaborative voices.

Catherine Clément returns here to the central theme of *Opera, or the Undoing of Women*, to describe music as a "great seducer, a pied piper of the dream state" that is opera. She grounds her original condemnation of music's seductive power in a new theory of how, even while its music swallows up plot and word, opera can also communicate social meaning musically by exploiting an established hierarchy of voice types and dramatic associations. The traditional images of helpless soprano, vulnerable romantic tenor, baritone as law-giver, etc., are so deeply entrenched that even when individual works depart from the pattern the archetypes remain. It is in this space between the archetypal and the specific that meaning can emerge; and so *Fidelio*, first conceived as a revolutionary plot, could in the twentieth century be staged in the space of a few years both as an allegory of Austria (Leonore) joyfully uniting with Hitler (Florestan) and as its opposite, a celebration of the Nazi defeat. This flexibility is made possible by a tension between Beethoven's trousered, vocally omnipotent Leonore and the traditional soprano archetype: behind even Leonore's most forceful vocal moments, the image of a soprano victim remains, always available for exploitation by a director, singer, or conductor.

Martha Feldman locates the political meaning of opera seria in a different kind of tension between text and performance. She sees the libretti of eighteenth-century *opere serie*—in particular their construction around a benevolent father-king and an absent mother—as wishfully reflecting the values of the absolutist regime in Naples, while the anarchic listening practices of the audience show that the very familial and social structures glorified in the plots are falling apart. But opera and history also move in parallel, and Feldman suggests that the French Revolution's execution of the royal fantasy-parents and the contemporaneous rise of the bourgeois family ushered in a new kind of operatic drama. In posing this opposition between the fixed system of meaning set up by the conventionalized seria plots and the "excesses" of their mode of consumption, Feldman uncovers multiple meanings in works usually seen as one-sided reflections of state power and transfers some control over their meaning to spectators.

The three contributors to the symposium on staging Mozart's operas offer concrete illustrations of how performance can alter the gendered meanings of even the most classic operatic texts. The authors agree that Mozart's heroines are less obviously victimized than the nineteenth-century characters Clément has focused on, but nevertheless see the dilemma of modern Mozart directors as one of balancing an accurate historical grounding of the roles, which frequently dictate submissive feminine behavior, with the desires of late-twentieth-century spectators to see these women as believable and sympathetic characters, perhaps even as role models. Mary Hunter and Gretchen Wheelock show how Konstanze's extreme coloratura in *Die Entführung aus dem Serail* can be made to denote either madness or force of will depending on the soprano's gestures. Wye Allanbrook focuses on what she deems a less successful example, Peter Sellars's evocation of the subtext of domestic violence in Zerlina's "Batti,

batti," an aria that in its original context can be heard as about feminine power.

Heather Hadlock engages with a different kind of Mozart reception in her study of Massenet's 1905 opera *Chérubin* as an updated portrait of Mozart's Cherubino. She documents increasing anxiety about trouser roles over the course of the nineteenth century, stemming from a nervousness about the solidity of gender divisions at the fin de siècle. While Mozart's Cherubino could usually be dismissed as a sexless child, Massenet's Chérubin was more threatening because he/she appeared in an artistic climate that both embraced and feared lesbian desire. Although this new milieu finally made it possible for Chérubin to voice his desire in a love duet, he is nevertheless relegated at significant moments to singing from offstage or from the shadows, as if to protect viewers from the visual shock of a trousered lover. Paradoxically, this concealment of the alarming body emphasizes the very aspect of Chérubin that can never be gendered male, his (her) voice.

Where Hadlock explicates *Chérubin* with reference to an actual history of what specific women were thinking and doing in Paris circa 1900, Roger Parker looks at the *idea* of history as represented within French grand opera. Parker listens to Verdi's *Don Carlos* in counterpoint with Anselm Gerhard's claim that French opera became increasingly personal and interior over the course of the nineteenth century, gradually abandoning its preoccupation with historical events and choral spectacle.[31] Noting that Verdi's opera belies this trend in certain respects, Parker follows some clues in the music sung by Verdi's Elisabeth to propose an alternative definition of history in opera, one more keyed to musical process and to the ways women could exercise power, both on and off the stage.

Peter Brooks discovers a similar power of musical self-determination in *Don Carlos*'s other female lead, the princess Eboli. Brooks reads Eboli's aria "O don fatale" as an operatic instance of the "talking cure," in which text and music gradually transform the "hystericized" voice of Eboli's self-deceiving recitative into the "cure" of lyric outpouring at the end of the aria, bringing both voice and psyche to self-awareness. Where the *body* of the hysteric can only reflect past trauma through physical symptoms such as paralysis, stuttering, or nervous coughing, the "hystericized voice" can go further: operatic song can undo the hysterical impasse, mimicking the analytical process by uncovering concealed trauma and venting it through narrative coherence and vocal substance. Taking off in part from Brooks's notion of the importance of gesture in melodrama and opera, my own essay tries to locate a source of female power not in voice but in body—in physical gesture and music that imitates gesture. Focusing on Verdi's *Aida*, I suggest that recurring themes and orchestral music that "mimes" physical movement can at certain special moments endow the female body on stage, usually seen as gazed upon and objectified, with a performative and musically constitutive force.

In contrast, Katherine Bergeron posits an opera almost without bodies when she interprets *Pelléas et Mélisande* as a drama of the unconscious in which Golaud is the only "real" character. Bergeron reads Maeterlinck's notoriously sketchy, motivationless plot as a Freudian allegory, in which the mysterious Mélisande represents the "nothingness" of desire, around which Pelléas as ego and Golaud as superego circulate. Bergeron turns to the hair scene to explore the ways Debussy figures this relationship and ultimately enacts its resolution musically, and her close attention to the music has almost the effect of an "analysis" in that other sense of the word: the progress of a winding, melismatic "desire" motive through the duet's several stages illuminates the unfolding of Pelléas's attempt to immobilize his desire (literally, by tying her up) even as he begins to mirror her slippery cries in his own music.

Lawrence Kramer's article works simultaneously on two levels, the interpretive and the programmatic. Following Derrida (in *Positions*), Kramer proposes that "efforts to conceptualize the place of gender and sexuality in opera" have moved through a preliminary, oppositional phase dominated by "feminist critique" and a transitional phase that recognizes the inadequacy of the oppositional model. Kramer argues, however, that we have not yet entered the final Derridean phase of "dissemination," which aims for "a movement above, though not beyond, the interplay of power and resistance" (190). As models for what such a criticism might look like, Kramer narrates "three scenes" of sexual transgression in the opera house, with protagonists as diverse as Walt Whitman, Freud, and *Götterdämmerung*'s Hagen. Kramer's three scenes do indeed move "above" oppositional discourse, but they do so largely by ignoring institutional manifestations of power and diving deep within the individual (male) psyche to demonstrate that opera in the nineteenth century was centrally involved in both policing and overstepping the boundaries of bourgeois sexuality.

Linda and Michael Hutcheon, too, draw on psychoanalytic theory, both old and new, in their attempt to make a place in opera studies for dance and the body. Their discussion of Strauss's *Salome*, in particular the Dance of the Seven Veils, uses turn-of-the-century psychosexual research, contemporary visual and literary material, and recent theories of the gaze to suggest that during her dance Salome is as much mistress as victim of the gaze. Although the musical processes and the cultural values they uncover are quite different, their conclusions are strikingly similar to those of my own article on *Aida*, questioning the tenets of feminist film theory and exploring the possibility that, in the sounding world of opera, to be looked at is not always, not only, to be objectified.

Joseph Auner stages a different kind of encounter between modernism

and the feminine in his discussion of Krenek's *Jonny spielt auf*. Auner sees
Krenek's opera as a commentary on (or revision of) Andreas Huyssen's opposition between the masculine identity of modernist art music and feminized mass culture. At first glance, Krenek's confrontation between the
Schoenbergian composer Max and the black jazz musician Jonny seems to
reverse the relationship, with Max portrayed as an impotent composer of
glacier-like music while Jonny is a vital, spontaneous sexual success. However, the opera's music undermines this set of associations by representing
Jonny's jazz band only as heard from offstage, while Max's parodically modernist onstage opera aria is lent an immediacy that no other music in the opera
possesses. Finally, Krenek refuses to decide between his two polar opposites:
since Jonny and Max never meet, the opera ultimately retreats from the issue.

If Auner's interpretation suggests that music and libretto can advance
conflicting views on race, gender, and aesthetics, Philip Brett locates clash-
ing ideologies even within the (crucially pluralized) "librettos" of Britten's
Peter Grimes. He begins his study of the libretto's genesis simply by trying
to arrive at an accurate division of creative responsibility, not only between
Britten and his librettist Montagu Slater but to account also for the significant contributions of Peter Pears and (at an early stage) Christopher Isherwood. But Brett's project extends far beyond historical reconstruction,
to untangling the opinions about pacificism and sexual morality each collaborator brought to the text. Most strikingly, he shows that certain allusions to adolescent sexuality deleted early in the creative process actually
continue to exert an influence over the finished libretto, with the result that
the opera's early reception parallels metaphorically the "open secret," critics responding as much to the residue of what had been expunged as to
what was actually said.

4

Ruth Solie has recently mapped the converging paths of feminist and
"new" musicology, proposing that feminism has been a "mother" to the
political orientation and analytical modes of "new" musicology.[32] The
voices gathered in *Siren Songs* certainly seem to support this view—if not
of the birth of new musicology from the efforts of feminism, at least of a
substantial common ground shared by the two. I hope that the essays collected here also do something to counter the fear that accompanied Solie's
genealogy: that feminism might eventually be absorbed altogether into the
new musicological methods, so that younger scholars would embrace the
methods made available by feminism, but will "have a hard time actually
keeping women as the focus of their historical investigations or keeping
gender front and center in their thinking."[33]

As one of those metaphorical daughters of Susan McClary (and, indeed, of Solie herself) and as the actual daughter of a feminist scholar, I am particularly conscious of both the temptations and the dangers of relaxing into paradigms of mainstreaming and postfeminism. And while the essays collected here show without a doubt that gender studies are indeed a center of imaginative thinking about opera these days, they also do much to allay any fear of compromise or sense that the resolve to critique opera's power structures might be softening. On the contrary, I would suggest that this new work on gender and sexuality has shaken up the historical and analytical tenets of opera studies, so much so that it has become impossible to write about certain aspects of opera without taking account of gender.

Among the numerous dimensions of the opera/gender relationship outlined in this volume, two of the most fundamental and recurrent are the rethinking of the concept of the author/composer and that of the interaction between music and words. As several of the articles demonstrate, scholars have begun—partly out of a desire to add women's voices to the history of male-authored opera—to pay attention to the creative contributions of singers to the operatic text, as well as to the perspectives of audience members and female patrons. An awareness of gender—and of the instability of gender—has begun to explode the old (and implicitly gendered) rivalry between words and music, lending new energy to the familiar but rather inert concepts of opera as "multivalent" or as composed of "three systems" (music, words, staging).[34] And finally, feminist concern with representation and visual objectification has thrown new and urgent emphasis onto the whole visual dimension of opera and onto the staging of the body. Once seen as an art form that excelled at perpetrating—and aestheticizing—crimes against women, opera has begun to reveal itself on the contrary as embodied, a site for multiple interventions and theoretical experiment. Its seductive siren song can be heard now not as disarming and intoxicating its auditors, but as beckoning toward unexplored territories, inviting us to imagine new voices and messages behind its melodies.

Through Voices, History

CATHERINE CLÉMENT

As a philosopher who was educated in France during the heyday of structuralism, my approach to opera is an idiosyncratic one. Music is far and away the most difficult field to analyze. Why? This question in itself is a philosophical problem. Rather than a science, music is a confused and passionate art form, perhaps more suited to anthropological than philosophical methods of explication; and within the realm of musical aesthetics, the global vision of opera, thanks to the irresistible power of the voice, occupies the mysterious place of the heart in a body, which, according to Christian tradition, is also the place of the soul. It cannot be proven, but—like a religious illusion—nor can it be doubted. But if we take into account opera's "religious" component, its emotional power and the devotion it inspires, then we can try to analyze its voices according to the method historians use to understand religious movements: by studying the use they make of history. Such an approach uncovers the deep ambiguity of opera, in terms of gender, power, and social factors, as well as uncovering a perverse relationship with history itself.

THE LYRE AND THE FLUTE

According to most European philosophers, it is impossible to think *philosophically* about music. Whoever they are, wherever they are born, European philosophers think not "about" music itself, but "around" it, until they reach an impasse. Even Hegel, who was famously equal to any philosophical problem, concludes his dialectic at the very borders of music; and writes in his *Aesthetics* that the essence of music is to express "the oh! and the ah! of the soul." "Oh" and "ah" are neither concepts nor ideas; and the word "soul" is rather unusual in the Hegelian vocabulary, which normally prefers "Spirit" or "Bewusstsein"—consciousness. I cannot take the time here to quote all the philosophers who, one after the other, concede to music the philosophical right of inaccessibility—that is, the right of resistance to philosophy itself. Nevertheless, I would like to mention two contemporaries, both French: Claude Lévi-Strauss and Vladimir Jankélévitch.

Before becoming an anthropologist, Claude Lévi-Strauss taught philosophy, and even if he would prefer not to be defined as such, his work seems to me to be that of a true philosopher. After having described the effects of music on human nature as scientifically as possible in his *Mythologiques;* after having analysed perceptions of musical time, duration, its physiological effects on the internal organs; after struggling to define its rules and concepts, Lévi-Strauss finally renounces all attempt to understand, sighing that "music will remain the supreme mystery of human sciences."[1] And Lévi-Strauss is only one of many to conclude that there is no scientific basis for understanding music. Indeed, this mystery is at the core of the entire oeuvre of the great French philosopher Vladimir Jankélévitch. In his *La Musique et l'ineffable,* he describes the mysterious power of music, quoting Franz Liszt's lied "Die Macht der Musik."[2] Explanations are impossible, but descriptions are possible, and the more poetic the better. Whatever music is, whether material or spiritual, emerging from passion or calculated from the rules of harmony, it acts powerfully on humanity, with a sweet and sour effect like that of a medicine or a poison—what Plato calls *Pharmakon* in his famous dialogue.

This is precisely why many philosophers are so cautious about music. The first in a long history, Plato expels from his ideal Republic a certain type of music. A certain type: for under the still powerful Greek influence on our ways of thinking, one finds even today a philosophical opposition between two types of music. The opposition suggests Nietzsche's separation of the Apollonian and Dionysian arts, but Jankélévitch rightly reminds us that in classical Greece the true distinction was not between Apollo and Dionysus, but between Orpheus and Dionysus. Orpheus the magician calmed the beasts with his harmonious instrument, the lyre; he could set lions to the plough and panthers to the carriage; in the same manner he tried to soothe women. However, if his magic worked on the wild animals in the forest, with women he failed. The Bacchantes, devotees of Dionysus, driven to frenzy by his divine flute, cut Orpheus into pieces and slashed his flesh. The flute triumphs over the lyre, Dionysus over Orpheus.

The lyre is sober, quiet, severe, and masculine; on the contrary, the flute is excited, passionate, ecstatic, and feminine. When Plato prohibits "music" from his city, he naturally means the second type, the oriental: in Greek *thrènôdeis harmoniai.* It was with a flute that a magician hypnotized rats and children in the German city of Hamelin and drew them to the river, where they drowned. "Flute," too, is the symbolic name for seduction, referring to the secret voice of a plaintive woman hidden in the instrument. Jankélévitch concludes that for most philosophers "the *lamento* and the *appassionato* do not belong to the moral sphere." *Lamento* and *appassionato:* we are not far from opera. And if Jankélévitch is correct that *lamento* and *appassionato* are outside the sphere of the moral, then so is opera.

Let us think about opera's innumerable moral ambiguities. The most striking example of the historical treachery that opera can practice must be *Fidelio,* Beethoven's beautiful work about freedom and the courage of women. After the Nazi invasion of Austria (the *Anschluss*), when Hitler entered Vienna in 1938, the city's main opera house, the Staatsoper, announced a performance of *Fidelio*. Why? Because through Nazism, the opera's directors claimed, Austria had won . . . liberty. Like Leonore, they said, Austria is a faithful wife, waiting and fighting for her husband . . . Hitler. Field-Marshall Hermann Goering, who was later condemned in Nuremberg and hung for crimes against humanity, attended the Staatsoper's official performance; and according to some newspaper critics, he himself could have played the role of the benevolent governor, Don Fernando.

Seven years later, after the war, in order to welcome the restoration of its freedom, Vienna celebrated by performing . . . *Fidelio*. But this time Hitler had metamorphosed into the tyrant Pizarro. And when the old Staatsoper building, damaged by bombs, was reopened ten years later, what work was chosen to mark the occasion? Again *Fidelio*. Thus within less than twenty years the famous prisoners' chorus served the causes of Hitler, the Russian army, and that of a "new" Europe. Today in Vienna, *Fidelio* has a new nickname: "the chameleon opera."

A spiritual chameleon: the phrase could describe the phenomenon of music itself, and because of music's elusive power, it might also describe that peculiar form of theater called opera. Because of music's expressive slipperiness, the stories told by opera have a special strength, full of ambiguity. Through opera, History speaks with a very strange voice: unlike theater, whose talent is to enlighten, opera's vocation is to darken History, to make it less intelligible. And there, in my view, resides the central question of gender in opera. Let me first address two points: how opera displays worlds on stage and how opera displays History.

CROWDS, CHOIRS, ROLES, AND POWER

On stage, through sets, costumes, and lights, every performance of an opera displays its own world, its specific vision, its style. But in any opera there is also what might be called a vocal backdrop, defined by the composer. Let us call it *a society of voices.*

Most frequently, an opera defines its particular world through the chorus, whether visible or invisible. The concept of *world* may seem vague; perhaps the German concept of *Gestalt* can clarify how such a world functions for the "consumer" of opera. We spectators see a people—a community—but also tribes and bodies, each with its own role in that opera's version of history.

The Musical Soul of the Operatic Community

The community is represented by crowds singing with a huge, vague voice, often expressing political feelings, but never political ideas. In Musorgsky's *Boris Godunov* or *Khovanshchina,* even if the men and women of the chorus sing different words, they all unite in expressing a rather simple psychic mood that might be summarized as either joy-and-hope or despair-and-sorrow. This is the mythical voice known as "the voice of the Russian people": as a collective being, like the collective Christ described in the poetry of Aleksandr Blok; the people hope, suffer, and weep, obeying the basic myth of the ecstatic Russian Orthodox passion. One can hear similar feelings, expressed even more straightfowardly, among the imaginary Chinese crowds in Puccini's *Turandot:* alternately cruel and compassionate toward the princess, floating with the rhythms of her complicated identity, whether inflexible or tender, the crowd is Turandot's collective mirror. In some operas the people express a quiet and solemn joy, as does the community at the end of Wagner's *Die Meistersinger*—and it is useless to recall how these peaceful feelings were distorted by the Nazis, in the city of Nuremberg itself. On the contrary, the famous chorus of the Hebrew slaves in Verdi's *Nabucco* expresses both hope and pain. Normally, the voice of the people belongs to both genders, feminine and masculine. Rarely, one hears an exclusively male melody, as in *Das Rheingold,* where the Nibelungen, a community of slaves, are all "Übermenschen," shouting and suffering.

Men, Women, and Tribes

When the chorus expresses itself as a *tribe,* their melodies tend toward the masculine, obeying the anthropological reality of tribes themselves. Nevertheless, the concept of "tribe" applies symbolically to a coherent group of human beings with their own rules and culture; one could also use the word "band," or even "gang." Unlike the mythical communities I described a moment ago, opera rarely allows women to share the tribal space: the heritage of these imaginary tribes seems to bring out the worst aspects of opera, cruelty and violence. The best example is Hagen's band of warriors in *Götterdämmerung:* rude and tough voices, without room for compassion. On the other hand, *Parsifal* presents a compassionate masculine "tune" among the "tribe" of the knights: there again, in the sacred circle, there is no place for a feminine voice, except the voice that is heard falling from the dome, strictly invisible. And in the realm of good classical humanism, we cannot escape the chorus behind Sarastro in *Die Zauberflöte:* whether tribe or band, this highly spirited and noble "gang" has nevertheless stolen a child from her mother.

Wagner was who he was: antisemitic, uneasy with femininity, fond of masculine tribes. Mozart was a freemason in a period in which freemasonry was strictly forbidden to women. But Georges Bizet shared certain revolutionary values with the Paris Commune: it is not surprising then to hear men and women singing together in *Carmen*'s tribal band of gypsies, a number of whom, both men and women together, will break with the social system, apply their own rules, and act as smugglers. Carmen is, of course, among these. In this operatic world, even if the men are the rulers, there is a space for women. What happens in a chorus is full of meaning: either archaic and forbidden to women, or open to them and thus advocating progress.

Official and Visible Bodies

Let me turn to the locus of power, to discuss what I would like to call official bodies. These characters are the most strictly ruled by history: they are members of parliament, priests, soldiers, nobles. In Verdi's *Don Carlos,* when the crowd awaits the king's entrance, we see a huge procession of these "official" bodies, accompanied by bizarre music—solemn, slow, and pompous. The whole range of Spanish society is gathering on stage to attend an *auto-da-fé,* the great social spectacle of Jews burnt alive on a Christian pyre. The army in *Aida* is similarly aligned with power: one hears neither lyre nor flute, but the triumph of trumpets, brass instruments especially marked for war and victory. And in Puccini's *Tosca,* when the whole of the Catholic body solemnly enters the church for a Te Deum of victory, the real incarnation of power, Baron Scarpia, lurks nearby in the dark. The reality of power is never really visible, never truly located in a collective entity.

In fact, the choruses of these official bodies, among which one must include noble women in a royal court, represent a tribe that has defeated all the others, centuries before. Any tribe can become a body; any body has been a tribe long ago, and can become a tribe again. What about the guild of Meistersingers? Are they a tribe, a band, or a body? In fifteenth-century Nuremberg, the masters were an official body. Later, they disappeared. In between, they were probably a threatened tribe. And for Wagner, they are the visible symbol of the values of ancient societies, much more admirable in his eyes than anything in the modern world. But this is not Wagner's fault. Opera has indeed a special taste for the past.

INDIVIDUAL VOICES AND SOCIAL ROLES

No scheme that correlates voice types—soprano, tenor, baritone—and types of characters will apply to every opera in the repertory, but some generalizations are possible. As Gilles de Van puts it in what he calls his "little Verdian grammar," "we are far from a situation in which every opera fits this scheme [of voice types], but the exceptions form part of a logic governed by the interaction of factors; and those exceptions finally settle into a pattern that does not deny the code itself."[3] So let us try to establish another code, with its own exceptions and its own logic.

Soprano: Persecuted Victim

In the operas of the nineteenth century, almost all heroines are victims, persecuted by men, baritone or bass. The situation of women in the real world has hardly followed a continuous line of progress and liberation, but has sometimes improved, sometimes receded into darkness, as we see from our perspective at the turn of a new century. After the Enlightenment followed the severely regressive nineteenth century and the rude twentieth century, in which European women were forced to pay the substantial price of history and wars. It is hardly surprising that opera reflects this situation. Humiliated, hunted, driven mad, burnt alive, buried alive, stabbed, committing suicide—Violetta, Sieglinde, Lucia, Brünnhilde, Aida, Norma, Mélisande, Liù, Butterfly, Isolde, Lulu, and so many others . . . All sopranos, and all victims.

But let us mention immediately the most important and symbolic exception of the early twentieth century: Turandot.

Tenor: Courage and Rebellion

Young, courageous, imprudent, heroes of a rebellion against the social order, fighting for love, most tenors are the masculine equivalents of sopranos, together with whom they often die. Perhaps the most self-conscious of all tenors is Tristan, both opposed to and synonymous with Isolde. Even if they begin differently—Tristan doomed to death, Isolde both a foreigner and a sorceress—the real aim of their mortal disease of passion is to blend the two of them into one unique, dead being. Tristan hesitates between obedience and rebellion, and finally decides to choose love, a choice that also implies rebellion, suffering, night, and death.

The tenor rebels are many: *Il trovatore*'s Manrico against his brother, Don Carlos against his father, Pelléas against his brother Golaud, Tannhäuser against Christianity, Don José against the Spanish army, Walther von Stolzing against the Meistersingers, and Tristan against his king. Each one is in love with a forbidden "lady," to use quite deliberately the vocabulary of courtly love, as a reminder of the powerful influence of thirteenth-century poetry even on nineteenth-century notions of love. Since the thirteenth century, our culture has been permeated by the myth of an impossible love between the lady and her servant. Whether or not Carmen can be considered as such a lady is a perplexing question, but undoubtedly as a "black" gypsy, as a sorceress, and as a free woman, she is forbidden to Don José. And while nothing remains of courtly love, a vague trace of this social and symbolic fight against order and law survives, in a celebration of what I will call "prohibited feelings."

Again there are some exceptions: Mime in Wagner's *Ring,* and both Shuysky and the Innocent in *Boris Godunov* are tenors without being heroes.

Baritone: Organized Opposition

Older, more prudent, they hide their rebellion and calculate their plots. Their voices have symbolically reached the ideal of maturity of European men: not too young, not too old. They do not really succeed in contesting the ancient order; often they fail and sometimes they die. They are often placed in the difficult position of go-between in a conflict. Strongly articulate, violent, full of anxiety but with a powerful philosophical mind, such are Don Giovanni, Macbeth, Posa in *Don Carlos,* Scarpia in *Tosca,* Amfortas in *Parsifal,* Iago in *Otello,* and even Giorgio Germont in *La traviata.*

The glaring exception might be Hans Sachs (*Die Meistersinger*), who succeeds in changing the old style of the masters' songs, but only at the price of painful self-denial.

Mezzo-Soprano: Resistance, Witchcraft, and Treason

Like the baritone, the mezzo is far from a fresh young voice. Like the baritone, the mezzo possesses active thought; she is articulate. And again like the baritone, she is capable of violent contestation. I insist on this similarity—"like the baritone"—for perceptions of the mezzo often focus on her "masculine" way of life. Carmen poses resistance to each and every order: "Libre elle est née, libre elle mourra" [Free she is born, free she will die]. Indeed, the best definition of the mezzo is through that freedom—freedom to murder, and freedom to meet death if necessary.

Azucena (*Il trovatore*) is a sorceress fighting her powerful enemy; Marfa resists the renovated Russian orthodox religion; the passionate Eboli betrays her mistress; the jealous princess of Bouillon kills Adriana Lecouvreur; Dalila, resistant to Jewish tyranny in a period in which the Jews were the masters, betrays Samson; Marina in *Boris Godunov* leads a conspiracy against Russia; and Dame Quickly in *Falstaff* is a superb go-between, betraying Falstaff and plotting for women. In this category, the exception might be Charlotte in Massenet's *Werther,* who appears as pure, innocent, and unhappy, like a soprano. But we can perhaps explain Charlotte with the help of another famous mezzo, Brangäne, whose example makes clear how a pure heart can betray—for this is exactly what Brangäne does on the ship when she deliberately gives the lovers the love potion instead of the poison her mistress has requested. Without knowing it, Charlotte is also treacherous: she faithfully betrays both her husband and her true love, Werther. Whether consciously or unconsciously, the mezzo often betrays.

Two voice types remain: the bass and the contralto. These are the deepest voices, and each has a precise function. I would place both in the same category: voices from beyond the human world.

Voices of Spirit and Power

With male voices this is clearly audible. The deepest male voices are not far from certain Asian voices, either Tibetan or Japanese, like those used in the Noh drama. They do not really impersonate, but rather act in a sacred field, shamanistic or religious. In opera, most of the great priests are basses: Ramfis in *Aida,* Oroveso in *Norma,* Zaccaria in *Nabucco,* Nourabad in *Les Pêcheurs de perles,* Dossifei in *Khovanshchina.* Moreover, all spiritual counselors, advisors, and representatives of churches or sects are basses: Titurel and Gurnemanz in *Parsifal,* the Grand Inquisitor in *Don Carlos,* Pimène the monk and Rangoni the Jesuit in *Boris Godunov.* Often, too, they are powerful but unhappy fathers: Philip in *Don Carlos,* Timur, Calaf's father in *Turandot,* Monterone in *Rigoletto.* In *Siegfried* Fafner is a bass: an old sleeping monster, but possessing a spiritual power. And although emasculated, Klingsor in *Parsifal* retains the strong spiritual power of a devil: like Mephistopheles in Gounod's *Faust,* he is a bass.

The spiritual power of the feminine voice is much more complicated. One version is heard in Erda's contralto in the *Ring:* asleep in the depth of the world, the old Earth goddess is the prophetess par excellence. Another version is the woodbird in *Siegfried:* invisible and clear soprano, this magic voice plays the role of the eternal flute described by Jankélévitch, seducing Siegfried and leading him to Brünnhilde, the sleeping beauty. Other manifestations of this same type are the role of the Angel in Messiaen's *Saint François d'Assise* or the Queen of the Night: a coloratura soprano, expressing sorrow and anger through athletic vocal exercise, the divine queen nevertheless loses her spiritual power. And although Turandot is a conventional soprano on the surface, the first notes of "In questa reggia," in which the origins of her deadly vow are traced back to the tortured soul of her raped grandmother, are unforgettably piercing. However deep or bright they may be, the female voices that express spiritual power are always extreme, as if related to the psychical state the ancient Greeks called hubris—a violent desire, supposedly inaccessible to humanity and strictly consecrated to the gods themselves. Whether deep or stratospheric, these voices verge on the divine.

Voices of Weakness

If the voices of spiritual power often reside in the realm of hubris, certain voices escape the categories I have outlined. These are the tenors without heroism. Sometimes they are ambitious and cowardly, like Prince Shuysky in *Boris Godunov* or Mime in *Siegfried,* but they may also simply be weak, like the old emperor Altoum, Turandot's father: his role is very small, but the character is made striking by the contrast between his feeble voice and his daughter's formidable strength. Finally, the best example of the special strength possessed by these exceptional weak voices is that of the great and sacred figure of the Innocent in *Boris Godunov:* simpleminded, therefore by definition committed to speak the truth, and weeping for the Russian people.

Not surprisingly, these feeble voices are closely related to the supposed weakness of so-called femininity. They run the gamut of nineteenth-century stereotypes of women: fearful, grasping, treacherous, weak, and complaining. Conversely, one can recognize a certain feminine weakness in the voices of mezzo-sopranos disguised as young boys: Cherubino in *Le nozze di Figaro,* and Octavian in *Der Rosenkavalier.*

HOW HISTORY SPEAKS THROUGH VOICES

Let us return to our starting point: the tension between the lyre and the flute, between the male timbre and the female. And let us examine the ways history is represented in opera.

Often the worlds shown on stage are completely imaginary. Sometimes they even lack geographical reality, as with the kingdom of Allemonde, ruled by the old Arkël—another bass—and by his son Golaud, in *Pelléas et Mélisande.* This is also the case in the *Ring,* in *Parsifal,* and *Lohengrin.* Sometimes, without any concrete references, the imaginary world nevertheless partakes of a kind of geographical reality: Seville in *Don Giovanni,* Peking in *Turandot,* ancient Egypt in *Aida.* But many operas have something of a factual historical background. Many tell not only stories, but histories. But if so, why does opera deliberately commit so many crimes against history? How is it that history, unlike painting, novels, or even cinema, is always "corrupted" by music?

Consider Verdi's *Don Carlos,* based on a well-known play by Schiller, which had itself already heavily disfigured the historical reality of the young heir to the Spanish empire. In Schiller's play, as in Verdi's opera, the tenor Don Carlos is a brilliant, beautiful, and unhappy young prince, in love with his stepmother who was formerly his fiancée, stolen from him by his own father, the king. Verdi's music provides this moving character with a kind of transfiguration: Don Carlos becomes the ideal and eternal hero of love and freedom, immolated on his father's altar with the help of the Inquisition. But who was the real Don Carlos? He was a poor handicapped child, mad enough to wear huge boots in the heels of which he could hide a dagger. Every day, when a servant would help the prince put on his boots, the prince would click on the boot with a finger and kill the servant. The real Don Carlos was a dangerous simpleton, whom his stepmother, Elisabeth de Valois, soothed with her compassion. This compassion is the only seed of truth in the play and opera. History tells us nothing of love, nothing of hatred for the father, and naturally nothing of any will to freedom. History and opera are almost complete opposites.

The history of Joan of Arc as told in Verdi's opera is similarly bizarre. The king of France, Charles VII, is in love with Joan, and she with him, but in order to protect her country, she refuses to marry him. How could Verdi and his librettist, Solera, transform a wild virgin, a peasant, and a warrior into a possible wife for a king? The answer certainly has something to do with the myth of impossible love, but also with competing definitions of history. Except for the famous destruction of the temple, nothing about Verdi's *Nabucco* is true. There was never a Babylonian king who converted to Judaism, and there is no trace in history of the two daughters with which Verdi and Solera endow their Nabucco.

In both cases the historical seeds of truth are easy to uncover. The historical relationship between Joan of Arc and Charles VII looks unusual in the modern Western world; and in order to explain how a simple maid convinced the king himself to attack the powerful British army, love seems more plausible than the old feeling of devotion to God, even if in Verdi's time this sentiment was quite alive. As for *Nabucco,* one can find in the Bible the famous lamentation of the exiled Jews on the borders of the river of Babylon as a source for the chorus "Va pensiero," but one would also discover there that, once settled in Babylon, these exiled Jews became advisors to the kings of Babylon, enjoying honor and friendship, just as Joseph had in Egypt. Here opera's peculiar version of history transforms the idea of friendship into its complete opposite, enslavement.

These questions may sound naive, but this is true of all the eternal questions about realism in art. The fact remains: opera has never respected the reality of history. Nevertheless, I would like to conclude with one more tale of history's corruption by opera, returning to my favorite "chameleon": *Fidelio*.

This opera is based on what is probably one of the most precise pieces of history ever depicted on the operatic stage. In 1793, during the Terror, Madame de Semblançay disguised herself as a man in order to enter the jail in the city of Tours where her husband, the count René, was imprisoned. The *accusateur public*, official envoy of the Revolution, was then Jean-Nicolas Bouilly, writer, freemason, and revolutionary. Count René de Semblançay had been thrown into jail by another revolutionary leader who wanted to steal his properties, a common enough occurrence in those times. Happily, Bouilly discovered the truth and freed his friend Semblançay.

Five years later, after the Terror had ended, Bouilly wrote his play *Léonore, ou l'Amour conjugal,* in which he cast himself in the modest role of Don Fernando, the benvolent governor. And in 1805 this play became the source for Beethoven's *Fidelio*. By this time, most German intellectuals, dismayed in succession by the Terror and the Napoleonic wars, had become disillusioned by the French Revolution. Beethoven's own disillusionment with Napoleon is notorious. When he began to write *Fidelio*, still under the influence of the freemasonry he had encountered in Bonn as a young man, he also recorded his "revolutionary feelings." These revolutionary feelings can be heard in *Fidelio,* as they can in the Ninth Symphony's "Ode to Joy." Revolutionary feelings: the expression is a strong one and has to be taken seriously.

For once in this overview of opera's brushes with history, we encounter here a precise moment of reaction to the French Revolution, an event that was strategically turned into a play by Bouilly and just as strategically chosen as an operatic subject by Beethoven. Nothing could be more premeditated than Bouilly's *Léonore* and Beethoven's *Fidelio*. We have already seen how the Nazis in Austria could make use of it to depict Austria as Leonore, Hitler as Florestan, and Goering as . . . Bouilly. Again the difference between history and imagination is enormous: the author of the libretto had been a hero himself during the French Revolution, and a century and a half later, he would be transformed into Goering!

This is how music plays the eternal role of the great seducer, the real pied piper of Hamelin. Whatever the libretto, the music dominates and carries the audience away with a dream. The audience is not there to think about history, but *volens nolens,* in spite of consciousness, moral values, in spite of all, a transformed history speaks on stage throughout music.

This at least is very real: this collective dream on stage. And depending on where they are situated in history, an audience may hear and understand the characters and their gender politics differently. The Viennese audience in 1938 accepted *Fidelio* as an opera about Hitler's victory. How was it possible to disguise Beethoven's ideal and Bouilly's experience, how could the proud, brave, victorious Leonore be reconfigured as a passive and defeated Austria welcoming her Führer? Perhaps the answer lies in those old conventions of voice and character: could it be that a century-long tradition of representing sopranos as victims was powerful enough to draw even Leonore into its web, to alter her image so totally and so convincingly? Less than ten years later, the same Viennese audience demanded another image, another Leonore: they were ready to hear the same opera as a story about their own liberation, and the opera's image as a narrative of victory was restored.

The public will always accept a description of the world that is tailored to its own historical dreams. Happily, the floating collective dream that is one of the strongest characteristics of opera as a genre leaves a large realm of freedom open for stage directors. It quite correctly allows them to set a work in some other historical world—to transport the *Ring* into the world of the emergent European capitalism as Patrice Chéreau did at Bayreuth in 1976, or *Così fan tutte* to the agitated world of a Long Island diner, as Peter Sellars did recently. As long as they do not kowtow to any political regime, as long as they do not behave like the Vienna Staatsoper in 1938, directors have every right to change the composer's historical dream: they even have the right to use opera to play on our own historical dreams, to convey to us a completely different message.

There is no other way: either directors cling to the factual historical moment in which the opera was born and are thus condemned to repeat an old, dead history, or else they adjust to *our* dreams, to the questions of our world. I would even go as far as to say that, as long as they have their own moral values, stage directors have a political *duty* to adjust the collective dream of any opera to suit the times. Reciprocally, if one of them behaves as did the Staatsoper's administrators in 1938, the public has a moral duty to reject him. Whether or not they adjust to the current issues and questions, directors must deal with the social role and stereotypes imposed by voices themselves.

For inside the field of the collective dream, the voices play their secret roles, like actors in a play blocked out by an invisible director, far more powerful than the real director. This invisible stage director might be called the unconscious, or, to borrow from Lévi-Strauss, "the savage mind." This is the reality of the mirror. Unwillingly, we could accept the eternal violence of femininity in the Queen of the Night's voice; we could bear to listen to the eternal suffering of the Russian people; we could accept Carmen dying, and Butterfly committing suicide. We would be forced to listen to the eternal tension between the lyre and the flute; we would delightfully attend the eternal battle between society and passion, men and women, power and rebellion. No wonder, and no cause for complaint: this is precisely what a part of us wants to hear.

The Absent Mother in Opera Seria

MARTHA FELDMAN

1

OPERA SERIA WAS FOUNDED on the myth of the good king. As a proto-typical tale aimed at legitimizing the prevailing political ideology of absolutism, the myth of the good king crystallized various propositions about the divinely ordained nature of the world and the role of the male monarch as a virtuous engine of its control. The king was the prime mover on earth, politically and morally, in a cosmic order that cascaded downwards from God through him to the different social orders below.

Such at least was the message codified, disseminated, and naturalized through the narratives of the classic Metastasian libretto, whose propositions—so it told the listener—were *not* up for review. This was an ironic message in the context of most eighteenth-century Italian theaters, since even as the myth (and its many variants) aimed to foreordain and foreclose its viewers' outlook on the world, in so doing it seems also to have freed them to listen when and as they pleased. Far from watching myths play out on the stage with the constant vigilance of modernist viewers, Italian spectators of Metastasian opera rarely gave their undivided attention.[1] It appears, then, that audiences' attentions were as anarchic, erratic, and unpredictable as the operas' narratives were axiomatic, inert, and repetitive—that, indeed, these two conditions were inherently linked.

In this sense, life in the opera house was hardly coextensive with the drama seen onstage, since the often tumultuous manner in which *opere serie* were experienced was at odds with the messages the works bore. These divided realities provide a useful caution that neither the domain of audience experience nor that of political narrative can be overlooked without loss to an analysis of the phenomenon of opera seria as a whole. Indeed it seems clear (as I have argued elsewhere) that discontinuous lis-

I am grateful to participants at the conference Representations of Gender and Sexuality in Opera (State University of New York at Stony Brook, September 1995) and to members of the study group on "The Anthropology of Music in Mediterranean Cultures" who attended the meeting Music as Representation of Gender in Mediterranean Cultures (Venice, Fondazione Levi, 9–11 June 1998) for ideas shared with me when I presented different versions of this essay in oral form. Special thanks are due to Lorenzo Bianconi, Philip Gossett, Mary Ann Smart, Martin Stokes, and the anonymous reviewers of this essay.

tening was possible only because endless, insuperable patriarchy was a foregone conclusion.[2]

Or so it was meant to be: other signs in Italian theater life, as we will see, betrayed deep ruptures in the field of patriarchal relations that ruled the old regime. To glimpse them, we should first recall the semiotics of space in the standard public theaters of eighteenth-century Italy, where a monarchical loge often formed the focal point for various rows of boxes, each looped around it in a semicircle, like embroidered lengths of ribbon. The classic example of such a theater was the Teatro San Carlo of Naples, built by the Bourbon king Carlo III in 1737; figure 1 shows its original architecture as it survives today.

Along the lower tiers in theaters like the San Carlo, boxes were typically owned by a noble family, with family constellations reproducing the patriarchal order articulated by the grand loge of the monarch. This same pattern repeated itself at various levels of the social order, from sovereign to nobles and on down, each box corresponding to that of the monarch and forming yet another microcosm of his family. The boxes of families higher in social station were normally situated in lower tiers of the hall and vice versa (although there were exceptions to this rule).[3] Families at higher social levels (the nobility and some wealthy civilians) generally owned their boxes, or (at minimum) leased them annually. All in all, the principal *unit* of theatrical viewing was the family; and the principal figure of power and authority within the family unit was of course the husband.

But the institution of marriage was in a peculiar state of crisis in eighteenth-century Italy, and many, if not most, husbands would not have been found in their family boxes. In the newly consolidated bourgeois public sphere, men of station were frequently drawn away by demands outside the domestic realm—by their traffic in commodities, their political engagements, and the new commerce in opinion and ideas.[4] Marriages had to respond to new economic pressures, new spheres of public exchange, and hence new patterns of existence, whose duties were largely inconsistent with the old courtly practices of baroque theatergoing. At the same time, older social forms remained strenuously in place, as if to ensure that aristocratic wives be accommodated with all the niceties of old courtly etiquette. For these and other reasons, a general state of disjunction between marital form and its content was inevitable. Indeed, if anything, the impulse to endow bourgeois marital form with courtly accoutrements seems to have increased as the content of marriage was depleted. In this respect, at least, the patriarchal order articulated by the visual arrangement of the hall was in practice drained of much of its message. Marriage, moreover, was only the most visible among a complex of family crises in *settecento* Italy: with the crisis of marriage came a crisis of motherhood, a generalized condition of doubt over whether the new public fantasy, which had begun

Figure 1. Naples, Teatro San Carlo, view of the back and sides of the
theater gallery, showing the royal box. Photo from Franco Mancini,
Il Teatro di San Carlo, 1737–1987, vol. 1 (Naples: Electa Napoli,
1987), 101. Reproduced with kind permission of the publisher.

to idealize the domestic sphere, was actually being realized by the contemporary habits of the aristocratic mother.

At the same time, over the course of the eighteenth century, the Italian
opera libretto had its own strange history of managing some of these crises
within its particular generic and representational parameters. When opera
seria was first codified within the hallowed halls of the Arcadian Academy

at the turn of the century, its most prominent practitioner, Apostolo Zeno, showed no special aversion to representing mothers onstage. Zeno's *Griselda* (1701), *Merope* (1712), and *Andromaca* (1724), for instance, all represented mothers—and valorous, protective ones at that. Yet once the genre was codified by Pietro Metastasio in the 1720s and 1730s, a canonical repertory of libretti came into being (to be set again and again throughout the century) in which almost nobody had a mother, and almost nobody seemed to notice.[5] It was only rather late in the century that mothers sometimes began to reappear, and when they did, they were most often shown in a terrible guise.

The figure of the mother will emerge as my theme toward the end of this essay. But it is not possible to understand the ambivalent and changing position of these operatic mothers without first understanding something of the quintessential father figure as structurally embodied in the divine king. As a generative figure, the father preceded even the mother in the minds of early-modern Europeans. To see how this was so, let me turn to what might be regarded as an archetype of the opera seria myth, Metastasio's *Artaserse*, to ask how the sovereign functioned as a pervasive engine of motherless kinship within the operatic imaginary.

2

The story of *Artaserse* typifies the Metastasian plot structure in oscillating continually between the demands of public duty and private desire. At the heart of this oscillation lies a tension that can only be subdued by resolving the fate of love interests, a process that tests and ultimately affirms the monarch's authority to decide affinal relations. Since the reigning monarch, King Serse, is mysteriously murdered offstage at the opera's outset, his son, prince Artaserse, becomes the immediate heir to the throne, at the same time as he is embroiled in one of the plot's two love interests: he loves a noblewoman named Semira, while his sister, the princess Mandane, loves Semira's brother Arbace. A symmetrical alliance involving a direct exchange of the young lovers between the two families seems destined early on, but for most of the opera the exchange exists only *in potentia*. Accession into the royal family by the brother-sister pair Arbace and Semira is confounded by an obstacle to their marriage imposed by their own father, the secret murderer (we later learn) of King Serse, who had acted to defend his son Arbace's honor against doubts about his worthiness as a suitor for Mandane's hand.

Details of the story need not concern us here. Rather, it is important to realize that within the context of a complex social order, the plot poses a specific problem of the *paterfamilias:* how can absolute loyalty to each consanguineal and symbolic father be maintained—and with it, loyalty to the practical and ideological exigencies of the father relation more broadly—in the face of demands that contradict and even negate one another? How can Arbace stand true to his father (who, for strategic reasons, has ended up framing him as the murderer) and yet also stand true to his murdered king and to his prince—also a friend and soon-to-be (fatherly) king? How can the princess Mandane be loyal to her beloved Arbace—who was soon to be her spouse and thus the head of her family—and yet also remain loyal to her murdered father (if, as she fears, Arbace is indeed his murderer)? How, in short, can the social order reproduce itself in the face of ineluctable conflicts, which always arise from attempts to resolve competing genealogical paradigms?

The liminal figure in this conundrum is not the one occupying the pinnacle of the hierarchy—namely, Artaserse—but his subject and friend, Arbace. Once the scent of guilt descends upon him early in Act I, his exoneration, and the devastating trials of conflicted loyalty he undergoes, become the keys to a general pacification of everyone in the realm, principals and onlookers alike: through Arbace's exoneration, the way is cleared for the two marriages, and the opera can end with the populace singing praises to king Artaserse. Analogues to Arbace's fate can be found in numerous other Metastasian plots (for example, Megacles in *L'Olimpiade,* or Ezio in the opera *Ezio,* to name two)—plots in which a beleaguered novice proves to be upwardly mobile through his virtuous nature, and thereby also to be an ideal object of identification for the new bourgeois viewing subject. Throughout the story, Arbace braves his wrenching dilemmas precisely so that he may establish his credentials as a worthy initiate into manhood and hence (beyond the reach of the plot) as a candidate for paternity, and moreover for the paternity of royal offspring. All the principal players undergo their own trials by fire, the women included; but because Arbace's trials rage fiercest, he experiences the most dramatic rite of passage, one that can be completed only once virtue triumphs by paying tribute simultaneously to multiple father figures. This is consistent with other Metastasian plots, in which females can, and usually do, inhabit a liminal role involving moral evolution, but are never the opera's leading moral figure. The prima donna was normally *suddita seconda* as far as sovereignty went—a partner in realizing the succession of the dynasty, yet in no sense a unilateral, much less equal, body.

In the midst of these trials, conflicts are mediated through an ethical hierarchy with obligations that point ever upward from lovers, friends, counselors, and confidantes, to fathers, brothers, and sisters, and finally to kings. As a rule, kings trump kin and kin trump nonblood relations in resolving conflict. Accordingly, the moral prerogatives postulated through this scalar movement also place public concerns above private ones, with the king at the apex of the earthly order as public representative of wider social interests. Larger clan relations are thought to bind king and kin, as well as other alliances, to help ensure the perpetuity of the patriarchy.

The king alone among all figures occupies at once the two categories of sacred and profane. In accordance with long-standing Western tradition (as described most famously by Ernst Kantorowicz), he is human with respect to person but divine and eternal with respect to office. This was not so much true in a legal sense (as it had been in medieval English and French traditions) as it was a matter of general consciousness, albeit one that was gradually being undermined, notwithstanding the tenacity of ideological tradition.[6] Accordingly, the direct link of the king to the sacred is instantiated in Metastasio's *Artaserse* through a host of symbols. When Artaserse attains the crown, he bestows sublime love on the people in exchange for their earthly loyalty (Act III, scene 11). In the midst of the rite he is to drink from a "sacred cup" by which he imbibes the eternal polity into the king's body and consolidates his connection to the sacred.[7] Mediating the two realms, his double position between sacred and profane is seen to function as an aid to securing new affinal relations, new princely offspring, and thus the general harmony and durability of the kingship.

At the same time the king works as an earthly link to the sacred *through* his subjects, and principally (again) through the heroic young male. Well into Act III, this link is affirmed in the major twist of the plot, when Arbace's sword becomes the divine rod of iron that breaks the back of his father's duplicitous accomplice, who has been conspiring to rouse the people against the king. Eventually the incident proves decisive in resolving dilemmas of alliance, but its immediate function is to offer proof that divine providence shines on the new reign.

3

In this respect, Arbace's liminal role is relevant not merely to him but also to others. More precisely, it is not just transformative *of* him but transforming *for* others, who depend for their own enlightenment on his extraordinary capacity to realize subjectively, through honorable action, the virtue immanent in the body social. Yet the enlightenment of those others—and specifically of eighteenth-century viewers—could not be achieved simply by altering certain objective facts of life depicted onstage. It depended on the effects of a communicative process to which human passions were fundamental. This is something audience members came to know by the very manner in which Arbace's intervention against insurrection was made known to them: rather than Arbace's heroism being shown onstage, his actions are reported by Mandane, whose account reveals the medium of passion to have been critical to the pacification of the populace (and, implicitly, to Arbace's subsequent moral ascent). A key feature of her account is that at the brink of his final upward resolution Arbace preserved the populace from unrest not with reason but with impassioned oratory: "On some with threats he wrought, on some with prayers; oft changed his looks from placid to severe" (III, 13). Arbace's fervor is finally the instrument that restores order to the kingdom and joins him to the royal family through his love for the princess. Occurring at the very moment when the polity is most threatened, passion becomes the kingdom's warrant against doom.

In this respect the magical effects of passion that Mandane recounts can be seen as a narrative token of the force that drives opera seria—the emotion collected and poured forth in singing and hearing arias. In the face of that lyric force, storytelling became relatively insignificant as an immediate agent in affecting most listeners, except perhaps when audiences were constrained to listen in a sovereign's presence. And even then, I would insist, following the plot did not mean acknowledging that the myth of the good king was *true*. Rather, it was proof positive of its power as myth, an affirmation that the medium of the message was effective, and that myths deserved to be legitimating because in some sense they were successful in objectifying certain subjective needs and conditions. It was for this reason that the person of the monarch (to recall Norbert Elias) was repeatedly made sovereign through the imitation of his behavior by his subjects.[8] By extending a condition of his bodily person, his subjects also extended his controls and benefits—of luxury, abundance, and virtue—into the body politic. Everyone collectively thereby became the monarch, who was dissolved into the new sovereign of the people.[9] When the king was present, performances demonstrated simultaneously to him and to his subjects the efficacy of the propositions at hand; when he was absent, performances iterated kingly force by virtue of reenactment.

The process of generating passions, magically linked to the sovereign's moral and spiritual condition, made sovereignty more than a mere site of power and charisma. It rendered sovereignty centerless, invisible, and pervasive—internalized by the sovereign's subjects. Consequently the sovereign's physical presence became all but unnecessary and the immortality of his spirit was ineffably demonstrated.[10]

If anything, the operatic plot contributed to this invisibility by dispersing propositions and symbolic currencies so thoroughly as virtually to absolve audiences of any requirement to evaluate events on stage for evidence of verifiable realities. That work was sooner done by genres that operated dramaturgically on more narrative terms. Narrative was necessarily minimized in a genre whose truth claims were decided in advance. Opera seria in its classic form asserts a social order that exists naturally, inevitably, and

endlessly. As it progresses, it merely turns the pages of eternal time, its outcome preordained and its messages and denouements hardly susceptible to
validation by earthly mortals. The characters in an opera seria therefore
need not be situated in *real* histories of family, place, or time. They are abstract actors of a transcendental truth, divine messengers of absolutist
metaphysics. Like Athena, they spring without origins from the head of
Zeus—literally, for the Father is so engendering that mothers typically
could be dispensed with altogether.

In this sense, seria's moral lessons had limits. They reminded people how
to show deference to the king and other superiors, especially fathers. They
could demonstrate how to court future spouses, how to treat brothers, how
to identify and resolve conflicts between family and state. One thing they
did not teach—or taught only by negation—was how to view mothers.

4

Mothers would have given centerless kingship a knowable core. Far from
grounding itself in realistic polities and genealogies, opera seria thrived on
roaming representations of kinship and power in which omnipresence was
all—father, bishop, king, general; dynasty, oligarchy, principality, or papal
state. As such, the claims of opera seria broke down within a material world
of effects and of things. Its taken-for-granted nature depended on highly
saturated and pliable signs—the divine king, noblesse oblige, the magnanimous prince, the royal crown, the divine sword, the altar and sun, the sacred cup. Enormously pliant, opera seria sounded the absolutist order in a
general way while numerous changes were rung on the messages it was understood to express.[11]

In its classic form, the messages of opera seria were inscrutable precisely
because they were transmitted in mystifying ways. Seria could more easily
articulate such generalized messages by (paradoxically) disarticulating the
process by which a viewer might test such truths, the modes that might lead
viewers either to certify or to spurn them. Thus perspectival illusions could
disregard the exigencies of human form; audiences could ignore the genders that inhabited characters on the stage; and kinship structures could
circumvent the realities of human generation. Far from "promoters" and
"producers" using material evidence and narrated stories to prove its
propositions to listeners[12]—"the king is omnipotent and magnanimous,"
"princes are valiant lovers," "subjects must imitate codes of honor similar
to those of their royal superiors," and so forth—those propositions could
better be ratified through the illogical magicalities of operatic staging.

The high points of opera seria therefore occur when the critical junctures
of plot—moral transformations and political turns—coincide with extra-

ordinary outpourings of feeling. The emotional effect Mandane's rhetoric attributes to Arbace resembles the effects that seria itself enacted on its listeners by means of lyric expression. Arias by turn articulated and resolved conflicts, not through rational deliberation but through expressions of moral outrage, demands for justice, and outpourings of love that were concentrated effusively at the ends of scenes. Arias dissolved narrative into lyric magic, as recitative culminated repeatedly in outbursts of unfathomable, mystically empowered song.

This special role of song was defined as well through spatial location. Sharply demarcated musically, arias were performed at the forestage or *proscenio,* that border zone between stage and house typically flanked by proscenium boxes, which helped transcend the more everyday operations of plot and action. Lyric moments thus inhabited a liminal space where normal time and action were suspended, where feeling annihilated reason, and where the passion collected in the recitative could be unleashed at the scene's end. In this way, arias epitomized the myriad formal disjunctions that caught the attention of eighteenth-century writers on opera seria— between reciting and singing, story and song, opera and ballet, character and gender. To outsiders, it often seemed as if all of opera seria's forms had astounding license to disjoin other forms—indeed, to shake outer form loose from meaning altogether.[13]

5

So too, we might say, the lives of couples who watched from their boxes. For just as arias and the emotions they conjured up were disjunct from the narrative flow, the lived content of aristocratic marriages had largely been rent from its representation. Indeed by the eighteenth century, the institution of marriage in Italy had been laboring in a state of extraordinary tension for some time. Although wives now moved freely and frequently throughout the expanding public sphere, marriages within the Italian aristocracy were still typically arranged by parents.[14] Future husbands were often little known, if at all, to the females who were to wed them, a situation that was intensified by the fact that girls were often educated in convents and thus prevented from making acquaintance with men in the outside world, much less from knowing anything about marriage.

In reality, a marriage market that had long been depressed in Italy gave the lie to the idealized model of family, central to representations of eighteenth-century Italy. Too little capital was available for marriage. Many women ended up as spinsters or nuns, many men did not marry, and many women lived out most of their lives as widows, never able to remarry.[15] As the aristocracy experienced growing uncertainty, fiscal and social, financial expedients dictating the bottom line increasingly governed choices of husbands. At the same time, an expanding public sphere created new family conditions that often took husbands away for business and public life while wives kept up social appearances on the promenades, in carriage rides, at the theater, and in daily visits to church, where they continued to play their role as vessels of virtue by upholding religious practices for aristocratic (and, in some official symbolic sense, Italian) society as a whole. By the turn of the eighteenth century, the contradictions of early-modern married life had finally been stretched to their tolerable limit through the exploitation of a compensatory arrangement, which provided aristocratic wives with surrogates for husbands who were preoccupied with business affairs and who traditionally kept separate mistresses.

Enter the *cicisbeo,* an extreme manifestation of late courtly society. Roughly defined, the *cicisbeo* (often called synonymously the *cavaliere servente*) was a male escort in Italian noble society who fulfilled a wife's perceived needs for company, intimacy, and above all public partnership.[16] While extremely little is known of them, it seems that *cicisbei* could be either married or single, and were typically drawn from the noble class, possibly at times chosen by common accord between husband and wife. They often entered long-term relationships with a single married woman—relationships that in some cases lasted for decades—although *cicisbei* could also be engaged on an occasional or short-term basis. Those who assumed long-term positions took part in numerous activities, some of which, in centuries past, had had little or no existence in couples' lives and others of which had formerly been reserved for spouses: taking the wives they served on visits and outings to public theaters and cafes; attending morning toilet, when a wife was dressed and groomed by her maids, and thence to church; and helping to serve her at mealtimes.[17] Some of these activities were immortalized in Pietro Longhi's characteristic (if somewhat sardonic) portrayals from the mid-eighteenth century (see figure 2).[18] So widespread was the fashion of nonspousal escort that some women complained that they were forced to endure the *cicisbeo* over the company of husbands they preferred.[19] Yet as Charles De Brosses remarked, "it would have been a kind of dishonor had one not been publicly ascribed to her"[20]—and thus it happened that the order of marriage was disordered through a social rule.[21]

It seems unlikely that *cicisbeismo* met with immediate acceptance once the practice got underway, even in those parts of Italy where it evidently proliferated; nor that its place in society was ever safe from censure. The only extended scholarly publication on the phenomenon to date, Luigi Valmaggi's anecdotal monograph of 1927, traces a gradual but partial endorsement in moralist literature, starting from the outraged tirade of Carlo Maria Maggi in the late seventeenth century to an apologia by Paolo Mattia Doria near the mid-eighteenth century, followed by mounting resis-

Figure 2. *La dichiarazione,* copy after Pietro Longhi, oil on canvas (ca. 1750); Venice, Museo Correr. Reproduced with permission.

tance and renewed invective as the century wore on.[22] Maggi claimed in his "Ritiramenti per le dame" that far from being innocent, the practice (still novel in his time) was a sin against God, an *invitation* to sin given the best of intentions, and an assault on women's religious work, which gave women generally a bad example.[23] The principled grounds of objection were resolutely religious. But already by the second decade of the eighteenth century Giandomenico Barile, in his *Moderne conversazioni giudicate nel tribunale della coscienza* (Rome, 1716), was willing to mollify his global critique with a revealing, if limited, justification: exchanges between women and their *cicisbei* should not be silenced for being evil or scandalous so long as they took place between persons distinguished by nobility of birth and integrity of habits.[24] For Barile, birthright was enough to excuse an otherwise repugnant practice. Within a short time, it seems, the phenomenon could be characterized not as illicit, but as a form of "noble servitude" and the *cicisbeo* assumed the status of an honored escort—even in cases wherein a larger theological critique endured.[25] Thus by the time Doria published his *Dialogo* in 1741,[26] the ground had been laid for a justification by class that situated the *cicisbeo* equivocally at the endpoint of a quasi-feudal tradition while also trying to distance him from it: courtly manners were preferable (so Doria's argument went) to the old feudal modes of so-called honor—the "barbarous and dissolute" way of living previously in use in Italy, which allowed duels, violence, and abuses of various kinds to be admired, even though they were more suited to bandits than men of virtue. Doria went on to deny charges linking escorts to sex and to rehabilitate the practice by aligning it with models of Platonic love.[27]

This discourse in defense of the *cicisbeo* played to a surprising extent upon sentimental nostalgia for the dying tradition of chivalric service linked to an old feudal world, even as the *cicisbeo* was being repositioned on new terrain: not the hilltops and castles of the lord's estate, but the urban salon and the public theater; and not the more stable subjective ground of masculine valor but the increasingly precarious one of servility in swishy lace and ribbons. The seemingly feminized nature of servitude, widely attached to *cicisbei*, stirred up tensions throughout the century. The anonymous author of the "Reflessioni filosofiche e politiche sul genio e carattere de' cavalieri detti serventi" portrayed the *cicisbeo* as "the shadow of the body of the woman served, whom he never leaves wherever he goes."[28] Another account, this one by Joseph Baretti, a transalpine Italian who lived most of his years in London, detailed the elaborate rituals of servitude as they were played out in daily church-going in order to underscore how extravagantly the *cicisbeo* shadowed and foreshadowed his lady's every move.[29] Arriving for morning services at ten or eleven, the woman was ushered through the church portal by her faithful escort, who preceded her so as to raise the curtain at the entrance door. He bathed his finger in the holy water and came to place it on her, she responding with a little bow. After mass she would stay seated for several moments, then genuflect, make the sign of the cross, recite a short prayer, and give the book from which she had read to a domestic or to the *cicisbeo*. She would then take her fan, rise, make the sign of the cross again, bow to the main altar, and exit preceded by her *cicisbeo*, who would again present her with holy water, raise the curtain to exit, and extend a hand for the return home.

Even though many fashionable circles considered it essential that women not be seen in public without a male escort (and, conversely, it had become unseemly in the same circles for husbands to be seen performing marital tasks in public),[30] these extreme avatars of servitude could not fail to be problematically aligned with the old world of courtly etiquette and the subordinated character of the female sex. Thus while the *cicisbeo* must have helped make good use of male surplus in the marriage market by relieving husbands of marital chores, he was also victimized by his ambiguous status. Adorning and subjugating himself to the woman he accompanied, he became simultaneously (if insidiously) assimilated to her sex. In the later decades of the eighteenth century this assimilation was the most common target of moralists' barbs; the *cicisbeo* became a bird in flight, a fop, fatuous, vain—so coquettish as to be barely male.

As a figure uncertain in deed and in kind, moreover, he came to symbolize sexual ambiguity in its most depraved state and, worse, to flaunt his embodiment of it in a kind of vulgar spectacle. One moralist summarized this objection by comparing the spectacle of *ciscisbeismo* to a "national disease" in which all Italy had become the "*stage or theater* of a bordello."[31] But the objection was voiced in the face of the *cicisbeo*'s relatively unmarked incorporation into marital arrangements, in which he clearly took part precisely because of the performances he could provide: extravagant displays of honor, feints of spousehood that so thoroughly imitated its ideal form as to surpass the limitations of the real—compensations for absence, in short, through an exaggerated show of presence.

In the end, his ambiguity and his utility both derived inseparably (and ironically) from the spectacle he made of normativity, a spectacle that betrayed itself through its intemperate excess.[32] In truth, of course, he represented "norms" that were far more contested and less "normative" than his behavior could suggest. In this respect, the *cicisbeo* was not so different from the castrato, another member of a caste of deviants who—abstracted as the perfect male (most typically the prince or noble hero)—was called upon to represent a mythical patriarchy in a mythical homeland.

Like the castrato, the *cicisbeo* gave a command performance each evening at the theater, where he accompanied his "woman" to her family box. There, in the standard practice of eighteenth-century theater, the inner hall staged the audience as much as the *palcoscenico* staged the opera, each box curtained, framed, and flickering with its own candlelight.[33] Across the panorama of such little "theaters," the *cicisbeo* and his lady sat boxed like marionettes, and it was here that he appeared stereotypically—and ever more dubiously—as the supreme gallant.

Most striking in the invective that rained down on the practice of *cicisbeismo* later in the eighteenth century was the way it had come to signal ever-deepening social ills. Now seen as a corrupt proxy of the good husband, the *cicisbeo* became ruinous to the souls of women, a defiler of womanhood, wifedom, and motherhood. Under the sway of the *cicisbeo,* wives were thought to rebel against husbands and even lose their natural love for their own children. In time the *cicisbeo* became an icon of antiaristocratic discontent, attacked along with the vanities of aristocratic women.[34]

Not surprisingly, a sharp decline in the practice coincided in the last decades of the century with the period when the aristocracy was at its most vulnerable, and when its censure became inseparable from the larger moral project of reconstructing the family, a project in which literati such as Vittorio Alfieri played a clamorous role.[35] In this prerevolutionary imaginary, "true" love—of hearth and home—had been ravaged by the falsehoods of aristocratic dissimulation, of which the *cicisbeo* was simply the most glaring manifestation. But worst of all, *cicisbei* were ruinous to the ethical core of the nation, which was beginning to be understood—partly under the influence of prerevolutionary France—as "a family writ large."[36] In the new morality etched by reformers, religious and revolutionary alike, mothers were to be the moral educators of their children; and in this work *all* women, aristocratic and plebeian, would be created equal.[37]

6

Although this was the rhetoric of the French Revolution, it was one that had currency throughout most of western Europe by the 1780s and especially the 1790s. The discourses of the family that surrounded the Revolution bring out the implications of the absent mother and the king-as-father in a blaze of clarity. As Lynn Hunt argues, French society moved in the later eighteenth century from imagining its rulers as fathers to condemning the fathers of the ancien régime with near-pathological fear.[38] Within the imaginary collective of the ancien régime, virtually all princes and ladies had served as fantasy parents.[39] By the latter half of the century, however, such fantasies had come to be regarded as dangerous daydreams, phantasms of adolescence. Simultaneous with this new attitude, French culture was experiencing a shattering ambivalence about the role of fathers, figurative and real. Since the magical nature of kingship was inseparable from the axiomatic nature of fatherhood, parental authority generally—especially, though not only, paternal—had to be reevaluated.[40] Deference, as taught to the king's subjects and the father's children alike, could no longer be granted automatically. Each person was now in principle a contracting social being, responsible for his or her moral relations with the larger world.

The watchmen of the people's newfound liberty were to be the brothers of the republic—in a Freudian sense, children of the fallen father—banded together to ensure fraternal rights at any cost: "fraternité ou mort." The central drama of the Revolution was therefore the killing of the king, an act effected notionally on 21 September 1792 when kingship was legally abolished (and with it the very word, still regarded by many as what one deputy called "a talisman whose magical force can serve to stupefy").[41] To ensure that *both* the king's bodies were exterminated, however, only an execution framed in the regal terms of ritual sacrifice would do. Louis's last words on the scaffold augured the utility of his own death in precisely sacrificial terms, bidding that his blood be "useful to the French" and a way of "appeasing God's anger." A great crowd stood witness to the event, dipping their spikes and kerchiefs in the blood after the dripping head was hoisted aloft by the executioner. Soon afterwards, the radical weekly *Révolutions de Paris* claimed that the blood of Louis Capet had cleansed the French of a thirteen-hundred-year stigma, while depicting Liberty as a voracious pagan goddess whom one cannot "make auspicious . . . except by offering in sacrifice the life of a great culprit."[42]

Note that the "brothers" never denied the king's magical status: on the contrary, they set out to "devour" and thus encompass and transform him into and through themselves. As Hunt points out, following the historian David P. Jordan, the announcement in the *Journal des hommes libres* the day after the execution cast the event as pivotal not so much in the remaking of the French political system as in the remaking of French systems of belief: "Today people are at last convinced that a king is only a man; and that no man is above the laws."[43] By killing the king, the brothers depleted his magic and he became ordinary. Once dead, the king's head and body were quickly thrown into a grave and covered with a double layer of quicklime to aid its rapid decomposition. The space previously occupied by the king now marked a "sacred void" that would be filled by the collective body of individual citizens, equal in their rights, whom his death had helped to create.

How sisters would figure in this new body of citizens is a problem for others to take up; but it is telling that mothers too had failed the French symbolically and had to be held to account for fathers' failures. Central to the dramatization of this charge was, of course, the figure of Marie Antoinette. In 1793 the queen was indicted for a variety of sexual crimes, presaged in the popular realm by representations of her in pornographic and moralizing literature that had been flooding Parisian bookstalls through the 1780s and early 90s (see Figure 3). The litany of charges was exhaustive: adultery, homosexuality, sodomy, bestiality, incest. The queen's body bore an unbearable polysemy, a polysemy identified in her ability to dissemble. Hence a second set of charges accused her of "having taught the king to dissimulate—that is, how to promise one thing in public and plan another in the shadows of the court."[44] Her sexualized body was a mask. A malleable symbol, it was aristocratic and feminine, like the body of the courtier (or, in Italy, like the body of the *cicisbeo* and the castrato), and therefore meretricious; but it was also monstrous because part male and yet castrating.[45] The sacred void that loomed with the destruction, symbolic and literal, of the king and queen left only one measurable space for women when all was said and done, a space of pure monumentality. Women would be the Nation, Freedom, Reason, Virtue, the Statue of Liberty bearing her torch—an infinitely imitable figure because unreal.

de mes transports reconnoissez Isrelle
Dieux, tant dappas excitent ma tendresse

Figure 3. Marie Antoinette in sexual embrace with a man and a woman; engraving from *La Vie privée, libertine et scandaleuse*, 1793; Paris, Bibliothèque Nationale. Reproduced with permission.

7

By the latter half of the century both France and Italy were awash with tales of renegade fathers, errant and absent mothers, and orphaned children conveyed in both sentimental literature and *opera semiseria*. Familar examples of the latter include Paisiello's *Nina, ossia la pazza per amore* (1789) and Paer's *Camilla* (1799), both based on libretti by Marsollier des Vivetières and both objects of frenzied popularity on Italian soil.[46] Shifts in opera seria were slower to come. Since Metastasio had virtually expunged those few mothers who had been admitted to the genre by Zeno and others around 1700, opera seria later in the century tended at first to transform the family it depicted—first by lessening fathers morally or by killing them off. King Mitridate is a case in point: in Cigna-Santi's *Mitridate* of 1767 (set by Mozart for the Regio-Ducal Teatro of Milan three years later), the king is a tyrant who manages to redeem himself and (magically) his kingdom too; in Sografi's libretto (1796; rev. 1797), on the other hand, Mitridate is a monstrous enemy of justice who dies by his own sword to the relief of the populace—a revolutionary revision, if ever there was.[47]

In opera seria mothers came in for a only small share of parental demonization, since even late in the century the genre rarely resuscitated them. The striking countercase of Semiramide widely restored to the stage one mother whose motherhood Metastasio had all but suppressed in his *Semiramide riconosciuta*. By the mid-1780s, Semiramide had been changed into the notorious virago, familiar from Voltaire's play, in which she murders her husband, plots an incestuous marriage, and is stabbed to death by her son. A Milan version of 1784 by Moretti with music by Mortellari was content to have her lover assassinated. But the infamous Giovannino libretto *La vendetta di Nino, ossia La morte di Semiramide,* staged at Florence two years later in a dramatic setting by Alessio Prati, culminated in matricide onstage.[48]

The absent mother, banished by Metastasio, had thus returned as a twin to those representations of Marie Antoinette emerging around the same time across the Alps. Not that Moretti/Martellari or (even) Giovannini/Prati tried to demonize Semiramide through a prism of sexuality—not explicitly, to be sure. If anything, theirs was a chamber of horrors, with roots in the *ombra* scenes crafted by Mattia Verazi in earlier years. Yet it was a chamber designed to make viewers quiver with abomination, to be no less repulsive to the viewing subject—and no less undermining of his or her subjective order—than the spectacle of the queen's alleged atrocities in bed. Exit the *cicisbeo,* enter the bourgeois family, the panacea of the new social order and the order in which the new-made person was to emerge.

That it became possible to conjure up fathers and mothers as irredeemably guilty, and thus recast the plights of sons and daughters, was one token of a new subjectivity in later eighteenth-century Europe, a subjectivity that valorized the capacities of the individual for moral reflection, judgment, and self-improvement. As the individual's world became ever more scrutable, the happy ending of the familial history was demystified. With it, too, the old schismatics of representation, staged and not—which displaced singers from sets, characters from singers' genders, husbands from wives, and mothers from children—began to ease. Where once the theater reached past the worldly, with sets so abstruse and limitless that no singer could inhabit them, with sopranos resounding unaccountably from male bodies and ballets tucked radiantly but extraneously between operatic acts, now a new logic of representation imposed itself. The earlier ways had come to signal the perilous feints of the old order. And the scrutinies that reviewed them and forced them out were so many signs that the crisis of absolutism had been eclipsed by the coming crises of modernity. But that is another story.

Staging Mozart's Women

WYE JAMISON ALLANBROOK, MARY HUNTER,
GRETCHEN A. WHEELOCK

KONSTANZE AND ZERLINA, "Martern aller Arten" and "Batti, batti." Both characters and both arias may give modern audiences—especially those with even an inkling of feminist consciousness—pause. Konstanze goes on and on (and on) in ways that seem out of proportion to the comic-opera threat she is under. She sings with extraordinary power and virtuosity, blasting the Pasha into dumbfounded silence, or at least into wondering whether he just dreamt this. But she can only exercise this extraordinary power from a position of being attached, even possessed. Zerlina, on the contrary, seems to be asking her lover to beat her up as a way of reassuring him that she still loves him, having gone willingly into an illicit affair that turned out badly. She may fully expect not to be beaten, but she manipulates Masetto by assuming a posture of total submission. Both arias explore or express something about the nature of female power in the late eighteenth century, and what they have to say raises interesting questions for staging. Is it a salutary discomfort they may induce? Should producers and singers "do something" about it, and if so what? How does the act of performance endorse, undercut, or relate in any way to the dramatic and social content of the work? And ultimately, what is the responsibility of those who put on Mozart's operas to take and "perform" a position on their values? Can a performance resist? Should a performance endorse? How separate should the actual performer be from the performance of a (possibly distasteful) role?

The three short papers below represent our thoughts on these subjects as we prepared them for a panel discussion. Although we all worried about "performance," we started from rather different assumptions about where the performance takes place, and thus who was the principal "performer." Gretchen Wheelock's paper points out that Konstanze's extraordinary "performance of constancy" arises from the fact that, historically, women have been expected to display their culturally assigned roles in order to hold on to their social status. Thus, the compositional and performative extravagances of Konstanze's "Martern" are necessary and proportional responses to the power of the Pasha to degrade her. Moreover, the fact that she must (and can) marshall a response proportional to his power effectively robs him of a voice: she appropriates in her aria of defiance the conventional opportunity for a thwarted ruler's rage aria. In this framework, Mozart (via the character of Konstanze) is in a sense the principal recreator (or performer) of this social function, and the job of the singer is to communicate as powerfully and effectively as possible the significance of the cultural performance embodied in the vocal one.

Wheelock reads this aria as a powerful statement of resistance on Konstanze's part—a resistance that, ironically "works" only because it is also a statement of constancy to Belmonte. This is a position that contemporary conduct books clearly reinforce. In addressing the relevance of a production in which the excesses of staged display bring the act of performance itself to the fore, Wheelock argues that a performance in which the real-life singer can be distinguished from the fictional character (a common feminist strategy in reading victimized women) can provide an ironizing perspective on Konstanze's vocal power. Indeed, when one singer (Edita Gruberova) returns for a curtain call, Wheelock sees her as replicating in her obedience to the conventions of operatic behavior Konstanze's captivity to the social conventions of constancy. In this aria, then, the richest site for feminist exploration is not the interstice between the modern singer and the historical character, but resides, rather, within the historical frame of the opera, and at the interface between performing an aria (a vocal and rhetorical activity) and performing a culturally scripted function.

Mary Hunter uses the singer/character distinction to think about what sorts of woman's work can be achieved, and what sorts of female viewpoints suggested, in the relations between a modern voice and consciousness and a historical character. Her contribution proceeds from the (unstated) assumption that since Mozart's female characters are rarely victimized to the extent of most vocally nineteenth-century tragic heroines, the questions about "feminist" stagings of these works, or about the discovery of the powerful singer behind or alongside the powerless character, will necessarily be different from those in nineteenth-century opera, where the demise of the most powerful female character is almost a given. Two questions that might arise in staging an opera where the heroine gets what she wants, but where all she wants is her man, are whether a production (or a singer) can comment on the conditions that make marriage the only possible happy end, and whether the singer can project a set of desires or values distinct from, or larger than, those of the character, thus throwing the situation of the character into relief. Another question relevant to feminist stagings of operas where the women move along a pretermined trajectory toward the right mate is the relation between the dramatic location of a character and her position with respect to the auditorium audience. Taking as examples a performance of "Martern aller Arten" in which the producer clearly decided not to let the singer convey a set of values different from the character, and a version of "Batti, batti" in which Zerlina projects erotic power over Masetto but is thoroughly objectified in relation to the auditorium audience, the essay begins to suggest how issues of female power in Mozart (both within the narrative and in the hall) might be addressed in production.

If Hunter's contribution depends on thinking about the potential gap between singer and character (or between the production and the drama itself), Wye Allanbrook's essay looks into the space between then and now, between a situation in which Mozart's musical gestures evoked a visceral understanding of their social implications, and a situation in which we can now choose whether or not to draw attention to, and make sense of, their multiple meanings. This contribution proceeds from the idea that Mozart's sense of male-female power relations was highly nuanced, and that a production that respects and communicates the various levels of persuasion, teasing, seriousness, and play in the music of "Batti, batti" will give an audience both a sense of historical grounding and a transhistorical understanding of human relations. Allanbrook argues that Peter Sellars's production of this aria chooses not to listen to the rhythmic and social gestures of the music, but rather to concentrate on the surface demand for violence. The failure of Sellars's production to do justice to this aria raises a larger question of updating; can a singer in modern dress in a modern setting in any production take Zerlina's position seriously without invoking the politics of domestic violence? And is domestic violence the issue to raise when the aria is (at least immediately) about Zerlina's power over Masetto, rather than the other way round?

In one sense, of course, the question of how to stage the "then" of Mozart's world versus its "now" (or our own present, refracted through Mozart's and his librettists' texts) is at the heart of all three contributions, despite their differences. It could be argued that for Wheelock and Hunter, the ideal "feminist" stagings of Mozart would convey a sense that the world of these operas is in many ways irretrievably different from our own, perhaps especially with respect to its sense of gender relations. These contributors would want a production to give a sense of the integrity of the values of a historically and morally distant world, but would also want production choices and performance strategies to communicate the ideas that these values are culturally specific, that they can be respected without being endorsed or promulgated, and that our own mores can play into a production as commentary. Allanbrook, on the other hand, might argue that Mozart's world is sufficiently rich and complex and continuous with our own that ideal productions would suggest no necessary distance from the values of Mozart's operas, but would, rather, embrace the subtleties of the music to bring out the complex negotiations of power between men and women, negotiations that are as meaningful now as they were then, despite the differences in the social structures that contain them. These ideals about how productions of Mozart's operas might intersect with a range of feminist consciousnesses do not map perfectly onto the more frequently discussed (and too easily polarized) categories of "authentic" and "modern" performance, but comparable questions of familiarity and distance, or aesthetic quality and emotional impact, arise when thinking about gender representation in these operas as when considering instruments and ornamentation. Although none of us exactly says it, we all consider gender representation an integral component of performance practice.

Perhaps fortunately both for us and for Mozart's operas, there are no definitive answers about how to retain and convey the integrity of an "original" while still treating with honesty and respect the sensibilities of the times in which that original is re-created. The following short contributions do not attempt to supply answers, either individually or in juxtaposition, but rather try to refine and complicate the questions that performers and producers of old works in new times have no choice but to consider.

KONSTANZE PERFORMS CONSTANCY
Gretchen A. Wheelock

Konstanze's voice in Mozart's *Die Entführung aus dem Serail* is probably best remembered for its blazing coloratura and extensive range in "Martern aller Arten"—an aria also famous for its length—in which the heroine faces down the Pasha Selim's threats of torture after she has refused his love. Presenting an enormous challenge to the athleticism of the singer's vocal chords, this number has been variously regarded as a dramaturgical mistake,[1] a director's nightmare,[2] and a regrettable concession to the "flexible throat" of the first prima donna, Caterina Cavalieri, to which Mozart himself alluded, though not in connection with *this* aria.[3] "Martern" is, in any case, practically guaranteed to stop the show, a fact that is documented even in filmed versions of the opera. In the production directed by August Everding and conducted by Karl Böhm, with Edita Gruberova in the starring role, for example, the camera continues to run as the diva is brought back onto the stage for a prolonged bow to thunderous applause—a discontinuity that replicates live performance.[4] Needless to say, the Pasha Selim's remarks following Konstanze's astonishing display are omitted in this production: for him to ask, "Was this a dream?" would open an even wider gap in dramatic continuity once the fact of performance has been made so very prominent. In fact, in three of the four videotape productions of *Die Entführung* I watched in preparing this paper, the Pasha is rendered speechless, and in two of these he leaves the stage before the aria is over.[5]

Many have remarked on the fact that the Pasha Selim is musically mute in this opera, but it seems especially remarkable that he has no aria at this critical juncture in the drama, as Konstanze rejects his suit in no uncertain terms. Given the provocation of this moment, Selim should fire off a raging, vengeful aria as sounding proof of his threats (as does his immediate predecessor, Soliman, in Mozart's Singspiel-melodrame *Zaide,* as well as such other rulers as Mitridate and Lucio Silla in their respective *opere serie*). Instead, Konstanze seizes the moment and hijacks her captor's opportunity to vocalize his rage: taking the words right out of his mouth, she turns them back on him to voice her defiance in an aria that silences the tyrant for nearly ten minutes.

There may be various reasons to account for the Pasha's "voicelessness" in this opera, but I don't think that Mozart was incapable of writing a suitable aria for him, as has been suggested.[6] Nor do I agree with the assertion that the spoken word is more demonstrative of Selim's ultimate power.[7] Indeed, in this instance the Pasha Selim seems decidedly reduced by his lack of a voice. A more likely explanation might be sought in the nature of *Konstanze* as subject, role, and performance. For not only does the constant heroine take over the Pasha's words and potential aria, and even elements of his own "Turkish" music,[8] she also takes on a new and powerfully mixed voice: in turn imperious and imploring, athletic and elaborate, martial and *empfindsam,* she is equal partner to both *concertante* and *tutti* complements of the orchestra. This expansion to a more comprehensive command of musical expression and rhetorical force effectively erases her captor's voice and neutralizes his power over us. Konstanze is the more capable of commanding our attention—and of extending that attention to unprecedented lengths. For no other character did Mozart ever write such a long and demanding aria as this.

Traditionally, coloratura and virtuosity have been regarded as relatively empty of feeling, or at least as less revealing of a character's inner emotions than those expressive, lyrical arias that lay claim to the "heartfelt." Seen as mere display, coloratura is perhaps suspect for its tendency to focus attention on the *singer's* performance and instrument, upstaging the dramatic force of the character and her music. On balance, we more readily take the heroine's solitary lament as proof of genuine feeling, more reliable as a private confession than the bravura aria's public display.

However one might choose to argue this question, I want to look at "Martern aller Arten" as precisely calculated to call attention to itself as a performance. Here the hyperbole of extended coloratura can be heard as an exercise of vocal muscle akin to pumping iron, a display of both endurance and rhetorical force needed to exhibit the culturally assigned role of "Constancy." In my view, that historical perspective can be captured in a modern production that allows the aria to be visibly *about* performance itself, highlighting its excessive demands as markers of a culturally scripted display. Before considering the possibilities for such a staging, I want to recall some of the features that seem to me relevant to the function of the aria as a performance within the drama and to speculate on what is at stake in Konstanze's resistance.

Certain features of "Martern aller Arten" suggest the graft of a concert aria onto Singspiel: its length of nearly 300 measures (320 in the original version[9]); its concerto-like structure, complete with an opening ritornello of 60 bars; its ceremonial *tutti* scoring of full orchestra with trumpet and drums, together with a complement of solo concertante instruments; and its extended flights of coloratura are uniquely "excessive" in Mozart's operas—even the Queen of the Night has less elaborate trappings in arias one-third as long. Unusual as well, and a trespass of convention in genres of both serious and comic opera, is the assignment of two arias in a row to the same character—here requiring the prima donna to perform two vocally demanding numbers back to back. Indeed, in the context of this opera, Konstanze's bravura aria might be particularly suspect as overkill: she has already sung two arias that demonstrate her fidelity to Belmonte—the first recalls for the Pasha Selim (and the audience) her past love, and the second is a monologue of present sorrow and longing. But the Pasha's insistence, in pressing his attentions on Konstanze and in requiring an answer from her, forces her hand. Her answer is, of course, not only a stunning display of the female voice but also a demonstration of the strength of Western feminine virtue under siege by sinister forces of Islamic culture. Thus, Konstanze must perform the virtue her name advertises as a shield against the Pasha Selim's threats of torture, but more especially to assure the Viennese audience of the strength of a gentlewoman's moral resolve, even in the face of dire consequences.

In Bretzner's original libretto, as Thomas Bauman notes, there was no angry interchange between the Pasha and Konstanze at this point in the opera, much less another aria for the heroine.[10] Rather, Konstanze and her maid Blonde were to sing a duet, an apostrophe to "Hope, Comfort in time of Sorrow," which Blonde signals as a favorite ("so melting, so tender") of her mistress. Mozart chooses instead an aria that serves as a demonstration, a performance for the Pasha Selim and for the audience, in which Konstanze's open defiance reveals unexpected strength of character as well as an appropriately public style.

One might well hear the excesses of "Martern aller Arten" as a projection of Mozart's real-life anxieties about his own Constanze, perhaps as a desire to enact her stout and fearless rejection of the advances of another suitor. As is well known, Leopold Mozart's objections to his son's choice of Constanze Weber for a wife caused a rupture in their relationship during the period of *Die Entführung*'s composition. Maynard Solomon notes an additional rupture between the young couple: in a letter of 29 April

1782, Mozart severely reprimands Constanze for allowing a young man to measure her calves during a game of forfeits.[11] Mozart's demand that she admit the error of her ways provoked a temporary rift and breaking off of the engagement. Perhaps, then, the musical portrait of Konstanze filled Mozart's own need to figure a woman of unshakable virtue, an exemplar that would answer even his father's objections. In any case, Mozart pulled out all the stops for this number midpoint in the opera, providing a fully staged musical analogue to the conduct literature of the day that exhorted gentlewomen to cling to constancy as their best hope for upholding moral order—and their own social status.

No matter how strenuous and impressive Konstanze's imploring and defiant exertions, she is obviously not a free agent. She is in captivity singing for freedom to remain true to her beloved, and as such she must marshall the full range of a heroine's passionate constancy. What was really at stake in this transaction?

The authors of eighteenth-century conduct books make it clear that the consequences of a woman's inconstancy were especially grave. According to one such writer, "The greatest crime on the woman's side, is the breach of the high trust her husband reposes in her for his offspring. . . . it is the highest infidelity to betray this sacred trust."[12] Nothing less than patrilineage was at stake, and the fear of bastard children being taken for legal heirs. Women's constancy thus shored up private and public morality, as well as the social and political stability of property and state.

In addition to warnings about the consequences of adulterous and premarital sex, many writers of conduct books and medical treatises took it as axiomatic that women were naturally predisposed to love and sexual appetite. And by an additional trick of predisposition, "if nature for just reasons has given the fair sex stronger inclinations, it has also given them a natural modesty and check upon them which we [men] have not." In the double bind of "an amorous softness, in a sex whose nature is more bent that way," women must allow their "natural" modesty to curb such predispositions in order to help men remain faithful.[13]

So too, Konstanze must resist the Pasha Selim's advances and persuade him to respect her promise to another. The range of her rhetorical arsenal is as impressive as the range of her voice (from the B below middle C to high D). But however heroic her resistance to the Pasha's threats, however heroic her voice, Konstanze has no recourse to real heroic action. It is not as though her outburst of martial fanfares portends a sword-fight with the Pasha. Her only hope is to convince him that as an enlightened ruler he must respect her wishes for his own good. As we know from previous exchanges between the two, however, he finds her resistance . . . well, . . . *irresistible*. (As he reflects following Konstanze's first aria, "Ach ich liebte"—itself full of virtuosic display: "Her sadness, her tears, her steadfastness enchant my heart ever more, make me even more desirous of her love.") This fits well with the gendered "catch-22" of Konstanze's staunch rejection: not only must she honor the love she has pledged to Belmonte, even if it kills her, but her staunchness makes her more attractive to the rejected one—and, most importantly, to the eighteenth-century audience as well.

Turning to the aria itself (see figure 1), we find that "Martern" presents the "constant" heroine as a strategist of changing and sharply contrasting affects, previewed in the long opening ritornello. Defiance yields to imploring gestures, then to scornful resolve and mockery, and the welcome release of death, only to retrace the imploring and then resolute sections in a faster paced and brilliant conclusion. Whereas Konstanze's divisions in the first stanza (on "ich verlache") support defiant scorn of the Pasha's threats, more extensive flights of coloratura occur within the second key area's imploring section, where the words "**Se**gen" (blessing) and "be-**loh**ne" (reward) are elaborated in the lines, "May Heaven's blessing be your reward." Here, where the brilliant style succeeds *empfindsamer* sighs, coloratura enters into dialogue with the concertante instruments. In the faster, final *C* section, Konstanze appropriates the Pasha's imperious manner in taunts that mock his authority ("Go ahead, order away, . . . Death will set me free"). The sheer volume of sound is impressive here, as the solo concertante instruments drop out and Konstanze's defiant voice marshalls sweeping gestures of the full orchestra to her cause.

In staging this number, directors have adopted various means of representing Konstanze's plight and heroic response. Video productions in particular offer a range of devices to frame our view of her and the Pasha Selim, and among those I have seen there are marked differences in representing both captor and captive in this opera. The Glyndebourne production, with Valerie Masterson in the starring role, uses the most literal imagery in a parade of props that are meant to display the Pasha's power. The camera moves from closeups on Konstanze to show the bird cage that occupies the Pasha's attention behind her. As he inspects candidates for his bird harem, a human victim passes across the stage in a rolling torture rack. Perhaps these rather obvious props are needed to remind us that the Pasha is capable of inflicting bodily harm, since his appearance is far from sinister—or Turkish, for that matter. A passive observer, he remains at the back of the stage throughout Konstanze's aria, and at the end pensively twirls a flower in his fingers rather than crushing it. Our last image is of the cage with its newly acquired bird added to the others, as applause signals the end of Act I in this altered version of the opera.

I will address only briefly Humphrey Burton's direction of "Martern" in the Royal Opera's video production (discussed below by Mary Hunter). In this version of the opera the relationship between Konstanze and Selim is

Figure 1. Konstanze's Aria

Ritornello 1 (mm. 1–60): I, Allegro

A   Solo 1 (mm. 61–73): I [defiance in martial motives; derision in virtuosic elaboration of "verlache"] (bold type = coloratura):

    1 Martern aller Arten   Tortures of every kind
    2 Mögen meiner warten,   May await me,
    3 Ich ver**lache** Qual und Pein.   I **scoff** at agony and pain.

Ritornello 2 (mm. 74–76): I

Solo 2 (mm. 77–92): Transition: I⟶ V/v [bold assertions undermined by agitation of syncopation, chromaticism, and instability of minor mode]:

    4 Nichts soll mich erschüttern,   Nothing can shake me,
    5 Nur dann würd' ich zittern,   I would tremble only
    6 Wenn ich untreu könnte seyn.   If I could be unfaithful.

B   Solo 3 (mm. 93–128) with soli: V [*empfindsamer* pleading yields to virtuosic elaboration extending from top of vocal register to bottom]:

    7 Lass dich bewegen,   Let yourself be moved
    8 Verschone mich!   Spare me!
    9 Des Himmels **Segen**   May Heaven's **bles**sing
    10 Be**lohn**e dich!   Be your **reward**!

Ritornello 3 (mm. 129–40): V

(B)   Solo 4 with soli (mm. 141–60): Retransition to V/I, using ll.7–10 of text

C   Solo 5 with tutti (mm. 161–85): I, Allegro assai [new material recalls defiance of opening section: decisive short phrases, triadic, angular vocal lines with emphatic orchestral support]:

    11 Doch du bist entschlossen.   But you are determined.
    12 Willig, unverdrossen,   Willingly, untiring,
    13 Wähl' ich jede Pein und Noth.   I choose every pain and peril.
    14 Ordne nur, gebiethe,   Order away, command,
    15 Lärme, tobe, wüthe,   Make a fuss, storm, rage,
    16 Zuletzt **befreyt** mich doch   In the end death will set me
        der Tod.   **free.**

B2   Solo 6 with soli (mm. 186–230): I, Allegro
    Return of B1, varied; exchange of vocal and concertante materials

C2   Solo 7 with tutti (mm. 231–85): I, Allegro assai
    Return of C1 extended by closing material

Ritornello 4 (mm. 286–93): I, tutti reiteration of closing material from end of C2
    (geht ab)   (exit)

---

full of sexual tension and ambiguity from the start. Replicating European courtly life in a foreign landscape, the clearly European Pasha makes his first appearance in white wig and dressed in white breeches and weskit, as similarly wigged and frocked musicians sing his praises under a canopy of parasols. Taking his arm, Konstanze's behavior toward her captor is flirtatious, inviting us to consider his actions and the passion of her later defiant aria in the rather different light of a reciprocal attraction.

The casting of a black Konstanze (Carolyn Smith-Meyer) in Harry Kupfer's Dresden Opera production focuses the political implications of captivity in more modern terms. Black slaves are seen in the background in previous numbers and the fierce-looking Pasha Selim (Werner Haseleu) resembles a cross between Napoleon and Hitler. The posturing of both characters in "Martern" is deliberately stylized, stiff and repetitive, with Konstanze singing much of the aria on her knees. Groveling at Selim's feet, she alternately implores him with clasped hands and clutches his robe, he awkwardly backing away and finally leaving the stage altogether. The lingering impression is one of an abandoned Konstanze singing her defiance to herself.

I find the Everding staging of Gruberova's performance striking in a number of respects, but most especially in its emphasis on the dual view of performance—Konstanze's and the prima donna's.[14] Here we have a formidable adversary in the Pasha Selim. His change of costume from his Act I robe of white to all-black dress in Act II signals a change from restrained suitor to sinister tyrant, especially in contrast to Konstanze's white gown with blue (for constancy?) sash.[15] Standing first at the back of the set, and seen only in silhouette, he appears fully capable of cruelty and physical violence. The scenery parts for his entrance, giving the impression that he is powerful enough to move buildings, and he grabs Konstanze's arm roughly in the dialogue that precedes her aria. But during the aria itself, various lighting effects, especially the spot lighting, bring performance into self-conscious focus. As the set parts to reveal the open sea behind, each character is equally held in a spotlight during the pantomime of the extended ritornello. But it is Konstanze who appropriates the light, leaving the unvoiced Pasha Selim consigned to the fringes of darkness, as she composes herself (and her dress) for her long-delayed vocal entrance. At the same time, however, Konstanze is pinned down by the spotlight, while the Pasha is allowed to roam, stalking her from the periphery, and eventually leaving the stage altogether before her aria is over.

Although Konstanze, in a quite calculated manner, gets down on her knees to beg for mercy in the *empfindsam* passages of both ritornello and the aria's B section, and even crawls toward Selim on her knees, she makes her most direct appeals to the audience out front, and most obviously during those passages of athletic melismas, elaborate coloratura, and brutally extended high notes. The lights come up gradually to flood the stage in the last powerful and defiant section, as Gruberova stands front and center, her arms extended to the audience; it is here, especially, that Konstanze, Cavalieri / Gruberova, and Constancy can be held in a kind of trifocal counterpoint of available perspectives on performance. The Pasha having left the stage, Konstanze has only the audience to address, in keeping with the opera seria convention of the exit aria. In Everding's production, the lingering view privileges the prima donna, as Gruberova returns to the stage to acknowledge shouts of "bravo!" and prolonged applause.[16]

Indeed, Gruberova has stopped the show, bringing into focus the act of performance as more than simply negotiating Mozart's powerful and grueling vocal number. Here we witness a female presence of voice sufficiently powerful to exceed the frame of character and role. As the Everding production points up, however, having made her defiant exit, Gruberova must return to the stage to acknowledge the success of her appeal with listeners. Thus, even though the diva may outperform the demanding text that is her vehicle for display, she is also captive to operatic conventions and to the tastes of audiences for vocal spectacle. So, too, Konstanze's vocal and moral steadfastness is configured as a larger-than-life display of womanly virtue, an iconic ideal to counteract that "amorous softness" feared by listeners of Mozart's day. Captive to the Pasha Selim and the audience for whom she enacts the steadfastness of Constancy, Konstanze is nonetheless a commanding presence, the epitome of the defiant bravery that Belmonte, for all his ardent longing, fails to display. And it is she who appropriates aspects of the Pasha's imperious manner and even elements of his "Turkish" music while silencing his voice. Yet, to recognize Konstanze's remarkable performance as challenging the stereotype of a languishing heroine does not change the fact that her aria performs a cultural function, prefiguring that of Fiordiligi and the central preoccupation with women's constancy in *Così fan tutte*. The ultimate irony of a resisting reading of "Martern aller Arten" lies in the very emphasis on this function as a performance, as transparently purveying gendered constructions of a constancy that is solid as a rock.

"THE GAZE" AND POWER IN "MARTERN ALLER ARTEN" AND "BATTI, BATTI"
Mary Hunter

I want to begin with a slight digression arising from my teaching. Recently, and for the first time, I cross-listed my general opera course with Women's Studies. This meant not only that twelve out of fourteen students in the course were female, but also that they were looking for something from the course that students in music courses at a liberal arts college are not normally looking for (at least not so explicitly) and that was role models—specifically, "strong women." Toward the end of the course (after *Otello* and before *Lulu,* I think) several commented that they hadn't found any, and, moreover, that most of the female characters they had been exposed to were "wimpy." This didn't mean they didn't like the pieces, just that they had expected feminist exemplars and had gotten, basically, warnings. There are, of course, enormous questions here about the relation between teaching and advocacy, about just what they meant by strong women, about the effects of teaching with videos rather than with either sound recordings or live performances, and so on, none of which I can address here. I bring the story up not to suggest that there is anything earthshaking in their observations, nor, on the other hand, to deride them, and certainly not to indicate that I have the answers about how to teach opera as women's studies (indeed, the following remarks are partly motivated by the sense that my responses to them failed). I bring the student comments up, rather, as an entry point to the question of how productions and performances of operas—Mozart's in particular, since that is our assignment—might make contact with an audience that takes female "strength" as an article of faith.

My first strategy was to play my mother, and to point out that it can take more strength to submit than to defy, more independence of mind to be loyal than not, and so on. These basically Victorian arguments did not begin to cut the mustard with my students; Desdemona was still of no interest to them as a role model. My other arguments, coming from feminist work in opera that "discovers" the singer behind the character, both as a historical figure who negotiates complex business affairs and as the agent or author of her physical, aesthetic, and moral responses to her character, did have some effect, I think.[17] But arguments about the singer behind/beside the character don't really address the question of how representations of women doing their cultural assignments of constancy or cuteness, docility or (in dire straits) defiance, play to an audience conditioned to look for role models—an audience, moreover, told repeatedly, both explicitly and implicitly, that classical music, in conveying aesthetic and moral "universals" (the best that has been thought and said) provides such models.

Obviously I do not think that Mozart operas are in any very obvious sense "about" role models, and I don't want to argue that the primary job of directors and singers is to produce such behavioral templates—to make Mozart's characters behave in ways that today's young women can wholeheartedly admire. However, questions of staging inevitably raise issues of sympathy and identification, which in turn raise the question of who is being asked to do the sympathizing or identifying, and what they bring to the task. In other words, my students may not simply have been saying that they didn't admire the characters they had seen, but that the productions we had watched did not leave or make room for any sympathies grounded in their own experiences.

Opening up a space for female (if not exactly feminist) sympathy is what Elin Diamond is after when she appropriates for feminism Brecht's notion of the theatrical *Gestus* or the controlling tone of a theatrical moment.[18] If one agrees that productions of canonical works can or should leave room for various sorts of feminist consciousness in the audience, the question then is what that space might be in works such as the Mozart operas. To put it crudely, the possibilities seem to be to make the women strong, or to contextualize or objectify their apparent weaknesses such that a production does not seem to be endorsing them. (And Elin Diamond's ideas are clearly closer to the latter option.) Obviously, the two possibilities need not be mutually exclusive—such classically feminist devices as cross-gender casting or reassigning utterances to different characters (what if Masetto sang "Batti, batti"?) both redistribute the gendered balance of power (making the women strong by redressing or revoicing them) and suggest the historical constraints that shape "normal" behavior (what does it mean that a Masetto-like character couldn't normally sing "Batti batti" in a Mozart opera?)

Of the two possibilities, I am less interested in the first than the second. Making the singer stronger than the character by emphasizing the sheerly performative aspects of an utterance, or making a production revolve around the vocal power of the singer playing the heroine seems to me both less plausible and less possible in Mozart than in much nineteenth-century opera. The voice in Mozart is, as Gary Tomlinson might say, simply less noumenal than it is in nineteenth-century grand opera. This is partly because of the generic differences between comedy (or even opera seria with a happy end) and melodramatic tragedy; in the latter, I would suggest, the extremes to which characters are driven produce vocal "excesses" that, perhaps paradoxically, allow and even encourage a separation between character and singer. Furthermore, the rhetorical qualities of late-eighteenth-century style demand a reasoned as well as a purely emotional response: vocal sound and the particularities of text are much more closely wedded, even at moments of the highest expressivity. In general in Mozart's operas, I would argue, moments of "noumenality" are just that—moments—and not the dramatic fundament of the characters.

On the other hand, Mozart operas seem to me to present many possibilities for producing moments, scenes, or whole works in ways that encourage what Brecht and his followers call "the A[lienation]-effect." That is, a degree of distance between the audience and the spectacle that emphasizes the artificiality of the fictional world on-stage, encourages critical thinking about the values of the narrative, permits the audience members to watch themselves watching, and leaves room for an actor (implicitly or explicitly) to step out of role and comment on his or her fictional circumstances, to express his awareness that he is being watched. The value of the A-effect in thinking about feminist or female-oriented productions of operas is that it reminds us of the ways staging decisions draw one into (and thus endorse the values of) the fictional world of the opera. It connects to feminist theories of the gaze by both de-naturalizing and foregrounding the questions of who is looking at whom and what that looking means in terms of power. Productions that distance the audience or the characters from the fictional world of the stage, or that self-consciously play with the gaze, can suggest that while the female characters may not be strong in a late-twentieth-century sense, they live in (and may project a consciousness of living in) a world whose social divisions and opportunities are radically different from our own.

Humphrey Burton's Covent Garden production of *Die Entführung aus dem Serail,* especially (and perhaps exclusively) in "Martern aller Arten," generates an A-effect that may not exactly intend to send a feminist message, but that certainly leaves room for feminist sympathies, or for a sympathetic response larger than the hope that Konstanze will be able to remain faithful to Belmonte.[19] The aria takes place on the front third of Elijah Moshinsky's set, the rest closed off by a curtain. There is no other scenery, and the only prop is a chair for the Pasha. Konstanze (Inge Nielsen) is dressed in a simple white empire-line dress, her dark brown hair tumbling loosely down her back. She could almost be in her nightclothes. The Pasha, by contrast, wears a splendid cloak, which billows out around him as he strides across the stage. During the long ritornello, the Pasha forces a kiss, and Konstanze, after disentangling herself, chases him, grabbing on to his cloak while he ignores her (compare Wheelock's comments, above, about her earlier flirtatiousness). As the vocal section of the aria begins, the Pasha seats himself center stage, refusing to meet Konstanze's gaze while she becomes increasingly hysterical, ending the aria by collapsing in a heap at his feet. The odd (even alienating) conjunction of her revulsion at the kiss and her desperate attempts to get his attention—from cloak grabbing to coloratura—suggest the absoluteness of his power: not only can he force his lips on this woman, but he can refuse her his eyes, the only path through which she might hope to exert any power over him. The gaze is explicitly an issue here, the more so because the stripped-down stage, with the focus explicitly on her (lack of) power to compel his attention, forces us to "watch ourselves watching." While the spectacle of a woman negotiating an aria as difficult and desperate as "Martern aller Arten" is normally totally engrossing—the singer's bodily efforts completely sacrificed to our gaze—in this production the Pasha's refusal to watch (listen) compromises our engagement with the spectacle, making us unusually aware both of the dynamics of enjoying virtuosity and of the ways in which women have historically succeeded in winning their cases—by making themselves be looked at. Finally, this production unmasks what may seem to be a moment of steely resolve and heroic bravura as a desperate plea for sympathy; as, in other words, what female performative power in opera always comes down to.

Whereas "Martern aller Arten" is an aria of desperation and repulsion, "Batti, batti" is in a sense its opposite: an aria of conciliation.[20] Nevertheless, the arias are connected in a number of ways. Both are performances of constancy, and both are exercises of a certain sort of authority from a structurally powerless position. Konstanze's cultural assignment is quite simple—to perform the primary female virtue of constancy for us by repelling the Pasha. Zerlina's assignment is more complicated than Konstanze's, in part because she has already been inconstant with Don Giovanni, but more importantly because of her class and her consequent incapacity to function as a straightforwardly admirable character (or, indeed, a role model). Unlike Konstanze, who performs constancy by repelling a clear intruder, Zerlina is trying to reestablish constancy with her proper lover by provocatively proclaiming his right to beat her; in other words, her job in this situation is to perform an erotics of chattelhood. Perhaps ironically, it is this chattelhood that connects her with Konstanze, who can assert her independence from the Pasha only because she already belongs to Belmonte. The erotics of "Batti, batti" are quite different from those in "Martern aller Arten" because they are directed toward her onstage interlocutor—her "forwardness" and openness about sexuality permitted only because Zerlina is a peasant. Her freedom to take the sexual initiative depends in part on it taking the form of submission to Masetto, but also, and equally, on her subordinate status in the larger social system. (In late-eighteenth-century opera buffa, serving girls seduce but ladies can only succumb.) The less obvious aspect of Zerlina's situation is that by asserting her possession by Masetto, she earns the right to a little space of her own in which she can imagine another life. This may seem like an advantage, but she (like other serving-class characters) can only enjoy this imaginative independence because in a stratified society it doesn't matter what she thinks; she is not burdened by being a role model.

What is striking about stagings of this scene is that they seem to divide chattelhood from erotics almost completely. Whereas the Peter Sellars production (discussed by Allanbrook below) concentrates exclusively on Zerlina's possession by Masetto, rendering her completely powerless and erasing all hint of sexuality, Göran Järvefelt's Drottningholm production (with Anita Soldh as Zerlina) concentrates exclusively on the erotics of the occasion. Here, Zerlina crawls around the stage with her bottom in the air, waggling it at both Masetto and the audience. Masetto is completely won over almost as soon as she begins to sing; she has complete control over the moment, and the "beating" is never construed as a moment of violence. One might argue this production represents a sort of female strength: it certainly shows sexual initiative. At the same time, even (perhaps especially) on the video, Zerlina is offered to the audience as completely as she offers herself to Masetto. There is no attempt to indicate any complexity of feeling on her part (to make her "strong" by representing this behavior as her version of the best way to put the pieces back together; that is, by endowing her with subjectivity). There is also no attempt to contextualize the moment by indicating complicity with other women, or a complex awareness of being watched by an audience. Thus this production manages to objectify Zerlina without contextualizing or de-naturalizing that objectification, leaving no room for feminist comprehension, let alone feminist sympathies.[21] Whereas a certain complexity of feminist reaction can emerge from the reflexive watching of watching in "Marten aller Arten," this performance of "Batti, batti"—even given a sympathy for female sexual agency—makes room only for banal reflections on the female form and the susceptibilities of bumpkins. Mozart, as Allanbrook will say, deserves better—but so do my students.

ZERLINA'S "BATTI, BATTI": A CASE STUDY?
Wye Jamison Allanbrook

In the dark street of a South Bronx neighborhood Don Giovanni shoots up; as he writhes on the ground after taking the hit, the camera pans to a dingy stairwell with iron banister that descends to Zerlina and Masetto's basement apartment. A conversation between an unseen Zerlina and Masetto can be heard, punctuated by occasional slaps. Zerlina appears on the staircase, her hand pressed to her face, and leans against the prison-like bars of the banister. She is weeping. She bids her "bel Masetto" to beat her—in fact, to continue beating her, as is clear from what we have just heard—and promises to stand there "like a little lamb" ("come agnellina")—a scapegoat—awaiting his blows. The invitation seems to shame Masetto, who looks ruefully at his offending hand. Zerlina kisses that hand, presses it against her swollen face, and sings of the happiness they will enjoy after her submission. She does not look at him during this delusionary tale, but stares beyond, into the middle distance, with blank eyes. Not until the final cadence do her eyes come alive, does she return from that distance. She smiles at him and they kiss.

Zerlina is clearly a codependent here, in a relationship that alternates drearily between beatings and reconciliations. Although cast as the seductress, she is in truth the seduced, persuaded over and over—it's clear this is a frequent occurrence—to acquiesce in this vicious cycle of abuse, the perpetual victim of poverty and the male violence it engenders. There is no agency on her part; the dead eyes, staring into the middle distance, make that clear. Seduction requires life and motion. When after the aria Masetto curses "that witch's" uncanny capacity to seduce him, we sense his self-delusion; he would like to feel seduced, but there is no true sensuality here. Instead they are both enclosed in this dead space, both sentenced ceaselessly to reenact the bleak scenario we have just witnessed.

Zerlina's willingness to submit to male abuse can only be painful to a modern audience. The masochistic mode in which she presents herself is simply unacceptable if the aria is presented in any form other than the one shown here—that of a case study of a dysfunctional relationship; there can be no good reason to represent on stage in an approving fashion a woman's erotic request to be beaten. The aria must be recuperated, as this production attempts, by turning it into a case study of codependence, of the crippling results of a woman's lack of a sense of self-worth. The pitiless eye of the video camera brings this reading into the tight focus of television drama: all is close-up—a lingering gaze on that dead gaze. It might be a scene in *ER,* so gritty is the setting, so naturalistic the representation, so immediate its application.

Unfortunately, to arrive at this reading, the director, Peter Sellars, had to ignore every musical cue. Mozart's aria might just as well not have been sung. The singer seems divorced from her song; the close-up technique forces rhythmic stasis. There exists already built into this aria the double perspective, the ironizing point of view, that Hunter and Wheelock would like to see suggested in productions of Mozart operas. Composed into the music, it needs only to be teased out by a skillful director. Zerlina's aria opens, as I have argued elsewhere, with the rhythms of a gavotte, which mime an arch parody of submission.[22] "Beat me, beat me," she surely does invite, and the onomatopoeic plosives of the text are foregrounded by the gavotte's gentle but unmistakable beating rhythms—"*B*atti, *b*atti, *b*el Masetto." Historically this French court dance, with its mincing hesitation step, was a memory of an antique courting ritual, involving bouquets proffered and kisses withheld. So in contrast to the phonemic mimesis of beating, the dance rhythms suggest the opposite of submission. Here already is doubleness and ironic play—an invitation to male violence tendered in the courtship mode. And the musical text multiplies the strata of meaning even further: beneath this perverse little machine of a gesture courses the sonorous *counter*-accompaniment of a baroque-style cello obbligato, wholehearted and flowing, seeming to speak for the interior self. The two entities are never entirely assimilated into one texture; they remain rhythmically separate, each doing its own work. The obbligato grounds the gavotte, counters its coy rhythms, brings substance to the teasing erotic artifice of its stance.

Returned from a sore temptation, a brush with the court and its cour-
tesan ways, Zerlina sees her reality clearly. The new life that had momentarily glittered before her would have offered the greater violence, the
more serious loss of self. She inflects her rhetoric to make the best of her
situation—a situation that she rightly sizes up as the rest of her life. The
successful rhetor must be a knower; with knowledge comes the power to
persuade—to seduce, if you will. In an ideal performance we arrive at
Masetto's grumbled comment about witches with complete assent; successful rhetoric is a kind of witchcraft. The delicate balance between the
erotic promise of the gavotte with its coyly sadomasochistic surface and
the deep-toned, whole-hearted obbligato makes us aware that Zerlina's
offer is other than it seems. It is an invitation to a possible life she is offering here. (If the subtlety of the gesture leaves any doubt about the
irony of the mode in which she is couching her invitation, the musical text
gives us more conventional clues further on, such as the near-seria parody of the vocal sally on the text "I'll let you tear out my hair"—"Lascerò
straziarmi il crine.") By making a joke about beating, Zerlina is throwing
the surly distrust of Masetto's sexual jealousy right back at him. Only a
very strong woman can make a joke about female submission, and by
making it she reduces the threat to a cartoon gesture that Masetto sheep-
ishly grants is inappropriate. By naming violence, she unmans it. At the
climax of the first section she declares what she knew was the inevitable
outcome: "Ah, I see you don't have the heart!" (Ah, lo vedo, non hai
core!) This exclamation is the preparation for the resolution, in the second section, of the double-layered gavotte into a single-layered and sunny
6/8 pastoral; it contains a swoony falling-fifth move to the subdominant
on the word "passar" that offers its own less kinky erotic promise in a private Arcadian space. The cello obbligato falls in with the pastoral rhythms,
ceasing to offer a gestural counterpoint.

Eroticizing a request to be beaten is in this situation a daring gesture—
a show of strength, as I think the music makes clear. We need not look
away from it with the embarrassed distress of our postmodern wisdom, explain it away as "the way they thought then." Zerlina is a strong and resilient character who picks things up quickly. She knows to fear male violence now, and to protect herself from it. Masetto's attempt to force her
back into the Don's clutches just after this aria in order to do a little market research reminds us of just how vigilant she will have to be. She knows
that Masetto is "stralunato"; male sexual jealousy causes a vicious failure
of soul. In "Batti, batti" she negotiates this carnal mine field with remarkable canniness.

I have never seen a performance of the aria that thoroughly lives up to
my image of the ideal, although most of them stop sensibly short of Sellars's misguided attempt at social realism. (By the way, I should say that

there are many moments in Sellars's three Mozart productions that I admire—some extravagantly; it is just that his cultural opportunism makes him wildly erratic, causing him in this aria to go completely wrong.) The aria is not a lyrical, flowing piece, despite the cello obbligato. The singer should play against the obbligato; it is a graft on the gavotte, not an essential element. Singers usually remain blissfully unaware of the gavotte rhythms, which should not be slurred and lyricized, but pointed up both vocally and gesturally. There should be a slight rubato on the approach to the strong beat, especially in the opening phrase—the hesitation of the hesitation step. The aria should be sung not with tears, but with an acknowledging smile—Zerlina's acknowledgment to Masetto—*and,* more importantly, to the audience—of her awareness of the game she is playing. Also, Zerlina should not approach Masetto, should not caress him—not seem to importune him in any fashion, at least until she breaks into the pastoral. She must keep her distance in this demonstration. A slide into real erotic closeness here would compromise her separateness; it would make legal tender out of a currency she never means to offer.

Sellars's opera videos subvert the possibility of theatrical distance by zooming in on the singers with close-ups that show every pore, and replace the wide-open spaces of the stage with the suffocating immediacy of the television screen. The medium provides the message here; video supports the close-up technique, which in turn suggests the case study mode. Paradoxically, zooming in on Zerlina depersonalizes her rather than deepening her character; it turns her into a statistic—a battered wife, a victim of spousal abuse. If ironic distance is not possible, then the image of sexual submission offered in "Batti, batti" will certainly offend, and some recuperation will be necessary. And it will be difficult to know what to make of the tender eroticism of the later "Vedrai, carino," when she finally does touch Masetto and draws him to her like a lover. Should we be frightened for her? Is this dangerous pattern of behavior repeating itself? Somebody call the cops . . .

Let the director step back, restore the proscenium arch, and take care to choreograph the rhythmic strata of the aria. Then "Batti, batti" stages a woman whose power does not come from vocal projection, from coruscating roulades delivered through the bars of her gilded cage, like the *fioriture* of Constanze. Its source is articulate wit and irony of text and gesture. Mozart seems to have felt a freedom to ironize with his lower-class and peasant women that he did not have with the noble ones. Both Konstanze and Donna Anna are locked into their single-minded seria stances; they are tragic monoliths. Hence they are suitable candidates for a close-up, which will not distort their earnest exaltation. Zerlina and Susanna are not; their multidimensional depictions need to be witnessed *in situ,* in act, rather than in a stiff cameo appearance. Is this, as Mary Hunter suggests, a product of the fact that what these nonaristocratic women think does not matter? I would like to suggest instead that in the tensile strength projected by their modest displays these women present us with the models that we seek.

The Career of Cherubino,
or the Trouser Role Grows Up

HEATHER HADLOCK

> . . . so much easier in Shakespeare's time, wasn't
> it? Always the same girl dressed up as a man, and
> even that borrowed from Boccaccio or Dante or
> somebody. I'm sure if I'd been a Shakespeare
> hero, the very minute I saw a slim-legged young
> pageboy I'd have said: "Odsbodikins! There's
> that girl again!"
> *(Dorothy Sayers,* Whose Body?[1] *)*

THE CONVENTION of female performers masquerading as slim-legged pageboys or unusually handsome knights, well-established since Shakespeare's time, remained surprisingly popular on the operatic stage into the nineteenth century. The closest parallels to earlier theatrical practice may be found in those operas whose heroines—prevented by circumstances from appearing in their true guises—dress themselves as men and sally forth to rescue a husband or lover from danger, or from temptation. Yet such rescue plots are relatively uncommon, for female travesty in nineteenth-century opera was far from a unified phenomenon, and at least two other categories are needed to account for it. In both these other scenarios the gender masquerade takes place "outside" the plot, and that plot presents the female performer consistently as a male character—although, as we shall see, the putatively male character's soprano voice often gives him access to feminine realms of the action. In numerous Italian works composed during the last period of opera seria, after the decline of the castrati who had played heroic roles, female singers designated musicos played warriors, lovers, kings, and even fathers.[2] These cross-dressed heroes would retrospectively be celebrated as possessors of the super-potent contralto voices admired by Théophile Gautier:

> Que tu me plais, ô timbre étrange!
> Son double, homme et femme à la fois,
> Contralto, bizarre mélange,
> Hermaphrodite de la voix![3]

[How you please me, oh strange timbre! / Double sound, man and woman at once, / Contralto, strange melding, / Hermaphrodite of the voice!]

Gautier celebrates the contralto's ability at once to envoice the lady, her heroic lover, and still a third character type:

> C'est la châtelaine qui raille
> Son beau page parlant d'amour;
> L'amant au pied de la muraille,
> La dame au balcon de sa tour.

[It is the lady of the manor who mocks / Her handsome page talking of love, / The lover at the foot of the wall / The lady at her tower balcony.]

This *beau page parlant d'amour*, first and most famously exemplified by Mozart's Cherubino, is the most persistent female cross-dressing role in opera, and from Gautier's poetic image we may derive the type's essential features. The variety of names for the practice, variously known as the "trouser role," "breeches part," or "pants part," *Hosenrolle* or *travesti*, testifies both to its international appeal and to the necessity of the singer's having slim, boyish legs. Equally essential for the *beau* effect is a light and clear voice, regardless of tessitura, differing in timbre from both the contralto and the heftier dramatic soprano expected in heroic musico roles. The page's "talk of love" is typically translated into melancholy or flirtatious staged songs, directly or indirectly addressed to an inaccessible beloved, of which Cherubino's "Voi che sapete" remains the archetype.

The difficulty of situating the page *en travesti* within modern opera's sex-and-gender system may be seen in Catherine Clément's taxonomy of voice and character types elsewhere in this volume, which relegates the page characters to the marginal category of "weak" voices. This weakness seems to derive as much from the character's typical place in the plot structure as from his youth or the generally light music composed for him, for as we shall see, pageboys are neither directly involved in the central heterosexual love plot nor able to alter its trajectory toward tragic death or comic resolution in marriage. Clément's analysis derives from—and reinscribes—a uniquely nineteenth-century framework, namely, the straightening out of relations between gender, voice, performer, and role that constituted the transition from opera seria and the bel canto aesthetic to modern romantic opera.[4] As long as we rely implicitly on George Bernard Shaw's summary of opera as the story of a soprano and a tenor who want to go to bed together, and a baritone who wants to stop them, other voice types will necessarily appear subordinate, fitting awkwardly into the system. Yet we might more productively define the category-confounding page *en travesti* not as a "marginal" (connoting a dispensable and merely decorative function) but rather as a "liminal" presence within opera's increasingly gendered spheres of action. My purpose is to reorient our gaze away from Clément's master narrative of women's undoing and onto the cross-dressed soprano, who, while she rarely occupies center stage for long, does tend to survive the prescribed fate of heroines.

Such a reorientation—the attempt to look directly at the page—poses its own challenges. Opera is unique, perhaps, in how little visual verisimilitude it demands: we expect to look through or disregard a singer's body and instead "see" the voice. Yet trouser roles require a more elaborate scaffolding from which to suspend our disbelief, for in order to accept the character *en travesti* as *male*, we must rationalize away the evidence of both our eyes and ears. In contrast with male travesty practice, which expects the audience to see, hear, and laugh at the discrepancy between performer and role, one can never be certain just what degree of double vision the audience is meant to bring to its scrutiny of the woman-as-pageboy. Such characters, particularly when they speak of love, often appear in shadow: the cross-dressed female body and its desires, though repeatedly characterized as harmless, are just as frequently veiled from sight. The pageboy casts the audience into a figurative darkness, a clouding of the mind's eye that results from the never-explained clash between the page's visual and vocal incarnations; in some sense, the trousered soprano who plays the page is also doomed perpetually to obstruct our view of him. How does this liminal figure, who was born in the last days of the ancien régime and who persisted through nineteenth-century French operatic tradition into the modern era, repeatedly escape and complicate the conventions of gendered representation? And how did it become possible, in Jules Massenet's *Chérubin* of 1905, for the "beau page" at last to grow up into "l'amant au pied de la muraille"?

> Se l'amano le femmine, han certo il lor perché.
> *(Lorenzo Da Ponte,* Le nozze di Figaro, *Act I)*

Beaumarchais's preface to *Le Mariage de Figaro* addresses the "moral inquisitors" who may be scandalized by his Chérubin, insisting—with a charming double entendre—on the innocence of "my page" and placing responsibility for any "shameful" interpretations on the spectator. Chérubin's forbidden yearnings after "all the women in the castle" are called harmless because of his immaturity, which places the page outside the sex and gender order: "Perhaps he is no longer a child," Beaumarchais explains, "but he is not yet a man."[5] The page's desires may safely be represented on stage because they accomplish nothing: they are only "lost words" addressed to "the trees, the clouds, the wind which bears them away."[6] Mozart represents these "lost words" in arias that may be considered as failed serenades, expressions of desire that fail to produce the desired effect in their recipients: the women to whom the page's ardent songs are addressed respond with laughter and teasing rather than equally ardent song. Chérubin's voice can reach out to women, but his hearers do not offer their voices in return because, Beaumarchais explains, the page's adolescent yearning inspires amusement or pity rather than reciprocal *desire:* "Haven't I seen the ladies in our very balconies love my page to distraction? What do they want of him? Alas! nothing: it is an interest, to be sure; but, like that of the Countess, a pure and naive interest, an interest that is . . . disinterested."[7]

Beaumarchais, then, excused his page's naughtiness on the grounds that Chérubin can be seen but not heard—precisely the opposite of the modern bafflement at a Cherubino whose voice we hear clearly, and whom we might be able to see and judge if only that distracting woman would get out of the way. But to deny either the audibility or the visibility of the page will lead us to Beaumarchais's implicit conclusion: that Chérubin, "not yet a man," has no sex at all. If we take the playwright at his word in his preface, we may accept the travesty casting on the terms of a heterosexist logic that defines the woman in trousers as a creature who can at most achieve a sexless imitation of masculinity, a creature whose body doesn't matter, and whose discovery (and near discovery) in a series of highly compromising positions is pleasantly scandalous rather than fatal. The Count's reactions to him, according to this same logic, are comic precisely to the degree that they are overreactions: the "restless and vague desire" that is the essence of Chérubin's character cannot threaten the prevailing sex and gender order. Both the play and the opera, however, suggest that we should not be too credulous.

For neither work, replete with scenes of veiling, revelation, and disguise, ever allows us to relax our scrutiny of Cherubino's body; indeed, both works invite us to look at that body whenever it is present, and to imagine it when it is temporarily removed from sight. The action of looking at the page dominates the first half of the opera, beginning with the Act I trio, whose whole action condenses around the Count's statement, "Vedo il paggio" (I saw the page). Cherubino's silent body is as indispensable to this trio as are the three singers' voices, and that body is also a "silent partner" in the Act I finale, Figaro's "Non più andrai," which merrily strips the page of his feathered hat and sash and replaces them with a soldier's uniform. This substitution of one set of masculine signifiers for another, like the removal of the uniform and its replacement with feminine accessories in Act II, seems designed to remind us of the original masquerade: that we watch an actress whose putative maleness is constructed only temporarily. The very travesty casting that claims to guarantee Cherubino's "bodilessness" also reminds us slyly that there is a body there, and that underneath the costumes is neither an immature man, nor an imitation man.

Beaumarchais declared the spiritual affinity between Chérubin and women in his brief character sketch: "The role can only be played, as it has been, by a young and very pretty woman . . . we do not have in our theatre any young men mature enough to understand its nuances."[8] (Since 1921, the Comédie-Française has abandoned these instructions and cast men in the role of the page, but Mozart, at least, fixed the character's original ambiguity by writing Cherubino's role for mezzo-soprano.) Nor is the page's affinity with women merely spiritual, as the bedroom scene in Act II makes clear.

Susanna's aria "Venite, inginocchiatevi," during which she dresses Cherubino as a girl, concludes, "Se l'amano le femmine, han certo il lor perchè." The musical setting underscores this epigram, sung to the most tuneful phrase in an otherwise fragmentary aria, and textual repetition emphasizes the couplet's function as the "punch line" of the aria, but no one supplies an answer to the riddle: why *do* the women love Cherubino? And why do they find him most irresistible when he is disguised as a girl—a disguise that reveals the "young and pretty woman" behind the page's male clothes? The erotic energy that coalesces around Cherubino's silent, ambiguous body in this number threatens to destabilize the whole economy of sexual difference, for the page's appeal to women lies in his similarity to them. When Suzanne declares that the page is "pretty as a girl" and admires his white arms "like a woman's! whiter than mine!"[9] we may feel the pull of a homoerotic current that momentarily distracts from the main plot of heterosexual marriage and its complications. And Mozart's Countess feels it too; perhaps the most important "action" of Susanna's aria is the silent drama between Cherubino and the Countess, whose gazes—directed and stage-managed by Susanna—seek and finally hold each other. Susanna directs the Countess, "mirate il briconcello" (look at that little rogue), and for a brief moment the Countess returns Cherubino's searching gaze—at last the lady, too, "sees the Page." The Countess is flustered and intrigued by this pretty creature—notice how she keeps sending Susanna away in the brief recitative that follows! It is worth noting, too, that recent research on the French court in Beaumarchais's time has turned up evidence of self-declared *anandryne* (literally, no men) aristocratic salons, and that Beaumarchais's depiction of the Countess, Suzanne, and Chérubin playing dress-up behind closed doors may have been a more pointedly satirical scene than has been recognized previously.[10]

However, this scene is not allowed to progress very far, for the arrival of Count Almaviva forces Chérubin back into the Countess's closet. It is perhaps all too easy to pun on this word, "closet," and to feel ourselves on familiar ground: a female body is in the closet; it must be a lesbian. But making Cherubino "a lesbian" does not do justice to the panic that ensues in the moment after the Countess sees the page's "vague and restless desire." The abruptness of the Count's arrival, which provides a dramatic rationale for banishing Cherubino from the scene, might better be seen as evidence of an authorial crisis, a limit to what can be represented. When the woman beholds Cherubino's desire without laughing, the page ceases to be a pretty toy and becomes instead a sort of monstrosity that must be cast out of the scene.[11] Indeed, Cherubino's embodied erotic aspect never emerges from that closet, for subsequent revelations of the page in *Figaro's* third and fourth acts will simply re-play events already seen. And although Beaumarchais's sequel to *Le Mariage de Figaro* centers on the Countess and the illegitimate child she has borne to Chérubin, he never depicted Chérubin's maturity: the adultery between the Countess and the page takes place "outside" the text, in the imaginary space between two plays. The sequel, *La Mère coupable,* opens with the announcement of the former page's suicide, as if only the death of the grown-up Chérubin could make it safe to acknowledge that he had existed at all.

The page's erotic identity in opera was to remain suspended through most of the nineteenth century, which consigned him to solitary yearning, to gazing, and to "singing about love to myself," yet this is not to say that opera represents no intimate moments between women; rather that the soprano pageboy was typically excluded from them. The music that might have been sung by the Countess and Cherubino remains unheard until Act III, when it surfaces in a safer representational context—namely, in the friendship between the Countess and Susanna. In their "Letter Duet," as Wye Allanbrook remarks, the women "seem at play together in a sheltered and intimate place."[12] The page will remain excluded from this "place," this operatic topos of female love and friendship, for another century or so, but if we note certain details about this duet, we may recognize echoes of it when we meet it again at the fin de siècle. The poem that the Countess and Susanna write "says" virtually nothing, but this *nothing* evokes a sensuous nighttime space, and the cryptic final line bears all the meaning, as the Countess's ellipsis becomes a speaking silence: "Che soave zefiretto / Questa sera spirerà / Sotto i pini del boschetto / . . . Ei già il resto capirà." The invocation of the Count as the absent recipient of these words "justifies" the sensual synchronization of women's breath and bodies in this gentle and reflective music, which suspends both time and plot as the wordless melismas and close, consonant harmony between the women seem to exceed verbal signification.

***

Le nozze di Figaro's two-soprano duet and its yearning page *en travesti* would travel on separate tracks into opera of the nineteenth century. The duet, either as a declaration of friendship between female characters or a love scene between the prima donna and a musico hero, would become something of a bel canto genre piece, whose persistence and generic features Hector Berlioz described disparagingly in 1859. Berlioz, who had seen Bellini's *I Capuleti e i Montecchi* in Florence in 1831, later recalled his disgust at what he perceived as an effete adaptation of Shakespeare's tragedy, and expressed particular disdain for the convention of duets in which "two feminine voices . . . produce those successions of thirds which are so dear to Italian ears." He attributed this taste to the Italian audiences' "childish sensualism," remarking that "low voices [were] disliked by this public of sybarites, who were attracted by sweet sonorities as children are by lollipops."[13]

It seems ironic, then, that the page, whose defining features were youth and sensuality, was largely excluded from these pieces. Grand opera confined its travesty characters to the permanent adolescence in which we left Cherubino, propagating the type in such roles as Urbain in Meyerbeer's *Les Huguenots,* Oscar in Auber's *Gustave III, ou Le bal masqué,* Thibault in *Don Carlos,* Siébel in Gounod's *Faust,* and Stefano in his *Roméo et Juliette.* The page, in this repertoire, frequently stands in for men spying on and peering at women, a voyeuristic drama staged most literally in the second act of *Les Huguenots.* The page Urbain leads the blindfolded Raoul into Queen Marguerite's garden full of bathing beauties, and rejoices in an aside that while all the semiclad women stare at Raoul, he (Urbain) can at last gaze freely at them: "Grâce à lui l'on m'oublie, et je puis en ces lieux contempler les danger qu'on dérobe à mes yeux!"[14]

This scenario, in which the page's function is to conduct the adult man into a forbidden female realm, exaggerates the voyeuristic elements implicit in *Le nozze di Figaro*'s Act II bedroom scene. It requires the taboo presence of the page—who is always at risk of expulsion by adult male authorities or by the women themselves—to define a feminine scene as *private* and thus to charge it with desire, reminding the spectator that "he" too witnesses forbidden events. Additionally, the travestied page is a trim young woman in tights, which provides a double pleasure: the spectator may look at women "through" the gaze of the ardent boy, and look "at" the woman who impersonates the boy. In a related contemporary phenomenon, romantic ballet assigned masculine lead roles to ballerinas, although contemporary critics justified the strategy on aesthetic terms: since dance had to be beautiful, they argued, and beauty was by definition feminine, both the art and its audiences had to be protected from the twin abominations of male ugliness and effeminacy. Dance historian Lynn Garafola, somewhat more cynically, describes the stage of the Paris Opéra at midcentury as a "private seraglio" where men in the audience looked and women on stage were looked at; travesty roles reinforced this dichotomy because heterosexual romance plots could be enacted on a stage full of women.[15]

The travesty tradition in French serious opera, however, fades away around 1860. To continue tracing Cherubino's descendants after the mid-century, we must travel some unfamiliar back roads through the subgenre of operetta, where women in trousers were an indispensable element of Second Empire naughtiness. Here operetta actresses impersonated two variations on the pageboy type: the sincere young lover of olden days and his more cynical modern cousin, the dandy.[16] Poetic and theatrical tropes associated with the dandy, including female travesty, lovesickness, alienation, nostalgia, and moonlight, will be most familiar from their late incarnation in *Pierrot Lunaire,* but they had clustered around the trousered woman much earlier, in the opéra comique of the 1870s. In its celebration of the artificial and the perverse, and its rejection of "natural" gender defined through reproductive sexuality, modernist dandyism enabled and celebrated the "impossible" body that Beaumarchais's Chérubin had not been allowed to occupy.

The trousered Nicklausse, in Offenbach's *Les Contes d'Hoffmann* (1881), is perhaps the first soprano *en travesti* to cross over into the musical space of a two-soprano duet. The Barcarolle that Nicklausse sings with the femme fatale Giulietta is a long way from the Countess and Susanna's "Letter Duet," but may be heard as an allusion to that duet and to bel canto convention: like the earlier piece, it has a hypnotic 6/8 meter, a repetitious accompaniment that suspends time, and a poem that enigmatically evokes a sensuous "elsewhere." Above all, its intimate affect derives from its imitative, interchangeable melodic lines and from the intertwining breaths of the two singers. We may want to distrust such a display of two-soprano sensuality, like earlier representations of the page at play in feminine spheres, as an invitation to voyeurism. But Nicklausse, unlike his predecessors, is not looking at women anymore—for the duration of the duet, "he" *becomes* a woman. Indeed, when Nicklausse has been played by a baritone (as was common in the mid-twentieth century), the second line of the barcarolle has been reassigned to a soprano from the chorus; endowed with a true male voice, Nicklausse can no longer cross over into the female musical space of the barcarolle. Perhaps the true perversity of moonlit music is that it invites listeners, like Nicklausse, to enter it as participants rather than as intruders. Modern responses to this barcarolle always note its strange allure: Carl Dahlhaus, for example, calls its euphony "untrustworthy," claiming to hear corruption just beneath the attractive surface.[17]

Such a characterization of the barcarolle echoes the negative connotations that came to be attached to female travesty itself at the fin de siècle, when images of female "sexual inversion" began to dominate both literature and medical discourse. The six lesbian poems that had been officially censored from Baudelaire's *Les Fleurs du mal,* for example, were restored in an 1881 edition, and the lesbian, in such unsavory guises as vampire, ghoul, and Oriental voluptuary, flourished in the decadent imagination. In 1894, the academic and artistic world hailed the "discovery" of a series of poems called the *Chansons de Bilitis,* attributed to a contemporary and lover of Sappho; the subsequent revelation that these "ancient" songs were fraudulent in no way diminished their popularity.[18] Medical and legal writings on female "criminality" and "sexual inversion" by sexologists including Albert Moll, Richard von Krafft-Ebing, and Cesare Lombroso appeared in French translation between 1893 and 1896.

More important than this efflorescence of imaginary lesbian monsters, however, was the contemporary emergence in Paris of a female salon culture that claimed the figure of the page as its own icon of woman-oriented desire and eroticism. Travesty was no longer a phenomenon confined to the stage, for the ardent page became a favorite role, in life and in literature, for the community that included Colette, Natalie Clifford Barney, and Renée Vivien (a pseudonym chosen by Pauline Tarn). Literary critic Karla Jay has argued that through literal and imaginary cross-dressing, these women invented and claimed a radically new sexual persona, neither that of a conventional woman nor of an imitation man.[19] The operatic page had acquired a real-life equivalent: Chérubin, offstage, grew up into an icon of women's sexual love for other women.[20] Wearing trousers also freed these women to construct new poetic voices, for the page not only yearns, but sings eloquently about that yearning. Vivien's first two collections of poetry, for example, appeared under the androgynous initial "R."; in 1903, however, she first published under her female pseudonym, "Renée." The theatrical pageboy tradition even seems to have provided a model for the reception and refusal of women's "travestied" desire for women, as we see in the remarks of critic Charles Maurras in 1905. He made Vivien into a new Chérubin, another singer of failed serenades that go unheard because, in addressing another woman, the poet can only be talking to herself: "The feminine spirit," he wrote, "returns to itself and expresses itself in formulas, in order to understand and describe itself. *It does not love. Instead of loving, it thinks of love, and of itself.*"[21] Such criticism attempted to force the modern lesbian back into an eighteenth-century mold, dismissing her transvestite costume and her no-longer-vague desires as a childish masquerade of "mature" heterosexuality, but it was too late: real-life "pages," singing to other women with undisguisedly female voices, ushered Chérubin into the modern age.

The theatrical world responded with its own representations of the page's passage to adulthood, and my "genealogy" of Cherubino and his successors will conclude with an examination of how Massenet's 1905 *Chérubin* represents the page—still played by a "young and pretty woman," but now embedded in a modern web of associations around the image of a cross-dressed woman who desires women, and is irresistible to them.[22] This *comédie-chanteé* represents the page, for the first time, as a successful lover rather than a solitary dreamer. The plot picks up where Mozart's opera left off: Chérubin, dismissed from Castle Almaviva, is now an officer in the army. A new environment has not defused the page's erotic threat, however; rather the threat has *diffused* up the social order, for Chérubin is entangled with three forbidden women—a countess, a baroness, and "L'Ensoleillad," a dancer who is the king's mistress—and pursued by their three jealous protectors. Over persistent objections from his librettists, who wanted a tenor hero, the composer insisted that Chérubin remain a soprano role. In a pre-performance interview, Mary Garden playfully emphasized her own pleasure in trouser roles, remarking that, "I always loved to play comedies. . . . At school . . . I always played the male roles, with a big voice and a great big beard."[23] The nineteenth-century tradition of women *en travesti* for the delectation of the male viewer was not abandoned, for as one review noted, Mademoiselle Garden "wears the trouser with a rare degree of *sveltesse*."[24] Yet the musical setting and the staging of the piece suggest that this attractively "embodied" Chérubin was a spectacle to be handled with some care. Although Chérubin has grown up, his voice has not changed: the page has matured, but he has not become a man. The sexualization of the trousered woman has two related though apparently contradictory results: when this character loves another woman, her *body* must be removed from sight, but the full passion of her *voice*—detached from the costumed body by careful staging—can at last be heard.

Pace, pace, mio dolce tesoro:
Io conobbi la voce che adoro,
E che impressa ognor serbo nel cor.
(*Lorenzo da Ponte*, Le nozze di Figaro, *Act IV*)

The first sign of Chérubin's new potency is the treatment of the page's two serenades, now anything but "lost words" dispersed on the wind, and provoking every response but laughing indulgence. The first act's intrigue revolves around a *canzonetta* that Chérubin has written to an unnamed lady and then mislaid, and whose discovery puts the whole company in an uproar as every woman hopes it is for her and every husband prepares to avenge his honor. (Chérubin deploys this same *canzonetta* ironically in Act II when, rather than using it to draw a woman to him, he sings it from offstage to lure a trio of jealous husbands away from the garden where he is trysting with L'Ensoleillad.) The second serenade initiates the Act II finale, as Chérubin sings beneath the window of L'Ensoleillad, the king's mistress.[25] Already, the priority of *sight* is challenged, for the woman cannot see Chérubin's shiny boots and sword—she can only hear: "Qui parle dans la nuit confuse? Quelle est l'ombre sur le gazon?" (Who speaks in the obscure night? What is that shadow on the lawn?) Furthermore, Chérubin's soprano *voice* becomes the center of sonorous attention and the whole bearer of the character as the orchestra drops out after the first quatrain (see example 1). If this serenade, with its unaccompanied *parlando* melody, awkward rhymes, and incomplete second quatrain, bears out Chérubin's disingenuous conclusion that "Je suis très naïf encore," it also demonstrates a native gift for seduction, for his choice of a G-minor tonality in the scene's E♭-major context picks up on L'Ensoleillad's "sentimental" swerve to the mediant in her brief soliloquy just before. Perhaps because the moonlight has already rendered his lady susceptible, this serenade works, as the adolescent Cherubino's serenades had never worked before: it draws L'Ensoleillad downstairs, and a mutual seduction commences, a musical lesson in love.

L'Ensoleillad, encouraging her bashful admirer to *carpe diem* or, more precisely, *carpe noctem,* teaches Chérubin how to sing a real love song, and here for the first time in the opera we hear the lush harmonies most typical of Massenet, who has until this point represented his eighteenth-century comic subject with a spare, faux-classic musical style. In contrast with the former page's clumsily improvised serenade, the lady's invitation begins with a shapely refrain, again harmonized in her sentimental style, in which she transforms the serenade from a phenomenal performance into a performance of spiritual connection: "Mon âme te parle et ton cœur m'écoute" (My soul speaks to you and your heart listens). With her move to the relative minor, promised by the opening measures, her "realistic" block-chord accompaniment is likewise transformed into a faster-pulsing, more elaborate orchestral texture nonetheless marked *sempre sostenuto tranquillo.* After the first quatrain she abandons her regular rhyme scheme for a free evocation of the night's allurements, unifying her poem with imagery of singing birds and sighing winds, and with repeated exhortations to "Admire . . . Ecoute . . . Ecoute"; throughout, she alternates between passionate arching melodic lines and intimate murmurs, leading up to the peroration, "Amants trop bavards, hâtez-vous d'aimer!" (Garrulous lovers, hurry on to love!). Chérubin learns this lesson well, leaping in with the refrain "Ton âme me parle" before L'Ensoleillad has even reached her final high note, and they finish the refrain in unison (see example 2). Thus the implicitly erotic sonority of the two-soprano duet is at last matched to stage action—yet at the very moment of vocal synchronization, the lady and the former page vanish from our sight. When they embrace at the climax of

EXAMPLE 1
Massenet, *Chérubin;* Act II, Final

EXAMPLE 1
(*Continued*)

EXAMPLE 2
Massenet, *Chérubin;* Act II, Final

EXAMPLE 2
(*Continued*)

EXAMPLE 2
(*Continued*)

EXAMPLE 2
(*Continued*)

EXAMPLE 2
(*Continued*)

their duet, the stage directions indicate, "The moon is veiled. Embracing . . . the two lovers withdraw into the woods."

The comic episode that follows, in which the count, baron, and duke arrive to hunt for Chérubin, seems designed to differentiate the rapturous musical idiom that L'Ensoleillad has taught to Chérubin from the rest of the opera. The three bumblers mutter to each other in staccato patter, and when Chérubin leads them astray in the forest by singing snatches of his Act I serenade, we remember what a trivial ditty it was compared with the suave "Ton âme me parle." The men's noise frightens L'Ensoleillad, who runs back inside, and when Chérubin reappears, action music in the orchestra illustrates rather literally his ascent up the ladder to her balcony. Not until Chérubin reaches L'Ensoleillad again do the ascending scales accompanying his rapid climb metamorphose into *appassionato* surges.

With the resumption of the duet, the opera's strategies for managing the spectacle of an adult Chérubin in love reach their peak of complexity. The lovers have almost become equal partners, and as they implore "Amour" to let darkness hide them again, we hear what progress Chérubin has made in L'Ensoleillad's rhapsodic language. He completes her first strophe and begins a second, parallel strophe that the two "write" together, alternating lines:

L'ENSOLEILLAD:	Amour! amour! quand tu t'en mêles,
	Les jaloux peuvent survenir;
	Les amants qu'on veut désunir . . .
CHÉRUBIN:	. . .Tu les rapproches d'un coup d'aile.
	Amour! amour! Entends ma voix;
L'ENSOLEILLAD:	Phœbé luit trop sur nos visages,
CHÉRUBIN:	Les jaloux vont nous voir du bois . . .
L'ENSOLEILLAD:	Cache la lune d'un nuage.[26]

[Love, love! When you're involved, / Jealous ones want to intrude; / The lovers whom they wish to separate . . . / . . . you unite with one stroke of your wing. / Love, love! Hear my voice; / Phoebe shines too brightly upon our faces, / The envious ones will see us from the woods . . . / . . . Hide the moon in a cloud.]

At the granting of this request, the duet culminates, like the previous one, in a unison outburst (see example 3), and the poster from the original production captures the ambivalent staging of the moment: while the girlish lovers are represented as a charming spectacle, their contact is literally "barred" by the railing of the balcony. As at the conclusion of the earlier "Ton âme me parle," the mise en scène veils the spectacle of musical consummation, as "the moon is obscured."

What are we to make of this finale, with its strategic "disappearings" of the trousered woman's body? The staging seems designed to shield the spectator from the still-taboo sight of Chérubin's encounters with L'Ensoleillad; to borrow Terry Castle's phrase, these lovers have been "ghosted"—hidden behind walls or cast into shadow like the moon.[27] Yet even as the careful obscuring of this spectacle betrays its potency, the music

EXAMPLE 3
Massenet, *Chérubin;* Act II, Final

EXAMPLE 3
(*Continued*)

EXAMPLE 3
(*Continued*)

EXAMPLE 3
(*Continued*)

of the duet undermines the staging's repressive strategy altogether. Removing the body also removes all signs of Chérubin's putative masculinity, and the very darkness that veils his image also reveals the truth *behind* that image: the disembodied voice that serenades beneath the window, that infuriates the men and sings with L'Ensoleillad, belongs unmistakably to a woman, and only Chérubin's slightly darker timbre distinguishes the trousered soprano from her partner.

Massenet further underlines the lovers' resemblance by setting both their duets at the unison, an unusual choice that may be illuminated with reference to Berlioz's above-mentioned critique of female duets and to Massenet's own *Cendrillon* (1899), written only a few years before *Chérubin*. For Berlioz, the only passage in Bellini's *I Capuleti* that momentarily transcended mannerism to represent authentic passion was Romeo and Giulietta's unison outburst in the final *concertato* of the Act I finale. The lovers swear their faith as the Capulet faction violently wrests them apart, and their doubled soprano melody, soaring over staccato mutters in the lower voices, makes audible their indivisible union despite the separation imposed upon them: "Se ogni speme è a noi rapita / di mai più vederci in vita / questo addio non fia l'estremo / ah! ci vedremo almeno in ciel."[28] Although the love scene in *Chérubin* is in no sense modeled on the finale to *I Capuleti*, Chérubin and L'Ensoleillad articulate the same bond of similarity and sympathy when they appeal in unison to "Amour" on behalf of "Les amants qu'on veut désunir," and the absence of parallel consonances in their vocal lines may reflect a deliberate effort to avoid the connotations of "childish sensualism," rendering their love scene modern and passionate rather than archaically "sweet."

A more immediate precursor to Chérubin and L'Ensoleillad's scene may be found closer at hand in Act III of *Cendrillon*, where—as in *Chérubin*—three parameters define the relationship between a pair of lovers: their visibility to each other and the audience, their physical proximity, and the space between their vocal lines. In *Cendrillon*, song bridges the physical distance and darkness between Cinderella and her lost "Prince Charmant," soprano lovers who have come separately to the enchanted garden of the *Bonne Fée* for help in finding each other again. Although they cannot see each other (thanks to the fairy's stage management), their voices touch, first in a unison appeal to the fairy and then in an exchange of solo pleas. Without seeing, they recognize each others' voices and declare, "ta voix me pénétre d'une extase suprême" (your voice penetrates me with a supreme ecstasy), a poetic image that anticipates the speaking souls and listening hearts of Chérubin and L'Ensoleillad. The climax of their love scene is also a unison plea, "Laissez-moi le/la revoir! par pitié! Bonne Fée! laissez-moi le/la revoir!" In each of these love scenes, stage movement, physical barriers, and especially lighting are manipulated to prevent the lovers from ever visibly embracing while singing in unison. At the climax of the love scene in *Cendrillon,* when the lovers finally see each other "with a cry of joy" and rush into each others' arms, the vocal texture changes and for the first time they abandon their unisons and ecstatic imitative fragments, defaulting to those old-fashioned ("childish") parallel thirds before sinking into a magical, innocent sleep. Similarly, the unison outburst and embrace in *Chérubin* can only take place after "the moon is obscured." Nor is the passionate moment allowed to last, for almost instantly, the comic intrigue picks up again: lights come on inside the inn, windows fly open, and the lovers must separate, this time for good.

Yet for that brief rapturous moment, the lady and her lover *en travesti* had outgrown the innocence of parallel consonances; vocal similarity had given way to a literal merging of two selves. Despite the eighteenth-century costumes and characters, and the comic business that frames and interrupts this duet, the relationship between Chérubin and L'Ensoleillad is informed by a thoroughly modern eroticism. In this unlikely quarter—a refined and Mediterranean *comédie-chantée*, dominated by faux-classic dance meters and patter declamation—we may even detect an unexpected outbreak of Wagnerism: this love scene, in which the individualities of "Chérubin" and "L'Ensoleillad" merge under the sign of Eros, acts out the erotic poetics of *Tristan und Isolde,* with its dissolution of the "I" and "thou."[29] One might even argue, only half-facetiously, that *Chérubin* takes the Tristan model to the literal conclusion that *Tristan* itself (with its lovers whose voices, try as they might, rarely get within a half-step of each other) could not achieve.

More important, though, is the fact that Chérubin's voice, doubling that of L'Ensoleillad, reminds us of Suzanne's original recognition of the pretty page, with his features "like a woman's."[30] Not the cross-dressed body, but the undisguisable voice has been the real actor in Chérubin's escapades, and so Chérubin's adulthood fulfills its transgressive promise: even as Massenet's staging upholds the ban on our seeing Cherubino as an erotic spectacle, we may hear the "love that dares not speak its name" raise its soprano voice in song. Cherubino grows up, not into another version of Count Almaviva (as Kierkegaard predicted), nor into another Don Giovanni (as the Philosophe ruefully remarks at the conclusion of *Chérubin*), but into something unrepresentable at the time of his conception in the late eighteenth century. The love scene bears out journalist Louis Schneider's prediction, shortly before the première, that Massenet, the celebrated "painter of women," should be the ideal composer to capture Chérubin's appeal to feminine sensibilities—but not, perhaps, for the reasons Schneider had in mind.[31] Chérubin, with his svelte form, ardent poems, and soprano voice, "himself" belongs in the gallery of fin-de-siècle feminine types.

It would seem perverse to conclude this discussion of Cherubino's descendants without mentioning *Der Rosenkavalier,* for more than any other pageboy character, Octavian has been central to recent arguments about opera's "queerness."[32] Yet if Octavian is the best-known of operatic trouser roles, he was also an exception to the implicit rules that had governed representations of desire *en travesti,* and his role breaks with that tradition as well as recalling it. Strauss and Hofmannsthal, unlike their predecessors up to and including Massenet, no longer treat female travesty as a problem or a challenge, and their opera contains no trace of ambivalence about the practice: their (excessively) frank staging of the relationship between Octavian and the Marschallin puts the female lovers in a spotlight, clearly intended to titillate.[33] Their "Cherubino" no longer undresses behind a screen, and this very shamelessness, this abandonment of over a century of shadows and veils over the page's body and desire, leaves less to "read."[34] Our vision of the page can only ever be partial—not because a female performer obscures our view of an actual (yet imaginary) male character, but because so many strategies have been employed to obscure the suggestion or trace of lesbian desire. Indeed, the page's "lesbian" aspects may be defined by the obscurantist strategies that attend operatic representations of the grown-up page, the obsessive management of every detail of the visual and vocal spectacle.

Indeed, although my attempt to make the modern Chérubin visible may seem to participate in the recent project of seeing lesbians everywhere in opera, I would insist instead on the historical specificity of the page *en travesti.*[35] Perhaps even more curious than the veiling of the page's erotic presence is the complete nonchalance with which trousered female performers are presented in other traditions: mezzo-heroes and lovers in opera seria and the bel canto repertory, for example, sing their love duets in broad daylight; they wear their masculine costumes securely. These roles present new puzzles by their very lack of mystery, and they may require even more searching scrutiny than Cherubino. The list is long—Handel's princes, Rossini's armor roles, Gluck's Orfeo restored for Pauline Viardot-Garcia, to name only a few—but none of these are precisely "like" Cherubino, and no all-purpose answer exists for the various questions they pose about opera, gender, and representation.

Elisabeth's Last Act

ROGER PARKER

An [historical] event is not a decision, a treaty, a reign, or a battle, but the reversal of a relationship of forces, the usurpation of power, the appropriation of a vocabulary turned against those who once used it, a feeble domination that poisons itself as it grows lax, the entry of a masked "other."[1]

Doing history means building bridges between the past and the present, observing both banks of the river, taking an active part in both sides.[2]

"IN QUESTO DRAMMA NULLA VI È DI STORICO"

As is very well known, Verdi's *Don Carlos,* first performed at the Paris Opéra in 1867, underwent several authorial revisions, the most radical of which occurred in the early 1880s, and in which, as well undergoing many more minor alterations, the opera lost almost its entire first act.[3] This act is a prologue: Carlos the infante of Spain and Elisabeth, daughter of Henry II of France, unknown to each other but betrothed through an arranged marriage, meet by chance in the forest of Fontainebleau; they fall in love and are of course ecstatic with joy to find out in a magnificent recognition scene that they are also engaged. If only life were more often like this. But of course their joy is short-lived: the act ends in confusion as it is announced that King Philip, Carlos's father, has magnanimously decided to marry Elisabeth himself. The rest of the opera takes place in Spain, and (albeit with generous sub-plots) plays out the unhappy consequences of these events: Carlos's despair at dealing with a wife become mother (a kind of Oedipus in reverse, the infante infantilized), Philip's gathering insecurity, and Elisabeth's consuming guilt and sense of duty.

Many commentators have described the pros and cons of this loss. The Fontainebleau act develops a relationship, and sets out a musical ambience, that is in some ways crucial to the rest of the opera: without it, Carlos and Elisabeth are harder to understand, not least because their subsequent utterances have prominent musical references to this first meeting. On the other hand, and as the opera's first critics were not slow to point out, *Don Carlos* is—even by the standards of *grand opéra*—extremely long, and this act, which is essentially a prologue to the main action, is easily narrated.[4] What is more, in the later, four-act version, the outer acts project a new and powerful symmetry. Both are set in the monastery of Saint-Just; the new Act I (the original Act II) opens with censorious monks chanting over the mausoleum of Emperor Charles V (Philip's father and Carlos's grandfather), a solitary monk adding vehement condemnations; the final act begins with very similar musical material, and ends with Carlos, cornered by the Inquisition, saved by that same monk, who emerges from the tomb now dressed in the garb of (according to some sources, actually transformed into) the emperor. Here is coherence of another kind; not so much of character and motivation, but of structure and tone—the opera becomes more monolithic, its central message that much easier to identify.

There was some trouble about this mysterious monk-cum-emperor, who was an invention of the first librettists, not appearing in Schiller's source play. In the first version of the opera, Verdi made sure that he would appear only in the very last moments, because, in his words, "Philip must not be allowed too much time to consider whether this is a ghost or a living person."[5] In the score he is described merely as "Le Moine," although everyone seems to recognize him as Charles V.[6] There were few remarks for or against among the critics of the Paris première, though one has the suspicion that they were mostly beyond comment by this extremely late stage in the evening. But at the time of the 1880s revision, and possibly in belated reaction to a considerable fuss those same critics had made about the opera's blatant historical inaccuracy, the denouement became more of a problem. Verdi led off the objections: "Charles V alive has always shocked me. If he's alive, how is it that Don Carlos doesn't know him? And what's more (again if he's alive), how could Philip be an old man, as he says he is? It's an imbroglio that has to be disentagled."[7] Camille du Locle, the librettist, countered with the fact that Schiller's original was so free with history that this was a trifling matter, and that, anyway, the historical Charles had been mysterious about his last years, and so it *could* have happened this way after all.[8] Verdi reluctantly agreed, and although in the end he shortened the denouement quite radically, the monk remained, and is this time explicitly called Charles V in the stage directions.

But the monk seems to have sparked off a round of questions about the whole idea of historical accuracy. When in 1883 Verdi sent off the final version of his revised opera to his Italian publisher Ricordi, he did so with the following gloss:

Charles V appears robed as Emperor!! It isn't very likely. The Emperor had been dead for a number of years. But in this drama, so splendid in form and in its high-minded concepts, everything is false.

<u>Don Carlos</u> was a fool, a madman, an unpleasant fellow.

<u>Elisabeth</u> was never in love with Don Carlos.

<u>Posa</u> is an imaginary being who could never have existed under Philip's reign.

<u>Philip</u>, who amongst other things says:

<u>Garde-toi de mon Inquisiteur</u> . . .

<u>Qui me rendra ce mort!!</u>

Philip wasn't as soft-hearted as that.

> In other words in this Drama there is nothing historical, nor is there any Shakespearean truth or profundity in the characters . . . so one thing more or less won't do any harm: I myself don't mind this appearance of the old Emperor.[9]

What are we to make of this? Perhaps Verdi was joking, or merely fed up with the endless argument. But, even in jest, he advanced categories we may find difficult to understand: a drama can have "historical" truth; or there can be "Shakespearean" truth in the characters; or, it seems, there can be neither of these things. What can the last category then consist of, the one into which *Don Carlos* falls? It might of course be a merely negative trait; though that seems unlikely. But what that is positive can emerge from a lack of "historical" and "Shakespearean" truth? I think there may be an answer in Elisabeth's aria, which opens the last act. But before considering that, we will need to explore some background.

PUBLIC MAN

Anselm Gerhard's recently translated book on Parisian grand opera, called in English *The Urbanization of Opera,* is one of the most ambitious contributions to the history of nineteenth-century opera to have emerged in the last twenty years.[10] As its title suggests, the book's major thesis is that many of the changes taking place in opera during the nineteenth century can best be explained not by the term "bourgeoisification" (which Gerhard pronounces too vague and historically too diffuse), but rather by the process of "urbanization," the gathering sense of an "urban space of experience" that encouraged composers and audiences gradually to favor certain styles of operatic representation over others. I can't here go into the levels of detail through which this proposition is argued, persuasive as many of them are, but must immediately turn to a related thesis, one that is sometimes tied quite closely to the first, is sometimes more loosely juxtaposed, and on occasion comes close to dislodging it in importance.

This is the more familiar idea that the nineteenth century saw an important turn away from what Richard Sennett has famously called the idea of "public man": an increasing tendency for urban dwellers to seek coherence not within the "public" world of politics and economics, which had so often betrayed them and was ever more obviously beyond their control, but rather within the "private" world of the family and of personal relationships generally.[11] This tendency, Gerhard argues, has a clear connection to changes in European opera generally, and eventually led to the "decline" of French grand opera: indeed, went hand in hand with what Gerhard calls—following Dahlhaus and others—"the wholesale withdrawal from Meyerbeerian historical tragedy into the interior world of private, personal tragedies."[12] A little later he is more specific:

> Just as *grand opéra* became ever more complicated, so breathtaking technological progress and other phenomena (not all rationally explicable) that accompanied the uncontrolled expansion of the capitalist economic order contributed to a general sense of vulnerability in a dangerous world. Thirty years earlier, in comparable circumstances, dramatists and novelists had invoked the power of fate to explain the inexplicable, but that was worn out by over-use and had lost the power to dispel such fears. The logical next step was to banish thoughts of what one was powerless to explain from one's conscious mind. The wage-earner confined his participation in public life to the absolute minimum necessary, left political decisions to "professional" deputies elected for that purpose, and concentrated his efforts on defending his own private space against harmful outside influences. . . . The authoritarian paterfamilias, concerned for the moral and material well-being of his children, became a stereotype character of novels and plays, short stories and full-length operas.[13]

This offers a bold sweep through nineteenth-century history, one that makes opera newly relevant and also, though I'm not sure Gerhard would want to use these terms, one that offers us a model in which opera can be seen not merely reflecting broader cultural concerns, but also potentially *creating* them, providing language and representational models within which these new private emotions could then flourish in the "real" world. What is more, far from remaining on this general level, Gerhard bodies out his thesis with persuasive close readings, in particular of the difficulties and equivocations that appear in "transitional" works such as Meyerbeer's *Le Prophète* and Verdi's *Les Vêpres siciliennes,* and of what he sees as Verdi's eventual emergence into a drama of unambiguous interiority with *Un ballo in maschera.* And although he doesn't press the point, this line can of course be continued, through Wagner, into obsessively interior early twentieth-century works such as *Pelléas et Mélisande* and *Erwartung,* and perhaps even into today's postmodern visual culture, which for Gerhard is inhabited by "consumers who do not distinguish between television images of political reality and the fictional horrors of feature films."[14] (Such remarks take up a strand of Sennett's argument perhaps even more relevant today than it was when he wrote the book some twenty-five years ago:

The Fall of Public Man repeatedly and impatiently mentions our modern-day habit of assessing political leaders in essentially personal terms—of looking harder at "credibility" than at political acts or even in some cases political competence.)

As I said, these broad pictures can be compelling, perhaps especially when they seem to carry with them gloomy, fin-de-siècle imaginings of a present cultural decline: from the historical canvas of *Les Huguenots* to (say) the bleak timelessness of *Pelléas* or *Erwartung* is powerful enough; and if the line continues all the way to *The Jerry Springer Show* and "Monicagate," then for some it will be just that much harder to resist. So I hope it won't seem churlish if I point out that, at least so far as Verdi's development is concerned, there are plausible alternatives or at least troubling exceptions, ones that may fit less smoothly with the grand narrative but may, perhaps even for that reason, nevertheless prove to enrich and complexify opera's relationship to its time. While there is, for example, little doubt that *Un ballo in maschera* fits the interiority thesis very well, what can be said of the last opera Verdi wrote for Paris? What of *Don Carlos*?

In some ways it also falls nicely into place. Gerhard himself offers a telling reading of the Act I scene narrated at the start of this paper. Philip's fateful decision to marry Elisabeth is announced, and hardly have the young lovers reacted before an offstage chorus of celebration is heard approaching. The crowd comes onstage, bringing with it one of those magnificent processions that seem to act out before us the hierarchies and paraphernalia of public life.[15] Eventually Elisabeth is obliged to accept Philip's offer, and a great tableau is set up, the noisy choral celebrations interspersed with the anguished reactions of the two principals. We have, in other words, the makings of a classic Meyerbeerian scene of individuals pitted against society, a violent clash between the private and the public. But then something curious happens: the crowd escorts Elisabeth away, the music dies to pianissimo, and the scene ends with a close focus on Carlos lamenting his "destin fatal." As Gerhard comments:

> There could hardly be a more convincing demonstration of the fact that it was absolutely necessary for the chorus to retire to the wings . . . when the dramaturgical conception placed the isolation of despairing individuals centerstage.[16]

On some levels—overwhelmingly the visual and sonic ones—the force of Gerhard's argument is very clear. However, the scene also of course advances a musical argument, one that, music being what it is (or should I say has become?), may potentially tell a different story. As is very common for scenes in which Verdi wished to set in extreme juxtaposition two opposing emotions (in this case the despair of the lovers versus the celebrations of the crowd), he articulated the contrast through extremely simple rhythmic elements. After their first shocked exclamations, the lovers employ almost exclusively the triplet figures obsessively announced in their dark allegro agitato. "L'heure fatale est sonnée!" (see example 1a). The chorus, on the other hand, are throughout characterized by a jaunty dotted rhythm whose repetitiousness takes them to the edge of banality (see example 1b). The "battle" of these two rhythmic ideas is played out, both in the voices and in the orchestra, over almost the entire closing ensemble. But then, at the very end of the scene, with the chorus retreated and Carlos left alone, something of great motivic significance occurs (see example 1c). Over a coda-like orchestral elaboration of the chorus's theme, Carlos loses his triplets. First his line disintegrates, becoming breathless and fragmented, and then, at the last, he sings out the chorus's dotted rhythm to the words "O destin fatal," complete even with their characteristic chromatic lower neighbor.

Of course a moment such as this can be made to mean in a variety of ways. One can easily imagine a "formalist" reading that would talk admiringly of tonal and thematic logic, of the achievement of "closure" on subtle musical levels. But within the extreme economy of Verdi's rhythmic characterization, another interpretation of Carlos's adoption of the chorus's motive could be that in these final lines he has despaired and capitulated. While a more conventional, noisy close could have held the lovers' musical resistance to the last, in this quiet coda the rebellious anguish, the *difference* expressed in those triplets becomes exhausted, and in their place is a tired acceptance of what the crowd, the public face, the political will, decrees; in the most obvious way, then, that dotted rhythm and chromatic lower neighbor mark Carlos's acceptance of public discourse: the exterior world has not retreated with the retreating chorus; it has, rather, invaded all the more completely the individual's affective world, becoming at once a more potent and a more malign force. This interpretation, though of course hardly immune from debate or even refutation, can at least rest comfortably with others: it is a way of looking that does not necessarily aspire to contradict Gerhard, for example, but merely to suggest that a further nuance, an accumulation of complexity, can emerge after attention to music's lexicon within the operatic object.

L'AUGUSTE EMPEREUR

My next port of call en route to Elisabeth's last act continues directly where the music stopped, pausing for a moment on the opening of Act II (or of the whole opera in the shortened four-act version). Although there are hints of motivic continuation across the act-break, in particular with those again-prominent dotted rhythms that characterized the festive chorus, the

EXAMPLE 1a
Verdi, *Don Carlos;* Act I, Final

EXAMPLE 1b
Verdi, *Don Carlos;* Act I, Final

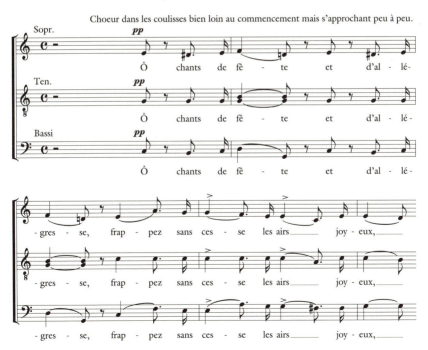

EXAMPLE 1c
Verdi, *Don Carlos;* Act I, Final

"public music" of the previous act, this new scene, geographically and visually so different from the first, presents a radically altered world outlook. A unison passage on four horns, austere and portentous, gives way to a solemn *psalmodie* intoned by offstage monks, singing from the chapel of the monastery of Saint-Just. Before us a solitary monk kneels before the tomb of Charles V. The monks present a deeply nihilistic view of the world's progress.[17]

Charles-Quint, l'auguste Empereur,
N'est plus que cendre et que poussière.
Et maintenant, son âme altière
Est tremblante aux pieds du Seigneur!

[Charles V, the august Emperor, / is no more than dust and ashes. / And now, his proud soul / trembles at the feet of the Lord!]

For those who know the rest of the opera, the music of this act-opening is densely motivic, in particular through its multilayered emphasis on b6̂-5̂ (D-C♯), which many commentators have identified as an important recurring element in the work as a whole (see example 2).[18] Also to be noted are the multiple harmonic contexts for A as a note of melodic climax. When the monks' chant arrives, the b6̂-5̂ goes into the inner parts, and that prominent A is taken up melodically to become the focus of an insistent modal mixture of A-A♯, the latter note then "composed out" in its enharmonic equivalent B♭. Those weary modal mixtures of the chant are also significant: they too play an important part in the opera as a whole. Here, though, I would like to register their peculiar blankness. When the A♯ emerges, it does not relieve the gloom of the minor mode, but merely seems to generate a dark echo, a resonance that brings no hope. It is, as the words tell us, a bleak view of history: everything will turn to dust and ashes.

The resonances of this taking-on of history could, of course, lead in many directions through this vast opera. It could, for example, encourage us to contemplate the tragedy of Philip, who starts the fourth act with a famous aria, "Elle me n'aime pas," that again fits very well with Gerhard's thesis, and which he discusses briefly.[19] The set piece takes place near dawn, the king leaning wearily on a table that overflows with official papers, the nearly spent candles marking the end of a long night wrestling (we assume with little success or pleasure) with the duties of state. The stage seems set for a contemplation of the melancholy verities of public life, but Philip begins instead with a simple, tragic statement, "she doesn't love me," an utterance all the more affecting and interior through its absence of conventional poeticism. Famously, Philip's subsequent historical thoughts, in particular his dreams of a royal puissance he so singly lacks, lead nowhere: in the end, he closes where he began—he can do no more than return to his impassioned outburst of personal loss, a retreat from the public ambitions that have deluded him, a descent into the labyrinth of the soul.

Or we could, as I have discussed at some length elsewhere, look again at Rodrigue, marquis de Posa, who in his Act IV death scene takes up those two prominent motives from and of the past, the ones laid out so powerfully at the start of Act II. In expressing love for his friend Carlos, Posa transforms for a moment their grim ambience, making them musically

EXAMPLE 2
Verdi, *Don Carlos;* Act II, Scène et Prière

EXAMPLE 2
(*Continued*)

something else, freeing himself momentarily from their grip.[20] But Posa's life is cut short, his public mission unfulfilled. And the final act of *Don Carlos* begins, as I said earlier, with a return to the dark ambience that started Act II. Into the cloisters of Saint-Just steps Elisabeth de Valois.

A MASKED "OTHER"

Most of the rest of this paper concerns Elisabeth and her aria that starts this final act, but by way of introduction I need to return for a last time to Anselm Gerhard, this time to the fall not of "public" man, but of public "man." The historical shift toward interiority that Gerhard relates so persuasively to the story of French opera needs, as do all such narratives, some points of stasis against which to measure change; and one of these concerns the role played by women. As Gerhard says:

> From [the 1830s] onward, in later *grands opéras,* and also in Italian opera after 1850, the pattern of the meek, self-denying maiden was the rule, even in those cases where the female protagonist is first depicted as an active heroine, or even a woman of doubtful virtue. . . . Violetta, the courtesan presented in Act I of Verdi's *Traviata* as a woman used to getting her own way with men, falls in with the ruthless demands made of her by Alfredo's father in Act II so readily that she appears to have been positively waiting for the opportunity to sacrifice her happiness and her love for Alfredo on the altar of patriarchal authority.[21]

To read plots thus is—I need hardly recall in the context of this collection—an old, old story; but in the case of Gerhard it can engage only tangentially with the main thesis, which of course has as its protagonist precisely those agents of patriarchal authority, those enforcers of the "bourgeois" theatrical representation of women. Passive as represented on the stage, then, women are also represented here as passive in historical terms: reacting to, rather than creating, the dynamic changes in manly subjectivity that take place around them. As Gerhard and many others have pointed out, this fictive representation was very far from what reality we can find in the historical situation of women, or even in many of the other public discourses—psychological, educational, sexual, what you will—that circulated during this period. But I also want to question whether the operatic object in its entirety is quite so secure a place for the patriarch. Taking up strands already mentioned in connection with Carlos's "interior" ending to Act I, I want in other words to argue that this representational model may also be in some sense discordant with some aspects of its operatic manifestation; again because, in the operatic world, characters are not limited to the verbal and the visual—in opera, characters also sing.

As has been for some time well known, Elisabeth was in fact a comparative latecomer to the Act V opening: the powers that be—patriarchal or otherwise in this instance—had planned something much more conventional. In the original prose scenario for the opera, and in the first draft libretto, an imposing aria for Carlos was imagined. It began with a verbal sign of that powerful reminiscence of the monks' solemn prayer at the start of Act II (which we must therefore assume was a gesture initially thought up by the librettists), from which emerges a further apostrophe to the spirit of Charles V, a personal prayer from Carlos, for strength to continue the political struggles espoused by his friend Posa, who now lies dead:

> (*Au lever du rideau, l'orchestre rappelle le motif de la prière des moines autour du tombeau de Charles-Quint. Carlos, pensif, est appuyé aux grilles de la chapelle.*)

> > Ô portiques muets, tombeaux, voûtes glacées,
> > Eteigner de mon coeur les ardeurs insensées;
> > Ombre de mon aïeul sous ce cloître endormi,
> > Fais-moi digne de toi . . . digne de mon ami.[22]

> [*As the curtain rises, the orchestra recalls the motive of the monks' prayer around the tomb of Charles V. Carlos, pensive, rests against the grilles of the chapel.*

> O mute porticos, tombs, icy vaults, / extinguish from my heart its senseless passions; / ghost of my grandfather, sleeping under this cloister, / make me worthy of you . . . worthy of my friend.]

In the libretto draft there follows a pair of reminiscences of past meetings with Elisabeth. Carlos then sees her approaching, and before she arrives ends the scene with a reprise of the quatrain quoted above. Verdi rejected this grandiose conception, calling it "an *hors d'oeuvre* which is out of place in a fifth act,"[23] thus adding further evidence to document his famous propensity for dispatch as the denouement of a drama approached. In its place came a much reduced scene for Carlos, in which the protagonist still recalls those earlier love duets, but now without the grandiose opening quatrain, and in a vocal style that barely emerges from recitative. The once-imposing scene is, in other words, reduced to little more than an introduction to the ensuing duet between Carlos and Elisabeth.

This version was sketched musically, and the sketch survives; but then, at an unknown date, Verdi together with his librettists had an important change of mind, canceling Carlos's recitative and putting in its place a lengthy aria for Elisabeth, one whose proportions and overall shape very much resemble those of Carlos's aria in that first libretto draft, and in which, again, reminiscences of love are enclosed within an imposing opening quatrain and its reprise at the close. What caused this change of plan, this decision not only to substitute characters, but also to present a substantial aria at the start of the act, a route Verdi had explicitly rejected earlier? Various hypotheses have been put forward for the change of character, most often that the tenor scheduled to create Don Carlos was proving less than satisfactory; even before the substitution Verdi was already working to improve and enlarge the role of Elisabeth,[24] and it seems likely that the new aria was a radical step in the same direction, bolstering her part, broadening and deepening her character, at a late date.[25]

A glance at the text of that imposing opening quatrain might easily make us think that this increased exposure granted to the opera's heroine merely serves to strengthen the "passive heroine" topos mentioned earlier, particularly in comparison with the draft aria for Carlos. Both apostrophize the tomb of Charles V, but while our hero had boldly asked for strength in the coming struggle, Elisabeth merely asks that her oh-so-female tears be heard:

> Toi qui sus le néant des grandeurs de ce monde,
> Toi qui goûtes enfin la paix douce et profonde,
> Si l'on répand encore des larmes dans le ciel,
> Porte en pleurant mes pleurs aux pieds de l'Eternel!

[You who knew the emptiness of the pomp of the world, / you who enjoy at the last a gentle, profound peace, / If one still sheds tears in heaven, / by weeping bring my tears to the feet of the Eternal One!]

As already mentioned, there are striking musical resemblances to the start of Act II; but there are also striking differences. As can be seen in example 3, the prelude begins with an instrumental version of the monks' blank chant, but, on the third system, as the curtain opens to reveal Elisabeth, a new affective musical presence appears, an agitated string theme that repeatedly rises to a climactic A♮, eventually sweeping away the chant. When Elisabeth finally sings, she too gestures musically to the past: her opening solo is clearly a recomposition of that austere horn unison that started Act II, but again there is a change: this time the music modulates, becomes itself a preparation, leads to a remarkable lyrical flowering as Elisabeth asks the dead emperor to intercede for her ("Si l'on répand"). The modal mixture here, the move from F♯ minor to F♯ major, will—especially emerging as it does from the orchestral introduction's motivic context—inevitably recall the monks' chant. But here, finally, the blank echo of their weary move to A♯ is banished, or rather, is substituted with the luminosity of this F♯ major episode, and in particular by Elisabeth's climactic high A♯ in the final phrase of this section. And the fact that this grandioso moment also dispenses with words—"porte mes pleurs, *ah,*

EXAMPLE 3
Verdi, *Don Carlos;* Act V, Scène (Elisabeth)

EXAMPLE 3
(*Continued*)

EXAMPLE 3
(*Continued*)

EXAMPLE 3
(*Continued*)

"porte mes pleurs" seems if anything to invest it with even greater individual power.

As you see in the last measures of musical example 3, this first vocal achievement is immediately countered by the return of A♮ in that agitated string theme. The new sonority serves as an entry to the middle section of the aria, taken up with reminiscences of past musical material, in particular of the two moments and the two places in which Elisabeth and Carlos had expressed their love for each other earlier in the opera: the first from their duet in the Fontainebleau act, the second from their duet in Act II. Much of this section is borrowed from the sketch for Carlos's scena, and although there are telling differences, I am constrained to pass them by. This is not to say, though, that these very obvious, verbally signalled quotations from the past are unimportant; in the present context, contained as they are within these imposing lyrical pillars, they allow Elisabeth to gather some important strands of her musical past around her, thus arming her all the more securely to address the music of that dark, history-laden place in which she stands.

The reprise of the A section (see example 4) has three important differences from its initial statement. First, Elisabeth's opening lines, originally a lone call, unaccompanied, are now supported by the brass: those solemn, reiterated chords that started the prelude are now, as it were, at her service, even urging her on. And then her lyrical flowering returns, but this time with a remarkable, diaphanous orchestration that, in the economy of Verdian usage, gives every impression that what we hear is now itself a reminiscence. In other words, those A♯s are now fully within Elisabeth's world; so much so that she can recall them in some kind of serenity. And then, at the last, there is a remarkable coda. The anguish of those A♮s returns momentarily, but they can no longer disturb our heroine, who banishes them with absolute certainty, and then with absolute calm. That dead echo that sounded as the monks wearily chanted has again been made living, and all the more so because of the extreme *daring* of these last moments: first the leap of a major tenth—up to A♯ and onto the structural dominant; and then that last, pianissimo high A♯, again articulated as a wordless cry. This high note, one of the most perilously exposed in the soprano repertory, seems to me at the still center of the act. The singer who achieves it achieves a very great deal, both personally and in terms of the character she embodies. And of course, as with other moments we have considered, the gesture can be made to mean in diverse ways. But according to this reading, Elisabeth has taken the deadening past and, before our ears, converted it into the affective present, an affective present that is hers but, with the extraordinary intensity and daring of that final pianissimo A♯, also becomes ours.

PAS PRÉCISÉMENT L'HISTOIRE

It's time to gather together some threads, if not a quiet coda of my own. There are several possible conclusions to this paper, several possible morals to be drawn. On a rather obvious level, the message of Elisabeth's aria could merely reinforce a sense hinted at earlier: that large-scale narratives about the position of opera in culture, necessary though they are and

EXAMPLE 4
Verdi, *Don Carlos;* Act V, Scène (Elisabeth)

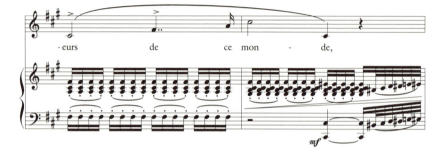

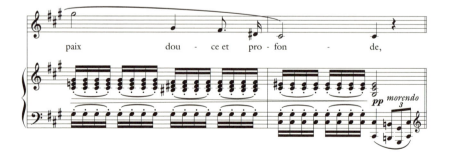

EXAMPLE 4
(*Continued*)

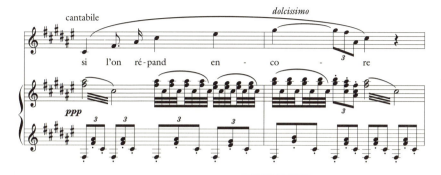

EXAMPLE 4
(*Continued*)

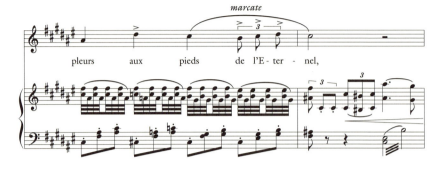

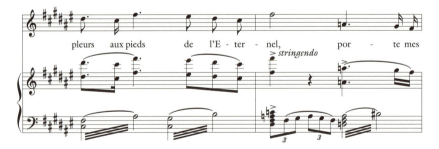

EXAMPLE 4
(*Continued*)

will remain, are best thought of as sites on which to register (good-natured) discontent, or at least only skeptical and only contingent approval. As times change, so the narratives will themselves change; and in the case of nineteenth-century opera, these changes may be encouraged by the intense present-ness the works retain in our own culture, in particular by the interpretive fluidity that now habitually accompanies certain aspects of their texts, and also perhaps by virtue of the fact that we are now more ready than we once were to find at the heart of opera's competing systems of communication a resistance to single-minded explanations. In this case, for example, it is quite clear that a simple survey of subject matter and broad dramatic treatments will indeed tell us that a concern for representing "history" on the nineteenth-century operatic stage gradually lost ground between about 1830 and about 1880, being replaced by an increased interest in individual subjectivities; but opera is not merely, perhaps not even primarily, a matter of plots, and when the musical element is added to the equation it can often confuse the matter, in the examples outlined here at least suggesting that the "historical" can be absorbed into the individual, so making its influence within the operatic event all the more powerful.

But the case of Elisabeth's aria has a further story to tell, one reminding us that historical narratives, being inevitably and always the products of particular ideologies, will tend to hierarchize along ideological grounds, dictating matters as basic as who is "a protagonist," or what constitutes "an event." Following this line of thought, it would of course be possible to extend my reading of Elisabeth's last act, now perhaps conventionally, as an "empowering" moment for the heroine, and perhaps to move from there into a rehearsal of the voice-plot nexus that has so animated operatic criticism over the last few years. In terms of Carolyn Abbate's now-celebrated distinction, "plot-Elisabeth" may indeed remain tied to the stereotype of the passive female heroine; but "voice-Elisabeth" (or, nearer my terms here, "music-Elisabeth") becomes an important dynamic force in the economy of the opera's world.[26] Unlike Carlos in Act I, she is not defeated by the force of history; unlike Philip in Act IV, she does not retreat into the interior, private emotion; in fact she becomes most human and alive precisely when she confronts the past and makes it her own present.[27] In the Foucauldian terms of my opening epigraph, Elisabeth becomes that "masked other," a character that has marked an historical "event" not in the conventional sense of fighting a battle or signing a contract, but in the sense of appropriating a vocabulary once owned by the voices of authority. And if this formulation will strike some as now having too powerful a scent of May '68, then perhaps my second epigraph will provide an acceptable alternative: unlike Carlos or Philip, Elisabeth "does" history, "building bridges between the past and the present, observing both banks of the river, taking an active part in both sides."

It would in some ways be fitting to close there but, especially in the context of the present volume, I prefer to end by fulfilling an earlier promise, returning to that Verdi letter quoted near the start, in which the composer stated that in *Don Carlos* "there is nothing historical, nor is there any Shakespearean truth or profundity in the characters." The absence of "historical" truth is easy to explain. As those critics of the first Parisian performances endlessly reminded their readers, Schiller's play (and Verdi's opera) had very little to do with mid-nineteenth-century perceptions of the historical truth about sixteenth-century Spain, being based on earlier, ideologically driven propaganda disseminated by Spain's enemies.[28] The matter seemed to cause little embarrassment, if many column inches. But the idea of characters and their "Shakespearean truth" is more difficult. In a famous letter of the same period, however, Verdi made his perception of Shakespeare somewhat clearer:

> It may be that [Shakespeare] found Falstaff just as he was, but it would have been difficult for him to find a villain as villainous as Iago, and never, never such angels as Cordelia, Imogen, Desdemona, etc., etc., and yet they are so true![29]

To what precisely are those angels true? They are not true to life, cannot conform to any woman; they are, rather, "essentially" true, conforming to the vision of the female, an "essential" and also "essentializing" vision that was endlessly represented on stage. I like to think that that is part of the reason why Verdi thought this opera lacked "Shakespearean" truth: because the aria he had given Elisabeth in the last act causes her to emerge musically from the passivity of her visual and verbal representation, cease to be "essential." Of course objections can be found, powerful counternarratives that have powerful resonances in the opera. As some will be quick to point out, at the end of the opera that tired, history-laden monks' chant is restored, has the final word—whether bleakly and chorally (the first version) or in an imposing brass fanfare (the second version). That mysterious old monk comes out of the tomb to protect and enfold Don Carlos. What has Elisabeth to do with all this? Earlier in that letter about the "historical" truth of the opera, Verdi stressed that the final scene should end precipitately. At the appearance of the old monk, Philip has nothing to say and Elisabeth "can do nothing other than die; and as quickly as possible."[30] Well, she does not quite oblige—for once the plot saves her. True to type, though, she does no more than thank heaven, doubtless with hands clasped in the approved, submissive manner. But in light of the way she started Act V, in light of those high A♯s, I want to argue that her final gesture doesn't have to be the inevitable plea to patriarchal authority. About fifteen minutes before, we heard her being implicated in the deal: she thanks a patriarchal authority she has had the power to influence.

___ Body and Voice in Melodrama and Opera ___

PETER BROOKS

I WANT TO REFLECT here on some key elements in the expressionist aesthetics of melodrama and opera—genres that are deeply intricated one with the other, historically and aesthetically, yet also seem to pull in different directions, to aspire to very different privileges accorded to body and to voice. It is on the relation of body and voice in the two genres that I want to meditate for a moment.

In the work I have done on melodrama, I have repeatedly been struck by the bodiliness of that genre. As an expressionistic mode, melodrama achieves its effects through making overt, present, visible—through acting out. Inevitably, acting out takes place on and through the body. Meaning is embodied. The body, in its postures and gestures, its emphases and distortions, must offer a visible, legible register of the message, reinforcing the other registers of the message—speech, stage set, music. Melodramatic acting on the nineteenth-century stage is something that we would now find ludicrously hyperbolic, accustomed as we are to the more intimate, domesticated melodrama of the television screen. We can recapture some of its elements mainly through the early silent cinema, and through grand opera.

Melodrama's recourse to meaning embodied, I have argued, has something to do with the historical emergence of the genre from earlier forms, pantomime and *pantomime dialoguée,* created in a situation where the popular theater had no legal right to the word, which was the exclusive privilege of the patented theaters. Whatever the historical causes, melodrama regularly sought occasions for the mute role and the mute scene, where plot and meaning had to unfold exclusively through action and gesture, without the supplement of the word. More recently, I have given some attention to the latter-day realization of a mute semiotics in the silent film, particularly in the work of D. W. Griffith. Griffith's cinema is indeed technically similar to that bastard form that precedes and prepares melodrama, *pantomime dialoguée,* in that the intertitles offer a skeletal structure of verbal meanings that the film enacts and embodies. The intertitles are quite like those banners and placards often presented in *pantomime dialoguée,* the display of the semantics of a situation, which often simply doubles the message the audience can deduce from the mute action itself.[1]

It was in fact a French stage melodrama of 1872, Adolphe Dennery's *Les Deux Orphelines,* that provided the story line for Griffith's great film of the

French Revolution, *Orphans of the Storm,* concerning two young women raised as sisters: Henriette, the daughter of peasants who almost disposed of her as an infant on the steps of Notre Dame Cathedral, and Louise, whom they rescued from those steps when they decided to keep their own daughter, and who has gone blind. Henriette and Louise (played by Lillian and Dorothy Gish) travel from the provinces to Paris in search of a medical miracle, and instead encounter dark intrigue and nightmare risk before recognition establishes Louise's aristocratic birth, and produces the happy ending.

Henry James reviewed the New York production of Dennery's melodrama, which he found a poor rendering of the original, but nonetheless "worth seeing simply for the sake of sitting in one's place and feeling the quality of a couple of good old-fashioned *coups de théâtre* as your French playwright who really knows his business manages them."[2] Both *coups de théâtre* are preserved in *Orphans of the Storm,* and though you don't have the film before your eyes to see their effect, I want to use them, briefly, as examples. One is the moment when the good brother, Pierre—thus far the ineffectual protector of the blind Louise, who has been kidnapped by his villanous mother, La Frochard—finally goes into revolt against the evil brother, Jacques, with the words: "As you say yourself, we come of a race that kills!" This needs intertitling, since it is not semanticizable through gesture alone—though what is nonetheless most memorable in the scene is Pierre's expression of manic joy and defiance, and his bodily movement of self-assertion, his casting off of years of subjection. After we have seen the message in the intertitle, we read its enactment on the body itself.

The other *coup de théâtre* noted by James needs no words at all. It is the moment when Henriette in her apartment recognizes the voice of Louise—turned into a beggar by La Frochard—singing in the street. In Griffith's film, this develops as a major sequence. As Henriette converses with the countess (who will turn out to be Louise's mother, of course), Louise appears in a long view, at the very end of the street, groping her way forward, forcing herself to sing under La Frochard's command. Henriette's face meanwhile begins to register recognition, almost as if preconsciously. Then Henriette begins to tremble, her whole person seized with the drama of discovery. The scene unfolds in the mode of panic action, as Henriette leans from the window, with gestures of yearning, hope, desperate seeking. The spectator has the impression that she may precipitate herself bodily into the street, while in the street the blind Louise casts about for the source of the voice calling to her.

It is a moment where the bodies behave nearly hysterically, if by hysteria we understand a condition of bodily writing, a condition in which the repressed affect is represented on the body. Indeed, Griffith's cinema is always on the verge of hysteria, and necessarily so, since hysteria gives us the maximal conversion of psychic affect into somatic meaning—meaning enacted on the body itself. The psychic overload, the hyperbole of the moment, is then confirmed by the arrival of the soldiers to arrest Henriette and throw her into prison, by means of the *lettre de cachet* obtained by the father of her noble suitor, the chevalier de Vaudrey. This serves of course only to increase and justify an aesthetics of hysteria, since there can be no discharge of the overwhelming affect, as Henriette and Louise are again separated—and also the recognition that is on the verge of taking place between the countess and Louise is again delayed.

I have argued that there is a convergence in the concerns of melodrama and of psychoanalysis—and indeed, that psychoanalysis is a kind of modern melodrama, conceiving psychic conflict in melodramatic terms and acting out the recognition of the repressed, often with and on the body. Now I have become convinced that the hystericized body offers a key emblem of that convergence, since it is a body preeminently invested with meaning—a body become the place for the inscription of highly emotional messages that cannot be written elsewhere, and cannot be articulated verbally. Hysteria offers a problem in representation: Freud's task, from the *Studies on Hysteria* onwards, is learning to read the messages inscribed on the hysterical body—a reading that is inaugural of psychoanalysis as a discipline. Griffith appears to understand that whoever is denied the capacity to talk will convert affect into somatic form, and speak by way of the expressionist body.

The hysterical body is of course typically, from Hippocrates through Freud, a woman's body, and indeed a victimized woman's body, on which desire has inscribed an impossible history, a story of desire at an impasse. Such an impasse will be typical of Hollywood domestic melodrama. It is pertinent as well to Griffith's bodily enactments of moments of emotional crisis, and in general to the moments in which melodrama distorts the body to its most expressionistic ends. A notable example in *Orphans of the Storm* comes when Henriette is in the tumbrel, on the way to the guillotine, and makes her last farewell to Louise, who is in the street—a sequence formally intertitled, as a kind of set piece, "The Farewell." As she leans from the tumbrel for a last embrace from Louise, and their lips meet and are held long together, Henriette's body appears to be in an almost impossible position, tilted from the cart, rigid, already nearly inanimate, like a mummy or a puppet, a bleached image, *pallida morte futura*. It is a pure image of victimization, and of the body wholly seized by affective meaning, of message converted onto the body so forcefully and totally that the body has ceased to function in its normal postures and gestures, to become nothing but text, nothing but the place of representation.

Yet if melodrama foregrounds in this manner the body as meaningful mute text, it also, in other ways, reaches toward the vocalization epitomized in the operatic aria. The soliloquy of the villain and the soliloquy of the innocent persecuted victim—classically, a young woman—became set pieces in melodrama. The content of many of these soliloquies is trivial; they exist to set an expressive tone. Villain and victim give voice to their natures, their states of being. They announce the tonal registers they bring to the play. When one considers how these soliloquies were underlined by the orchestral score, one can say that all that is lacking for them to become operatic arias is melody. And when we reach romantic drama written in verse—which so often reads as an ennobled melodrama, melodrama with class—the soliloquies often seem to be on the verge of taking off into song. Victor Hugo's soliloquies are the best example here: his extraordinarily supple and lyrical versification reaches toward song—seems ever about to become aria. It is easy to see why Hugo's dramas were so easily adaptable to operatic libretti. And of course the authors of standard melodramas also provided a number of plays that, though written in prose, proved easy to turn into operas.

I seem to be suggesting, then, that opera in the nineteenth century develops, realizes, two apparently contradictory tendencies of melodrama: on the one hand, the extreme embodiment of meaning, meaning represented bodily, and on the other hand, meaning become lyrical self-expression, aria, song that conveys a state of being. Here in fact we may encounter one of the apparent paradoxes of opera: the extremity, the hyperbole, with which it embodies voice. Not that voice is of course really separable from body in any live performance. But in a recital of lieder, for instance, body is effaced; it is voice we attend to. Whereas what you get in opera is a body thrust upon your attention—a costumed body, staged and lighted, representing a certain person in a certain dramatic situation. Here in fact is the glory, and also the embarrassment, of opera: the claim that visual embodiment and voice coincide in the singer. Those who dislike opera do so precisely because they prefer singing voices to be disembodied, pure voice; they cannot accept a convention that, as we all know, can lead to a knob-kneed, fifty-year-old tenor condemned to wobble around the stage in Egyptian fighting gear, or a voluminous soprano made to represent a teenage virgin. The demands made on voice and body for dramatic representation are not the same, and the claim for their coincidence will very often demand a large dose of faith on the part of spectator/listener, a willingness to accept an as-if that would seem to be excluded from a genre that traditionally seeks, in its stage settings and effects, such a large measure of illusionism.

Lovers of opera do of course accept that as-if. They do not close their eyes as the overage and overweight Radames launches into his adoration of Aida. On the contrary, they revel in the weird excess of the situation. They revel in a form that combines illusionism with clear impossibility, the height of artifice with the most natural of instruments, the human voice.

Opera is the impossible genre, where we are estranged into a heightened element in which emotions make claim to expression in some version of the romantics' understanding of the original language which—according to Rousseau, Herder, and others—was song and gesture.

If it seems evident that opera, like melodrama, hystericizes the body—distorting it and arresting it in postures and gestures that speak symbolically of powerful affects—what about voice? Does it make any sense to speak of the hystericization of voice? After all, the hysterical body that presides at the invention of psychoanalysis is typically speechless, since repression has denied it the possibility of speaking its desire directly. It is a pantomimic body. Typical hysterical symptoms include aphonia, nervous coughing, and concurrent problems with parts of the body—temporary paralysis of a limb, for instance, or facial neuralgia. That which is denied to consciousness and thus to speech writes itself in symbolic form on parts of the body. As Freud comments in a well-known moment of the *Dora* analysis: "He that has eyes to see and ears to hear may convince himself that no mortal can keep a secret. If his lips are silent, he chatters with his fingertips; betrayal oozes out of him at every pore."[3] The analyst must of course supplement his observation of the body and its symptomatic acts with listening to the analysand's speech. It is a premise of the "talking cure" that the analysand will eventually, by way of distortions, displacements, condensations, recounted dreams, denegations, parapraxes, and the rest, speak of the desire that cannot directly say its name.

The operatic aria, like the melodramatic monologue, speaks the name of desire directly. It may be the most unrepressed speech of desire that art allows. And yet, it can have something of the weirdness of hysteria as well. The hystericization of voice in opera, especially in the aria, derives, I think, from the extremity I have alluded to. I mean both the extremity of the situation in which the character finds himself—more pertinently, usually, herself—and also that extremity that comes from the paradoxical conjunction of artifice and naturalism in the genre itself. The extremity of the character's situation is obvious enough: operatic libretti exist to move characters from one moment of excruciating crisis to another with a minimum of necessary development in between, and the moment of crisis is the place for musical illustration, where a few words can be unpacked into a major piece of song. The extremity of the genre, I've tried to suggest, is inherent in the very risk of a sung drama, that impossible heightening of life where it takes on the form of dreams (and don't we all from time to time dream of our lives as transmuted into opera?), in a world where one can sing, over and over again, with all the possible embellishments, "I love you" or "He betrayed me."

Opera achieves what one might call the spectacularization of both body and voice. Traditional operatic production—as at the Metropolitan Opera—

invests heavily in spectacular scenery and costume, in a way I often find over-burdened and unimaginative but which is certainly faithful to the ideal of spectacle that characterized nineteenth-century melodrama and opera, as opposed to Renaissance and neoclassical theater—be it Shakespeare or Racine—that gave clear precedence to the word. And of course the Met invests still more heavily in the spectacular voice, the dramatic and coloratura soprano diva most evidently. Like the hystericized body, the effective operatic voice is capable of acting out emotion. I use this psychoanalytic term to suggest a certain quality of representation that gives the impression not merely of imitating affect but of reproducing it before our eyes. We know we are in the realm of the highest artifice, witnessing the most professional, highly trained imitation of passion imaginable. Yet we are, while the song lasts, inhabited by that passion in a manner that few other art forms can realize. Freud opposes "acting out" to remembering as recollection: acting out is remembering in the form of repetition, reproduction that abolishes the distance between mental ideation and physical action. Such, I think, may be the effect of the great operatic moment.

An example may be useful here. A multitude could make the point: "mad scenes," of course, but many other moments of realization of extreme passion as well. Let me consider briefly the famous aria of the mezzo-soprano, the Principessa Eboli, in Verdi's *Don Carlo*: "O don fatale." Eboli through her jealousy is condemned to a villainous role. She is a victim in an impasse that produces treacherous actions—though she also proves capable of the nobility of redemption through self-sacrifice. She is thus a character who will display a full range of extreme situation and emotion. Her great aria comes when she has just confessed to the queen, Elisabeth, a double betrayal: her denunciation to king Philip of the love between Don Carlo and the queen—his step-mother—and her own liaison with the king. As a result, she has been given the choice between exile and the convent. Betrayal, then, lost honor, and the end of her life at court with her beloved queen converge in this excruciating moment, this impasse where all her desires reach dead end.

In Schiller's *Don Carlos,* the source of the opera, Eboli's realization that she will never again see the queen is followed by a mute tableau: Eboli falls on her knees, "mute and motionless," before the door of the queen's bed-chamber. Then "she rises suddenly and rushes away with her face covered." With a sure sense of transposition, the librettists, Joseph Méry and Camille du Locle—two professionals of melodramatic scripts—in the place of the mute scene wrote the material of the aria.

"Ah! più non vedrò, ah più mai non vedrò la Regina!" (Ah! I will never again see the queen!) Eboli begins, in a great outburst of regret and passion. Then she launches into her curse of her own beauty, fatal and cruel gift from an angry heaven. It is almost a shriek: "Ti maledico, o mia beltà"

(I curse you, oh my beauty) (see example 1, at the end of this chapter; I cite the Italian here, as the most frequently sung version of the opera, though the first version was in French). Eboli's voice then moves into the gravity of self-accusation, a sombre judgment of her accursed and irreparable situation, punctuated by the refrain cursing her beauty. All hope is gone, only suffering remains:

> Speme non ho, soffrir dovrò!
> Il mio delitto è orribil tanto
> Che cancellar mai nol potrò!
> Ti maledico, ti maledico, o mia beltà!

[I have no hope, I must suffer! / My crime is so horrible / That I will never be able to expiate it / I curse you, I curse you, oh my beauty!]

More quietly now, she reviews her betrayal of her queen. Only the cloister, she concludes, shall hide forever her unassuageable grief—the weight of that gravely underlined *dolor:*

> Solo in un chiostro al mondo ormai
> Dovrò celar il mio dolor!

[I must retire to to a cloister / To conceal my suffering from the world forever.]

(In the French version, it is the *pour toujours* that the music underlines—the eternity of the punishment awaiting her.) Then this tortured consciousness is traversed by the recollection of Carlo's situation: his execution by the king impends, no doubt tomorrow. Tomorrow? A day remains. A hope revives her: to save Carlo in the time remaining. Her whole being suddenly turns to the project of salvation—Carlo's, her own. The action of hope—*la speme m'arride*—works, in the manner of grace, an instantaneous conversion. And the aria reaches its desperate, triumphant, and fully hysterical conclusion:

> Ah! un dì mi resta, la speme m'arride!
> Sia benedetto il ciel! Lo salverò!

[Ah! a single day remains to me, hope revives me! / Blessed be heaven! I shall save him!]

As so often in both melodrama and opera, in the situation of extremity and anguish we encounter the deadline: the ticking clock that will mean the difference between despair and salvation. (The French text here in fact says "*Béni ce jour*"—Eboli blesses the hours remaining to work her act.) Eboli rushes from the stage with this cry of hope and redemption, of a hopeless life redeemed by a final act of self-sacrifice. She will make good on the cry at the end of Act IV, when she indeed saves Carlo.

In the course of the aria we run through a register of emotions from de-spair to hope, from self-condemnation to the chance of redemption, from base egotistical passion to self-sacrifice. The aria gives the best imitation of hysterical conversion, of acting-out, that I know. It spectacularly voices the symptoms of Eboli's condition and situation. It creates extremity. From that original tumultuous outburst of "Ah! più non vedrò, ah più mai non vedrò la Regina!" we move to the emphatic, ringing indictment of her beauty, then through the dolorous assessment of her fate—"Solo in un chiostro . . . dovrò celar il mio dolor!" to the sudden realization of the fate of the man she has betrayed along with herself, and the nearly instanta-neous conversion of self-pity into the resolution of self-sacrifice in order to save Carlo, and the mingled madness and hope, despair and redemption of the exit line, "Lo salverò!" and the brassy finale.

Here the hystericized voice does something that the hystericized body cannot do—something that the mute text of pantomime or silent cinema, or Schiller's mute tableau, cannot perform. That is, it doubles the hysteri-cal symptoms with their cure. The aria offers us at once the symptoms of the hysterical impasse and the working-through of the impasse. Voice un-leashes passion, and thereby brings—for the spectator as well as for Eboli—the solution, in the lyrical assumption of self and situation. That is, the voic-ing of the situation of curse and extreme desolation clarifies, not merely Eboli's emotional destitution and agony but as well the one act remaining for her to perform, an act that in its very extremity of heroism both incor-porates and redeems her hysteria. In the voicing of the impasse and the lyri-cal working-through of its resolution, in the musical assumption of self and situation, we have a version of hysteria and cure peculiar to opera, peculiar to the power of song.

Roland Barthes, discussing the aria that puts Sarrasine into ecstasy in Balzac's tale, uses the recondite word *cénesthétique*—coenaesthetic—to describe the effect of song: the coenesthetic concerns a person's percep-tion of internal, bodily physical sensations. Barthes writes:

> Song (this characteristic has been ignored in most aesthetics) has something coenaesthetic about it, it is linked less to an "impression" than to an internal sensualism, one that is muscular and humoral. Voice is diffusion, insinuation, it passes through the whole extent of the body, the skin; insofar as it is pas-sage, abolition of limits, of classifications, of names . . . it possesses a particu-lar power of hallucination.[4]

Barthes's "internal sensualism" is, I think, a sensation of both the listener and the singer, one that indeed links singer and listener in the illusion of a shared bodily experience. "Internal sensualism" suggests the peculiar power of song to undo the hysterical impasse. It also suggests why the ro-mantics in their aesthetic speculations placed music first in the hierachy of the arts. As Schopenhauer put it, in music the will overcomes its strivings to reach a state of will-lessness. All passion spent.

We might want here to open a reflection on those scenes from romantic literature in which listening to opera brings for the listeners an emotional clarification of their situation, a recognition of passion: as when, in Stendhal's *La Chartreuse de Parme,* Fabrice del Dongo and Clelia Conti, separated but in love, shed tears to Cimarosa's *Il matrimonio segreto.* But that would require another essay.

To conclude this one: it is as if the hystericized voice of the operatic aria—where voice has become, in the manner of the melodramatic body, symptomatic of an extreme situation, an emotional impasse—expresses and resolves passion, works it through in an internal dialogue of passion and measure, that of song. Can we really speak of an hystericized voice in opera? Yes, but only if we note that hysteria has here been given form, has theorized itself, so to speak. Both Dora and Freud are present in "O don fatale," both symptom and talking cure.

EXAMPLE 1
"O don fatale," from *Don Carlo*

EXAMPLE 1
(*Continued*)

EXAMPLE 1
(*Continued*)

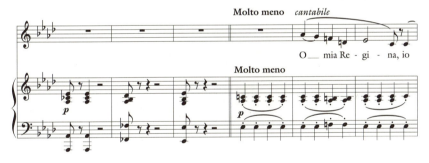

EXAMPLE 1
(*Continued*)

cor. So - lo in un chio - stro al mon-do o - ma - i do - vrò ce-

-lar il mio do - lor! Ohi - mè! Ohi - mè! O

mia Re - gi - na, so - lo in un chio - stro al mon-do o-

-ma - i do - vrò ce - lar il mi - o do - lo - re!

EXAMPLE 1
(*Continued*)

EXAMPLE 1
(*Continued*)

EXAMPLE 1
(Continued)

ciel!_____ Lo__ sal - ve - rò! Un dì_____ mi

res - ta, un dì_____ mi res - ta, ah si -

- a be - ne - det - to il ciel!_____

Lo_____ sal - ve - rò!...

EXAMPLE 1
(*Continued*)

VERDI'S RECURRING THEMES REVISITED

MARY ANN SMART

VERDI'S 1871 OPERA *AIDA* has always been known for its pomp. The elephants traditionally called for in the Act II triumphal procession have become a symbol for all of opera's most gaudy and expensive excesses, and in *Aida* the elephants are just the beginning, a convenient metonymy for the harem dancers, pagan priestesses, and the other spectacular scenic effects that mark *Aida* as a product of Verdi's midcareer infatuation with the overblown visual scope of Parisian grand opera. In recent years, however, *Aida* has achieved a different kind of notoriety, thanks to Edward Said's critique of the opera's orientalist agenda. Said's analysis focuses mainly on the historical circumstances of the opera's commission for the inauguration of the Opera House in Cairo, and on Verdi's efforts to lend *Aida*'s ancient Egyptian plot and setting an air of authenticity by drawing on up-to-the-minute archaeological research for both music and stage settings.[1] Said argues that, unlike Verdi's earlier operas on historical and political subjects, *Aida* inhibits audience identification and inspires only a feeling of neutrality in spectators.[2] He attributes the opera's expressive failure partly to Verdi's growing insistence on control over all aspects of operatic production, both musical and scenic, which he sees as duplicating and reinforcing the authoritarian practices of colonial rule reflected in the opera's picturesque presentation of ancient Egypt for a European audience.[3] The result, for Said, is a fundamentally unlikeable work of art.

Even leaving aside this last severe value judgment, there is much to quibble with in this analysis, beginning with the naive trust Said places in Verdi's calculated statements about his own compositional aims and his assertion that the opera's première was met with nothing more than cool disinterest.[4] However, I would like to focus here on one detail of Said's critique that I believe resonates with other, more technical criticisms of the opera.[5] His complaints about the opera's "airlessness and immobility" and its "wall-like structure," which he connects to its genesis as a colonialist project, may be inspired by some of the same musical features that have caused musicologists to keep a cool distance.[6] On the most obvious level, this suspicion probably springs from *Aida*'s unembarrassed embrace of extravagant staging and visual display: musicologists trained on the metaphysics of German symphonic music tend to be uncomfortable with those endless ballets and triumphal marches. But scholarly unease with *Aida*'s musical language also runs deeper, provoked by Verdi's reliance on old-fashioned and rather mechanical compositional techniques such as strict counterpoint, and especially by his use of an ambitious system of "identifying themes" associated with the principal characters. Verdi had used such an extensive grid of referential motives (or musical "calling cards") only once before, in his 1844 setting of Byron's *The Two Foscari,* and in both cases the technique has met with almost universal disapproval, with critics more or less evenly divided between resistance to the overliteralness of tying a musical theme so closely to a single verbal (or dramatic) idea and unfavorable comparisons with Richard Wagner's much more elaborate leitmotivic technique.[7] One of the ideas I shall explore in this article is the possibility that that these two sources of dissatisfaction with *Aida* may be intertwined: that the identifying themes are intimately tied to the physical movement of the characters they represent, and thus grow out of the opera's extreme emphasis on staging and the importance it places on the display of bodies—in dances and processions, but also in more ordinary circumstances such as entrances, exits, and scenic tableaux.

1

My starting point will be Aida's first appearance in the opera, where her identifying theme is placed at the center of an unusually tight web of semantic meaning, with the characters' sung words, the stage movement, and the orchestral motive all coinciding to identify this melody unequivocally as attached to Aida.[8] As Aida enters, into the middle of an agitated conversation between Radames and Amneris, a solo clarinet plays the short-breathed chromatic melody that will come to be associated with her (see example 1). We see her approach slowly from the rear of the stage, and her entrance is announced by a proliferation of verbal signals: Radames murmurs "Dessa!" and Amneris remarks on the direction of his gaze, then states the name "Aida."

To ears accustomed to Wagnerian leitmotifs, there is something almost embarrassing about such gestures. The various layers of meaning seem to interlock too neatly, blatantly labeling the clarinet motive as Aida's and flattening out the three layers of words, music, and stage action into a single, unequivocally physical message: "look at Aida." In other words, rather than supplying a quasi-linguistic commentary on the action or hinting at subtextual meanings (activities Wagner's motives have trained us to expect), the orchestral theme underlines an action already visible (and commented on verbally): as Joseph Kerman put it more than thirty years ago, Verdi's

EXAMPLE 1
Aida, Introduzione

identifying motives often function as "sonorous ... extension[s] of the characters' physical and psychological selves."[9] Kerman found Verdi's treatment of recurring themes too literal, especially in the early operas, and he dismissed their use in *Aida* as "stiff and uninteresting," a judgment consistent with an operatic aesthetic that values psychological development above all else.

As the title of his most famous book suggests, Kerman tended to measure opera according to the standards of spoken drama—"*Opera as Drama*"—and specifically against those of drama in the realist tradition.[10] But while much German opera, from Mozart to Richard Strauss, may reward such comparisons, nineteenth-century *Italian* opera relies on stylized and emphatic modes of expression that recall earlier and more popular genres of spoken theater: indeed, the closest theatrical parallel to Italian opera's penchant for shouting out its gestures might be what Peter Brooks has called the tendency toward "overstatement" in French melodrama.[11] Even more than opera, melodrama spells out its meanings, sometimes on several levels at once, leaving little to be decoded by the spectator: characters forthrightly name their emotions and state their allegiances; plot twists are marked with eminently legible gestures or facial expressions, and even symbolized by bodily signs such as scars or birthmarks.

In example 1 above, such "overstatement" could be said to operate on two levels. First and most transparently, Aida's theme here—as in later occurrences—tends to be treated as synonymous with her physical presence: it is never heard except when she is on stage, its main function is to accompany her entrances, and it is absent from as important an evocation of the heroine as Radames's soliloquy, "Celeste Aida." Of course, most of Verdi's recurring themes work this way; but the Aida motive is unusual in also capturing the heroine's physical presence through a form of mimesis: its at once languishing and timid phrases and constricted intervallic reach almost seem to choreograph her cautious advance onto the stage.[12] At this early stage of the opera, the motive seems entirely concrete, repelling symbolic meanings but iconically matching Aida's body, her movement as she walks on stage, and perhaps even the gaze of others, both on stage and in the audience, turning to watch her as she does so.[13] This is not to suggest a one-dimensional interpretation of the motive as *restricted* to its association with Aida's physical presence; as we shall see, when it recurs later the Aida theme accrues symbolic meaning—associated most consistently with Aida's love for the enemy warrior, Radames—while also continuing to function as a sort of melodic stage direction, outlining Aida's gestures, pace, and posture.[14]

This image of the orchestra guiding our gaze toward Aida each time she enters raises troubling questions of voyeurism and the representation of female characters on the operatic stage, evoking both cinematic theories of the male gaze and Carolyn Abbate's imaginative attempts to hear certain orchestral utterances as emanating from the characters themselves, rather than from a controlling male authorial perspective.[15] According to the first approach, the orchestra might be seen as an analogue for the gaze or the camera lens, its imitation of Aida's movement drawing attention to her body, forming an objectifying trap from which she can escape only by countering the orchestra's unchanging portrayal with a forceful singing voice.[16] Abbate's approach is better attuned to inherently musical means of expression, but she similarly sees the orchestra as capable of entrapping a heroine, and by extension of limiting music's meanings. Or, to be more precise, it is our conventional, ingrained strategies for deciphering orchestral accompaniment that Abbate criticizes: she argues that to read orchestral music in opera either as leitmotivic commentary or as a chain of mimetic gestures is to tie music too closely to plot, and thus potentially to draw all opera's various points of view into the service of a single, word-dominated composer's voice.[17]

Abbate's resistance to the entrenched operatic habit of hearing the deepest truths about plot and character in the secret language spoken by the orchestra opens up empowering possibilities for gender critique of opera. But Aida's slinky and utterly embodied orchestral motive is hardly the kind of escape from orchestral control she has in mind. Abbate's own analyses tend to focus on exactly the opposite kind of orchestral utterance: reminiscences of leitmotives that confound neat symbolic labeling and so sound disembodied and oracular, or instrumental voices that conceal their sources and seem to emanate from a magical space behind the stage.[18] On the contrary, the Aida motive's close ties to movement and visible stage action might qualify for what Abbate considers to be the *least* interesting form of musical representation: "miming" music, or music that shadows plot and text so closely that no dissenting voices can squeeze through.[19] Indeed, an Abbatean approach would probably prefer the other recurring musical idea associated with the heroine, the twice-heard prayer "Numi, pietà," which, with its sustained pianissimo high notes and sense of suspended animation, presents just the sort of disembodied and mysterious vocal outpouring in which Abbate tends to locate feminine power.

One of my purposes in what follows is to suggest an alternative way of listening to Verdi's physically embodied (or "miming") motives, building on Abbate's visionary approaches while also seeking theories that might be better suited to the highly manifest gestures that are the basis of the Italian repertoire. My exploration of Verdi's cheerfully overt motives, and of some ulterior meanings we might attach to them, will proceed in three large sections. I begin with a turn to early Verdi for a brief consideration of what we can learn from the identifying themes in *I due Foscari,* where contrast between the physical movement suggested by the orchestral motives and the portraits painted by the characters' vocal music is at a maximum. The central section of the article dives into technical detail, to trace the "career" of Aida's identifying theme, both through the symbolic meanings that collect around it and through some of its more submerged transformations. To conclude I will take up Aida's other recurring theme, the sung prayer "Numi, pietà," as a starting point for considering what we know of Verdi's intentions for the staging of *Aida* and what these instructions can tell us about his representation of Aida's body and her melody.

2

I due Foscari is generally considered to be one of the young Verdi's ambitious failures, but its motivic excesses can serve as an enlightening background against which to understand *Aida*'s more subtle practice. The plot is remarkably simple for early Verdi, focusing on just three principal characters—or four, if the sinister collective of the Venetian Council of Ten can be counted as a character. Jacopo Foscari has been exiled from Venice for treason, but drawn by an irresistible love for his native city, he has returned and been thrown into prison. Most of the opera is concerned with the unsuccessful efforts of his wife, Lucrezia, to have him freed, and with the bitter meditations of Jacopo's father, the aging doge of Venice, on the burdens of power and age. Even more than in most early Verdi operas, each character is defined by his or her obsessive hold on a single idea—for Lucrezia the determination to free her husband and protect her son; for Jacopo a nostalgic love for Venice; and for Francesco disillusionment with power and corruption.

Verdi assigns one identifying theme to each principal character, with one more for the chorus. Except for the chorus motive, these themes are played only by the orchestra—never sung by their "owners"—and are heard, like the first occurrences of the Aida motive, only when the characters they identify walk on stage; mercifully, they do not accompany every entrance. This strict association with entrances also has implications for the motives' placement, dictating that they appear almost exclusively in the opening recitative sections of arias and are segregated from the surrounding discourse, never impinging on the lyrical sections of the arias and duets.

A strange result of this separation is that each character is effectively introduced twice, first orchestrally, then vocally; and for both principal soprano and tenor, these two registers contradict each other sharply. Although both characters are introduced *vocally* in styles entirely typical of their gender and character type, the purely orchestral identifying themes are free to convey less stereotypical messages.[20] The prima donna soprano, Lucrezia, is first seen rushing on stage inflamed with rage, accompanied by what is by far the most active of the opera's recurring themes; but the force of character suggested by that motive is immediately undermined by the delicate vocal style of the aria that follows and is never really recaptured in Lucrezia's music later in the opera (see examples 2a and 2b). As if in a mirror-image of his wife, Jacopo's identifying theme (featuring solo clarinet) droops and sighs, mimicking both the torture victim's halting steps and his lackluster emotional state and contrasting sharply with the athletic tenor revealed once he begins his aria (examples 3a and 3b). It seems clear not only that both Lucrezia's and Jacopo's motives are based on an emphatic sense of physical presence and movement, but also that this is hardly one of those cases where voice can be equated with female power, while (as Abbate's theory might have it) to be "spoken for" by the orchestra is an automatic sign of passivity.

The *Foscari* motives are usually dismissed as a failed experiment, both because of their disjunction with the vocal expression and because they do not develop over the course of the opera. A standard historical explanation would see the motives' lack of expressive integration as the result of a collision between Verdi's "forward-looking" concept of using identifying motives in the first place and the entrenched operatic convention of the double aria, which enforces a rigid form of self-identification for each principal

EXAMPLE 2a
I due Foscari, Coro, Scena ed Aria (Lucrezia)

EXAMPLE 2b
I due Foscari, Coro, Scena ed Aria (Lucrezia)

Tu al cui sguar - do on-ni - pos - sen - te, tut - to es-ul - ta, o tut - to

ge - me; tu che so - lo sei mia

spe - me, tu con-for - ta il mi - o, il mi - o do -

-lor.

EXAMPLE 3a
I due Foscari, Scena ed Aria (Jacopo)

character, based on a stylized alternation of lyrical song and fiery vocal dis-play.[21] But there may be an equally important antecedent in the practice of melodramatic "overstatement" I referred to a moment ago, as an extreme example of Verdi's melodrama-influenced tendency toward "shouted" ges-tures. For not only do the identifying motives duplicate each character's style of movement (tempestuous for the soprano, languorous for the tenor), they are also semantically charged in the manner of those birth-marks and heavenward gestures in the French plays, capturing the dramatic *idées fixes* that dominate each character. In this sense, the *Foscari* motives'

EXAMPLE 3b
I due Foscari, Scena ed Aria (Jacopo)

much-criticized failure to develop over the course of the opera becomes an expressive strength, their tendency to return literally and to insist on a single idea each time they appear providing what we might think of as semiotic points of orientation in the drama.

But the *Foscari* motives seem yet richer, their significance deeper than a mere analogy with a literary genre now fallen out of favor can suggest, because they also exploit an effect not available to their counterparts in spoken theater. The clash between the identifying motive and vocal style implies a splitting-off of voice from body, or perhaps a *displacement* of the character's "true" voice onto the mimetic orchestral motive. Even more decisively than Aida's clarinet theme, the contrast between Lucrezia's motive and her aria throws the meanings carried by voice and body, voice and orchestra, into question. In other words, the orchestral motive that "mimes" Lucrezia's entrances and draws attention to her body is also marked as the site of her power, suggesting that doublings of stage action and music can just as easily signify an *excess* of power or voice as they can a silencing or restriction of meaning.

My conclusion, then, is primarily a theoretical one, concerned with an interpretive lesson we can learn from *I due Foscari* about the relationship between women's voices and their bodies, and about the access identifying themes can provide to a character's physical presence, a register perhaps less available to vocal music, shaped as it is by stylistic convention and the technical dictates of a particular singer's voice. The very fact that Lucrezia Foscari's body—as captured by her frenetic identifying motive—can become such a site of power within the opera's motivic system suggests a third role for the orchestra in opera, neither as quasi-authorial source of hidden meanings, nor as surrogate for the camera lens. And although nothing in Verdi's later experiment with orchestral identifying themes poses quite such an acute disjunction between voice and orchestra, voice and body, Lucrezia's example can perhaps point to a new way of hearing the recurring themes in *Aida,* and specifically of interpreting Aida's shadowing by the orchestra.

3

One immediately striking difference between *Aida* and *I due Foscari* lies in the character of the motives associated with their heroines: even though both carry a strong sense of bodily motion, it is difficult to hear the gentle Aida motive, with its short-breathed and tentative chromatic gestures, as communicating power. Indeed, Aida's motive closely resembles the sinuous and gently seductive melodies associated with oriental and dark-skinned women throughout the late-nineteenth-century operatic repertory, a melodic stereotype rarely imbued with any kind of power except the ability to attract and delight the gaze.[22] And perhaps equally important is the contrast in the *placement* of the identifying themes in the two operas, their relationship to the overall formal structure. As we have seen in *I due Foscari,* the separation of the identifying motives—confined to the recitative sections—from each character's primary vocal expression in the arias is crucial to their sense of a physical energy severed from (and contradictory to) the conventional gestures of vocal expression. It is what happens *between* the motives that we would probably call the "real" music of the opera: arias and duets with a formal logic (and a pure vocal force) far more compelling than that of the motives themselves. The identifying motives seem to supply a separate level of discourse, an alternative reality that is episodic, physical, and semantically charged.

As we might expect of an opera written almost thirty years later, when Verdi had begun to smooth out the entrenched formal divisions of number opera, the heroine's identifying motive in *Aida* is far more integrated with the "real," vocal music of the set pieces; it is progressively absorbed into Aida's vocal utterance after its first orchestral manifestation in the opening scene. Equally important, the theme is both formally and motivically embedded in the still fairly conventional sequence of arias and duets that structures the opera, often appearing as a bridge between two more stable sections of a form or providing motivic raw material for the music that surrounds it.[23] The most extreme example of this kind of motivic working comes in the opera's prelude, which engages in elaborate contrapuntal play with the Aida motive. Such abstract compositional manipulations, of course, weaken the motive's association with Aida as a physical presence, freeing it instead to accrue other, less strictly mimetic meanings later in the opera. But the initial sense of embodiment and gestural mimesis attached to the motive never completely falls away, but instead colors and inflects (even perhaps at times undermines?) the symbolic weight the motive gathers along the way.

As we have seen, in its first appearance after the curtain rises, Aida's identifying theme is purely orchestral and almost purely physical, drawing attention to her entrance without hinting at deeper levels of signification (example 1). The motive's next occurrence, in the middle of Aida's Act I soliloquy, "Ritorna vincitor!," seems to leap to the opposite extreme of signification, finally to be invested with the symbolic meaning we tend to expect from recurring themes. In the midst of the aria's schizophrenic fantasy of military victory, Aida has surged up to a high B♭, as she envisions an Ethiopian triumph in the coming battle. Suddenly realizing that such a victory would mean death for Radames, she stops short and asks herself "Che dissi?" (what have I said?) as the solo clarinet recalls her theme, transposed down a tone and played "more slowly than the first time" (see example 4). She joins the clarinet on the crucial words "e l'amor mio" (and my love), suggesting a symbolic reading of the motive as no longer representing Aida's body in motion, but now specifically relating to her love for Radames. This may be the opera's most "Wagnerian" moment, in the sense that Aida seems to lose physical force as her motive gains semantic specificity: music becomes more closely tied to plot and the composer's controlling voice asserts itself, where once the same music seemed to spring unmediated from Aida's body.

Aida's motive is next heard in her Act II duet with Amneris, where the

EXAMPLE 4
Aida, Scena (Aida)

melody undergoes a series of elaborate motivic manipulations that seem to merge the contrasting mimetic and symbolic functions seen so far. As in the opening scene, the theme is first heard as a bridge between sections—here linking the chorus for Amneris and her slaves to the duet—and it is again placed in a tautological context, duplicating visual and verbal evidence provided as Aida walks slowly on stage and Amneris comments on her advance (example 5). But this time the motive clearly does more than just mimic or choreograph Aida's gestures: the parlante phrases for Amneris layered over the orchestra's performance of the motive begin in the redundant expository vein we saw at Aida's first entrance ("Aida verso noi s'avanza"), but quickly take on an interpretive slant, as Amneris reads a sadness in Aida's face that reawakens her suspicions of a love between Aida and Radames.

The motive gradually comes to dominate the opening section of the duet for the two women. It is heard next in a literal (but sped-up) incarnation, as Aida reflects on the simultaneous joy and torment of her secret love for Radames (example 6). The use of the aside hints at an emerging association between Aida's theme and disclosure or revelation. If in example 6 the only truth revealed is directed at the audience, the contorted version of the theme delivered in Amneris's ensuing statement (example 7) is clearly designed to win Aida's trust by projecting a veneer of sincerity. Amneris concludes her statement with a wholesale borrowing of Aida's closing phrase (see the last phrase of example 7), as she plays her manipulative trump card, hoping to provoke a reaction from her rival with the false announcement that Radames has been killed in battle.

In the duet's slow movement, Aida, having admitted her love for Radames, begs Amneris to treat her with mercy, and elements of her motive are freely recombined to form a longer-breathed melody with a stronger sense of harmonic direction (example 8). The transformation exploits both a sort of loose allusion, as in the transposition and inversion of the turn figures that begin both passages, and more literal references to the motive, such as the ascent through E-natural to F, followed by a stepwise descent, sketched by Aida at measure 9 and taken up more exactly by Amneris at her entrance.[24] By this point, then, the snaky, seductive motive primarily associated with Aida's body, now recast in more diatonic garb and given stronger harmonic grounding, has become a musical symbol of her love for Radames—and, more specifically perhaps, of her *disclosure* of that love. It would be too simple—and would perhaps place too much weight on some rather subtle motivic transformations—to interpret this progression as a sublimation of Aida's originally mimetic "body-motive" into a purely vocal utterance, but there is perhaps something of that effect in the way Aida's melody twists and turns here—as if the seductive music that originally stood for her body has taken up residence within her voice.

EXAMPLE 5
Aida, Coro, Scena e Duetto (Amneris, Aida)

EXAMPLE 6

Aida, Coro, Scena e Duetto (Amneris, Aida)

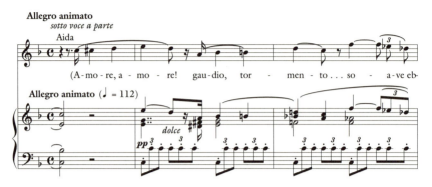

Clearly, each ensuing statement of the Aida motive in this duet moves further from the literal pitches and intervals of the motive as heard in its original form. As figure 1 illustrates, however, the various transformations of the theme all share a reliance on turn figures and chromatic winding in their first half (although the order of the chromatic pitches undergoes quite a bit of inversion and recombination); the second halves of each statement are more clearly related by a shared stepwise descent from the tonic to scale degree $\hat{5}$. And even though these last few variations are probably too subtle to be perceived without aid of the score and a sharp analytical eye/ear, I would suggest that they are just as significant as the motive's more obvious recurrences. Such hermetic motivic workings prompt us to pose the question of *why* Verdi would choose to construct an entire duet almost entirely from manipulations of this single motive, and why it should be this particular duet. Several possible answers spring immediately to mind: that this duet is above all concerned with rooting out and displaying the secret of Aida's love, a love previously associated with this motive; that Verdi is showing off, exhibiting the sophisticated compositional techniques that prompted Said to complain about the opera's "wall-like" structure; or that he "dignifies" Aida's identifying theme here by injecting it with symbolic associations and giving it vocal expression. And although it risks overreading, I cannot ignore the fact that Aida's motive here goes "underground," submerged but not erased by compositional expertise, at exactly the moment when Amneris wrings from her the crucial disclosure. The contradiction suggests that the motive appears here as a mere semblance of truth, pale and twisted compared to the vibrant "truth" of its original, physically grounded occurrences in Act I. This would make the whole duet a critique of the very sophisticated musical techniques it displays, demonizing them through their association with Amneris's deceptive strategies. It is a reading that would no doubt have outraged Verdi, but at the same time seems in tune with his overall aesthetic, his preference for manifest meanings over suggestion.

4

Aida's lyrical statement in this slow movement is not the final incarnation of her motive, nor the last word of her duet with her rival. Rather than concluding on this intimate plane, the Aida/Amneris duet is interrupted by a violent reminder of the opera's other plot, its parallel dimension of spectacle and display: chorus and band are heard offstage singing a reprise of the victory hymn ("Su! del Nilo") from the military pageant that closed the first scene of Act I, summoning warriors to the battlefield and crying for "death to foreigners." This intrusion from the "public" world precipitates

EXAMPLE 7
Aida, Coro, Scena e Duetto (Amneris, Aida)

EXAMPLE 8

Aida, Coro, Scena e Duetto (Amneris, Aida)

EXAMPLE 8
(*Continued*)

Amneris's exit, leaving Aida alone on stage to perform one last, radical transformation of her characteristic motive in her brief prayer, "Numi, pietà" (example 9). This, too, is a recurring theme, an almost note-for-note reminiscence of the ethereal peroration of Aida's first-act aria, "Ritorna vincitor!" "Numi, pietà" possesses everything the Aida motive lacks, completing the progression toward lyricism and away from bodily movement already begun in the duet: it is purely vocal in character, with the orchestra providing only a pale tremolo background; it recurs with the same text each time; its periodic phrases and diatonic language give it a songlike quality; and it is heard only when Aida is alone on stage. Even amid all this contrast, though, the skeleton of the Aida motive is audible, although with all sense of chromatic winding and of physicality now bleached away. Like the Aida motive, the prayer's first four bars prolong scale degree $\hat{5}$, but here the dominant is intoned, left, and returned to in wide, contemplative circles. And while the prayer's second half, beginning with the leap up to the high A♭, imitates the stepwise descent of the original motive's ending, the ambitus is now stretched across most of the soprano range, and the drive down to middle C over dominant harmony lends the phrase a sense of cadential direction and an emphasis on the tonic completely at odds with Aida's meandering theme (see figure 1, last system).

In a sense, then, the prayer borrows its contour from the Aida motive, but obliterates the earlier melody's characteristic features of chromatic equivocation and avoidance of closure on the tonic. Furthermore, the perfect stillness of the prayer seems diametrically opposed to the original motive's sense of movement, to its mimetic association with Aida's body and gesture. The periodic phrases, melodic repetitions, and prolonged pitches of "Numi, pietà" come closer to the mood of pure song than does anything in Aida's actual arias, positioning the prayer as a point of repose in the relentlessly unfolding action. In formal terms, this manifestation of the

a. from Example 5 ("Ritorna vincitor")

b. from Example 7 (Aida/Amneris duet)

c. from Example 8 (Aida/Amneris duet)

d. from Example 9 (Aida/Amneris duet)

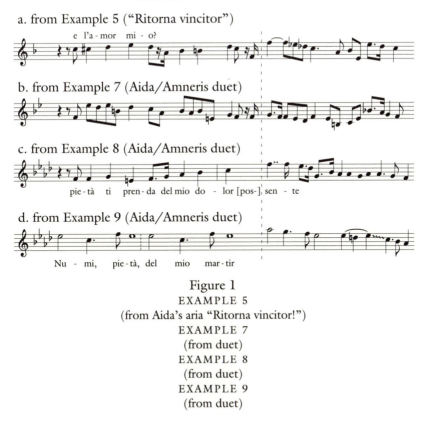

Figure 1
EXAMPLE 5
(from Aida's aria "Ritorna vincitor!")
EXAMPLE 7
(from duet)
EXAMPLE 8
(from duet)
EXAMPLE 9
(from duet)

motive can be seen as more than encroaching on the lyrically contemplative set piece: its stillness, shimmering accompaniment, and tone of summation reveal a family resemblance to the brief transcendent melodies, such as the "Bacio" music in *Otello* and Amelia's prayer-refrain in Act II of *Un ballo in maschera,* that Verdi had begun by this stage of his career to substitute for the now impossibly old-fashioned cabaletta.

Tempting as it is to hear this prayer as a moment of pure voice for Aida, retaining the outlines of "her" motive but freed of the semantic or mimetic associations that tied her down to plot and to physical objectification, in another sense "Numi, pietà" seems to have come full circle, to have been reinscribed as a sign in the sense of those overstated melodramatic gestures. In contrast with the conventional formal logic and carefully calibrated vocal arc of the duet's slow movement, this melody's sharp edges, its isolation and its sharp difference from its musical surroundings, seem to cry out for semantic interpretation, its meanings perhaps best read as pleading, extremity, despair . . . In fact, the stillness and self-containment of the prayer

EXAMPLE 9
Aida, Coro, Scena e Duetto (Amneris, Aida)

EXAMPLE 9
(*Continued*)

would seem to make it the perfect musical analogue for one of the most conventional gestures of French melodrama, the wordless appeal to heaven for support, were it not for the fact that the unusually explicit stage directions that accompany the melody both times it appears undermine any sense of such tidy correspondence between music and gesture.[25]

Until now, my invocations of Aida's "body" and "gestures" have been largely imaginary, based on the barest indications for entrances and exits contained in the score and libretto. But, as Said has noted, *Aida* is a product of the period when Verdi's fame and economic power were great enough to allow him control over every detail of a production. One consequence of this is the existence of a voluminous staging manual—the first for any of his Italian operas—prepared by Verdi's publishers for the opera's première. This formidable *disposizione scenica,* compiled by an editorial committee with input from Verdi, mainly concerns itself with choreography for the several ballets and triumphal processions. And while the *disposizione* is usually more reticent about the staging of more intimate scenes, it provides several clues to how the relationship among music, word, and gesture was conceived by the opera's creators.[26]

At the first appearance of "Numi, pietà," at the end of "Ritorna vincitor!," the *disposizione* provides a level of detailed choreography not specified for Aida anywhere else in the opera, instructing that:

> on the words, "*Pietà*," Aida staggers, anguished and afflicted, toward upstage left, so that on the last word, *soffrir,* she will be in the wings.[27]

The directions for the theme's second occurrence at the end of the Aida/Amneris duet are similar, and in this case are reinforced by even more specific instructions penned by Verdi himself. Still fiddling with the last section of the duet just before the opera's first performance in 1871, Verdi finally hit on the idea of bringing back "Numi, pietà" and wrote to the conductor, Giovanni Bottesini, explaining the change and musing that the return of the melody would work well "provided that when the motive . . . from the first act returns, [the soprano] sings it while walking falteringly towards the back of the stage."[28]

This is intriguing. It presents us with the idea of a recurring theme that, while decidedly not mimicking words or action in the manner of Lucrezia's identifying theme or Aida's first orchestral motive, nevertheless seems to *owe* its status as a recurring theme to its staging. The theme brings its gestures back with it, but more than that, Verdi suggests that it is the repeated gesture that will make the musical return worthwhile, will lend it impact. In direct contrast to the segregation between orchestral motive and vocal presentation in *I due Foscari,* the passage from Aida seems to represent an attempt to merge the two registers, making the vocal moment an occasion for looking as well as hearing. And perhaps more interesting, the scenic direction cuts across the stasis of the musical design, raising the possibility that, by the time of *Aida,* Verdi may have imagined a "syntax" of gesture, a language that was partly dependent upon musical structure, but also capable of creating tension and meaning by contradicting the syntax of the musical form.

What we confront with this strange creative impulse of Verdi's, and in a larger sense with the whole comparison of the gestural dimensions of *Foscari* and *Aida,* is, perhaps, nothing other than the arrival of "realism" on the operatic stage. What I mean by this is, of course, nothing like a truly naturalistic acting style, but rather a still very stylized stage technique that nevertheless rejected the blatant overstatements of melodrama. In terms of Verdi's compositional evolution this may be something of a commonplace, but the consequences of a realist aesthetic for staging and gender representation are provocative and unexplored. It seems clear that the intention behind the detailed stage directions for "Numi, pietà"—the faltering and the staggering, the last note sung when the singer had already disappeared from view—was to depict the weakness of the body, the physical disintegration that comes with the emotional extremity of Aida's position.

But without undermining this surface expression, the staging of the prayer also raises some more subversive, and more energetic, meanings. Something about Aida's plea to the heavens—the sublimation of the Aida motive, its position as a transcendent cabaletta substitute, and the "staggering" specified in the *disposizione*—recalls descriptions of turn-of-the-century actress Eleonora Duse, sublating her body through a highly personal stock of hysterical gestures that circumvented the expected correspondence between word and staging.[29] Feminist theater critic Elin Diamond has written of Duse and other actresses as using their manic gestural language to free their characters from the flattening effect of mimesis, an effect that is perhaps inherent in the very apparatus of theatrical representation, but that has a particularly overwhelming force in realist theater.[30] And although Diamond locates this disruption of realism through gestural excess in the style of particular actresses, the performance directions in the *Aida* staging manual perhaps have a similar effect. The strange—and strangely deliberate—contradiction between static, beatific song and agitated movement in "Numi, pietà" perhaps opens a space in which we can imagine ourselves to be communing directly with Aida, or with the singer impersonating her. Paradoxically, then, the very overabundance of authorial instructions for "Numi, pietà" may be what pries open a crack in Verdi's "wall-like" text, and ultimately even calls into question the complete and authoritarian control Said attributes to Verdi. For, in a genre as complex and as dependent on performance as opera, the kind of colonial control imagined by Said may be impossible: when an author offers such a wealth of guidance in score, libretto, staging manual, and personal letters, it is perhaps inevitable that the text should topple under its own weight, and the composer's own voice here and there be obscured or drowned out. It seems poetically just that for Aida, this moment arrives as she addresses a prayer for mercy to the gods that control her destiny; as she leaves the stage repeating "pietà, pietà . . . " the audience is left to wonder whether her prayer has perhaps been granted for a few moments.

Mélisande's Hair, or the Trouble in Allemonde

A POSTMODERN ALLEGORY AT THE OPÉRA-COMIQUE

KATHERINE BERGERON

"IT'S ALL MÉLISANDE'S FAULT," Debussy wrote to his friend Ernest Chausson early in 1894 in the midst of composing the first act of his opera *Pelléas et Mélisande*. Having neglected to answer a letter, he coyly offered Maeterlinck's heroine as the excuse. The taciturn Debussy, famous for having little to say, evidently found himself at a greater loss when trying to cope with the silences of his fictional *compagne*. He summarized the plight to Chausson in words that could easily have been spoken by the opera's ill-fated Prince Golaud: "I have spent days," he complained, "in pursuit of the 'nothing' that she is made of."[1]

Vacuous Mélisande, vexing Mélisande, one of opera's supremely unfulfilling heroines. Debussy was not alone in finding fault. More than a few critics have ascribed the weaknesses of Maeterlinck's drama to her problematic character, the crowning enigma of an enigmatic play overburdened with symbols. Having little to say and less to do, she appears hollow or capricious, her actions so devoid of motivation that even death cannot render them meaningful: her noiseless parting produces no emotion, no catharsis. Tellingly, Maeterlinck lists her name in the play's roster of characters without a single attribute, as if to emphasize her status as an outsider in Allemonde, a figure unencumbered by the ties of kinship binding all the other inhabitants of the castle. Nor do her words provide her with any more substance. Standing on stage while Pelléas or Golaud or Arkël deliver ponderous speeches, endless paragraphs of prose, she responds in monosyllables, at most a phrase or two: "Non." "Ah." "Je ne suis pas heureuse." If in its deliberate lack of action the second act of *Tristan* seems to move slowly, the disjointed dialogues throughout *Pelléas et Mélisande* stop the drama dead in its tracks. And it all appears to be the fault of Mélisande, the girl made from nothing.

What to do with this problem child? Directors face a task almost as difficult as that confronted by Debussy himself in attempting to represent her mysterious nature on stage. For the decision of how exactly one should play her character will in large measure determine (as Debussy readily understood) the meaning of the whole opera. Mélisandes of our time have ranged from ambulatory ghosts to ambivalent teases, but in the guise of lover she can sometimes appear as a kind of inversion of the other femme fatale of the nineteenth-century French stage: a disaffected and blond Carmen toying listlessly with her men. How are we to reconcile such interpretations with Debussy's own reading? In trying to solve the problem of Mélisande for themselves, some modern directors (not to mention critics) have perhaps paid too little attention to the clues offered by the opera itself, the temporal and audible symbols on the surface of Maeterlinck's play and enfolded within Debussy's musical score.

It is useful, then, to begin by reviewing the broad outlines of the opera in order to place Mélisande within the finer network of its symbols—especially those of the extended central scene of the lovers at the tower (Act III, scene 1). For this is the one moment in which Mélisande, always hard to pin down, appears momentarily to stand still, absorbed in the act of combing her hair. And it is in this arresting scene that Debussy, catching his elusive heroine for once at rest, finally catches *up* with her, and makes her into "something." If attending to Debussy's music can offer a special access to Mélisande, then a glimpse at a 1998 production at the Paris Opéra-Comique will show us how one director in particular succeeded not only in untangling the symbolic mass of her hair, but in separating whole strands of meaning woven into Maeterlinck's mysterious text.

ALLEMONDE/ALLEGORY

The mystery is close to home. The setting of *Pelléas et Mélisande* is the fictional kingdom of Allemonde, a country whose very name points to the mode of reading that the drama will ultimately require. As a portmanteau word combining "allégorie" and "monde," "Allemonde" seems to present us, quite simply, with a world of allegory, a symbolic mode that Hegel once described as something "icy and barren." It is probably significant, then, that the chilly realm also sounds a lot like *Allemagne,* the northerly region that was Hegel's home, and a place that—in French, at least—easily stands for all that is harsh and uninhabitable. The kingdom has the requisite castle housing an extended royal family: there is the blind patriarch Arkël and his sometime companion, the widowed Geneviève, who in turn is mother to two mismatched princes, Pelléas and his half-brother Golaud; the latter also a widower and father to a young son, Yniold. As in Bluebeard's castle, the in-laws seem to have fared badly. There are two unaccounted-for husbands and at least as many dead wives lurking somewhere in the building's collective memory. Is it they who occupy the horrible subterranean chamber, with its intolerable stench of death and putrefaction?

Every castle has its ghosts, of course; every royal closet its skeletons. But there is something funny about Allemonde, something that invites us to view the chateau and its inhabitants not as the props of a conventional fairy tale but as subjects of a very different kind of story. Roger Nichols rightly observes that the lines of descent between generations, particularly the familial bonds linking Arkël, Geneviève, and her two absent husbands are never made clear throughout the entire drama.[2] Moreover, only a passing comment informs us about the precise relation between her two sons. It is in fact Golaud who bothers to spell it out for us in a letter to Pelléas, read aloud on stage by Geneviève to Arkël during the second scene of Act I. "My dear Pelléas," he interjects, but the apparent eloquence of the gesture is immediately muted by the utterly pedestrian clause that follows: "you whom I love more than a brother even though we were not born of the same father."

The literalness of the moment is significant. If Golaud's identification with his half-brother strikes us as mechanical or unpoetic that is precisely the point. For Golaud himself is prosaic, practical, human. The one character who can always be counted on to have his feet planted firmly on the ground, he appears genuinely out of place in the dreamland of Allemonde. He asks questions (too many questions, as far as Catherine Clément is concerned.)[3] Compelled to put his thoughts into words, he tries to make things plain. When we meet him at the beginning of Act I, he is trying to talk his way out of a forest in which he has inexplicably become lost. In the next scene, the letter to his half-brother relates everything that has taken place since that moment—his discovery of Mélisande, their marriage, his plan to bring her home—all in ten, brief sentences. Golaud's letter may lack a certain literary refinement, but it certainly gets the job done.

This verbal efficiency simply complements that of the earlier scene in the forest, where Golaud has been hunting wild boar. Never mind that he loses his way and stumbles on a mysterious princess. He never loses sight of his identity. The first interaction between Golaud and the foundling Mélisande is telling in this respect. After several rounds of cross-examination Golaud manages to learn nothing more than her name; he, by contrast, rattles off his full title and institutional affiliation at the merest provocation. To her simple question "Qui êtes-vous?" he proclaims triumphantly, "I am Prince Golaud, the grandson of Arkël, who is the aged ruler of Allemonde." The gravity of the answer, which Debussy incidentally saw fit to score with vulgar diatonic triads, cannot but make this prosaic prince, especially in comparison to his diaphanous maiden, appear rather comic.

It is precisely this literalism that establishes Golaud's unique position within the drama. He wears his family name, his royal pedigree—in sum, his entire civilization—like a badge. Indeed, he cannot escape it. Even lost in the forest, the knight errant is a worldly figure, a character defined by his attachment to custom, habit, language. This is perhaps the single aspect of Maeterlinck's equivocal drama on which all critics unfailingly agree.

When Joseph Kerman describes him as "the one person who acts," he concludes with a string of verbs designed to show just how mundane, how impossibly bourgeois, that activity is: Golaud, he says, "hunts, complains of famine, inspects the foundations of the castle, struggles to save his marriage."[4] Yet even the much more impressionistic reading of Réné Terrasson (whose cultish book *Pelléas et Mélisande, ou l'initiation* seems to walk a fuzzy line between Schopenhauer and the New Age) delivers a similar conclusion. For him, Golaud is *l'homme matériel*, the practical man, the man of substance.[5]

Viewed in this way, the character of Golaud appears not only to oppose that sweet nothing Mélisande, but radically to contradict every other figure in the drama as well, all the ill-defined relatives floating in Allemonde's shadowy realms. Judging from the evidence of scene after scene, it becomes entirely plausible, then, to take Kerman's words and push them a bit further: Golaud may be the only character who acts because he is in fact the drama's only *character*. All those other people on stage might best be seen—as the disjointed family tree suggests—not as "real" relatives but as traces of those symbolic figures roaming about the invisible landscape that, already by the end of the nineteenth century, was known as *l'inconscient*.

We hardly need to be reminded about the important role played by the mystical world of the psyche (or the soul, as it used to be called) in Maeterlinck's oeuvre. It was a world he would develop far more systematically in his *Ariane et Barbe-bleu,* in which the collective chambers of Duke Bluebeard's castle represent the site of an even bleaker mental anguish than that found in the darkest regions of Allemonde. In the collection of essays that make up *Le Trésor des humbles,* Maeterlinck further clarifies this spiritualist aesthetic by lifting his thoughts from the theater to the universal aspects of the human condition. In one essay his description of a troubled soul so tellingly recalls both Bluebeard and Golaud that the statement reads more like a bit of drama criticism than a philosophy: "It is only too evident," Maeterlinck asserts, "that the invisible agitations of the kingdoms within us are arbitrarily set in motion by the thoughts we shelter."[6] However we read it, the passage's central image of invisible kingdoms should be enough to convince us that the Allemonde of *Pelléas et Mélisande* is ultimately an unseen world, its allegory of love and death an inner drama—a modern-day *Psychomachia* produced from the mind of the one character who thinks, and talks, too much.

This is precisely the vision offered to us in a marvelous production of Debussy's *Pelléas* staged by Pierre Médecin at the Opéra-Comique in April of 1998.[7] From the very first moment, the mise en scène leaves us in no doubt that the trouble in Allemonde lies entirely within Golaud himself, within the castle of his psyche. This interior castle is first revealed as the opening orchestral prelude draws to a close and the stage lights are illuminated: we see a claustrophobic box of a room, with Golaud crouched in one darkened corner. He is dressed *à la Belle Epoque,* in a tweed suit, his van doren and close cropped curly hair making him look a little like a middle-aged Debussy. As the set becomes brighter the plain box turns into a larger space, with an old leather chair and various bits of hunting paraphernalia positioned to one side, close to the front. It is Golaud's den. He sits facing the audience and starts to sing, when slowly, almost imperceptibly, the floor of the stage begins to fill with water. In fact the water continues to flow through the whole scene (as it does through all of the acts), making the stage floor into a kind of flat fountain, a trembling, liquid mirror that reflects back Golaud's image: he is a weary old man sitting in his chair, thinking.

The décor for the scene recalls, with a kind of uncanny fidelity, another Maeterlinckian vision of the interior life. "I have grown to believe," wrote the playwright in *Les Trésors des humbles,* "that an old man, seated in his armchair, waiting patiently . . . giving unconscious ear to all the eternal laws that reign about his house, . . . does yet live in reality a deeper, more human and more universal life."[8] More universal, he means, than the heroes of the conventional theater, all those passionate men who (as he would have it) strangled, conquered, avenged. Indeed, Maeterlinck's alternative idea of a quiet hero listening into the silence of existence must have offered suggestive possibilities for music, especially for a post-Wagnerian composer such as Debussy, enamored of a form of opera whose action would be advanced less through singing than listening—attending to the wordless deeds of an unseen orchestra. The picture proved equally suggestive, it seems, for Monsieur Medécin, who forces Golaud throughout the production—not only during the orchestral interludes but also, arrestingly, *between* the acts—to remain seated before the audience in silence. Listening thus becomes productive activity. Médecin makes us see that it is in effect Golaud who, like a composer, conceives the opera's action through his own silent thought, an action that can be glimpsed only from behind his armchair, through vertical blinds that open onto each scene.

What does all this cogitation produce? Quite simply, an inner drama whose basic structure looks all too familiar. If Allemonde stands as the primary symbol of Maeterlinck's drama, it is a symbol whose meaning was so fully developed by the later discipline of psychology that no late-twentieth-century reader could mistake its implications: Allemonde begins to look like the silent, interior kingdom we call the mind. Freud would not formulate his structural theory of the mind until long after the era of Debussy and Maeterlinck, of course, and yet the symbolism of *Pelléas* seems compellingly to anticipate the form of these later discoveries.[9] While there is nothing in Golaud's interior castle quite so tidy as the separate regions of unconscious activity that Freud in 1923 called the id, the ego, and the superego, the relations among the male characters—Yniold, Pelléas, and

Arkël—point to a range of functions that are at least as suggestive. The symbolic role of the archetypal Father (Arkël) is perhaps the most obvious: as the agent who monitors Golaud's interior world. Right from the beginning we witness the fear and trembling—in a word, the guilt—he evokes in Golaud. The letter scene makes this apparent when Golaud expresses confidence in his mother's forgiveness but, in the next breath, admits his fear of the king—an anxiety that is not at all overstated. For in response to Golaud's plan of bringing Mélisande home, this internalized conscience can say nothing more than nothing ("je n'en dis rien"), the austere reply capturing all the father's civilizing function. The figure of Yniold falls to the other end of the spectrum. An innocent child, he easily stands for everything Golaud has already lost and now longs to recover: the real experience, or truth ("la vérité"), that can no longer be found in the confines of his highly civilized world.

If Pelléas's symbolic function is at first more difficult to comprehend within this trio of forces, it may simply be for the reason that he continues to look a lot like a conventional operatic lover—indeed, according to a long critical tradition like a French version of Tristan.[10] But the events of the plot show him to have much less vigor than his Teutonic counterpart, and certainly fewer worldly concerns than his greying half-brother. Pelléas thinks only of himself. In the tower scene of Act III, his response to Mélisande's initial question "Qui est là?" is telling. He answers not with a resumé of the family pedigree (whose burden he, unlike Golaud, evidently does not experience) but with a statement that is, simply put, *all* ego: a thrice repeated "Moi, moi et moi." Who is there? Me, myself and I.

Once we are able to imagine Pelléas as the figure of ego—the free and imaginary dimension of Golaud's fully conscious self—even his status as half-brother begins to make more sense. For is not what we call the "self" always a mixed proposition, containing parts we believe we can recognize together with those that appear entirely foreign, like the face of a brother whose father is not our own? In Médecin's mise en scène, incidentally, this complex relation is suggestively evoked by his very choice of singers: Golaud is played for the first time by François Le Roux, a baritone whose operatic career was largely established through his numerous, memorable appearances in *Pelléas,* in which he had always played the role of the title character. The spectator aware of this history could thus hardly avoid viewing the much younger (and blonder) William Dazeley, who played Pelléas in the 1998 production, as something like François Le Roux's "alter ego."

The problem caused by this beloved and alien sibling, and all the other relations in Golaud's house as well, becomes only too obvious as the story unfolds: there is simply not enough room for them all to have their way. While Pelléas overtly pursues his pleasure, Yniold continues to play behind the scenes, and Arkël to exercise his blind authority. It is no wonder that the civilized Golaud begins to experience greater anxiety and guilt as he tries (and fails) to deal with all these unseen players. In a word, he suffers. When, Othello-like, he erupts with rage in Act IV, he expresses his emotion so suddenly and aggressively that the scenes would likely have prompted a sober nod from Freud himself. The moment leaves us in no doubt that the central theme of *Pelléas et Mélisande* is not the love between the title characters but ultimately the suffering—one might even say the neurosis—of Golaud. The theme is so powerful, in fact, that we could easily imagine this allegory of Allemonde refitted with a new title: something like "Civilization and Its Discontents."

The figure responsible for the greater part of this malaise is, of course, the one who refuses to be assimilated into the family tree. Yes, the trouble in Allemonde seems to be—once again—all Mélisande's fault. She is the one who upsets the critical balance within Golaud's interior castle, moving freely about its chambers to form separate, intimate relations with Yniold, Pelléas, and Arkël. Even so, she remains in some essential respects an outsider. In the decor by Andreas Reinhardt at the Opéra-Comique, she wears a costume whose sheer stylistic difference underscores this outsider status, placing her beyond the temporal frame that unites all the other characters. With her radiant white dress and bobbed hair she looks more like one of Man Ray's fashionable divas—or a "star" of the golden age of cinema— than a *belle dame* of the belle époque. She is made to stand, in other words, at some recognizable distance from the turn-of-the-century manners and mores that shape the image of Arkël (a kind of Freud look-alike in dark glasses), and Geneviève (dressed as if in mourning with a big, dark hat), and Yniold (in his blue sailor suit).

Not to mention Pelléas or Golaud. If Pelléas's white linen garb is perhaps meant to echo Mélisande's brilliance, the tweedy Golaud remains impossibly out of touch—and out of time—with his distant spouse. Indeed, Médecin's staging makes sure of it. When, during Golaud's bewildered monologue in Act II, scene 2, Médecin has Mélisande appear and disappear again through the blinds from behind his chair (figure 1), he seems to recall the meaning of her repeated command at their initial encounter, her words ("ne me touchez pas") only reinforcing what this fleeting vision again tells us—that she will forever remain beyond his grasp. In her continuous, restless movement she is thus like the water of the fountain alongside of which Golaud first discovers her, or of the sea on which they together set sail: she alone, it seems, has the power to start up his imagination, to put his thought in motion. In this sense, Mélisande might begin to appear like a personified form of that fluid psychic energy that Freud

Figure 1. *Pelléas et Mélisande,* Act II, scene 2; Opéra-Comique, 1998, directed by Pierre Médecin (photo: Pierre Richard).

sometimes called libido. Médecin himself would probably have been content to identify his glittering beauty with a word whose etymology (from *de* plus *siderus*) means quite literally a thing of the stars: desire.

So might Debussy. In a letter to Prince Poniatowski written in 1893, just a few months before embarking on the composition of *Pelléas,* we find the composer summarizing the miserable state of his own personal affairs with a sketch of desire that would seem to anticipate the role of his future Mélisande. "In the end desire is what counts," he quipped, adding, "you could write down a formula for desire: 'everything comes from it and returns to it.'"[11] The circular formula certainly recalls the character of the elusive Mélisande, for she too has no clear beginning or end, no easily narratable history. At first, Golaud has no idea where she came from; at last, he knows not where (or why) she goes. If Allemonde is indeed an allegorical symbol for Golaud's silent, interior life, it is a topsy-turvy realm, governed not so much by the archaic law of its blind king as by the far more incomprehensible movements of the shimmering object of desire that runs through Golaud's thought like a river.

HAIR

His kingdom within is ruled, in other words, by something unruly, the uncontrollable Mélisande having changed the course of Golaud's orderly and civilized life. Indeed, the unruliness of her nature is conveniently symbolized by the one physical attribute that causes her to stand apart from the other figures in the play: her long and luxuriant hair. To be sure, very long hair always exhibits a life of its own, a wildness that has to be tamed. Unbound, it is like the domesticated animal released to its natural habitat, an unmistakable mark of sexual freedom.

As Clément has elsewhere remarked, the story of *Pelléas* makes allusion to the animal nature of Mélisande already in the first scene, when Golaud finds her in the forest by the edge of a fountain, speechless and sobbing like a small wild creature.[12] But the analogy is developed even more directly, I would argue, through the strange and simultaneous event that occurs in Act II. Mélisande is again at the fountain, this time playing with Pelléas. At the stroke of noon, as her hair chances to tumble into the water and she drops her wedding band, something inside Pelléas evidently stirs. But Golaud himself is *thrown* at this very moment, his horse having suddenly and inexplicably bolted, as he later tells us, on some impulse to reclaim its freedom. Golaud's *chute de cheval* thus becomes associated, through a dreamlike logic of puns, with Mélisande's *chute de cheveux,* the dual event unmistakably linking her loose and unruly hair to the stirring of his animal instinct.[13]

By a far less circuitous route, Freud himself would develop this tie between hair and sexuality. In *Civilization and Its Discontents,* for example, he compares the sexual life of civilized man to the status of hair and teeth, which in our present moment of human evolution are, as he puts it, "in the process of involution as functions."[14] Through the slow process of civilization, in other words, these physical attributes no longer function solely for the purpose of survival; yet the very notion of "involution" suggests that a trace of that prior wildness—a scent of animal—still resides within. We find just such a scent wafting conspicuously through a passage from the 1905 *Essays on Sexuality* in which Freud, discussing the nature of sexual perversions, offers a suggestive theoretical speculation. Objects such as hair that have a strong smell, he explains, have a tendency "after the olfactory sensation has been abandoned to become exalted into a fetish."[15]

The sheer amount of energy lavished on hair by nineteenth-century artists and writers (not to mention the popular Victorian fad for jewelry made from the hair of a loved one) suggests that Freud was perhaps onto something.[16] Today the abundant tresses of the women painted by Puvis de Chavannes or Dante Gabriel Rossetti, flattened into familiar greeting card images, have lost their power to ignite the erotic imagination as they apparently once did. Yet the elaborate hair fantasies charted by certain fin-de-siècle poets seem to have retained, mostly through their tenacious imagery, a more obvious trace of this sexual charge. Indeed, two poems in particular, by Charles Baudelaire and Pierre Louÿs (both titled simply "La Chevelure"), offer us a potent vision of the pleasures to be discovered in the lover's unbound hair, a vision that may in turn help us to recapture a sense of the unsettling erotic energy associated with Mélisande herself.

Of the two, Baudelaire's poem, from the first book of *Les Fleurs du mal* (1857), is most explicit in its evocation of sensual pleasures. The primal and instinctual urges aroused by *la chevelure* become apparent, in fact, in its very first words, which forsake the cliché of golden locks for a much more direct and bestial image—that of a mane, or a mass of fur or fleece: "O toison, moutonnant jusque sur l'encolure!" (Oh fleece, billowing to your neck!). The woolly apostrophe expands into a threefold exclamation ("O boucles! O parfum chargé de nonchaloir!" [O ringlets! O perfume charged with languidness!]) whose last image recalls the most powerfully erotic dimension of hair: its smell. The substitution of visual metaphors for the olfactory image of a languid perfume, like the oily scent left on clothes or bed linens (an image Mallarmé himself would later use to evoke the seductive power of his Hérodiade), transforms the hair into a lingering reminiscence, a charged sensual memory that the poet wishes to shake from his lover's head like a handkerchief ("je la veux agiter dans l'air comme un mouchoir!").

This potent emanation motivates the imagery of each of the subsequent strophes, in which the remembered hair is described as an "aromatic forest" (un forêt aromatique) that in turn recalls all the exotic, faraway places "down there" (là-bas), whose hot perfume the lover will ride like a wave. Indeed, he imagines this redolent undulation carrying him away (Fortes tresses, soyez la houle qui m'enlève!), first to an "echoing port" (un port retentissant), later to an ocean, into whose jet-black depths the lover will plunge headfirst, to drink and "grow drunk with the mingled scents of coconut-oil, and musk, and tar" (Je m'enivre ardemment des senteurs confondues de l'huile de coco, de musc et de goudron). The ever more expansive chain of erotic images suggests that what we have in "La Chevelure" is, simply put, an elaborate sexual fantasy, the psychic movements of desire having turned "an appetite for sensations," as Leo Bersani puts it, into an inexhaustible series of imaginary forms.[17] By the end of the poem, in fact, Baudelaire appears to have transformed the lover's hair into something like the field of poetry itself, a site in which he will plant his precious jewels ("ma main dans ta crinière lourde / Sèmera le rubis, la perle, et le saphir") so that the object of his pleasure will grow ever closer, and never be "deaf to his desire."

This opulent erotic journey could not have been unknown to Pierre Louÿs, who in fashioning his own hair-inspired fantasy almost four decades later would translate Baudelaire's lyrical excess into a discrete and self-contained narrative form. The thirty-first poem of a long cycle he called *Chansons de Bilitis* (after the fictitious poetess of ancient Greece whose texts he claimed to have translated into prose), his "La Chevelure" relates, in between conspicuous quotation marks, an absorbing vision of hair presented as a lover's dream. The prose poem in fact presents the dream as a story twice told, first by a male lover to his beloved, who now tells it to us: "Il m'a dit: 'Cette nuit, j'ai rêvé. J'avais ta chevelure autour de mon cou. J'avais tes cheveux comme un collier noir autour de ma nuque et sur ma poitrine.'" (He told me: "Last night I had a dream. I had your hair around my neck. I had your hair like a black collar around my neck and down my chest.") The measured cadences of the three opening sentences, which relate the subject's imagined entrapment by hair, expand proportionally (six syllables, giving way to eleven, then to twenty-one) as if to mimic the dilating imagery of the dream, with its potentially endless chain of dream symbols. The expansion continues in the even longer period that follows, the subject's initial entwinement now reinterpreted as a kind of pleasurable possession: "Je les caressais et c'étaient les miens, et nous étions liés pour toujours ainsi par la même chevelure, la bouche sur la bouche, ainsi que deux lauriers n'ont souvent qu'une racine." (I caressed it and it belonged to me, and we were bound together like this, by the same hair, mouth on mouth, the way two laurels often have but one root.)

If the excitement of the caress is perhaps tempered by the distancing analogy of the laurel root, the shift of focus is but a temporary caesura in the movement of fantasy. Hastening toward its object of desire in the next and final stage of the dream, the *moi* experiences a union so profound ("tant nos membres était confondues") that the subject is completely undone, becoming indistinguishable from the other ("je devenais toi-même"), indeed, penetrated by the other like the dream that has entered and transformed him ("tu entrais en moi, comme mon songe"). With this moment of oblivion, of pure engulfment—like the penultimate strophe of Baudelaire's poem whose love-drunk subject plunges into oceanic depths—the dream of hair comes to an end, signaled by the closing of the quotation, and the decorous appearance of the historical past ("Quand il eût achevé"). Only one event remains to be reported, a final moment of closure that is also an overture. The dreamer (now in the third person) places a hand on the shoulder of his beloved (now the first person) and, as if still possessed by his dream memory, penetrates her again with his gaze. But the gesture is simply too much—the gaze so tender that it is chilling—and the narrator, who cannot return it, lowers her eyes "with a shiver."

The penetrating look, in other words, leaves her completely cold. This final act constitutes the crux of Louÿs's erotic poem, for it is here that we may recognize the most important dimension of the dream, namely, that it belongs to the dreamer alone. The second person evoked in that mental activity, like the woman whose musky curls Baudelaire evokes, is simply not present—in fact, not really a person at all—in the mind of the one who imagined her. This condition essentially reflects the nature of desire itself, which, as Bersani has described it, "is always a lack, [for] the object is never entirely present in desire; when it is, it erases desire." The vexing situation is helped along, however, by "certain fantasies [that] both provide the necessary stimulus to desire and partially satisfy it."[18]

The will to recover prior satisfactions in fantasy can be seen in the act of narration that reconstitutes the dream of Louÿs's imaginary lover. By telling the dream, he holds fast to his pleasure, just as the quotation marks "hold" the dream on the page, fixing in narrative form the satisfaction that he will hope to have again. As the central figure within the dream, *la chevelure* thus represents the symbolic possibility of such holding, the place where erotic energy is both released and tied back up in the web of fantasy. Indeed, the strand of long hair may be an apt analogy for the working of fantasy itself, representing the medium through which, as we see in Baudelaire's poem, desire can be spun out in countless forms that will ultimately weave another yarn, one whose promise of repeated pleasure will always be close at hand.

FANTAISIE / MÉLODIE

Médecin obviously knows that long hair is the stuff of pure fantasy, and
proves it through a notably quirky feature of the production: his Mélisande,
it has already been said, has short hair. It is a more than welcome decision.
Not only does he spare us all the distractions of the singer whose costume
typically includes a massive—and obviously fake—blond wig (the very sort
of distraction that forced Adorno to abandon the opera house for the sanc-
tuary of the long-playing record). But even more important, once faced
with this conspicuously shorn Mélisande, we are obliged to imagine her
longs cheveux for ourselves, and thus, in a very real way, to enter into the
same fantasy that motivates Pelléas during the powerfully erotic encounter
at the center of the opera known as the *scène des cheveux*.

Which means, of course, that we enter more fully into the fantasy of
music. For in the opera, the passionate odyssey through the lover's hair is
not just a poetic excursion but a musical one. Like Baudelaire's exotic
ocean voyage and Louÿs's dream, the imaginary journey in *Pelléas* begins
with the lover's arousal by hair, then leads by stages to more intense and
sustained pleasures as he touches, holds, and eventually ties it down. What
differs is the journey's scale. The musical setting enlarges the imaginary
scheme of events several times over, at once extending the action in time
and giving it a kind of depth, an audible and palpable sensuality. Debussy's
music thus allows us in a unique way to account for, indeed, to *feel* the distinct stages of Pelléas's symbolic entanglement. Or, stated in the terms of
our allegorical reading, we are made to experience the inexorable course of
the (imaginary) self toward its object of desire, and thus, finally, to understand what the trouble in Allemonde is all about. A look at a few of the
more striking moments of this famous scene will reveal just how deftly
music figures the problem of desire and ultimately enacts its resolution.

———

The scene begins with Mélisande alone in a tower of the castle, singing
about her hair: "My long hair falls to the bottom of the tower / My hair
waits for you the whole length of the tower." The imagery is reminiscent
of Mallarmé's Hérodiade, standing before her mirror and singing of the
"blond torrent of her immaculate hair," which Medusa-like "freezes her
body" and makes her "immortal." Médecin, at least, seems to have had
something like this in mind in his stark and almost surrealistic conception
for the scene. For Mélisande *is* immortalized in his decor, perched atop a
tower that is in fact an enormous totem (a taboo?) of her own serene image:
a huge head and shoulders frozen in stone (figure 2). The song Mélisande

Figure 2. *Pelléas et Mélisande,* Act III, scene 1; Opéra-Comique, 1998,
directed by Pierre Médecin (photo: Pierre Richard).

EXAMPLE 1
Debussy, *Pelléas et Mélisande;* Act III, sc.1

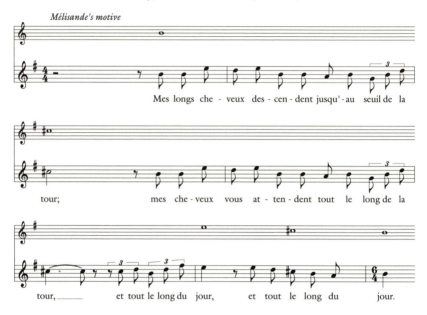

Mélisande's motive

Mes longs che - veux des - cen - dent jusqu' - au seuil de la

tour;   mes che - veux vous at - ten - dent tout le long de la

tour,_____ et tout le long du jour, et tout le long du jour.

sings is as timeless as her towering statue, a chant carved from an archaic mode that is actually a permutation of Mélisande's own motive (see example 1). Intoned without the accompaniment of a single instrument, her opening phrases sound completely uninhibited, naked, like a call of the wild, Rousseau's "animal cry of passion." For just a moment, the song seems to be free from this entrapment we call opera, coming from some other place and time like Mélisande herself: an utterance squeezed out, "expressed," as if from the very otherness of this woman whose name resonates with *melos*, pure melody. This timeless song of hair is desire's tune, a chant that comes from a deep interior that is nowhere in particular, a pure register of music that lies beneath the operatic surface like an instinct.

At this moment in Médecin's production Golaud is still on stage, sitting off to one side in his by now familiar leather chair. But there is a difference. For the first time in the opera he has fallen asleep. Médecin stages this musical fantasy, in other words, as a dream in which Golaud experiences the fulfillment of his most profound wish. The scene's sequence of events certainly lends credence to the idea; we can almost hear Golaud, after the fact, retelling the strange dream to us: "There was a woman. She was standing far above me on a tower. It was night. She was combing her hair and singing. A young man approached, who was myself . . . "

Pelléas does approach the tower at this moment, having responded to the call from afar. His movement toward Mélisande's "call" initiates the second phase of the fantasy, a long stage of arousal in which Pelléas attempts to get closer to this distant love-object. He begs Mélisande to come down from her perch, asking, without apparent embarrassment, to see her long hair: "Lean out of the window a bit so I can see your unbound hair." Her reply is both direct and indirect. She doesn't refuse; she says only "Je suis affreuse ainsi," a line that is often (and I think wrongly) interpreted by singers as coquettish flirtation. For Mélisande in fact speaks the truth. Her loose hair, a sign of wildness, *is* frightful, even monstrous. The cryptic flirtation is really a warning.

At the very moment she utters these words we hear for the first time a little melodic motif, a fleeting chromatic figure that is sounded in the orchestra as if to give voice to this warning. The instrumental figure, no more than a chromatic turn, returns throughout this first part of the scene, yet it will soon be heard underscoring Pelléas's demands, recurring each time he entreats Mélisande for her hand (example 2a and b). The motivic recurrence has a unique effect: it seems to suggest something about the deeply embedded relationship of these two symbolic figures, Pelléas's de-

EXAMPLE 2
Debussy, *Pelléas et Mélisande;* Act III, sc.1

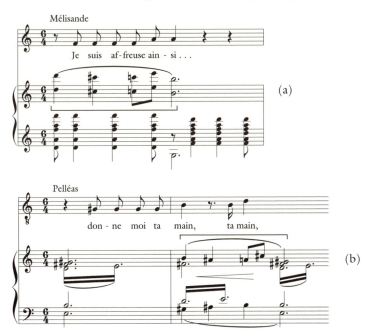

mand reflecting back the very thing that is "frightful" in his desire, in Mélisande's wild hair.

As it turns out, this little chromatic twist makes an appearance a few years later in Debussy's setting of "La Chevelure," one of the three poems Debussy chose to set from the large collection in Louÿs's *Chansons de Bilitis.* The motif appears in the first half of Debussy's song, at the moment when the poem's first person begins to dilate on his dream. Debussy marks the poetic expansion in the third phrase ("J'avais tes cheveux comme un collier noir") by an equivalent melodic expansion, whose right-hand piano accompaniment makes direct reference to the orchestral motif from the first part of the hair scene (see example 3). The more extended, and indeed more *audible,* form in which this melodic figure appears in "La Chevelure," written in 1897 (that is, some time after Debussy had completed his first draft of *Pelléas*), makes me wonder whether we might profitably use the song to cast a backward glance on the opera. For it seems significant that the entwining chromatic figure, which Debussy uses in the song to paint the subject's attempt to *hold onto* his dream, had also served a similar purpose in the opera, where it can be heard underscoring Pelléas's repeated (and quite literal) attempts to grab hold of Mélisande, and his awakened pleasure, by spinning them into a more fulsome fantasy.

The motive soon disappears. Pelléas's demands now take a different turn, the intensity of the scene increasing until it reaches a peak, a sudden moment of release triggered by an unexpected event: Mélisande's hair falls from the tower. In purely formal terms, this moment can be heard as a distinct point of articulation, a musical event that decisively brings the first long section to an end. Strikingly, the event is announced by a breathless cry from Mélisande herself ("Oh! Oh! mes cheveux descendent de la tour!"), which hangs on a high F♯ and G. The decorous shriek obviously recalls—indeed, it seems to resolve—a long-forgotten vocal register from the litany of saints in the second half of her opening chant (at "Saint Michel et Saint Raphael," see example 4), at the same moment that a gentle cascade of strings and distant horns announces the shower of gold. Médecin's tasteful rendering of this often ridiculous moment is entirely in keeping with the shimmering figure of desire to whom it belongs. Illuminating the night sky, a stream of shooting stars rains down from behind Mélisande's perch, finally supplying the symbolic substance that this woman of the stars has never really lacked: her golden light is a comet, which comes from the Greek *kome,* meaning hair.

This luminous articulation initiates a new phase of the dream, beginning with a reply from Pelléas that may just be the strangest moment in the whole scene. In response to the torrent of hair he says, "Oh! Oh! qu'est-ce que c'est?" as if he does not *recognize* the very thing he has been asking for all along. Even more disturbing is the warped sense of time that the accident

EXAMPLE 3
Debussy, "La Chevelure," from *Chansons de Bilitis*

EXAMPLE 4
Debussy, *Pelléas et Mélisande;* Act III, sc.1

EXAMPLE 5
Debussy, *Pelléas et Mélisande;* Act III, sc.1

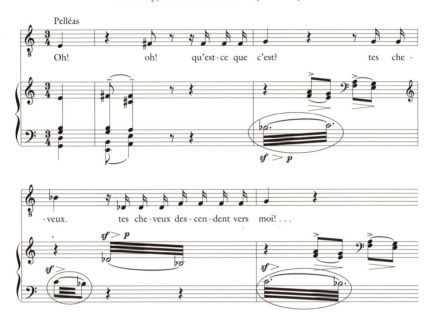

seems to initiate, for Pelléas's response is also oddly out of whack. It is only now, for example, that he cries, "your hair is falling toward me!" In other words, he repeats the event that has just transpired—and that we ourselves have just witnessed—in the present tense, temporarily cancelling the past. By turning the fallen hair into a present-tense narrative of falling hair, he thus extends his hold on it, staking a new claim on an event that took place perhaps too quickly for him to notice. This imaginative retelling creates in its wake an entirely ambiguous interval of time, a sort of temporal blank.

Accompanying this out-of-time response is an agitated dissonance, the interval of a major second repeated at different pitches in the winds and tremolo strings (example 5). The ambiguous harmony seems to match the ambiguous temporality of Pelléas's stunned "qu'est-ce que c'est?" but the significance of this musical sign will become even clearer as the scene develops. For the sound of the second can be heard as a kind of irritant—or better yet, an agitant—that propels Pelléas forward into a fantasy that draws out the fleeting moment of pleasure. As in Louÿs's "La Chevelure," the imaginary space is represented unmistakably through the image of holding Mélisande's hair.

Debussy paints this "holding" through a compelling shift of musical action. The musical flow is now redirected; the scene lifts itself into an

EXAMPLE 6
Debussy, *Pelléas et Mélisande;* Act III, sc.1

entirely new temporal register. A gentle pulsing motion emerges from the undifferentiated buzz as the harmonic dissonance resolves, the tension of the major seconds relaxing into a sweet stream of flowing thirds. And for the first time in the scene, as Pelléas proclaims his act of holding the hair in a repetitive quatrain ("Je les tiens dans les mains, je les tiens dans la bouche, je les tiens dans les bras"), we begin to feel a true sense of meter (see example 6). The dialogue between the characters has given way to a monologue for Pelléas alone (marked *moins vite*), whose gently rocking strings and sighing clarinet recall the infinite pleasure of Baudelaire's lover, rocking on the waves of hair, returning to the pure bliss of the cradle.

Caught in the primordial flow, Pelléas starts to swing. The new song he sings calls attention to its difference with an exotic musical event (beginning with the words "Vois, vois") that features, along with the vocal melody, a snaking oboe line set adrift over throbbing pedal tones. But almost as soon as this phrase begins, the harmony suddenly shifts, warming into the sound of a dominant seventh. We recall at once the rush of pleasure that comes in the form of an inexplicable warmth filling heart and knees. And this image yields to another, more striking one of blacking out ("I can no longer see the sky through your hair"), a passage painted black by Debussy with arresting blocks of sound, major chords on C and F♯, played by full orchestra. Here the song takes off again, becoming more ecstatic until a final outcry: "Your hair loves me more than you do." Yes, the dream seems to be working. As Pelléas holds onto his object, he consumes his desire in the temporary plenitude of song. But the pleasure is interrupted as desire seems to pull away, speaking for the first time in a long while. She says, "Laisse-moi, quelqu'un pourrait venir" ("Let me go, someone might come"), and the orchestra vanishes, leaving only a completely naked major second, a bleating sound in the low bassoons (example 7).

EXAMPLE 7
Debussy, *Pelléas et Mélisande;* Act III, sc.1

EXAMPLE 8
Debussy, "La Chevelure," from *Chansons de Bilitis*

Hearing the sound of the dissonant second as the orchestra falls away, I begin to feel that it perhaps had been there all along, pressing beneath the obscuring fantasy. Its return signals the end of the third stage of the dream and simultaneously begins the next. For as before, this irritant of desire gives rise to yet another pleasurable sequence—this one more voluptuous than the last. The moment of articulation once again resembles a musical strategy Debussy uses at the opening of "La Chevelure" (see example 8). There we find the ambiguity of the major second, hanging precariously on the edge of the narration, absorbed and ultimately softened by the ensuing accompaniment, an effortlessly rocking dominant ninth harmony. The ambiguous irritant, in other words, disappears in the space of this new and more pleasurable *bercement*. Desire's "lack" is filled.

In the *scène des cheveux*, this cradling can be heard as Pelléas ignores Mélisande's demand, and simply keeps moving: "No, no, I will not deliver you tonight. I will have you the whole night" (see example 9). The line is followed by a poignant, melancholy cry, a reminiscence of the call of the

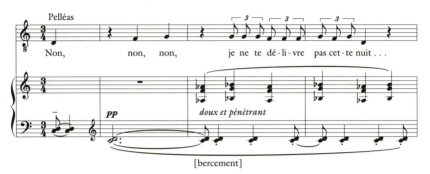

EXAMPLE 9
Debussy, *Pelléas et Mélisande;* Act III, sc.1

EXAMPLE 10
Debussy, *Pelléas et Mélisande;* Act III, sc.1

Figure 3. *Pelléas et Mélisande,* Act III, scene 1; Opéra-Comique, 1998, directed by Pierre Médecin (photo: Pierre Richard).

wild that initiated the scene, now reduced to two words: Pelléas, Pelléas. And as Mélisande calls back, the sound of the major second persists, as if to remind the self of the tenacity of desire—out of time, out of tune. The dissonance propels Pelléas into his most opulent imaginary refuge, a sweet vision of bondage, as he sings of weaving the hair into the branches of the willow tree ("Je les noue . . . au branches de saule"). With its stream of liquid thirds, the new vision is both a reprise and an expansion of the previous fantasy, the singing now so full and continuous that it turns into a true *mélodie*—indeed, the only *mélodie* in the whole opera (see example 10). In this extended moment, where fantasy is spun into a long, thin line, the "I" reflects back the *melos* that is Mélisande herself, and, as Médecin's mise en scène so poignantly shows, finally melts into its bliss (figure 3).

How does the cycle of fantasy end? In a word, abruptly. Without warning, Golaud comes back to his senses with all his darkly colored music, and tries

Figure 4. *Pelléas et Mélisande,* Act IV, scene 2; Opéra-Comique, 1998, directed by Pierre Médecin (photo: Pierre Richard).

to resume order and control. "What are you doing here?" he barks. "Vous êtes des enfants." Pulling back from his dream, he effectively represses his desire. This act of repression is made even more obvious in the next scene, when Golaud takes his half-brother into the castle's subterranean chamber, as if to put the desiring ego in its place, far from the surface of his consciousness. But the repressed, as we all know, has a tendency to return and return it does, with a vengeance. In the next scenes, we witness Golaud's renewed suffering as he tries to cope with what his civilized nature requires. When, in Act IV, Mélisande and Arkël have their tête-à-tête—when, that is, desire comes under the surveillance of the father—the sense of guilt has become too much to bear, and Golaud performs the most violent act of the whole opera. He seizes Mélisande by her precious hair, acting just like the primitive man described in Freud's *Civilization and Its Discontents,* who "throw[ing] the blame on his fetish . . . gives it a thrashing instead of punishing himself."[19] Indeed, we could almost believe that Médecin was trying to stage this very passage from Freud in the tableau that he offers at the Opéra-Comique. Appearing like the analyst himself behind a raging Golaud, Arkël stands over the scene and observes the struggle from a secure theoretical distance (figure 4).

Meanwhile, Pelléas forms a plan to pick up where he left off, to resume his desired pleasure of engulfment so abruptly cut off by Golaud's return. To consummate this pleasure implies, however, a terminus—in effect a dissolving of the ego—which is precisely what happens in the opera's culminating scene of love at the end of Act IV. The moment of the lovers' embrace, long deferred, brings on Pelléas's death. As should now be clear, this moment is a death of the self, the sort of *jouissance* that Baudelaire reified in his sonnet about sexual communion "La mort des amants."

Mélisande herself is wounded, although not quite snuffed out. Indeed, if desire has neither beginning nor end it can never completely die. To keep this in view is finally to understand the whole problematic dreamworld of Act V. We might read the sequence of events in this bizarre final act as a representation of desire's persistence in one more form—a form of that indefinite time zone we call "languor." For languor is the condition of desire in a wholly undefined space *between,* in a movement, as Bersani might say, from "one representation to another." Mélisande, as one image of desire, simply slips away. She ebbs. And as she does, she has already given birth to the next incarnation. This unexplained infant has caused even more trouble for critics than Mélisande herself. Only the blind Arkël seems to understand who she is. His concluding words foretell the endlessness of desire's perpetual movement—a movement that will inevitably torment Golaud forever—in a single sentence that both completes the drama and simultaneously acknowledges the beginning of another we will never see. "Now," he says, "it's her turn."

Opera

TWO OR THREE THINGS I KNOW ABOUT HER

LAWRENCE KRAMER

HOUSE LIGHTS DOWN

TWO OR THREE THINGS I KNOW ABOUT HER is a movie released in 1966 by Jean-Luc Godard. It consists of a series of images, interviews, and vignettes that sketch the life of a bourgeois housewife who is also a part-time prostitute. The woman does not, of course, "just happen" to be a prostitute. Like many others, she is working to support a habit—in this case precisely the habit of being a bourgeois housewife. The desire she withdraws from her sexual performances is reinvested in the material pleasures of ownership and consumption.

In form, Godard's movie is innovative. Its discontinuous, nonlinear, antimimetic technique, placed in the service of demystifying the facades of normal, or normative, life, can be said to prefigure the advent of deconstruction, which occurred just a year later, in 1967, with the publication of Jacques Derrida's *Of Grammatology*. In content, however, the movie is positively nostalgic, despite an abundance of ostentatious hard edges. It can seen as a variation on an old theme from nineteenth-century opera, indeed one of that art's core themes. *La traviata* had long since shown the intimate connections between prostitution and bourgeois yearnings—the yearnings of being bourgeois, the yearning to be a bourgeois. It had given those connections palpable, not to say palpitating, substance in its seductive music. And judging from the introduction to a recent PBS broadcast of *La traviata,* those connections, Godard notwithstanding, are still being mystified as the stuff of true love and romance.

With operas less explicit than *Traviata,* the same connections may underwrite the impression of profundity. Isn't it possible to understand *Götterdämmerung,* for example, as an archetypal bourgeois tragedy? One of the secrets of the potion that alters Siegfried's desires, and in so doing reveals their true content, is that by forgetting Brünnhilde Siegfried can retire from active duty as a mythic hero. He can settle down as a pillar of polite society with an attractive wife and a couple of good after-dinner stories about a dragon and some magic fire. But in order for that to happen there must first be a mutual commodity exchange: Gunther must pimp Gutrune to Siegfried, and Siegfried pimp Brünnhilde to Gunther. If only the saturnine Hagen hadn't had other ideas . . .

The chain of associations from Godard to *Götterdämmerung* can be taken to suggest that opera has an exceptionally equivocal relationship to sexually mediated normality, or, more accurately, to the identification of social normality with a certain psychosexual disposition. Since the nineteenth century, such normality has generally hinged on the centrality of one version or another of bourgeois identity, from which other modes of identity may be understood to deviate by degrees. I take this fact, however, to be more exemplary than definitive; my primary concern here is not with the content of normality but with normality as a social and psychical function. In saying that this is also one of opera's primary concerns, I may risk seeming to reinvent the clichés that declare opera to be a uniquely extravagant, incredible, or artificial art form. At the same time—though my sympathies make this a far happier risk—I may seem to ally myself with recent reevaluations that take operatic extravagance as a medium of resistance to social and sexual norms.[1] Both the clichés and the reevaluations, however, assume the prior existence of a stable, effective, unquestioned normality, the referent of both enforcement and resistance. It is precisely in *not* making that assumption that my own effort begins. Following Michel Foucault, I regard the device of the norm and the associated concept of normality not as elements intrinsic to all social organization, but as historically specific formations.[2] My suggestion is that opera, at least since the nineteenth century, has been actively involved in the production of normality, above all of a sexualized and engendered normality, as a mechanism of social regulation. Opera's distinction is that it openly, perhaps even compulsively, seeks to do what most other cultural and social practices seek unsuccessfully to avoid: opera, that is, puts normality into question in the very act of helping to produce it by various combinations of enforcement and resistance.

My aim in what follows is to offer some reflections on this process that will contribute to an understanding of its specificities, both historical and theoretical. These reflections will be discontinuous, nonlinear, and antimimetic—in other words, deconstructive. First, however, I will have to reflect a little on the possibilities of such reflection itself, both in general and in relation to recent musicological efforts to think about opera in terms of gender and sexuality. That done, I will return to opera proper—or improper, oblique to the proper in every sense of the term—and try to convey two or three things I know about her. Three things, actually, each of which emerges from a different scene in which opera is construed. The scenes depend, successively, on images, interviews, and vignettes from the world of nineteenth-century normality and abnormality. In the first, Walt

Whitman listens; in the second, Sigmund Freud reads; in the third, Hagen sings a song.

PRELUDE

Before the curtain rises, though, Derrida has to write. In *Positions,* a book collecting several of the interview transcripts by which he loves to reduce speech, literally, to writing, Derrida outlines what he calls "a double gesture" through which deconstruction must pass and continually re-pass. An extended quotation will be necessary here:

> On the one hand, we must traverse a phase of *overturning.* To do justice to this necessity is to recognize that in a classical philosophical opposition we are not dealing with the peaceful coexistence of a *vis-a-vis,* but rather with a violent hierarchy. . . . To deconstruct the opposition, first of all, is to overturn the hierarchy at a given moment. To overlook this phase of overturning is to forget the conflictual and subordinating structure of opposition. Therefore one might proceed too quickly to a *neutralization* that *in practice* would leave the previous field untouched. . . . We know what have always been the *practical* (particularly *political*) effects of *immediately* jumping *beyond* oppositions, and of protests in the simple form of *neither* this *nor* that. . . . On the other hand, to remain in this phase is still to operate . . . from within the deconstructed system. . . . we must also mark the interval between inversion, which brings low what was high, and the irruptive emergence of a new "concept," a concept that can no longer be, and never could be, included in the previous regime.[3]

Derrida notoriously offers a surplus of names for "the irruptive emergence of a new 'concept,'" but the one he favors in *Positions* is "dissemination," which he characterizes as "an irreducible and *generative* multiplicity" of meanings (45).

I will shortly suggest that the course of musicological efforts to conceptualize the place of gender and sexuality in opera has so far corresponded to Derrida's double gesture, but without fully realizing the disseminal character of the second phase. The reason for this new gap or interval (it is in no sense a failure) is that the disseminal phase does not constitute a unified field—as, on its own terms, it ought not to do. A deconstructive reading of Derrida's full text would suggest that his disseminal phase incorporates a double gesture of its own, a second double gesture that recapitulates the original movement from overturning to dissemination.

On the one hand, Derrida outlines what we might call a phase of mixture, in which an opposition breaks down when it encounters a concept it cannot assimilate. The result is to scramble and conjoin the terms that the opposition is meant to keep separate. Mixture is marked by the appearance of "undecidables": terms that "inhabit" an opposition without belonging to it and "*without ever* constituting a third term" by which the opposition could be resolved dialectically (43). The best known of these undecidables is *différance:* the movement through which the elements of "language, or any code, any system of referral in general" enter into the interrelationships of difference and deferral by which, and by which alone, they become meaningful. The movement of *différance* is wayward, unsimple, constantly "enmeshed in [a] work that pulls it through a chain of other 'concepts,' other 'words,' other textual configurations" (40). Yet it is not purely contingent because the production of difference and deferral is unremitting. Any classical opposition is inhabited by something that "indicates that each of [its putatively self-standing] terms must appear as the *différance* of the other, as [itself] the other different and deferred."[4] Opera, as it happens, furnishes a fine example in the classical form of its conjuncture of words and music. As Avital Ronell observes, "In the demand that their encounter make sense, opera figures the irreducible difference between words and music. Language, for its part, is left a little emptied by the encounter, for it discovers that it can never hear itself unless music plays the other of itself. . . . [But] music finds in language that it has been critically denied access to saying what it means."[5]

On the other hand, Derrida envisions a phase in which the terms dislocated by mixture enter into a pure conceptual mobility, an unbounded generativity from which previously unsuspected meanings proliferate. At a certain point (Derrida simply invokes a floating "then"), "the operator of generality named *dissemination* insert[s] itself into the open chain" of undecidables. In contrast to the phase of mixture, which is said to produce resistance and disorganization within a conceptual field, the more radical phase of dissemination "*explode*[s] the semantic horizon." Dissemination is even glossed as, in effect, the *différance* of *différance* itself: it is "seminal *différance*" (*Positions,* 44–45).

It seems fair to say that the phase of overturning was ushered into opera criticism by feminist critique. Catherine Clément's *Opera, or the Undoing of Woman* treated opera as a form grounded, not in the transcendence of shoddy librettos by beautiful music, but in the use of beautiful music to glamorize the suffering and death of women. Susan McClary's *Feminine Endings* grounded the operatic representation of madwomen in the need to control a fascinating but threatening feminine excess.[6] The trouble with this phase is that its work is initially hard to do, but once done, all too easy to do over. The result is a certain impatience with new readings. "Yes," it's tempting to say, "we know this, it's all very true, but there must be something else," meaning, of course, something more important. But what is important is to resist this temptation. As Derrida suggests, "It is not a question . . . of a page that one day simply will be turned, in order to go on to other things. . . . The time for overturning is never a dead letter" (41–42). There is, indeed, something more, if not more important, to occupy us about Norma, say, or Brünnhilde, than their suffering and death. But like witches, Norma and Brünnhilde still burn.

As to the phase of mixture, we can find it represented both in work that traces out the nexus of opera and homosexuality and in work that expands and complicates the initial impetus of feminist critique. On the queer side, we can point to studies of the gay appropriation of opera; Wayne Koestenbaum's anthology of "queer moments" in *The Queen's Throat* comes immediately to mind, as does Mitchell Morris's work on opera queens. There are also studies of gay and lesbian appropriation in, and sometimes by, opera, as in Philip Brett's readings of Britten or Elizabeth Wood's of Ethyl Smyth.[7] On the feminist side, there are studies that dwell not only on opera's undoing of women but also on opera's resistance to that undoing, a resistance that is characteristically present in the very work of undoing itself. Here we might point to McClary's work on *Carmen*, Ralph Locke's on *Samson and Delilah,* and my own on *Elektra* and *Salome,*[8] the last of which—notwithstanding the best efforts of Carolyn Abbate, who polemically flattens it into an account of "patriarchal meltdown"—explicitly tries to theorize the historical and critical necesssity of mixture.[9] Speaking generally, this phase justifies both Derrida's emphasis on resistance and disorganization and Michel Foucault's celebrated axiom, "Where there is power, there is resistance"[10]—always remembering, however, that where there is resistance, there is power. Above all, perhaps, mixture is the phase of an ambivalence that cannot, and should not, be overcome. It is an ambivalence that must be *practiced*.

That leaves us with dissemination—but the phase of dissemination has not yet arrived. For a glimpse of what it might look like, I offer, in a spirit of exploration, my three scenes with Whitman, Freud, and Wagner. What we might hope for from this phase is a movement above, though not beyond, the interplay of power and resistance, and an attitude free, though not forgetful, of ambivalence. This movement, however, neither promises nor seeks closure, only some new ways to open a conceptual field.

FIRST SCENE: WALT WHITMAN LISTENS

Whitman's favorite music was serious Italian opera, and he cheerfully admits that his taste for it is perversely erotic. When he lists his favorite scenes in "Proud Music of the Storm," nearly all of them turn out to involve despairing love and impending death. His response typically combines a voyeuristic fascination with erotically charged details and a masochistic identification with someone in anguish:

I see poor crazed Lucia's eyes' unnatural gleam,
Her hair down her back falls loose and dishevel'd.

I see where Ernani walking the bridal garden,
Amid the scent of night-roses, radiant, holding his
    bride by the hand,
Hears the infernal call, the death pledge of the horn.

$$(ll.78–82)^{11}$$

At their peak, these erotic responses fuse into an orgasmic sense of being filled, physically penetrated, by the operatic voice from which "passionate heart-chants [and] sorrowful appeals" (l.43) stream forth. This is from *Song of Myself:*

I hear the violoncello ('tis the young man's
    heart's complaint),
I hear the key'd cornet, it glides quickly in
    through my ears,
It shakes mad-sweet pangs through my belly and
    breast.

I hear the chorus, it is a grand opera,
Ah this indeed is music—this suits me.

A tenor large and fresh as the creation fills me,
The orbic flex of his mouth is pouring and filling
    me full.

$$(ll.596–601)$$

Opera thus seems to be the medium in which Whitman's sexuality achieves its greatest clarity and intensity. It is not that opera reflects his sexuality, or feeds his sexuality, but rather that it *becomes* his sexuality. In particular, Whitman's way of listening to mournful bel canto song gives him access to certain kinds of pleasure that he otherwise feels compelled to deny to his textual body.[12]

In the passage about the tenor from *Song of Myself,* the pleasure is homosexual, in particular a pleasure suggestive of anal penetration; note the chain of associations leading from the young man's heart's complaint, through the cornet singled out by its phallic key, to the gliding-in that shakes transgressive pangs through belly and breast. (The identification between the ear, traditionally the most spiritual of orifices, and the anus, traditionally the most corporeal, fulfils erotically a claim that Whitman has made rhetorically earlier in the poem: "I keep as delicate around the bowels as around the head and heart" [520].) When the tenor appears, his voice supplies the loving same-sex body, large and fresh, by which the listener is filled. It is even possible that a particular tenor role is the latent origin of this sequence. The identification of the young man's heart's complaint with the sound of a cello suggests the conjunction of a solo cello with Edgardo's dying lament in the final scene of *Lucia di Lammermoor*. The scene is one that focuses intense sympathy on the suffering young man through an on-stage group of male onlookers, and in this respect it may form what for Whitman is the Ur-scene, or primal scene, of operatic pleasure.[13]

Where the singer is a woman, the parallel pleasure is a lachrymose sentimentality that draws the poet into a posture of abjection. The focus of this sentimentality is motherhood; for Whitman, the diva is always maternal, even if she is singing *Lucia*. Consider, for example, "The Singer in the Prison," an embarrassing poem by latter-day standards but by the same token a revealing one. Here Whitman commemorates a concert he may have attended at Sing Sing, where a famous diva, flanked by "a little child on either hand," supposedly reduced an audience of hardened convicts to "deep, half-stifled sobs, the sound of bad men bow'd and moved to weeping, / And youth's convulsive breathings, memories of home, / The mother's voice in lullaby, the sister's care, the happy childhood" (44–46). As they often do in nineteenth-century texts, the spasmodic sobs and tears form the basis of a publicly sanctioned mode of hysteria.[14] Their presence allows a convulsive eroticism to appear as edifying moral grief, the ultimate reference for which is the childhood innocence preserved (only) in the image of the mother. (Consistent with the masochistic pleasure it incites, that image is sometimes slightly detached or cold.[15] The diva in Sing Sing is a "large calm lady" who "vanish[es] with her children in the dusk" immediately after her performance.) What Whitman adds to this cult of the *mater dolorosa* is the location of its eroticism in the operatic sound of the mourning maternal voice "Pouring in floods of melody in tones so pensive sweet and strong the like whereof was never heard" (3). The voice in this role counts as what Jacques Lacan calls the object a: the object and cause of a desire that only exists insofar as it can never be satisfied.[16]

The operatic passage from *Song of Myself* supplies the (fantasmatic) origin of the scenario in "The Singer in the Prison" when a soprano takes the place of the tenor. Combined with or dissolving into the orchestra, the female voice gives pleasure by wrenching Whitman away from his usual sense of identity and throwing him figuratively from planetary to oceanic space with casual and cruel omnipotence. The music is less something he hears than something he swallows; he feels it in his throat like a sob or a gasp or the classic *globus hystericus*, as lacerating and smothering as it is ecstatic:

> I hear the train'd soprano (what work with hers is
>   this?)
> The orchestra whirls me wider than Uranus flies,
> It wrenches such ardors from me I did not know I

> possess'd them,
> It sails me, I dab with bare feet, they are lick'd
>   by the indolent waves,
> I am cut by bitter and angry hail, I lose my
>   breath,
> Steep'd amid honey'd morphine, my windpipe
>   throttled in fakes of death.
>
> (ll.603–8)

The "honey'd morphine" sugggests the satiation of the infant "steeped" in the mother's breast that soothes away all bitter and angry wounds. The "indolent" waves licking the poet's bare feet present the same suggestion from a reverse perspective. (Mother Music tends you from head to foot, bathing and nourishing; like the singer in the prison, she goes with her children everywhere.) But music as honey'd (mellifluous?) heal-all is also music as sweetened poison. It must register as poisonous because by reducing Whitman to a helpless, preverbal state, it doubly suspends his subjectivity. It gags him both as a speaking subject and as a poetic voice. Traces of this gagging carry over, together with traces of bliss, into the verses that describe both. The images of steeping and throttling press back on the rhyming exhalations of "breath" and "death" that enfold them; the sighing vowel sounds of "steep'd amid honey'd morphine" adjoin the plosive-glottal bolus of "pipe throttled."[17]

Although Whitman is genuinely absorbed in (and by) the maternal image, his receptivity to male "tremulousness" is even more acute. This is how "Proud Music of the Storm" evokes a beloved scene from Donizetti's *La Favorite:*

> From Spanish chestnut trees' dense shade,
> By old and heavy convent walls a wailing song,
> Song of lost love, the torch of youth and life
>   quench'd in despair,
> Song of the dying swan, Fernando's heart is
>   breaking.
>
> (ll.86–89)

This vignette is striking for the undisguised purity by which it transcibes erotic pain as erotic pleasure, a pleasure conveyed viscerally in the hypnotic rhythms grouped around the word "song." Even more striking is the surge of syntactic distortion; the coherence of the passage as a statement collapses under the pressure of its urgency as a rhythmic event. Instead of producing the "normal" effect of poetic speech, the illusion that a referential transparency has fused seamlessly with a rhythmic impulse, this passage appears less as reference than as substance, a material manifestation of the poet's pleasure. It becomes a dab of honey'd morphine.

For Slavoj Žižek, this kind of passage constitutes what he calls a "phallic anamorphosis."[18] In other words, it is a structural deformity—a blot, stain, or nub—that "sticks out" of the work in which it appears. Except for the quibble on "sticks out," the phallic character of the blot has nothing to do with male anatomy. Žižek uses the term *phallus* in a strict Lacanian sense to refer to "a signifier without a signified." The effect of this opaque signifier is one of simultaneous discovery and concealment. The lack of the signified endows the text with mysterious depths of meaning—the very depths, so to speak, in which the signified has been lost. The opacity of the signifier marks the site of this loss and blocks all attempts to plumb the depths with certainty. As if on a perverse treasure map, the signifier is the spot that marks an X.

Lacan calls this "master signifier" the phallus by analogy to the Oedipal prohibition that both awakens and punishes primary desires. Whitman, however, is not a strict Lacanian. In producing the phallic anamorphosis, he also reunites the phallic function to an idealized image of the virile body, in particular the tenor's body. In the passage on *La Favorite,* this reunion becomes evident in the traditional phallic image of the torch, which, though quenched for the fictitious Fernando, is reignited in the tenor's torch song. All the verses need to do is sing along. Instead of seeking to plumb the depths of the mystery produced by the blot, Whitman simply enjoys the blot as substance, as fluidic pulsation, by linking it to a homo-erotic fantasy. In another poem, "The Dead Tenor," he even more explicitly juxtaposes the tenor voice as pulsating erotic substance, "So firm—so liquid-soft— . . . that tremulous, manly timbre!" with the same voice as the signifier of an indecipherable "lesson" that constitutes "[the] trial and test of all."

For Whitman, this combination advances the social experiment of American democracy by identifying cultural work, not with the repression or sublimation of sexuality, but with its channeling, the creation of a national circulatory system for the fluid dyamics of desire. As a sexual politics, this program requires the affirmation of both heterosexual love and the cult of maternity. Cultural supremacy, however, belongs to a specific form of homosexuality, the masochistic reception of the tenor voice.

The channeling of this sexuality is realized most complexly in the passage quoted earlier from *Song of Myself*:

> A tenor large and fresh as creation fills me,
> The orbic flex of his mouth is pouring and filling
>   me full.

$$(ll.601-2)$$

Another anamorphosis here: these lines compel special attention because on the surface they make so little sense. The tenor is not a piece of fountain statuary spouting water at the mouth. Nonetheless, it is the music pouring from the tenor's mouth that fills the poet full, and that corresponds to the earlier phallic gliding of the key'd cornet. At one level, the equation of the music with a kind of penetrating fluid is probably literal. Whitman was a believer in animal magnetism, and what he is recording here is probably the sensation of having his body charged (literally "thrilled") by an influx of electrical fluid.[19] Emitted from the tenor's mouth, the fluid passes as from a mesmerist to his subject, completing the charismatic circle of magnetic treatment. This process was often represented as having a phallic character. What allows it to act phallically for Whitman, however, is once again the overlay of a penile fantasy on the phallic nub. The imagistic blend of orbic flexing with pouring and filling endows the music with the "firm— . . . liquid-soft" character that grounds Whitman's homosexual desire. At its height, the operatic experience becomes an encounter in which two men, without touching each other except in the magnetic medium, come together in their "pensive" sadness and—come together.

SECOND SCENE: SIGMUND FREUD READS

Shortly before the end of the nineteenth century, one of Freud's patients, described in *The Interpretation of Dreams* as "a young man with strong homosexual leanings, which were . . . inhibited in real life," dreamed the following dream:

> He was attending a performance of *Fidelio*, and was sitting in the stalls at the opera beside L., a man who was congenial to him and with whom he would have liked to make friends. Suddenly he flew through the air right across the stalls, put his hand in his mouth and pulled out two of his teeth.[20]

The young man added shamefacedly that "the state of sensual excitement provoked by his [frustrated] desire" for a similar "friend" had once led him to masturbate twice in rapid succession. We can surmise that he acted twice in order to stage the masturbation as mutual, once on behalf of his own body, once on behalf of the absent body of his "friend." The young man, it turns out, had never made love to anyone, male or female, and "pictured sexual intercourse on the model of . . . masturbation." Freud, who can take a sexual hint, located the dream's transciption of this double masturbation in the pulling out of two teeth. He adds that the same action also gives a double visual form to a German slang expression for masturbation, *sich einen ausreissen*, "to pull one out."

But why set this scene at the opera? And why at *Fidelio* in particular? Freud's answer depends on noticing a small textual adventure. The finale of the opera contains a joyous phrase, "Wer ein holdes Weib errungen" (He who has won a lovely wife), lifted from Schiller's "Ode to Joy"; the same phrase thus also occurs in the finale of Beethoven's Ninth Symphony. What makes this important is that the young man described his feeling of flight as one of being "thrown" (*geworfen*) in the air, and that the key phrase in the symphony is immediately preceded there by another one:

> Wer der grosse Wurf errungen,
> Eines Freundes Freund zu sein
> [He who has won the great throw
> To be the friend of a friend].

On this reading, the dream identifies the young man's masturbatory scene as the "great throw" of homosexual love. Freud adds that this image of the throw is ambivalent. On the one hand, the throw represents rejection, the feeling of being "thrown out," and repeats in symbolic form the dreamer's compensatory act of double masturbation in the friend's absence. On the other hand, the throw fantasizes a blissful fulfillment of the dreamer's homosexual desire. We might even add that it fulfills his specific wish for a mutual masturbatory consummation—to pull *two* out, eines *Freundes Freund* zu sein.[21]

At this point Freud stops, but if we want to know something about opera we have to go further. When the young man displaces material from the Ninth Symphony into *Fidelio,* he sexualizes the social relationship of male friendship. The logic of the dream suggests a pair of complementary motives for this process.

First, the opera provides a compelling parallel to the dream's image of a bliss that becomes mutual by dividing into two identical parts. Florestan and Leonore find such a bliss in the duet, "O Namenlose Freude!" which is in every sense the climax of *Fidelio.* The peculiar quality of a self-twinning pleasure is figured not only in the intertwining and echoing of Leonore's and Florestan's voices, but also in their very articulation of the key phrase: "O namen-, namenlose Freude!" Even more important in this context, however, is the duet's *visual* doubling. The fact is so obvious that no one makes anything of it, but the duet is a drag scene: although what we *hear* is Florestan and Leonora, what we *see* is Florestan and the cross-dressed Fidelio, a man and a youth. In the "nameless joy" of this couple, Freud's dreamer may well have found an image of his own "unspeakable" desire.

That image, moreover—and here the second motive emerges—is an altogether idealized one, the very nucleus of a redeemed community as the opera presents it. In "real life," the young man found his desires shameful, but there is no trace of shame in his dream. With his great throw, he visualizes the literal uplifting, the sublimation, of his desires onto the edifying plane of Beethoven's music, and especially onto the super-idealistic plane of the Ninth Symphony. The displacement from the Ninth to *Fide-*

lio is a way of affirming that operatic sexual crossovers carry their own idealism, and that male friendship can freely be sexualized without losing its ideal character.

But the dream also contradicts this affirmation in a startling way. The dreamer appears in the act of masturbation when he puts his hand in his mouth and pulls out two teeth; but he also appears, proleptically, as the actual substance that "takes flight" from the "great throw" of the masturbatory climax. In other words, the dream identifies the young man with his own semen. What's more, it propels him, in that form, "right across the stalls," which is to say that it propels him right toward the adjacent orchestra pit and stage. It is literally *toward the opera,* and away from his friend in the stalls, that the dreamer-as-semen is traveling. Only by marking the opera with this sign and substance of his desire can he hope to gratify that desire. Only, it seems, by thus defiling and adhering to the opera can he render himself visible to his friend as an object of mutual desire, as Florestan is to Fidelio, and vice versa.

This aspect of the dream is obviously an index of the young man's desperation, and as such it demands an empathetic response. It may, however, also picture a recognition of something distinctive to opera. It is worth noting that although both Freud's interpretation and mine make reference to specific scenes in *Fidelio,* the dream does not. The young man as semen-subject is actually thrown toward the *locus of opera as such,* regardless of what appears there at a given moment. This perplexing gesture makes the most sense if we interpret the semen, not primarily as the bodily fluid produced by a particular sexual act, but as a representative of the adhesive quality of sexual desire in general—of what Whitman called "the fluid and attaching character" and Freud, of course, called libido. In a more recent formulation, Jacques Lacan characterizes the libido as an imaginary bodily organ he calls the "lamella" or "l'hommelette."[22] The latter term means both "omelette" and "little feminine man"; Lacan offers it as a witty play on Plato's myth that human beings were originally egg-shaped androgynes who were only later divided into the two sexes. Lacan, knowing how to make a good French omelette, also knows how to capture the floating, insistent, sometimes queasy character that desire assumes when imagined or intuited apart from its objects. He simply breaks some eggs:

> Let us imagine it, a large crepe moving about like the amoeba, ultra-flat for passing under doors, omniscient in being led by pure instinct, immortal in being scissiparous. Here is something you would not like to feel creeping over your face, silently while you are asleep, in order to seal it up.[23]

Isn't it possible that what is thrown toward the opera in the dream of Freud's young man is not something proper to the dreamer's body but the adhesive substance of *l'hommelette?* And since the throw targets no specific scene, but only the operatic conjuncture of music and drama, orchestra pit and stage, wouldn't it be possible to see in the throw a recognition that opera is always already the site of *l'hommelette,* always already covered at every point of its surface with the substance of desire?

Perhaps when Ernst Kurth described the harmonies of *Tristan und Isolde* as forming "a light, thin, and extraordinarily sensitive film,"[24] he recognized unawares not only the erotic substance Wagner produced by breaking a twinned subjectivity into a musical *hommelette,* but also the libidinal substance of opera in general. The singularity of this substance in *Tristan* is simply that the harmonies make it more humid, so that it gets in the listener's face more than usual.

THIRD SCENE: HAGEN SINGS A SONG

No one ever has a good word to say for Hagen. Most dramatic villains elicit at least a twinge of human sympathy; not this one. Hagen is more like Iago than like Shylock, both of whom he resembles in important ways. He is so awful that when he treats Alberich with contempt we even feel sorry for the old wretch with his plaintive refrain of "Hagen, my son." Besides, Hagen wreaks havoc not only dramatically but also musically, smearing blots and croaks across the texture of *Götterdämmerung* with his snarling basso profundo. He even has the chutzpah to interfere with the sublimity of the final conflagration by shouting "Hands off the ring!" (Zurück vom Ring!).

One has to admire Wagner's ingenuity with Hagen: this monster is hateful for what he does, not what he is, but there is no way to keep the two apart. And what is Hagen but the archetypal half-caste degenerate of nineteenth-century racialist anti-Semitism? Not a Jew in any literal sense, he is the object of cultural phobia that Jews are imagined to embody: the other who is not quite other enough, the Sigismund by which every son of Siegmund is shadowed.[25] Hagen is the half-assimilated pariah whose very existence bespeaks a contamination of once-pure bloodlines. He is the parasite who feeds on the virtues of a nobler but more vulnerable breed whose weaknesses he draws out with his superior, amoral cunning. You can tell, once again, by the baseness of his voice.

But perhaps the very virulence of this portrait should prompt us to give Hagen his due: "Stand up for bastards!" to call on Shakespeare again. After all, Hagen is the only character in *Götterdämmerung* who is absolutely true to himself, if to no one else. His integrity, however malign, may be more palatable than Gunther's tortured *ressentiment,* Gutrune's abject wheedling, and even Siegfried's tedious vanity. Only Brünnhilde's rage rivals Hagen's mania in purity—but Hagen is not engaged in self-betrayal as Brünnhilde is, and besides, the rage and the mania both have the same outcome: the spear in Siegfried's back.

The core of Hagen's purity is his absolute lack of sexuality. Alberich may have renounced love, but Hagen alone lacks desire—lacks it, indeed, with no sense of lacking anything. His intent to possess the ring is not even fetishistic; it is more like an empty placeholder, a purely formal function of his purely abstract integrity—just something, as he tells Alberich, that he has sworn to himself. Hagen's dark voice marks the void left behind where desire has been abolished.

It is no wonder, then, that when Hagen wants to round up some wedding guests he does so in the form of a call to arms. On learning that Siegfried, in Gunther's form, has come home after abducting Brünnhilde from her rock, and that she and Gunther are near, Hagen takes the stage by himself. Perched on a high rock of his own, he summons the Gibichung vassals with striking vehemence:

> Hoiho! Hoihohoho!
> Ihr Gibichsmannen, machet euch auf!
> Wehe! Wehe! Waffen! Waffen!
> Waffen durchs Land! Gute Waffen!
> Starke Waffen, scharf zum Streit!
> Not is da! Not! Wehe! Wehe!
> Hoiho! Hoihohoho!

This call deserves some reflection. It constitutes the one moment in the opera when Hagen "lets himself go" expressively, and baleful as it is, it is compelling, too. With the fate of the others in his grasp, Hagen sings a song. The "Hoihho, Hoihohoho" with which he frames his call has a saturnine jauntiness to it, a sunless exuberance that, just for a moment, can become infectious. It is certainly infectious for the orchestra, which reponds by overlaying the grinding bass geared to Hagen's voice with brassy outbursts and turbulent flourishes. In the swirling music of this scene, Hagen already enjoys possession of the ring of power, though he doesn't know it.

Hagen's song is yet another phallic anamorphosis, another blot that produces deep truths by seeming to distort their appearance. Why give stage time to the trivial act of calling the vassals? And why should Hagen himself stage the call as such a charade? He otherwise conducts his villainy with exquisite economy; the ham-handed joke of his wedding call is superfluous. We might say that his lack of desire hobbles him here by acting something like autism. Hagen can name desire but not comprehend it, so his invitation to a wedding flips over into a war whoop. Belligerence is something he does comprehend, or at least knows how to mimic. But the music of this scene bespeaks grotesque power, not blustering automatism. We are meant to remember the power when Hagen later uses his plangent "Hoiho" motive to prefigure the announcement of Siegfried's death. What the music of this scene says is that Hagen is telling the truth when he cries out that danger is coming. It *is* coming—and coming in the form of Gunther's bride.

Hagen's erotic autism, then, acts in this scene not as a lack but as a positive force or presence. As such, and strictly following the logic of the blot that both demands and resists interpretation, the autism points beyond Hagen himself to the other characters. They, after all, not he, are the ones who swirl in currents of lust, envy, delusion, jealousy, and rage. Hagen is simply *their* phallus, a kind of golem pieced together from the rejected pieces of *their* desires.

Chief among these pieces is Siegfried's desire for Brünnhilde, which is supposedly cloaked by Hagen's magic potion. In slightly anachronistic terms: when Siegfried accepts this drink from his new hosts, he acquires a repressed desire; he becomes a Freudian neurotic. This formula is the outcome of a symbolic one, according to which Hagen's potion (like its counterpart in *Tristan und Isolde*) only does what its victim wants; the "symbol" becomes most revealing when it is understood with the greatest literalness. On these terms, what Siegfried wants is to shift his desire for Brünnhilde onto a more conventional mate. This change of heart has nothing to do with the mimetic plausibility it so obviously defies; instead it represents the position that Siegfried must occupy to enter the social order of the Gibichungs, an order constituted by kinship alliance, the homosocial bonds of blood-brotherhood, and "normal" heterosexuality, the pivot on which all else turns. Hagen's potion in effect accelerates the process by which desire becomes socialized; the heavy-handedness of the symbolism exposes the machinery of normalization, the coerciveness of what Lacan would call the symbolic order. (Siegfried, victim of a Dickensian childhood, enters that order belatedly; hence the hurry.)

Like Hagen's "autism," Siegfried's lack of desire for Brünnhilde is not just a negativity, but a destructive force. The object of hostility is, of course, the former object of desire, whose presence at the desire's point of origin almost has the power to reawaken it. Siegfried's rejection of this reawakening fuels the cruelty of his actions. When Siegfried-as-Gunther reenters the ring of magic fire that once mirrored his desire and protected it from the world, Brünnhilde asks him who he is. His voice falters as he replies; the voice he assumes, deeper than his own ("dann redet er mit verstellter— tieferer—Stimme an")—the voice in which he hears Gunther but in which we can hear Hagen—quavers a moment ("mit etwas bebender Stimme beginnend"). Just for that moment, Siegfried's surly Gunther-music catches in his throat. The words that would reawaken desire are on the tip of his tongue. No matter: it is too late for old flames.

The sheer strangeness of the love between Siegfried and Brünnhilde helps make sense of this outcome. At the end of *Siegfried,* the couple achieves a sexual consummation that the music tells us is unparalleled. But no sooner has Siegfried loved Brünnhilde than both agree (in the Prologue to *Götterdämmerung*) that he has to leave her. His love for her constitutes a heroic ideal; it is meant to guide his conduct as an image, not to constrain him by domestic or sexual demands. Although Siegfried's relationship to Brünnhilde is consummated by a sexual act, it is not a sexual relationship. Only Gutrune offers him that. Torn between these women, Siegfried suffers from a particularly subtle and perplexed form of the infamous nineteenth-century division of all women into either objects of love or objects of desire. In seizing Brünnhilde for Gunther, he is trying to choose desire over love. But he can do that only if he violates the bond of love with the maximum of brutality. That is why the abduction scene assumes a ritualistic, quasi-sacrificial form, crowned by a piercing scream from Brünnhilde and her collapse "like something shattered" ("Sie schreit heftig auf . . . sie wie zerbrochen in seinen Armen niedersinkt"). And that is why the music of the scene is so full of gloating malevolence; the ponderous fanfares of heavy brass, pretending to judicial gravity, are Hagen's serenade. The violent two-note figure that punctuatues the end of the scene even bears comparison to Hagen's "Hoiho." Deep-voiced and false-faced, Siegfried is Hagen's mouthpiece here. Yet Hagen, through this mouthpiece, once again speaks the truth. Siegfried's abuse of Brünnhilde is the positive, aggressive form of his disavowed desire for her. In that form it will feed his garden-variety desire for Gutrune, to whom he will boast about his exploit when he gets home. It's a kind of foreplay.[26]

Poor Siegfried: he can't hold on to the phallus because his penis keeps getting in the way. Even after his marriage, he is tempted by the charms of the Rhinemaidens like Alberich before him. Except in the dragon- and fire-business, he is really a very ordinary fellow. His charisma can be restored only through his death—only, indeed, through his corpse: by the unknown power that raises his dead fist to keep the ring from Hagen's grasp, by the mourning community brought into being through the orchestra's funeral music, and above all by Brünnhilde with her heart and voice set on immolation. By comparison, Siegfried's own self-restoration in his dying moments is a smallish thing. Yet it is not a contemptible thing. In its own way, as Siegfried once again chooses love over desire, heroic truth over social fabrication, and as the orchestra wraps him in a shroud of lyricism, his death is a kind of minor *Liebestod*.

CURTAIN

In the readings offered here, these constructions of opera by Whitman, Freud's patient, and something in Wagner—it is not quite Wagner himself—all tend to support the same conclusion. Let me approach a first formulation by recalling Godard. In exposing the relation of prostitution to bourgeois luxury, *Two or Three Things I Know about Her* employs a classic technique of unmasking by which the abnormal is shown to be the hidden truth of the normal. Opera, in contrast, suspends the difference between the normal and abnormal, so that the two terms can neither supply each other's truth nor fail to do so.

In order to make this point more rigorously, I will frame it twice more, first deconstructively, then psychoanalytically. First, then, opera suspends the difference between the normal and the abnormal by presenting each of these terms as always already enmeshed in the movement of *différance*, always already the trace of a presence "that dislocates itself, displaces itself, refers itself [elsewhere]" en route to the semantic "explosion" of dissemination (24). Opera, indeed, opens up something that Derrida regards as impossible, a veritable "kingdom of *différance*" (22). For Derrida, *différance* is "definitively exempt from every process of presentation by means of which we would call upon it to show itself in person" (20). It never becomes perceptible in itself, but only in textual traces. Opera seems bent on revoking this limitation. Its *différance* appears materially, seductively, in and as the bodily interplay between singing voice, instrumental envelope, and receptive ear.

Second, opera suspends the difference between the normal and the abnormal by suspending the "deeper" differences supposed to ground this proximate one: the differences between policing and transgressing, edification and debasement, the symbolic and the imaginary, eros and the death drive. One consequence, already implicit throughout this essay, is that opera constitutively undermines its own aesthetic pretensions. Opera is always in danger of being exposed as a purveyor of what Freud called the "forepleasure" that screens fantasy;[27] opera as high art continually risks being reduced to an alibi for the practical art of psychosexual equivocation.

In response, we might look for evidence to support the alibi; some alibis, after all, are true. But we might also choose to believe our ears. We might recognize opera as part of a historical project that required the *ingredients* of aesthetic pretension and forepleasure, alibi and equivocation, regardless of how they fit together in any given case. Among recent critical theorists, Philippe Lacoue-Labarthe has emphasized the persistence of opera's quasi-sacramental aesthetic from the Florentines through Wagner and beyond, while Slavoj Žižek and Avital Ronell have emphasized the parallel persistence of irreducible difference, both within operatic subjectivity and in the "broken contract" between music and language.[28] These disparate insights are bound together by their common concern with the process of "binding" itself. Opera, on this reading, would register both an urgent and historically specific need for such binding, as if, in the age of opera, human subjectivity had somehow come undone. The most familiar name for that coming undone, a name that also applies to widening circles of experience during the age of opera, is modernity. Could it be, then, that opera is part of a broad cultural effort that first crystallizes in the early-modern period and has only recently, if at all, begun to wane? Could opera be part of an effort to deal with a human subjectivity understood—I would say *constructed,* designed to be understood—as a tendency to wander, a potential ab-errance or ab-normality, that becomes intelligible only by means of the techniques meant to regulate it?

Staging the Female Body

RICHARD STRAUSS'S SALOME

LINDA HUTCHEON AND
MICHAEL HUTCHEON, M.D.

AS AN ART FORM, opera has always been self-conscious about singing, despite the fact that, as Carolyn Abbate and others have emphasized, the convention of opera is that the singers are actually deaf to the "music-drowned world" in which they live.[1] The earliest operas—by Peri, Caccini, and Monteverdi—focused on Orpheus, the singing poet, and Wagner's *Tannhäuser* and *Die Meistersinger von Nürnberg* stand as nineteenth-century epitomes of opera about singing. But dance—the body in motion—has also been an important part of opera historically, and was a convention of French opera from the seventeenth century on. In the West, dance has been seen as a representation either of order (baroque and classical ballet, with their emphasis on physical control and discipline) or of madness and possession, excess and transgression (foreign or modern dance).[2] After all, the vocal arias of the dangerous gypsy Carmen are deliberately named after dances—the Seguidilla and the Habañera—and dance was frequently prohibited because both religious and secular authorities recognized and feared its power.

This essay examines one of the most provocative dancers in opera, Richard Strauss's Salome, and, through her, the role of the staged body in late-nineteenth- and early-twentieth-century concepts of social transgression, medical neurosis, and gender empowerment. Strauss's 1905 opera was based on the Oscar Wilde play of the same name (first published in Paris in 1893). It represents the fin-de-siècle, decadent revision of the biblical story of the beautiful (and very young) princess of Judea who dances for the lustful Herod in order to possess—and kiss—the decapitated head of John the Baptist, the object of her newly awakened passion.[3] It was shocking then; it still manages to be so today.[4] However, the critics at the time seem to have found the opera more shocking than the audience at

We would like to thank Erika Reiman and Jill Scott, our research assistants, for their provocative questions, their intellectually satisfying answers, and their fine "bloodhound" research noses. A singular debt of gratitude is due to both Sander Gilman and Ted Chamberlin for their acute critical readings of an earlier draft of this article and their learned suggestions (gratefully accepted) for further readings.

large, who greeted the first performance with thirty-eight curtain calls. There were fifty productions within two years.[5] Wilde's play was originally written in French in 1892 and then translated into English and famously illustrated by Aubrey Beardsley.[6] A production with Sarah Bernhardt was banned in London in 1892, ostensibly for portraying biblical characters on stage, but the play opened in Paris in 1896, the year following Wilde's famous trial and conviction. The German version premiered in 1901 in Breslau and found its perfect audience among the German avant-garde (who saw themselves as the supporters of the artist, persecuted by English law and English aesthetic conservatism): there were one hundred eleven performances in Germany in 1903 and 1904 alone. It was in Berlin at Max Reinhardt's Kleines Theater that Strauss saw the play in Hedwig Lachmann's prose translation (which he would go on to use for the libretto instead of a poetic version prepared by Anton Lindner). When someone at the performance suggested to him that it might make a good opera, he is said to have replied that he was already busy composing it.[7]

The opera he completed a few years later suffered a fate at times not unlike that of Wilde's play: it too was banned, this time, in Vienna (at the state theater) for religious reasons. It had to be bowdlerized in order to play in London, where Sir Thomas Beecham claimed: "we had successfully metamorphosed a lurid tale of love and revenge into a comforting sermon."[8] No synopsis of this decadent plot appeared in the Covent Garden program until 1937. The New York production was closed down by the daughter of J. Pierpont Morgan on moral grounds; the press described it as having a "moral stench."[9] It would appear that the general taboo regarding respect for the bodies of the dead was broken too scandalously by Salome's necrophilic and almost cannibalistic kiss of Jochanaan's lips.[10] In general, though, Wilde's decadent and lyrically lush libretto (even in German translation) contributed to the moral and aesthetic shock response as much as did the powerful, radically new sounds of Strauss's music. Together the narrative, the text, and the music worked to place not so much the *voice* but the *body* of Salome front and center—where the audience members (like Herod) cannot take their eyes off her.

To put this issue briefly in a larger cultural context: the body, says Terry Eagleton, "so obvious, obtrusive a matter as to have been blandly overlooked for centuries—has ruffled the edges of a bloodless rationalist discourse, and is currently *en route* to becoming the greatest fetish of all."[11] Perhaps, but for many the gains seem to outweigh the dangers of fetishism. Elizabeth Grosz, among others, has recently turned our attention to the "somatophobia" of the Christian and Cartesian traditions—their construction of the body as the source of danger to reason.[12] She has taught us that the body is a force to be reckoned with—a lesson that recent work on opera too has been heeding. While it may seem obvious that the staged body is central to any form of theatrical representation,[13] it is the voice—almost a disembodied voice—that has come to dominate discussions of opera, especially since the technological advances in audio recording and radio transmission. In a related move, opera criticism has been dominated by considerations of the music that voice sings—usually separated from the libretto's verbal text and the dramatic staged narrative. Musicologists confidently assert: "It is after all the music that an opera-lover goes to hear."[14] But, speaking for these opera-lovers, at least, we go to *see* as well as hear a performance, and that performance includes a verbal text and a staged dramatic narrative—for which that (admittedly important) music was especially written. Opera is an embodied art form; it is the performers who give it its "phenomenal reality."[15] Indeed, opera owes its undeniable affective power to the overdetermination of the verbal, the visual and the aural—not to the aural alone. And it is specifically the body—the gendered, sexualized body—that will not be denied in staged opera. (Think of the fascination with the castrato.)[16] No matter how much audiophiles may like to forget this, the voice does come from the body. And there are moments—especially in Strauss's *Salome*—when the singer does not sing at all: she dances and the orchestra supports her moving body, not her voice.[17]

The body of Salome was the obsession of late-nineteenth-century European, and especially French, culture.[18] Gustave Flaubert's 1877 story "Hérodias" created, in its portrayal of the sultry but strangely indifferent young dancer, the orientalized type that would so influence his compatriots. This Salome danced "like the priestesses of India, like the Nubians of the cataracts, like the bacchantes of Lydia."[19] Indeed, the body of this exotic dancing princess soon became the subject of operas, poems, stories, plays, sculptures, decorative objects, ballets, films, and paintings.[20] No painter was more obsessed with Salome's body than Gustave Moreau, who left hundreds of oils, watercolors, and drawings as testimony to his fascination.[21] In so doing he anticipated (and in part created) the tastes of a generation of writers, from Jules Laforgue to the young Proust, from Joris-Karl Huysmans to Oscar Wilde.[22] Two of Moreau's paintings from the year 1876 stand out from the others precisely because of Huysmans's immortalizing of them in his novel, *A Rebours* (translated as *Against Nature*). His hero, the dandy Des Esseintes, purchases these works in order to contemplate Salome's charms and dangers. One is an oil painting entitled *Salome Dancing before Herod* (see figure 1). It pictures the princess in an exotic, orientalized setting (copied from the pages of the *Magasin pittoresque*), as described in great and lush detail by Des Esseintes. Curiously, his subsequent depiction of Salome's body puts the static, painted image into motion: "she begins the lascivious dance which is to rouse the aged Herod's dormant senses; her breasts rise and fall, the nipples hardening at the touch

Figure 1. Gustave Moreau, *Salome Dancing before Herod*, 1876, oil on canvas, 56½ × 41¹⁄₁₆. The Armand Hammer Collection, UCLA at the Armand Hammer Museum of Art and Cultural Center, Los Angeles, California.

of her whirling necklaces; the strings of diamonds glitter against her moist flesh" and so on (and it does go on).[23] Of all the painters who had portrayed Salome over the centuries, only Moreau, claims Des Esseintes, has captured "the disquieting delirium of the dancer, the subtle grandeur of the murderess."[24] For this French male, Salome had become more than a biblical character or even a pornographic delight:

> She had become, as it were, the symbolic incarnation of undying Lust, the Goddess of immortal Hysteria, the accursed Beauty exalted above all other beauties by the catalepsy that hardens her flesh and steels her muscles, the monstrous Beast, indifferent, irresponsible, insensible, poisoning, like the Helen of ancient myth, everything that approaches her, everything that sees her, everything that she touches.[25]

He imagines Moreau thinking of "the dancer, the mortal woman, the soiled vessel, ultimate cause of every sin and every crime,"[26] before moving on to contemplate his second possession—a watercolor called *The Apparition*—which disturbs him even more. In this, the head of John the Baptist appears before the dancer who tries, as he puts it, to "thrust away the terrifying vision which holds her nailed to the spot."[27] This Salome upsets him because she is "a true harlot, obedient to her passionate and cruel female temperament; . . . here she roused the sleeping senses of the male more powerfully, subjugated his will more surely with her charms—the charms of a great venereal flower, grown in a bed of sacrilege, reared in a hot-house of impiety."[28]

If that feels a bit overblown (not to say misogynistic) today—in terms of sentiment as much as rhetoric—we need to remind ourselves of two things: first, of the strategic value of exaggeration to the decadent aesthetic, and second, of the astonishing impact of that description on all subsequent representations of Salome, especially that of Oscar Wilde, whose Dorian Gray saw Des Esseintes as prefiguring himself.[29] Huysmans's description of Moreau's paintings has been called the "principal engenderer" of Wilde's *Salomé*.[30] Des Esseintes may have been attracted to Moreau's "hieratic allegories whose sinister quality was heightened by the morbid perspicuity of an entirely modern sensibility," but we are attracted to another allegory suggested by the form (rather than the content) of Moreau's Salome paintings.[31] Art historians have commented on the radical disjunction in Moreau's oil paintings of this period between the large background blocks of color (developed in advance to get the chromatic harmony right) and the superimposed drawing of fine detail, often in India ink.[32] What is striking is that the superimposed detailed drawing does not always coincide with the color blocks: the delicate tracery appears almost independent of the colored form it seems intended to define. We would like to suggest that it was the strange disjunction between this detailed precision and the ill-fitting blocks of color (which offered suggestion rather than definition) that in part provoked the symbolist generation's dedication to his art.

Wilde's play could also be called a symbolist drama, a British esthete's version of what the French writers tried to do in capturing the fleeting, immediate sensations of inner life. This is where an allegorical reading, in the light of Moreau's formal disjunction, becomes possible. Wilde's delicate text is like Moreau's equally delicate India-ink tracery that attempts to cover the canvas surface with a kind of *cloisonné* enamel.[33] The large blocks of unruly color represent, in this allegory, the music Strauss composed for Wilde's text—strong, powerful music that feels at times utterly inappropriate for the delicacy of the libretto. If we were to imagine what a symbolist opera's music should sound like, we should likely think of Debussy's suggestive, evocative music for Maeterlinck's *Pelléas et Mélisande*. Instead, here the subtle, erotic, sophisticated prose of Wilde's translated text contrasts with the often abrasive orchestration, with what have been called its moments of "lewd bestiality" that respond more to the psychological implications than to the actual language of the play's text.[34] However, like Moreau's disjunction of detailed drawing and color blocks, the lack of fit between Wilde's text and Strauss's music is in some ways the very cause of the disturbing power of the work.

Caught trying to reconcile the brutal music and the delicate text, critics are quick to point to this lack of fit—condemning one side or the other, depending on their preferences.[35] Arguably, however, it is the disjunction itself that contributes to the opera's impact in performance. Without Strauss's music, Wilde's play remains an ornate lyric, a ballad—but not, on its own, all that dramatic: it takes the uneasy conjunction—and disjunction—with Strauss's music (astonishing in its "audacity of raw excitement and [at times] extreme compositional crudity"[36]) to make the play into a drama.[37] Strauss's instinct for the theatrical has always been clear, but in *Salome* the music's emphatic and dramatic vocabulary of harmonies, rhythms, and instrumentation often clashes with the luxuriant, voluptuous vocabulary of the verbal text.[38] And when the two opposites come together, as in Moreau's paintings, the power to disconcert lies in their noncoincidence.

There is a direct analogy here with the disjunction within the equally disconcerting character of Salome herself, as she incarnates and embodies on the stage a *psychic* lack of fit that makes her powerful and, finally, terrifying. But she does not begin that way. The Salome we first see on stage is quite different: an attractive, if willful, young girl.[39] Wilde intended his Salomé to be both the embodiment of sensuality and a chaste virgin, and all Strauss did was to accentuate the contradictions.[40] Productions of the opera, though, have tended to emphasize either the virgin or the whore, rather than sustaining the paradox or ambivalence Wilde seems to have intended: the virginal Birgit Nilsson performed differently than the vampish Teresa Stratas.[41] Salome is obviously the typical femme fatale in the long operatic tradition of Carmen, Kundry, Dalilah, and, later, Lulu—the demonic beauty who could lure men to damnation, and therefore aroused in her beholder fear along with attraction, terror along with desire.[42] Traditionally characterized by her almost oppressive physical presence as seductress, the femme fatale usually took on the identity of a historical or mythic character—such as Salome—likely in order to stress the universal or archetypal nature of her appeal.[43] The placement of these women in exotic, often oriental locales offered European audiences not only heightened mystery and complex associations of the physical and the spiritual, but also "easy, imaginative projections of sexual desires."[44]

As a negative, misogynistic version of the "eternal feminine"[45]—but embodying death more than life—the femme fatale was viewed as "deadlier than the male, coolly indifferent or aggressively lethal."[46] But while Salome might well have been, to use Lawrence Kramer's term, "everyone's favorite fin-de-siècle dragon lady," this is a femme fatale with a difference: as Ken Russell captured well in his film, *Salome's Last Dance,* she is an adolescent and a virgin.[47] We only come to see the contradictions as the opera progresses, as her character is unveiled as surely as the famous "Dance of the Seven Veils" reveals her body. But the Salome of the opening is beautiful; she is young; she is an impulsive, spoiled child who must have her own way, a pampered princess who lives very much in her own world, as befits the narcissism of the young.[48] Yet it is this same pubescent girl who develops an obsessive and lethal passion to kiss the lips of Jochanaan (the opera's Germanic-Hebraic name for John the Baptist). Indeed, upon first seeing his body, she sings a most sensual hymn of praise to its beauties that is rare in opera, a genre always ready to talk of love but so reticent when it comes to frank expressions of physical desire.[49] But again, part of the impact—for audiences then and now—derives from the fact that this frankness is articulated by and therefore associated with a chaste, pubescent, female body.

However, it is Jochanaan who first introduces the language of sexuality into the play and libretto: when he comes out of the cistern he begins his tirade against Salome's mother, Herodias, in terms of her sexual misdeeds—from looking at pictures of men to giving herself to Syrian captains and the young men of Egypt and, of course, to the abomination of her incestuous bed (she has wed her husband's half-brother). He then addresses Salome as the daughter of Babylon and Sodom, whose mother has filled the earth with the wine of her lust. It is only after this sexualized attack that Salome herself begins to use sexual and sensual language in her seducing description of Jochanaan. She begins with an extravagant description through biblical similes of the whiteness of his body, of which she says she is enamored ("Ich bin verliebt in deinem Leib")—a description that ends with her request to touch his body ("Lass mich ihn berühren deinen Lieb"). At this point the motif of Herodias echoes in the music, identifying the daughter with the mother's condemned sexuality.[50] Jochanaan's response to Salome is an implicitly sexualized attack on womankind for first bringing evil into the world. This rejection causes Salome to respond with a series of, this time, hideous images of his body—which she now says she hates. The music shifts at this point, offering "disturbingly heterogeneous orchestration, dissonant harmony and more angular vocal lines."[51] Having thus disposed of his white body, Salome turns her attention to his black hair. Her fulsome description and his subsequent rejection are followed, once again, by a revised depiction of his hair as a tangle of black serpents writhing around his neck, prefiguring the Medusa image that the final scene will powerfully evoke, as we shall see. Her attention then becomes fixed on the redness of his mouth, and she concludes her praise by asking to kiss it. His continued rejection of her advances is met with her stubborn will: "Ich will deinen Mund küssen, Jochanaan" (I will kiss your mouth, Jochanaan), she insists.

Gustave Moreau was not alone in seeing in the young, willful Salome a representative of generic Woman—that is, associated at that time with sensuality and unhealthy curiosity.[52] To understand both Salome's appeal to her earliest audiences (as well as the thrilling danger she incarnated), we need to understand the context of gender politics of the time, a time very different from our own. *Then* the medical and social discourses were all too content to reduce women to morally underdeveloped, childlike creatures, and so the dangerous Salome could come to stand, even in her youth, for all women.[53] As Cesare Lombroso articulated rather forcefully in his study of the "female offender" at the end of the nineteenth century: "women are big children: their evil tendencies are more numerous and more varied than men's, but generally remain latent. When they are awakened and excited they produce results proportionately greater."[54] Female libido was therefore taken to be "volatile, capricious, even rampaging . . . inherently dysfunctional, dangerous even."[55] Gender and criminality were clearly connected in fin-de-siècle medical thinking.[56] Nevertheless, the impact of Salome's actual youth is not to be discounted, for it is one of the sides of the psychic paradox that makes her so disturbing. And there was another medicalized discourse at the time that linked "the insanity of puberty" in females to "a destructive tendency" comparable to pugnacity in males.[57]

In addition, female criminal violence came to be directly associated specifically with female menstruation.[58] Control, according to Havelock Ellis, was "physiologically lessened at the menstrual period even in health, while it is much more lessened in the neurotic and imbalanced."[59] Ellis draws here on a longer nineteenth-century tradition of associating pubescent women, menstruation, sexuality, and insanity that is articulated most fully (and relevantly, for Salome's characterization) by Henry Maudsley in *The Physiology and Pathology of Mind:*

> Where the heritage of the insane temperament exists . . . if the individual is placed under conditions of great excitement, or subjected to a severe mental strain, the inherent propensity is apt to display itself in some repulsive act of violence. The great internal disturbance produced in young girls at the time of puberty is well known to be an occasional cause of strange morbid feelings and extraordinary acts; and this is especially the case where the insane temperament exists. In such cases, also, irregularities of menstruation, always apt enough to disturb the mental equilibrium, may give rise to an outbreak of mania, or to extreme moral perversion more afflicting to the patient's friends than mania, because seemingly wilful. The stress of a great disappointment, or any other of the recognised causes of mental disease, will meet with a powerful co-operating cause in the constitutional predisposition.[60]

Indeed, the connecting of insanity to gender, youth, and menstruation is a recurring theme in the medical literature of the nineteenth century.

In this context, the obsession with the moon in both the play and opera takes on a new and sinister meaning beyond even the usual notions of lunacy. The moon's role has been interpreted in many ways: as the favorite lighting for the decadent movement's nocturnal settings, as a symbol of mythic mutability, or even of the feminine extremes of the crone (Hecate) and the virgin (Diana).[61] But the moon's insistent presence here may also symbolically engage that contemporaneous medical discourse of female periodicity following puberty and its physical dangers for others. The moon dominates the stage as the curtain rises; each character who enters looks at it and projects upon it his or her own feelings at that moment—usually feelings related to the body of Salome. As the lovestruck Syrian, Narraboth, admires Salome's physical beauty, the nervous page compares the moon to a woman coming out of a grave ("Wie eine Frau, die aufsteigt aus dem Grab"). Narraboth sees in the moon a small dancing princess, with feet like white doves ("Wie eine kleine Prinzessin, deren Füssen weisse Tauben sind. Man könnte meinen, sie tanzt."). To this the page responds once again, in stark contradiction, that the moon more resembles a dead woman ("Wie eine Frau, die tot ist"). The role of the moon as a psychic screen upon which characters project their desires and anxieties is affirmed as Salome herself enters and admires it in terms of a silver flower that is cool and chaste ("kühl und keusch"), with the beauty of a pure virgin ("einer Jungfrau, die rein geblieben ist"). She will shortly associate the moon's chastity with that of Jochanaan's pale ivory body: "Gewiss ist er keusch wie der Mond." And, indeed, the moon becomes a constant point of reference in her hymn to his bodily beauty.[62] When Herod enters, seeking Salome and arguing with

Herodias who scolds him for staring at her daughter too much, he too ends up looking at the moon, which he sees as a mad drunken woman looking everywhere for lovers ("eine wahnwitziges Weib, das überall nach Buhlen sucht . . . wie ein betrunkenes Weib"). The more down-to-earth Herodias refuses to project, asserting that the moon is like the moon, and that is all it is ("der Mond is wie der Mond, das ist alles").

This constant reference to the moon in a context of lovers, chastity, death, and danger suggests another connection to that medical discourse of menses, but this time associated with abnormal sexuality, specifically with hyperaesthesia (or exaggeration of the sexual appetite). In one contemporary physician's terms: "In women it is during or after menstruation that the sexual appetite and consequently sexual hyperaesthesia are generally strongest."[63] These medical contexts might perhaps fruitfully be considered here alongside symbolic ones in interpreting this odd figuring of the moon as the focus of everyone's attention. As a pubescent female verbally linked to that moon, Salome is directly associated with menses and indirectly, therefore, with these various contemporaneous medical discourses of the pathological that link the menstruating woman with violence and increased sexuality. (As if to underline the connection, Wilde has his Jochanaan offer an apocalyptic vision of the day the moon would appear as red as blood, an image Herod appropriately recalls—and twice repeats—just before Salome begins her infamous dance.)

As the opera progresses, as layers of Salome's character are revealed, she becomes more and more disturbing. It will surprise no one that the woman whom Huysmans's Des Esseintes called "Goddess of immortal Hysteria" has indeed been interpreted as an hysteric or even a psychotic by post-Freudian critics.[64] But the contemporary discourse—of Richard von, Krafft-Ebing and Havelock Ellis, not to mention Jean Martin Charcot, Pierre Janet, and Freud himself—offers another context in which Salome would have been constructed in relation to pathological sexuality.[65] Even before Freud, the associations of women with hysteria included heightened suggestibility, emotional irritability and instability, hyperaesthesia, and impulsiveness.[66] Maudsley once again provides a canonical articulation that is suggestive for the opera's portrayal of Salome: "An acute attack of maniacal excitement, with great restlessness, perverseness of conduct, loud and rapid conversation. . . . An erotic element is sometimes evinced in the manner and thoughts; and occasionally ecstatic states occur. The symptoms are often worse at the menstrual periods."[67]

Such a list offers a kind of thumbnail character sketch of the willful young Salome, who must have her own way, who reacts as strongly to first seeing Jochanaan's body as to being rejected by him. Her lability is clear in her rapid oscillation between praise for his corporeal beauty—his body, his hair, his lips—and disgust at the same, when he rejects her advances. To underline the psychic oscillation, the music shifts at this point, offering disturbing orchestral, harmonic, and also vocal changes to alert the audience or listener.[68] While today it may be more fashionable to interpret hysteria, as does Elizabeth Grosz, as a form of resistance,[69] when the opera and play were written the pathological dominated the medical—and cultural—discourse of female sexuality.[70] And, as we shall see shortly, that pathology directly linked hysteria to the dancing body.

If the assumed norm at the time for women was, in fact, asexuality, as doctors claimed, and if women who sought men were deemed anomalies, imagine how transgressive Salome would appear.[71] Her open display of sexual desire for Jochanaan would have been seen by most as a sure sign of mental disease and proof (in the "elementary force" with which she was attracted to him) of her nymphomania.[72] The contemporary discourse on the excitable, insatiable women who, from their early youth, "throw themselves onto men" would have provided another significant context for interpreting Salome.[73] Today, we are more likely to believe that male desire created the image of the "insatiable nymph" and that male scientists then "discovered her existence as a medical fact," but at the time, to Krafft-Ebing, nymphomania was a "syndrome within the sphere of psychical degeneration," and this would then account for what another physician called the nymphomaniac's loss of "all sense of shame, all moral sense, and all discretion, as regards the object of her desires."[74]

Certainly, by the finale of her body-unveiling dance, when Salome makes her demand for the head of the prophet, her character too is unveiled in what, at the time, would have been seen as all its pathological glory. Presumably this is what led the first Salome, Maria Wittich, to protest what was asked of her: "I won't do it, I am a decent woman," she exclaimed.[75] Salome's character caused Romain Rolland to write to his friend Strauss that Wilde's play "has a nauseous and sickly atmosphere about it: it exudes vice and literature. This isn't a question of middle-class morality, it's a question of health."[76] He went on to call Salome "unwholesome, unclean, hysterical," as did many early critics of the opera, protesting in the name of health, but likely also reflecting the impact of Wilde's scandalous reputation and recent sodomy trial.[77] But the verbal signs of the influence of those medical discourses of pathological female sexuality are there nonetheless in that vocabulary of hysteria and unhealthiness.

Yet, the power of Salome as a character comes from her progressive, staged embodiment of that perverse disjunction between the pathological, dangerous sexuality of the castrating femme fatale and the innocence and willfulness of the young girl—and her biblical story.[78] That willful character can be seen in her stubborn repeating of her desires. When she decides she wants to see Jochanaan's body she thrice reiterates this wish, moving from "Ich möchte" (I would like to) to "Ich wünsche" (I want to) to "Ich will" (I will). Four times she insists she will kiss Jochanaan's mouth. Eight times she repeats to Herod her demand for Jochanaan's head as the payment for her dance. In her final monologue to that head, her childlike willfulness comes together with the dangerous pathology in all its power. She again repeats several times that she has said she wanted to kiss his mouth and now she is going to do so, for she lives, while he is now dead. When she does kiss him, she sings: "There was a bitter taste on your lips. Was it the taste of blood? No! Then, perhaps it was the taste of love. . . . They say that love has a bitter taste." ("was war ein bitterer Geschmack auf deinen Lippen. Hat es nach Blut geschmeckt? Nein! Doch es schmeckte vielleicht nach Liebe . . . Sie sagen, dass die Liebe bitter schmecke.") The vampiric associations with the femme fatale, preying on men "ill-equipped for the onslaught,"[79] here unite with representations of the willfulness of the child who decides she does not really care: "What does it matter?" ("Allein, was tut's? Was tut's?"): the important thing is that she has had her way, as she twice exultantly notes.

What would have been seen as pathological physical desire comes together with adolescent female power, as the orchestra plays what has been described as the "most sickening chord in all opera."[80] Throughout, the music too has mirrored the paradoxes of Salome's character: this entire monologue is grounded in C major/minor, the keys of "violence and death which are opposed to the C-sharp major/minor world of desire."[81] The ambivalence of her character is shown by her participation in both keys.[82] But by the end of the opera, as Salome kisses Jochanaan's mouth, the violence, death, and desire all come together and contrast with the text's emphasis on the willfulness of the chaste virgin who has learned the meaning of power.[83] Even before her famous "Dance of the Seven Veils," Salome has used her knowledge of that power, a power inseparable from her body. That dance is a calculated move in a game of exchange with Herod—one in which she offers her body as a sensual, sexual spectacle to his eyes, in return for a promise that will fulfil both her lethal willful stubborness and her consuming sexual obsession to kiss the mouth of the resistant prophet.

The "Dance of the Seven Veils" is the best known part of the opera and play.[84] Wilde's text, like the Bible, leaves the dance undescribed, and Marjorie Garber argues that "[i]n its non-description, in its indescribability lies its power, and its availability for cultural inscription and appropriation."[85] That may be true for the play, but for the opera the music is much more explicit, here as elsewhere: "Its Hollywood-exotic contours, bedizened with motifs from the opera proper, sometimes tempt directors to make an elaborate production number, far beyond the rather chaste little scenario that the composer sketched to guide himself."[86] In that scenario, Strauss had Salome posing like, once again, Moreau's *Salome Dancing before Herod,* and then provided her with a rather stylized choreography—with "menacing steps or lively paces" to go with certain bars of the music.[87] The dance's embodied representation on stage is probably guaranteed to be a failure for many viewers because "no staging can be the Dance in all its mythic force."[88] Strauss himself came to feel that many productions went "beyond all bounds of decency and good taste": "Salome, being a chaste virgin and an oriental princess, must be played with the simplest and most restrained of gestures, unless her defeat by the miracle of a great world is to excite only disgust and terror instead of sympathy." He felt that the music offered enough "turmoil," and so the acting should be "limited to the utmost simplicity."[89] At least in Strauss's eyes, this was not intended to be what Kramer calls "the first operatic striptease in history."[90] Why then did he write the music he did?[91] It may well have been that music that drew Peter Hall to direct (his wife) Maria Ewing to end up naked at the end of the dance (at Covent Garden), and Atom Egoyan to have his dancing Salome (at the Canadian Opera Company) naked behind a screen (see figure 2).[92]

Dance is, of course, of all the art forms, the most insistently bodily—and bodies are decidedly gendered.[93] The dance is the moment in the opera when the "sensual is made visible" as well as audible.[94] The wild music that signals the start of the orientalized dance is quickly subdued by Salome herself. Slow, seductive, at times waltz-like music (complete with orientalist castanets) speeds up again by the end, causing the bewitched Herod to cry out: "Herrlich! Wundervoll, wundervoll!" Drawing on authentic oriental music (as modified by European clichés about it), Strauss set up a tension between distance and recognition for the audience. Familiar waltz music is interwoven with oriental(ist) sounds that, to a turn-of-the-century European, at least, would have connoted sensuality—not to mention the luxury and cruelty associated with the Eastern "other."[95]

In turn-of-the-century Europe, though, dance had a particular cultural resonance that contributed to the memorable quality of Salome as dancer.[96] Not only did dance (in general) become "an emblem of the perfect work of art that fuses sensuousness and thought into one," but it took on a more medicalized and pathological meaning through its association with hysteria.[97] Charcot's famous images of the "attitudes passionnelles" and his colleague Paul Richer's drawings of the body of the female victim of "grand hysteria" are strikingly reminiscent in their poses of the positions of modern dance—that is, very different in form and effect from the controlled, disciplined form of classical ballet.[98] This may help explain the real fashion in these years for (modern) dancing Salomes such as Loïe Fuller and Maud Allan.[99] Fuller's dances, it has been argued, consciously attempted to confront the medical stereotyping of the "performative hysterical" female body, established by Charcot's famous Tuesday leçons—which were attended by members of the general as well as medical public.[100] Eliz-

Figure 2. "The Dance of the Seven Veils" with dancer Carolyn Woods
in silhouette behind projections by Phillip Barker in the Canadian
Opera Company's 1996 production of *Salome,* directed
by Atom Egoyan. Photo by Michael Cooper,
courtesy of the Canadian Opera Company.

abeth Dempster points out that modern dancers such as Isadora Duncan
and Ruth St. Denis

> constructed images and created dances through their own unballetic bodies,
> producing a writing of the female body which strongly contrasted with clas-
> sical inscriptions. These dancers, creating new vocabularies of movement and
> new styles of presentation, made a decisive and liberating break with the prin-
> ciples and forms of the European ballet.[101]

But to do so, they turned to representations of hysteria. It may not be at
all strange, then, that productions of *Salome* have always used modern
and/or orientalized choreography for their dances.

Given the literally "embodied" nature of dance, a dancing Salome was
not necessarily going to look like a singing Salome.[102] Nevertheless, the
dancing body has always been hard to ignore. Indeed, from the early
Church fathers on, one strong tradition was that dance was hedonistic, instinctual, physical, and consequently dangerous.[103] However, a different

interpretation can be seen in Nietzsche's assertion of the centrality of dance and music to the very birth of tragedy. While Salome's dance could be (and indeed has been) interpreted as a Dionysian dance of the body,[104] it is also explicitly presented in the opera as a token in an economy of exchange: Salome uses her dancing body as a means to an end—the fulfillment of her obsessive desire and her strong, childlike will.[105]

In the opera, as in the play, the body is the focus of the attention—and the eye—of both audience and characters.[106] The dancing Salome is certainly the object of the gaze—particularly the male gaze—as she had been from the Bible onward.[107] In general, though, the visual or, more specifically, the act of looking (as both surveillance and spectacle) is so omnipresent in the opera and play that this has been called the "tragedy of the gaze."[108] As Martin Jay has convincingly shown, "ocularcentrism" (or the dominance of the optic/visual) has a long and complex history in Western thought.[109] The visual has been considered superior to the other senses, in part because it is detached from what it observes.[110] For this reason, the observer has the power of objectifying what is observed, of mastering and controlling through distancing. Because of this connection between the act of seeing and power, the privilege of vision has been linked to sexual privilege:[111] the gaze has thus often been gendered male, leaving women as the objects of the gaze—either as exhibitionists or as the passively displayed. The representations of women in visual art, as in film, are (argues Laura Mulvey) "coded for strong visual and erotic impact so that they can be said to connote *to-be-looked-at-ness.*"[112] This coding means that to be looked at is a negative, a position of powerlessness.[113]

Salome the character and *Salome* the opera turn this now widely accepted view utterly on its head. Here, to be the object of the gaze is to have great power, as if "to-be-looked-at-ness" conveys mastery and control. This is certainly an opera obsessed with the acts of looking and even staring. It opens with the Syrian guard, Narraboth, staring at Salome as the page tries to distract him; the soldiers stare at Herod, wondering what he is looking at; Salome enters worrying about why her mother's husband stares at her the way he does.[114] The verb *ansehen*—to look at—dominates the text. Salome then stares at the moon, as Narraboth continues to stare at her. The one person who evades the gaze at this point is Jochanaan, who has been imprisoned deep in a cistern by Herod—who himself obviously knows the power of being seen and wants to deny it to his enemy and harshest critic.[115] But Jochanaan evokes in others—first the Cappadocian and then Salome—the desire to see him. Knowing the erotic power of looking—and being looked at—Salome seduces Narraboth with the promise of a future glance at him: "ich werde dich ansehn." This is a young woman who is not objectified by the gaze, but is instead empowered by it: she tells Narraboth to look at her, and when he does, he gives in to her request to bring Jochanaan out of the cistern, against Herod's orders. But Jochanaan too knows the power of the visual, and refuses to look at the staring Salome.[116] The gaze here is female, not male, and the power is in the beheld and not the beholder. Jochanaan refuses to give Salome the power that would come from his gaze: "Ich will dich nicht ansehen," he tells her, and demands to be taken away from her staring eyes. It has been suggested that this refusal to look at her is a metaphoric refusal to recognize her as a person, independent from her mother.[117] But, more significantly, it is a refusal to grant her the power of the "gazed upon," a power already central to this young woman's sense of personhood.

Given this, Salome's dance is a triumph, as all of us—audience as well as Herod—bestow power on her as we gaze.[118] Salome therefore does not reverse the centrality of the male gazer as powerful, as John Paul Riquelme argues,[119] but rather she alters the very power dynamics of the gaze itself: the person—of either sex—who gazes grants power to the one—of either sex—gazed upon. When Salome demands her reward in the form of Jochanaan's head on a silver plate, Herod tries to offer her instead a number of (oddly enough, gendered) visual treats that suggest a surrender of male visual control—jewels that significantly, her mother had never seen and a crystal no woman had ever looked into. But Salome refuses; she knows wherein lies the power of the gaze. It is this knowledge, however, that is the tragedy of both Salome and Jochanaan. When she addresses his decapitated head with its closed eyes, she asks why he never looked at her when alive; why, in other words, he never granted her the power that others did. Her narcissistic fury at being thwarted in her visual power (that comes with being looked at) is clear in the thrice-repeated personal "me, me, me you never saw" ("mich, mich, mich hast du nie gesehn"). The tragedy in this, for Salome, lies in her belief that, *had* he looked at her, he would have loved her ("Hättest du mich gesehn, du hättest mich geliebt"). Such had indeed been the beautiful young princess's experience thus far in life. In despair, she again asks why he didn't look at her ("Warum sahst du mich nich an?"), knowing that being looked at is as much a fulfillment of desire as looking can be. According to the libretto, no one (including the audience) ever sees Salome actually kiss the lips of the prophet: the act should occur in darkness as torches are put out and the moon (which itself had been gazed upon by everyone) disappears. The power of Salome's visual act is left to the imagination and the aural power of the music and voice, as we then hear Salome sing of having kissed his mouth at last.

The interpretation that Salome is master/mistress not so much of the gaze but of "being-gazed-at" (and that therein lies real power) runs contrary to the interpretations of both Lawrence Kramer, who sees her as ultimately losing the power of the gaze she usurped during the dance, and Carolyn Abbate, who sees her as a constant object of the gaze.[120] The male gaze has not been usurped because the power was never with it in the first place. Rather, in this case, to be the *object* of the gaze is to be empowered. As many have pointed out, this is indeed an opera full of obsessive voyeurs and warnings of the dangers of looking, but in stark reversal of the traditional theory, to look is to grant power to the one observed.[121]

To render, in this way, the visual more complex in its empowering dynamics is to suggest the need to rethink the relation between the aural and the visual in operatic performance, especially from the point of view of the audience—gazing at Salome's body as well as listening to her voice, granting her the power Jochanaan refused her. An early reviewer implicated the audience by suggesting a certain hypocrisy inherent in moralistic responses: "[t]he public stares hypnotically, like slaves of the tetrarch, at the bloodthirsty music, then throws the shield of indignation over it."[122] Whether today we would feel guilty pleasure or moral disgust at the end of *Salome*, the combination of the two extreme possibilities seems to have been central to the decadent aesthetic of Wilde's play and the libretto: "the last pages of the opera are surely the apotheosis of decadent malaise. They capture that crucial moment for the decadent aesthetic, the moment when ecstatic experience of forbidden pleasures transforms into revulsion."[123]

As drama, the final scene in which Salome kisses Jochanaan's mouth and Herod, in disgust and terror, orders her death, functions in complicated ways. We are perhaps as shocked by his act as by hers, but, given the growing horror that accompanied the gradual unveiling of Salome's character, her death may allow the audience to experience some satisfying cathartic release: the embodiment of the terrifying femme fatale is no more. As Susan McClary puts it, in musical as well as narrative terms: "The monstrosity of Salome's sexual and chromatic transgressions is such that extreme violence seems justified—even demanded—for the sake of social and tonal order."[124] With the aid of what has been described as a music of "exposed nerve ends" that nonetheless has a strong "erotic charge," the audience is both shocked and appeased.[125] It is, above all, implicated. The audience has actually been implicated well before this, and by the music as much as the text.[126] Herod's first invitations to Salome to dance had launched "generously into a tune that never comes, foundering equally upon Salome's indifference and Herod's short concentration-span." But the dance, when it does come, assuages our disappointment: "thus deftly aligning the audience at once with Herod's desires and Salome's knowledge that she possesses the means of steering them towards the realisation of her own."[127] The means, of course, include both her body and the power of having it gazed upon.

Already in *A Rebours*, Huysmans had made his hero identify with the gazing Herod: "Like the old King, Des Esseintes invariably felt overwhelmed, subjugated, stunned when he looked at this dancing-girl," the one in Moreau's watercolor.[128] His construction of her as the predatory, hysterical, but irresistible temptation of the flesh suggests that at least part of Salome's appeal was in her contradictoriness: as Gustav Klimt's paintings inspired by the opera suggest as well, the deadly young dancer was as much a degenerate object of misogynist fears as a sado-masochistic erotic ideal.[129] Huysmans's description also focuses the figurative eye of the reader on her body—though here in ekphrastic representation—just as surely as Wilde and Strauss's construction of her focuses the literal eye of the audience of the staged version on the performer's body.

Part of the unease of watching and listening to *Salome* may come from this implication in a relationship of empowerment that has fatal consequences. But for decades audiences have kept going to this opera, to see and hear the deaths of Salome and Jochanaan over and over. Abbate argues that, at the end, Salome's "musical speech drowns out everything in range, and we sit as passive objects, battered by that voice."[130] But we are always affected by more than the aural, and we are not passive: we too have been active in the granting of power to this contradictory and complicated woman—the vamp *and* the virgin—whose body we too have stared at for almost the full ninety minutes of the opera. We heard of her physical beauty in the first moments, and then she appeared—and we didn't take our eyes off her body until the shields of Herod's soldiers crushed her to death. These unusual weapons of execution—shields—recall the myth of Perseus and the Medusa, already signalled in Salome's description of Jochanaan's hair as like serpents. Like Perseus, the soldiers have been protected from the sight of a female body that commands the deadly power of being gazed upon. Salome's death, seen in this context, forms a complex irony as we remember Medusa's fate: decapitation by Perseus.[131]

As audience members we had no shields. We watched her dance, but we also watched her die.[132] As a staged work, *Salome* does not allow its audience to remain passive or distanced: our gaze, like Herod's, does not objectify but instead empowers this woman. In fact, it may be the reversal of the power of the gaze that contributes to the anxiety that Salome manages to inspire. Repelled perhaps, but also fascinated, we return and recreate again and again this contradictory story of virginal innocence and murderous passion—as told in a delicately bejewelled text set to brutally powerful music. In the politics of the gaze, Salome is like Medusa: to look upon her is to feel her power. While it is Salome who causes the beheading of Jochanaan, rather than being beheaded herself (though Wilde considered this the best way to end his play), most significantly, it is the Gorgon's head, *her body*—alive or dead—that has the power to turn people to stone: her body's power, like Salome's, lies in being gazed upon.

_____ "Soulless Machines" and Steppenwolves _____

RENEGOTIATING MASCULINITY IN KRENEK'S
JONNY SPIELT AUF

J O S E P H   H E N R Y   A U N E R

As HERMANN HESSE'S NOVEL _STEPPENWOLF_ BEGINS, the protagonist Harry Haller is alone and adrift, having rejected his "besotted humdrum age of spiritual blindness."[1] He finds refuge in the books that litter his attic room and in the "lovely old music" of his pantheon of immortals—Bach, Handel, Haydn, and above all Mozart—that seems to open a door to a world in which he can see God at work. Yet as the story unfolds Haller comes to distrust this musical tradition; he blames the power of the "matriarchal link with nature" in the German spirit for enticing intellectuals to rebel against reason and the word, and to revel instead in "wonderful creations of sound, and wonderful beauties of feeling and mood that were never pressed home to reality." The price of this revelry, this refusal to fight manfully against the "fatal relation" with music, is, Harry says, that, intellectuals cannot be at home in reality, but remain "strange to it and hostile."[2] This estrangement from the real world is dramatized in the sharp splintering of the protagonist's personality into two halves: the refined, artistic Haller and the Steppenwolf, the persona for all that is chaotic, instinctive, and impulsive. This split between man and that "beast astray . . . in a world that is strange and incomprehensible to him" leaves Haller at war with himself and his surroundings, with thoughts of suicide the only solace.[3]

Haller's alienation—presented most directly through his attitudes toward women ranging from incomprehension to hostility to contempt—is thematized in the novel through his disgust and fascination with the jazz he hears spilling out of the dance halls during his nightly rambles. Yet it is only through his encounter with this music, brought about by—and intimately intertwined with—his love affairs with Hermine and Maria and by his relationship with the exotic, dark-skinned jazz musician Pablo, that Haller is offered a way back to reality and "true manhood."[4] Dance music and all the worldliness it represents mark the path of liberation, with the

An earlier version of this essay appeared in _Critical Matrix: The Princeton Journal of Women, Gender, and Culture_ 10, nos. 1–2 (1996): 58–72. I am grateful to the journal for granting permission for this publication, and to its former editors Heather Hadlock and Anne-Lise François for their insightful commentaries.

first step symbolized by his purchase of a gramophone and the introduction of American jazz into the sanctum where he had previously taken refuge with Novalis and Jean Paul. Haller's attempt at enlightenment is ultimately a failure, culminating in fantasies of murder and destruction in the novel's hallucinatory conclusion, but Hesse holds out the possibility that Haller might yet reject his sense of tragedy, overcome his dual nature, and learn to live again in the world.

Hesse's story of a damaged masculinity that regards music as both peril and salvation finds many striking parallels in Ernst Krenek's opera *Jonny spielt auf,* which premiered with enormous success in 1927, the year of *Steppenwolf*'s publication. Novel and opera have significant similarities of character and plot, and, perhaps most obviously, in the symbolism they attach to "high" and "low" musical styles. Krenek's libretto embodies this musical opposition—with what Richard Taruskin has described as "sledgehammer" subtlety—in the figures of the composer Max and the black American jazz musician Jonny.[5] Like Harry Haller, Max charts a trajectory over the course of the work from a position of isolation and elitism to a new wholeness and worldliness with Jonny as his lodestar. Yet despite the many close similarities with *Steppenwolf, Jonny spielt auf* is a more problematic work in the definition of its characters and in the image of redemption it offers.

A significant point of divergence between novel and opera is the music Krenek chooses to represent his flawed hero. In *Steppenwolf,* the central conflict is between a broadly conceived "jazz" music and the eighteenth- and nineteenth-century German canon; only in passing does Haller mention "the academic music of the day," to which even the "repugnant" jazz is preferable.[6] *Jonny spielt auf,* in contrast, is more directly engaged with contemporaneous debates about New Music, *Neue Sachlichkeit,* and *Gebrauchsmusik,* thus substantially revising the novel's constellation of gender, race, and musical style. The opera's conflation of gender anxieties with debates about art and the relationship of the intellectual to the world fits neatly into Andreas Huyssen's analysis of mass culture as modernism's feminine Other, which locates the image of a masculine modernism in its sharp differentiation from a feminized mass culture.[7]

Many aspects of *Jonny spielt auf* manifest such a framework. The shallow violin virtuoso Daniello, typical of the foreign-born violinists associated with the popular salon orchestras of the day, describes himself as the "king of the violin"; when he plays his heart "is engulfed by the flames of women's desires" (51).[8] Depicted as a "greasy, levantine matinee-idol" (kitschige, südöstliche Männerschönheit) (50), Daniello and his entourage of adoring female fans represent the corruption and decadence of those who seek success in the world on its own terms. The two principal female characters—Anita, an opera singer and the focus of erotic desire for the three male leads, and Yvonne, a coquettish maid—are similarly placed squarely in the midst of everyday life. At the same time, however, Krenek uses jazz as a trope to undermine Max's position of purity and autonomy, and, by extension, that of modernism in general. The opera reflects a shift that took place in the 1920s, when the new American dance music seemed to offer a middle path between femininized mass culture and a modernist high art that was increasingly viewed as enervated and irrelevant.[9] Jazz, a symbol of both modern technological life and "primitive" vitality for European audiences, represented the possibility of a new masculinity squarely grounded in the "real" world. It is only through the infusion of Jonny's strength that Max and the decadent and worn-out Old World as a whole can be reborn.

Yet Jonny's moment of triumph at the end of the work, when a dancing mob sings that "the new world in all its splendor comes across the sea and conquers old Europe through dance" (95), raises disturbing issues about the means by which Max is brought back to life and his masculinity restored. Whereas Hesse's *Steppenwolf* challenges contemporary notions of gender, race, and class, *Jonny spielt auf* ultimately reinforces and perpetuates traditional oppositions of masculine and feminine, spirit and body, human and beast, civilized and primitive, white and black. Writing about the opera in 1930, a few years after its première, Krenek seemed to let these old dichotomies get the upper hand. Explaining the significance of the work's *Zeitoper* trappings of modern technology, such as the loudspeakers, telephones, and trains, he writes:

> Showing these completely soulless machines is the shortest way of demonstrating the antithesis which inspires the piece—the antithesis between man as a "vital" animal, and man as a "spiritual" animal—as incarnated in the diametrically opposed figures of Jonny and Max. In this sense Jonny is actually a part of the technical-mechanical side of the world; he reacts as easily, as gratifyingly exactly and amorally as a well-constructed machine. His kingdom is of this world, and as a matter of course he is the one who gains mastery over life here below, over the visible globe. He is in direct contrast to Max, who, starting out from spirituality, never comes to grips with the problems posed by external life, which today is so attuned to vitality.[10]

My purpose here is not to charge Krenek with some hidden racist agenda, but rather to explore how the gendered discourses he inherited and perpetuated could deflect the opera's intended message. One sign of this is the striking similarity between Krenek's remarks and the language of extreme conservative and antimodernist figures such as Hans Pfitzner, who described jazz as "soulless American machinism."[11] The opera ostensibly champions the liberating force of the modern world, but at the same time it reflects contemporary uncertainties about whether Americanism means liberation or doom, whether jazz brings deliverance or degeneracy, and, consequently, about the very nature of masculinity.[12] The opera's tremendous success—it received over forty-five different productions in the first two years of its existence—as well as the intense opposition it provoked from the National Socialists confirms its strong resonances for Weimar audiences. With the 1993 release of a new recording as part of London Records' "Degenerate Music" series, along with renewed scholarly interest in the opera and its fate, it has become more pressing to explore the message of this troubling work.[13]

The opera's opening scene immediately establishes the gendered terms in which it will operate. When we first see the composer Max, he has fled the crowds of a mountain resort hotel for the solace of a glacier. Max's affinity with the glacier is solidified in both text and music through the establishment of an important leitmotif associated interchangeably with Max and the glacier throughout the opera.[14] When Anita suddenly appears, having lost her way, her horrified reaction to the glacier reinforces its image as a refuge from the feminine. The vast expanse of ice, which Max praises for its rigidity, "as a symbol of form, of ordered nature, of contained life" (40), appears to Anita as limitless death. If Max truly represents what Krenek elsewhere described as the "ponderous, inhibited, Central-European intellectual," any ambiguity raised by the glacier's initial symbolism is dispelled with Max's opening line: "Du schöner Berg! der mich anzieht, der mich antreibt, zu gehn fort von der Heimat, fort von der Arbeit" (Lovely mountain! You attract me, you urge me to leave my native country, my work) (36).[15]

That Schoenberg felt himself to be attacked by Krenek, in other contexts at least, is evident in his own pun on Krenek's name in the foreword to the *Drei Satiren,* op. 28 (1926), where Schoenberg identifies a reference to Krenek's 1925 essay "Musik in der Gegenwart," with the phrase "wie der Medio*kre neck*isch sagt" (as the mediocre playfully say). An unpublished commentary by Schoenberg on the same essay demonstrates moreover the ways sexual imagery figured in these musical debates. His remarks, entitled "Krenek für leichte Musik," engage in extended wordplay on the word "leicht," meaning variously "light," "easy," "simple," as well as "loose" or "promiscuous."[16] Krenek's own thoughts on gender ideology and Schoenbergian modernism are presented less elliptically in his 1937 essay on Alban Berg's *Lulu.* Krenek interprets the character of Lulu as the embodiment of the *Ewig-Weibliche,* tracing Berg's influences to Karl Kraus and Otto Weininger—notably the same writers Krenek absorbed as a youth.[17] He writes that standing opposed to Lulu's "pre-logical sphere" which is the "real domain of the female nature" is the masculine sphere of the law, "thoroughly dominated, with inexorable logic, by language and the norms of art." In a striking echo of Harry Haller's castigation of music as linked to a matriarchal, irrational nature and opposed to the masculine world of reason, Krenek claims that "Alban Berg was always saved from sinking mindlessly into the intoxicating cult of the *Ewig-Weibliche* by his love of strict construction."[18] This image of "strict construction" as a defense against the irrational and anarchical has obvious resonance with some recent interpretations of Schoenberg's own development, in which the twelve-tone system has been characterized as an attempt to contain and frame the transgressive feminine excess of atonal works such as *Erwartung*.[19]

Max's glacier, the embodiment of Schoenberg's world of reason and law, thus serves as a vivid representation of Huyssen's masculine modernist art work, which by "fortifying its boundaries, by maintaining its purity and autonomy, and by avoiding any contamination with mass culture" maintains its adversary stance to the feminine bourgeois world of everyday life.[20] To underscore this symbolism, the opera singer Anita is associated repeatedly with heat, rushing blood, and water. Max says to her: "I am a stranger to the hustle and bustle of your life! This turmoil, like the waves of the sea, always restless, confused and pointless. . . . No form, no shape, no permanence, no strength" (85). Such language was widespread enough that even Max Brod, who disapproved of the new trends, borrowed its imagery to critique the adoption in recent literature and modern music of a "hard, cold, masculine tone," which he attributed to the disillusionment of the younger generation who, after the war, "justifiably learned to mistrust everything that partook of the passions of the heart" and to abstain from the chaos of daily life.[21]

Just as the desolate wilderness of the glacier symbolizes the high cost of creating a world apart from social reality, the opera soon makes clear that Max's devotion to the "schöner Berg" has left him deeply flawed. Reflecting the widespread sense of the decadence of both pre-and post-war modernist styles in the face of the more hard-edged *Neue Sachlichkeit*, Max's renunciation of both the world and the feminine principle means the loss of all sexual identity. Krenek's essay on *Lulu* hints at this process of neutering as an inevitable result of "the ruthlessly intellectual musical thought stemming from Schoenberg." For although it saved Alban Berg "from sinking into the naive, unreflecting swamp of the Jugendstil's matriarchalism," Schoenberg's twelve-tone method "caused the destruction of tonality, the break-up of the firm musical foundations which had supported the masculine type of artistic order."[22] Here too, there are connections between Krenek's interpretation of Schoenberg's music and Schoenberg's own use of sexual metaphors in his writings. In the 1922 edition of the *Harmonielehre*, Schoenberg compares the dualism of major and minor to the binary opposition of "male and female (*Zweigeschlechtlichkeit*) [which] delimits the spheres of expression according to attraction (*Lust*) and repulsion (*Unlust*)." For Schoenberg, such dualisms represent only a stage in an evolutionary process: "the angels, our higher nature (*Übernatur*), are asexual; and the spirit does not know repulsion (*Unlust*)."[23]

In *Jonny spielt auf* this asexual ideal is transformed into an infirmity. Already in the opera's second scene there are signs of Max's sexual inadequacies, when, after a night together, Anita and Max are shown trying to patch up some undefined problem. Max begins the scene by remarking, "everything is all right, I have cheered up"; later he asks, "have you forgiven me?" Anita tries to smooth over the difficulties, responding, "you make too much of everything. You are a man of the glacier"(41). But Anita grows increasingly dissatisfied in the following scenes; she repeatedly chides him for his "tragic view of life," and describes him as too weak and dependent, complaining in Act I, scene 3, when she has traveled alone to Paris, "oh, if only you were as strong as you are good" (53). But as she imagines him there and sings "Hold me tight!" it is Jonny who appears, claiming "Oh, I'm strong, you've no idea, just ask the girls in Paris!" (54) Max's flaws are underscored by the alacrity with which Anita entertains Jonny's advances, then spends the night with Daniello. In contrast to Max's weakness, Anita's independence clearly marks her as one of the "New Women" who were causing great anxieties in the 1920s. Fear of the uninhibited female is palpable in the *Neue Zeitschrift für Musik*'s hostile review of the opera's première, which reports in an outraged tone that Anita "belongs" in the space of five minutes to no fewer than three men, two of whom she has just seen for the first time.[24]

Max's attraction to the frozen glacier is elaborated in more subtle ways in the words and music of an aria from his new opera, which he and Anita rehearse in the second scene.[25] The aria's text captures the crucial elements of Max's personality: a desire to retreat from life to a world of dreams free from suffering and a strong dose of self-dramatization (see example 1). The exaggerated outpouring of *Weh* and *Schmerz* at the end mirrors Max's inability to hold his emotions in check throughout the opera, while the flowing tears that cannot be staunched underscore the danger he faces of dissipating into the feminine life of "turmoil, like the waves of the sea." Indeed, Krenek linked Max's extreme emotionality to the feminine, at the same time getting in another ironic dig at Schoenberg, when he referred to Act II, scene 5, in which Max waits all night in vain for Anita's return, as "Max in Erwartung."[26]

The aria's languid rhythm, indicated as *Andante triste*, and its wandering harmonies suggest what Susan Cook has described as a parody of chromatic atonal writing, a style Krenek referred to as "head in hands" music.[27] Both the text and the extreme chromaticism of the harmony anchored by

EXAMPLE 1
"Aria" from Max's Opera, *Jonny spielt auf,* Act I, scene 2

Max *(setzt sich an den Flügel)*
Ich leide so . . .
. . . um dich und doch fährst du weg!
(begleitet sie zum Gesang)
Anita
Ein Automobil, sofort!
(Dienstmädchen ab)
(Sie tritt an den Flügel.)
Bitte!

Als ich damals am Strand des Meeres stand,
suchte das Heimweh mich heim.
Ich suchte mein Heim in der Träume Land,
daß das Weh, daß das Weh mich ließe.
Doch ward meiner Träume ich nicht froh.
Das Leid blieb das Gleiche im Schlaf!
O Schmerz, o Schmerz, der mich
tödlich traf, tödlich traf!
Drum, o Träne, fließe, Träne, fließe,
drum, o Träne, fließe,
Träne, ah—ah—fließe, fließe.

Manager *(tritt hastig ein)*
Ich kam mit dem Auto her,
Sie zur Bahn zu holen.

Max *(sitting down at the piano)*
I'm so unhappy . . .
. . . on your account, and yet you leave me!
(He prepares to accompany her.)
Anita
Call a cab, immediately.
(Exit chambermaid.)
(Anita approaches the piano.)
Right!

As I stood one day on the seashore
I was assailed by homesickness.
I sought my home in the land of dreams,
hoping that my grief would be eased.
But my dreams gave me no comfort.
Awake or asleep, I suffered.
O pain, you have mortally wounded me!
Therefore flow, my tears, flow,
therefore flow, my tears,
Flow, ah—ah—flow.

Manager *(entering hurriedly)*
I've come with a car
to take you to your train.

eventual tonal resolution recall several works of the Second Viennese School from around 1908–10, including Schoenberg's *Second String Quartet,* op. 10 and Berg's *Four Songs,* op. 2. In contrast to Jonny's strongly rhythmic pseudo-jazz with its simple and firmly rooted harmonic structure, the indecisive and unstable accompaniment of Max's aria seems barely able to contain the florid and soaring vocal line. The accuracy of Krenek's parody is underscored by the strong similarity between the way the voice part destabilizes the harmonic structure and David Lewin's discussion of the "transcendent woman's voice" in Schoenberg's op. 10, *Erwartung,* and other works. For Lewin these works are marked by a specifically female "upper register *Hauptstimme* that controls the flow of musical events with a motivic through-line, specifically wresting control of that flow away from any fundamental bass."[28] In Max's aria the initial C-minor tonality, significantly established by a *Tristan*-like half-diminished seventh to a dominant-seventh progression, is repeatedly diverted to distant realms by the vocal line (see example 2). The accompaniment, notably deficient in the lower registers, while first attempting to provide triadic harmonizations, repeatedly resolves to nontriadic sonorities in order to accommodate the voice (mm. 372–77). At the end of the aria there is tonal resolution, but not before the bass line has become infected by the flowing motion of the voice.

EXAMPLE 2
Aria from Max's opera, *Jonny spielt auf,* Act I, scene 2
Used by Permission of European American Music Distributors

Although the ultimate function of Max's aria in the opera as a whole is complex and contradictory, Krenek leaves little doubt that we are to hear it as a symptom of Max's disengagement from the world. This is evident in its first appearance in Act II, scene 2, when the aria's conclusion is punctuated by the sudden intrusion of the Manager with his talk of cabs and trains as a stark contrast to the aria's otherworldly text. In Act II, scene 7, when a radio broadcasts the aria over the hotel loudspeakers, the assembled crowd admires Anita's voice, but remarks: "what a shame that she is so fond of modern music!" (101). As the aria reaches its most Schoenbergian chords, Max sings, "ist das der Wahnsinn?" And at the end of the aria the crowd rejoices "Gott sei Dank!" when someone changes the station to Jonny's jazz band.

As this last vignette makes clear, Max's deliverance from both his emotional weakness and asexuality comes through Jonny and his American jazz. For Krenek and many others in the 1920s, jazz appeared to offer the solution to the dual dangers of the "swamp of Jugendstil's matriarchalism" and the Schoenbergian glacier, by restoring tonality in a new masculine form "so fresh and powerful that a primeval sense would emerge from it."[29] The opera is only one example of contemporary works and writings that presented jazz and blacks as forces for regeneration. Ivan Goll, for example, described the arrival of Josephine Baker and the *Revue Nègre* as a rejuvenating rain of "Negro blood . . . slowly falling over Europe, a long-since dried up land that can scarcely breathe" and Kurt Pinthus compared the new masculine language of the New Objectivity to the body of a boxer, "with no lyrical fat, with no intellectual listlessness, hard tough, trained."[30] When jazz classes were introduced at Frankfurt's Hoch Conservatory for Music in 1927, they were similarly justified as a "transfusion of fresh [*unverbrauchten*] negro blood."[31]

In Krenek's opera, Jonny's power to overhaul the past is defined in part through his actions, the most obvious being his theft of Daniello's Amati violin, an act that is presented as a sort of cultural liberation rather than a crime. When, after many plot twists, Jonny finally comes into possession of the violin, he sings: "Everything of value in the world is mine. The old world created it, but no longer knows what to do with it" (95). In the final scenes of the opera it is also Jonny who liberates Max from the police, who have mistakenly arrested him for the theft of the violin. As Max is being taken to the police station, Jonny overpowers the policemen and drives him instead to meet Anita and catch the train that will start his journey to America, "the train that leads to life" (122).

But perhaps more important than what Jonny does is what he is. His character is unambiguously intended to be a product of his race. Although in later stagings in New York Jonny was portrayed as a white musician in black face, the original German productions presented the character as black (although the role was still played by a white singer). This led to disturbances at the 1929 Munich première, where Nazi protesters threatened to lynch the singer Alfred Jerger until they discovered that he was white.[32]

Krenek's discussions of Jonny emphasized his light-heartedness and lack of inhibition; he referred to him at one point as "a sort of sophisticated latter-day Papageno" and elsewhere as "a child of nature, totally free of inhibitions, acting on impulse at the spur of the moment."[33] Such a characterization is consistent with Jonny's first appearance wearing what is described as his "comic bowler hat," and with the minstrel show behavior he occasionally exhibits, most typically boisterous dancing and clowning. At times he also presents an artless sentimentality, as when he nostalgically sings a phrase from Stephen Foster about heading back to Alabama to see his beloved Swanee River. But there is much about Jonny that is less like Papageno than Monostatos: he is often depicted as violent, amoral, and animalistic. When at one point he says furiously to Yvonne, "I must have that violin," she replies, "all right, don't bite me!" (49) The American critic Herbert Peyser, admittedly no friend of the work, described the performance by a singer reputed to be one of the best Jonnys in Germany as a "simian burlesque." "When I protested to some German friends that negroes did not talk or act that way I was admonished that when they were in Europe they did."[34]

But Jonny's defining feature is his boundless and irrepressible sexuality. The linkage of jazz, American blacks, and unrestrained sexuality in the contemporary European imagination has been amply documented. A 1927 article on the jazz craze from the *Frankfurter Zeitung*, for example, describes the effect of a jazz gramophone recording at a fashionable party: from the first notes "a jungle flash hits the salon; the music thunderously electrifies silken calves and formal trousers . . . Saxophone blasts cast couples about, niggersong entwines them like garlands, lustful cries weaken their knees . . . an art historian anxiously feels himself turning primitive and the ground giving way under him."[35] Jonny's interactions with both Anita and Yvonne blatantly display the sexual power ascribed to him. At their first meeting Anita is nearly overwhelmed by the "rushing blood" that Jonny's strength and "barefaced bluntness" unleashes. Jonny also acts as a stimulant to the other male characters; when Daniello stumbles upon Jonny and Anita collapsed upon the settee, it is the sight of her "in that beast's hands" that seems to arouse him most, and he explicitly takes advantage of the sexual excitement Jonny has produced in Anita to complete his own seduction.

By placing him so firmly in the everyday world Krenek runs the risk that Jonny, like Daniello, will be feminized through his proximity to everyday life.[36] Yet for Krenek, the attraction of Jonny as the ultramodern/ultraprimitive man was precisely that he and his jazz offered deliverance both from a mass culture coded as feminine and from an emasculated modernism. Extreme plot measures are mobilized to protect Jonny from the realm of the feminine. Krenek resolutely severs Jonny's sex drive from any emotional encumbrances, depicting his character as acting throughout on pure self-interest, motivated solely by his own desires. To Anita he says, "Why won't you feel my strength? Just for one night! You need never see me again!" (55) Jonny's rage when his conquest of Anita is interrupted is easily assuaged by Daniello's surreptitious offer of a one-thousand franc note. The hit song "Leb Wohl, mein Schatz" from Act I, scene 4 could be taken as an anthem of Weimar sexual cynicism, with its chorus, "You can get on without me, I'll try to get on without you, and I'll never come back again" (57).[37] The same defense against femininization explains Jonny's strong misogynistic streak; he says to Anita: "I know what you white women are like: first you resist, then you're ecstatic, and then good bye! That's how you turn us into animals" (55). Suspecting Yvonne of deceiving him he says, "I knew it! Another proof . . . that women aren't to be trusted" (92).

———————

Krenek's depiction of Jonny draws upon many of the same ideas about jazz that Harry Haller presents at the beginning of *Steppenwolf*. On a late night walk, Haller wanders past a dance hall where he hears the sound of jazz drifting out on to the street, "hot and raw as the steam of raw flesh." He is repulsed, but the Steppenwolf in him is drawn as if smelling fresh blood.

> One half of this music, the melody, was all pomade and sugar and sentimentality. The other half was savage, temperamental and vigorous. Yet the two went artlessly well together and made a whole. It was the music of decline. There must have been such music in Rome under the later emperors. Compared with Bach and Mozart and real music it was, naturally, a miserable affair; but so was all our art, all our thought, all our makeshift culture in comparison with real culture. This music was at least sincere, unashamedly primitive and childishly happy. There was something of the Negro in it, and something of the American, who with all his strength seems so boyishly fresh and childlike to us Europeans.[38]

Over the course of the novel, Hesse systematically deconstructs these dichotomies between jazz and culture, between the dark-skinned Pablo and the pomaded Mozart, and between the whole framework of the "angry primal mother Nature and the troublesome primal father Spirit."[39] In *Jonny spielt auf*, in contrast, these oppositions are ultimately stabilized and reinscribed. Krenek himself commented in 1930 on this problem at the heart of the work:

only at the moment of greatest peril does [Max] decide to assent to life—but at this moment the opera ends. We shall never know what he does after this, because I did not know when I wrote it. The confrontation between the two spheres of life never takes place, Max's and Jonny's paths never cross, apart from the one fleeting encounter in the car which does not lead to any intellectual result. The duality of the world is presented without being brought to any crisis.[40]

What Krenek does not recognize is that it is precisely his initial notion of the world as "duality" that precludes any reconciliation.

As little more than a "soulless machine," Jonny becomes essentially a dehumanized puppet, a charge that could also be made of Daniello, Yvonne, and all the other characters with the exception of Max and Anita. Alfred Einstein made this point in his review of the Berlin première in 1927, saying that "in Krenek there are figures, marionettes, with which one can do anything."[41] When Daniello is run over by a train in Act II, scene 10, it must be one of the least affecting deaths in opera. And the character of Jonny is if anything even more hollow and artificial. Just as his defining characteristics are pieced together from tropes about the primitive, jazz, and the American black male, Jonny's music is constructed primarily from generic references and quotations, excerpts from "Swanee River," imitations of jazz, minstrel songs, and spirituals. Even when he lays aside these masks in moments of sexual passion or rage, his music still evokes a kind of *Rite of Spring* octatonic primitivism, as in his "tierisch" assault on Anita (mm. 886ff).

The stark contrast between Jonny's music and what Krenek called the "romantic idiom" of the other characters reinforces the opposition of the spiritual and animal spheres.[42] This results in what Taruskin has characterized as an operatic "Heisenberg problem" for *Jonny spielt auf,* and for *Zeitoper* in general. Because the elements of everyday life could "function convincingly within the world of opera only as an exotic import," they remain "exceptional, numinous and threatening."[43] The role of jazz as external to the real musical world of the opera is reinforced dramatically by Jonny's existence on the boundaries of the story. He enters through windows, lurks in hallways; we see him running across railroad tracks, and even at the conclusion he is placed outside and above the crowd, perched on the station clock. Jonny's outsider status is marked as well by his language, a peculiar mixture of English, German, and French; at one point he sings, "Auf Wiedersehn, good bye, my dear, / sleep well in deine Sack!" (63). This enforcement of boundaries explains the growing importance of the maid Yvonne as the opera progresses. After the initial scenes emphasizing the dangerous conjunctions of Jonny with Anita, in the later scenes the two are kept safely apart. Yvonne, naturally positioned in Jonny's sphere by function of her class, serves as the intermediary, acting as a go-between and instigating Jonny's rescue of Max.

This sense of Jonny's music as an intrusive force is strengthened by frequent distancing effects: the jazz band numbers, marked in the score as "Shimmy," "Blues," "Tango," and "Jazz," are only heard offstage or broadcast over the loudspeakers in Act II, scene 7.[44] To borrow Carolyn Abbate's terminology, Jonny's music is primarily "phenomenal"; even when his only audience is Yvonne, he is always represented as performing.[45] When the violin first comes into his possession, for example, he dances about in front of Yvonne, then "strikes a triumphant circus pose *ad spectatores*" before presenting his song of triumph "im Ton eines Neger-Spirituals" (94–95).

In contrast, Max and Anita are associated primarily with the more traditionally operatic "noumenal" music, that heard only by the audience in the opera house. Krenek touched on this distinction in his later rejection of the label of "jazz opera" for *Jonny spielt auf*:

> whatever jazz there occurs is brought in to characterize the professional sphere of the protagonist, Jonny, leader of an American combo. The music attached to the other characters, which to me were at least as important, is conceived in that early romantic idiom I had chosen as my model, occasionally touched up with dissonant spices and Italianizing Pucciniesque vocal exuberance.[46]

One obvious exception to this phenomenal-noumenal opposition is the aria from Max's opera, initially also part of the realm of phenomenal music that Jonny and the offstage jazz-band occupy. Yet in contrast to the music of Jonny's jazz band, Max's aria is performed *on stage* in the manner of a lied with the composer at the keyboard, creating a sense of immediacy and interiority that Jonny's music lacks.

Unlike the jazz elements that remain phenomenal, moreover, Max's aria gradually penetrates into the noumenal unconscious of the score. In the third scene, Anita returns to her Paris hotel with the memory of her performance of the aria still ringing in her ears. As she thinks of the distant Max, she cites both the music and words for the phrase, "I was assailed by homesickness" (suchte das Heimweh mich heim) (53), while the melody and accompaniment of Max's aria permeate the entire passage. A more complicated example of this collapse of "opera's conventional barrier between heard and unheard,"[47] occurs when Max attempts to distract himself by composing while waiting in vain for Anita to return (Act II, scene 5, mm. 270–81). Although he seats himself at a piano, he works silently on paper; the fragmentary reference to his aria, performed by the orchestra, must thus represent only his thoughts of Anita or some new imagined music that only Max can hear. In Act II, scene 7, the noumenal and phenomenal are further merged when the complete aria is broadcast over the hotel loudspeakers. Following directly on Max's imagined dialogue with the "Voice of the Glacier," depicted by an ethereal offstage women's chorus, Max is unable to determine if the "sweet" sounds of the aria he hears are real or imaginary.

This moment also marks a transition in the meaning of the aria. While the crowd assembled on the hotel terrace disparages the broadcast as "modern music," even these listeners seem touched by the beauty of Anita's voice: "when she sings it, it almost sounds like real music" (101). Despite the fact that the aria is clearly intended as a sort of parody, its return at several key points in the drama suggests this style as a norm at the center of a work that defines everything else as "Other." Through each of its appearances the aria acquires the aura of authentic utterance, in contrast to the patchwork of quotations and allusions that is Jonny's music. By Act II, scene 7 the aria has been performed and alluded to so many times that one comes to hear it as already somehow canonical. Significantly, although Max still must face his final trials in the last scenes, it is ultimately the experience of hearing his own music that snatches him from death back into life.

Because the opera does not challenge the "duality of the world" within which it operates, it never rises above the level of a kind of minstrelsy, whereby Max, and through him other "ponderous intellectuals," can find a persona to overcome inhibitions and to secure vicarious sexual potency.[48] Perhaps the best symbol of this is the often-ridiculed choice of Daniello's Amati violin as the target of Jonny's desire. By fetishizing the violin rather than a saxophone, for example, the opera accepts traditional conceptions of cultural value and attainment. Moreover, the way Jonny disguises the violin as a banjo by tying his bowler hat on to it and hiding it in a banjo case explicitly reproduces the dynamics of blackface minstrelsy. At the opera's climax he pulls the instrument out of the case to reveal the same old Amati. Even the glacier is eventually redeemed: from its original appearance as the epitome of sterility and isolation, it is transformed into a Wagnerian symbol of eternity and truth. The despairing Max is rejected when he tries to throw himself into the glacier, but it is clear that this is only a temporary condition until he has "filled the space" allotted to him.

It should come as no surprise that Krenek himself was profoundly ambivalent about mass culture and the "real" world he appeared to embrace in *Jonny spielt auf*. After a period of flirtation with "everyday life" he returned to the Schoenberg fold for the rest of his career. Krenek's 1939 commentary on the place of *Jonny spielt auf* in his development makes clear both the degree to which the opera was autobiographical, and how significantly he changed his views in later years. After an early interest in atonality, which he attributes to a desire to be "as radical as possible," Krenek suddenly discovered himself to be in full retreat:

I know now that the need for an "affirmation of life" was the innermost force that drove me to this movement. I soon came to feel that atonal music did not contain enough rich possibilities to be just to the positive side of life. From a purely technical viewpoint I was dissatisfied with the disorder and lack of organization which seemed to reign there; but that was a subjective cause, for I never had occupied myself thoroughly enough with the problem of atonality—I had simply employed it as a device which seemed to be as convenient as tonality.

Inspired by his contact with French music and Stravinsky, Krenek hoped for "better and gayer times," for the renewal of tonality through jazz, trends he linked to the period of deceptive stability in late 1920s Weimar. Although he acknowledges that he "conducted polemics against Schoenberg and the twelve-tone technique," he concludes that his contact with atonality must have been too strong:

> my conscience was not at rest. It became more and more evident to me that I had simply avoided a decision—that I had run away from a given problem.[49]

Krenek's conclusion resonates strikingly with the central metaphor of *Jonny spielt auf:* Max's flight from life to the solace of the "schöner Berg." But, in a reversal that seems entirely in keeping with the twists and turns of *Jonny spielt auf* what in the opera is depicted as a sign of weakness and renunciation is reconfigured in the composer's retrospective self-justification as an assertion of strength.

"Grimes Is at His Exercise"

SEX, POLITICS, AND VIOLENCE IN THE LIBRETTOS OF PETER GRIMES

PHILIP BRETT

Grimes . . . is very much of an ordinary weak
person who, being at odds with the society in
which he finds himself, tries to overcome it and,
in doing so, offends against the conventional
code, is classed by society as a criminal, and
destroyed as such. There are plenty of Grimeses
around still, I think!

(Peter Pears[1])

INTRODUCTION

THE MODERNIST CRITICAL AXIOM that, in Joseph Kerman's classic formulation, "opera is a type of drama whose integral existence is determined
from point to point and in the whole by musical articulation,"[2] was often
used, as we now realize, as a way of vesting sole authority in the composer,
a male. Much work has now been done on recuperating the singer (usually female). It is a particular irony of Benjamin Britten's fifty-year-old
repertory opera, *Peter Grimes,* that the singer who premièred the role of
the protagonist—and still the only one apparently capable of singing the
notes as written—was also the person who drafted the scenario, and even
wrote bits of the libretto. He happened to be the composer's lover, and his
auditions for that role were evidently as protracted and demanding as those
for the role of Peter Grimes, which was not originally conceived for him,
and was given to him well into the course of the project.

There could be no better parable in the twentieth century of the social
process by which operas come into existence, or, alternatively, of the bank-
ruptcy of the modernist model of criticism based solely on the composer

This is a new version of an essay entitled *"Peter Grimes:* The Growth of the Libretto" in
The Making of "Peter Grimes," ed. Paul Banks (Woodbridge, Suffolk: Boydell Press, 1996),
2:53–78 (this volume is subsequently referred to as *MPG*). Details of libretto revision explored there are here curtailed, but several of the arguments have been amplified.

and the score. It is true, as Philip Reed has written, that "when Britten sat down at his desk in the Old Mill, Snape, in January 1944 . . . he was on his own";[3] Britten himself cultivated an image that encouraged the modernist view. The reclusive magician of Aldeburgh, drawing to him those he needed to realize his ambitious operatic dreams (and tending to drop many who were spent) could be made to fit an almost Wagnerian image of operatic creation. But there was always a great deal to consider before the notes—the libretto and its ideas, most obviously, and in Britten's case also a physical sense of the stage and its design—without which they could not have taken shape, or would not have taken the shape they did. In the case of *Peter Grimes,* a whole two-and-a-half years of preparation, much of it spent in conversation with others, led up to that lonely moment in the Old Mill.[4] Furthermore, many presences hover above and around this score: some, like Pears and the librettist Montagu Slater, have a direct bearing on it, others, like the poet W. H. Auden and the novelist Christopher Isherwood, played the roles of intellectual godparents. More shadowy but equally powerful forces, I shall argue, are the uneasiness in the relations between individual and state during a period when Europe was emerging from one of its most agonizing wars, an uneasiness that in Britain naturally focused on the class system but that in Britten's case, as for many of his circle, also included unresolved questions surrounding sexuality. Even at the personal level, Britten's single most powerful statement about the intent of the opera included Peter Pears: "[a] central feeling for us was that of the individual against the crowd, with ironic overtones for our own situation . . . as conscientious objectors."[5] The remark was addressed to the social situation in which the two found themselves—pacifism, in this instance as on other occasions in Britten's life, doing double duty as a controversial but mentionable position for still-unspeakable homosexuality.[6]

The opera was conceived in Escondido, California, where the two lovers came across a copy of *The Listener* with the reprint of a BBC radio talk on George Crabbe by the celebrated English novelist, E. M. Forster. The story of this exotic and epiphanic moment is familiar enough.[7] Less familiar is the notion of how many people and connections were involved even at that initial moment—two musician-lovers inspired by the words of another English homosexual male of the same leisured intellectual and artistic class about a poet who evoked "the sea, the estuary, the flat Suffolk coast, and local meanness, and an odour of brine and dirt—tempered occasionally with the scent of flowers."[8] Predictably enough, the vivid drabness of the East Anglian coast where Britten had grown up and which Forster brilliantly evokes survived in the score. More remarkable are the intimations of those two Englishmen in California about the unpromising story of Peter Grimes as a subject for an opera.

Unpromising? It is difficult to say this in hindsight, but Christopher

Isherwood thought so when Britten approached him to write the libretto, and so he pleaded the claims of other work and the geographical distance between them as an excuse to get out of it. Replying to this refusal, Britten let Isherwood know that "incidentally, alot [sic] of your hints . . . have proved useful—thank you!"—a remark that allows us to count Isherwood as another contributor to the process and raises the distinct possibility that his influence had some effect in pushing the story in a more socially progressive direction.[9] Isherwood's various autobiograhical books show how clear he always was about the efficacy of anger in response to society's attempts to dismiss him for being "queer" (the term he preferred to use as a reminder of the need for that anger). Was it Isherwood, possibly, who first nudged the two young Englishmen toward a view of Grimes that ultimately led to a classic modern reinterpretation of the subject of oppression?

In George Crabbe's poem, Grimes is an unmitigated ruffian. He spurns his father, gambles and drinks, becomes a poacher and trespasser, but cannot finally be satisfied until he has "a feeling creature subject to his power." The three workhouse boys who serve this function as his apprentices "bear the blow of his outrageous hand" to such an extent that they forfeit their lives. Forbidden to hire more apprentices, Grimes sinks into melancholy, is tormented by visions of his father and dead boys, goes mad, and dies a pauper in a parish bed. As E. M. Forster later wrote, "Grimes is tough, hard and dull, and the poet must be tough with him, tougher than Shakespeare had to be with Macbeth, who possessed imagination. He must smash him up physically . . . and then place indubitable spectres in his path."[10]

Crabbe was a realist, and a social critic rather than a reformer. His Grimes merely takes advantage of what the law allows. Unlike the villain of a Gothic novel, he does not have to resort to kidnapping to place another person under his control: he has only to apply to the nearest workhouse. The townspeople are implicated in the situation:

> But none inquir'd how *Peter* us'd the Rope,
> Or what the Bruise, that made the Stripling stoop;
> None could the Ridges on his Back behold,
> None sought him shiv'ring in the Winter's Cold;
> None put the question—"*Peter*, dost thou give
> The Boy his Food?—What, Man! the Lad must live:
> Consider, *Peter*, let the Child have Bread,
> He'll serve thee better if he's strok'd and fed."
> None reason'd thus—and some, on hearing Cries,
> Said calmly, "*Grimes* is at his Exercise."[11]

When they do inevitably turn on Peter, the Borough folk are not interested in examining their own consciences; they want to find a scapegoat. We are reminded that Crabbe, though drawn back to Aldeburgh again and again, did not like the place or its people. As Ronald B. Hatch points out, "Grimes does not think he is doing anything out of the ordinary: nor do his fellow citizens. And in fact he is not. He is taking advantage of an accepted system. His individual savagery reflects the savagery of the society."[12]

That last sentence comes very close to something Britten told *Time* magazine in February 1948, just before the first New York performance of the opera: "The more vicious the society, the more vicious the individual."[13] But he prefaced this by saying that Grimes was "a subject very close to my heart—the struggle of the individual against the masses." Unlike Crabbe, who saw Grimes as the embodiment of an evil society, Britten and his partner identified their character as the victim of that society, treated him with compassion, and cast him as Everyman.

In this makeover, Grimes becomes an artist, a dreamer who can enter a pub during a heavy storm and sing about the stars, to the astonishment of the Borough regulars, who think him mad or drunk (Act I, scene 2). He is ambitious, though, to win their respect through the means he perceives them as admiring most, commercial success, and won't listen to the wise advice of the retired sea-captain Balstrode, one of the few to resist the communal pressure to ostracize Grimes. Ultimately, his drive to succeed leads him to break his pact and friendship with the retired schoolmistress, Ellen Orford, and drag his new apprentice, whom she is minding, off to fish on a Sunday morning. This precipitates a crisis in the Borough, whose hypocritical citizens have been carefully introduced in the prologue and first act: the pompous and lecherous coroner, Swallow; the ineffectual Anglican parson; the Methodist preacher, Bob Boles, who preaches temperance and drinks like a fish; the apothecary, Ned Keene, always ready to supply drugs under the table; and Mrs. Sedley, the "respectable lady" high on laudanum and low on charity, her nose in everyone else's business. A posse is organized (II, 1) and the men march off to Grimes's hut leaving the women (Auntie the publican, and her two loose-living nieces) to lament the foibles of men together with, and out of sympathy for, Ellen. As the posse reaches Grimes's hut (II, 2), distracting Peter, the apprentice misses his footing as he climbs out of the seaward door, and he falls to his death down the precipitous cliff. The result is inevitable: the Borough condemns Peter (while continuing to display its own moral turpitude), and he is driven to madness and suicide.

I want here briefly to outline the process of the construction of the librettos of *Peter Grimes*—several versions reached publication—and to deal with some strands of criticism that connect with them. The development of the drama falls roughly into three main stages. To some simplified degree, these stages follow the categories of my subtitle, which may therefore provide subheadings.[14]

SEX

The earliest scenarios, probably dating from that summer in Escondido, already display the main cast of characters—Grimes, the boy, Ellen, and a Landlord of the pub (who later became Balstrode)—as well as some of the features of the plot; but there are also some dead ends, such as a band of smugglers who disappeared from subsequent versions. Most striking is Pears's language about Grimes's relation to the boy: in the pub scene, for instance, "Ellen acclaims boy as her child, Grimes (aside) as his apprentice (prey?)." And a remarkable passage in the hut scene (II, 2) must be quoted in full:

> [Peter] admits his [the apprentice's] youth hurts him, his innocence galls him, his uselessness maddens him. He had no father to love him, why should he? His father only beat him, why should not he? "Prove yourself some use, not only pretty—work—not only be innocent—work do not stare; would you rather I loved you? you are sweet, young etc.—but you must love me, why do you not love me? Love me darn you."[15]

Pears must have recognized that this was going too far, for in another draft written on board the *Axel Johnson* the following spring as the young couple sailed to England, he changed the hut scene to emphasize Grimes's violence. Responding to his partner after he had heard part of the score, and perhaps acknowledging an earlier difference of opinion over the homoerotic question, Pears writes:

> The more I hear of it, the more I feel that the queerness is unimportant and doesn't really exist in the music (or at any rate obtrude) so it mustn't do so in words. P. G. is an introspective, an artist, a neurotic, his real problem is expression, self-expression.[16]

POLITICS

A second stage of the opera-making process is represented by the engagement of a librettist, Montagu Slater. Slater was not only a founder-editor of *Left Review* but also a Communist party member, and the alliance between what one might call the thirties homosexual/pacifist sensibility of Britten and Pears with the Marxist left had been foreshadowed by Auden and Isherwood and by other friends Britten had made while working in the film industry. In the musicians' case, it was an alliance that would not survive far beyond the completion of *Peter Grimes:* Slater was among many to be discarded as the couple moved toward the political center. Certain aspects of Slater's working habits, and his final act of aggression in publishing his own version of the libretto separately, may have accounted for this. At the time, however, the connection with Slater was an extremely important and effective one. It can probably be credited with giving Britten's first major opera a political twist that saved it from being "no more than a rather bloodthirsty melodrama"—Britten's own description of the first drafts in a letter to Isherwood.

Slater's contribution was most important in the two episodes in which the tragedy moves beyond simply impinging on the community and actually spurs the community into action: the procession to the hut and what happens between protagonist and chorus there; and the manhunt in the last act. Commentaries on *Peter Grimes,* although frequently paying tribute to its status as a chorus opera, tend to ignore the first two of these crucial elements of the plot, neither of which was present in the earlier Britten-Pears drafts and are likely therefore to have been Slater's own invention.

The posse that sets out to inspect Grimes's hut for no better reason than "popular feeling's rising" (as the lawyer Swallow puts it) is formed in direct contravention of the due process on which the rule of law is founded, and of the convention of privacy that governs the individual's relation to the state in a democracy. The posse's approach throws the already overwrought Grimes into a paranoid panic, generating anger that is predictably directed at the boy ("Wait! You've been talking / You and that bitch were gossiping. / What lies have you been telling?"). But the effect of this on the audience is offset by what becomes the second turning point of the opera (the first being Grimes's rejection of Ellen and his symbolic acceptance of his role as outcast and failure in Act 2, scene 1—"So be it, and God have mercy upon me!"—on a massive cadence in B-flat, the "Borough" key). Discerning the boy as "the cause of everything," Grimes decides to get out before the crowd arrives. The sequence of events makes it clear that even in his anger he has an eye toward the boy's welfare:

PETER: Careful, or you'll break your neck
              Down the cliff-side to the deck.
(*Rope in hand he drives the* BOY *towards the cliff door.*)
CHORUS: (*off*)   Now the liars shiver, for
              Now if they've cheated we shall know:
              We shall strike and strike to kill
              At the slander or the sin.
PETER: I'll pitch the stuff down. Come on!
(*He pitches ropes and nets.*)
              Now
              Shut your eyes and down you go.
(*There is a knocking at the other door.* PETER *turns towards it, then retreats.*

Meanwhile the BOY *climbs out. When* PETER *is between the two doors the* BOY *screams and falls out of sight.* PETER *runs to the cliff door, feels for his grip and then swings quickly after him.*)[17]

In other words, the community is directly implicated in the boy's death by means of the complicated symbol of "knocking at the other door," which momentarily distracts Peter from watching over him. Its significance must surely have been heightened by the sensitivity of many of its first audience to the devastating potential effect of this simple act, during the immediately preceding years, on the lives of those under the rule of the Nazis all over neighboring Europe. Separation from family or friends, confinement in a concentration camp, or even death were among the possibilities of such an intrusion. This was perhaps the single most decisive change in the drama after the decision to reclaim the title figure, and it is certainly the feature of the plot that has been least appreciated and examined.[18] The manhunt of the last act is no doubt more musically remarkable. But the intensity of that moment can only work as well as it does by being part of a series of increasingly intrusive, aggressive, and finally inhuman acts carried out by a narrow-minded, hypocritical community represented not only as in perpetual struggle with the sea but also as obsessed with conformity and enforcing "standards" to its own arbitrary liking. Without the preceding scenes, this last and most powerful crowd event would have risked seeming merely surreal.

VIOLENCE (WITH SOME SEX)

Although Slater constructed the social aspect of the opera along lines that (so far as we can tell) Pears and Britten had not previously imagined, he did not feel the need for a complete change of direction in the characterization of Grimes. He appears rather to have relished the hints of loose-living and sadism in Pears's drafts, even those of homoeroticism. To Ellen's question "Peter, tell me one thing, where / Young stranger got his bruise and weals," Peter answers "Out of my true affection"; and in the hut scene at the point where Peter, suddenly losing his temper, "takes a short length of rope and whirls it around," a manuscript draft in Slater's hand presents a Grimes who would have severely hampered the opera's chances of success:

PETER:　By God I'll beat it out of you.
　　　　Stand up. (*lash*) Straighter. (*lash*) I'll count two
　　　　And then you'll jump to it. One.
　　　　Well? Two.
(*The boy doesn't move. Then* Peter *lashes hard, twice. He runs.* Peter *follows.*)
　　　　Your soul is mine.

Your body is the cat o' nine
Tail's mincemeat. O! a pretty dish
Smooth-skinned and young as she could wish.
Come cat! Up whiplash! Jump my son
Jump (*lash*) jump (*lash*) jump, the dance is on.[19]

If this complicates Grimes in one way, the apparition of his father during the hallucinatory episode later in the scene adds yet another dimension to his psychological profile. And Slater kept this sort of detail (but not the above passage) when he published his own version along with many of the other passages in which Grimes addresses the boy in charged emotional language.[20]

Britten, Pears, and Eric Crozier, the stage director who at this point became important in the process, may gradually have realized that Slater had transformed the plot only halfway. He had introduced community wrongdoing and injustice effectively while retaining the psychological profile that set up the audience either to pity the protagonist or to hold him in contempt, but not to identify with him. If the idea of the "individual against the crowd" was to work, and if the drama were to become an allegory of oppression (both external and internalized), then the process of Grimes's self-destruction had to be felt to be the direct result of his social situation, so that everyone in the audience could recognize a little of themselves in him. A set of psychological circumstances that would make his sadism explicit, or suggest a fundamental cause in an Oedipal conflict, would undermine this process. "Once we'd decided to make it a drama of the individual against the crowd," as Peter Pears once explained to me when I asked him why the father and dead apprentices had been excised, "then those things had to go."[21] And so it was at quite a late stage, from the beginning of composition right through to rehearsals and even beyond, that the third transformation occurred in which Peter Grimes lost the psychological or even pathological groundings that Britten and Pears had initially imagined and that Slater could not now be persuaded to relinquish.

The alterations to the mad scene in Act III are emblematic of the final process in the evolution of the drama of *Grimes,* in which the protagonist loses all those features of personality that might "explain" him outside the action of the drama and the aura of the music. Slater portrays a craven individual who rolls out his psychological credentials ("This breakwater with splinters torn / By winds, is where your father took / You by the hand to this same boat / Leaving your home for the same sea / Where he died and you're going to die."), defensively excuses himself for the death of his apprentice ("You're not to blame that he went down. / It was his weakness that let go"), and harps self-pityingly on his failings ("The drinking's over, wild oats sown") as he answers to Ellen, his mother figure, in person. The eventual version, concocted by Britten with the help of yet another collaborator, Ronald Duncan (soon to be the librettist of *The Rape of Lucretia*), tells the story of the opera in the music of the opera, recalling the inquest, the evil message of the posse ("Bring the branding iron and knife"), the soliloquy ("The Great Bear and Pleiades' setting") and the round in the pub, and the friendship and betrayal of Ellen, culminating in the symbolic moment of capitulation to society, "And God have mercy upon me," brilliantly recalled sotto voce in E♭, a step further into Borough tonal territory, and addressed now ("upon *you*") to Ellen and his persecutors, suggesting absolution as well as capitulation. This leads Grimes in turn to the desperately repeated enunciation of his own name as a prelude to its and his own erasure, and a brief recall of the storm soliloquy, sign of his inner life, literally dragged down to the Borough's E♭ as it concludes. Here, powerfully, music ends. Grimes is a nonexistent entity, finally, apart from the community and its actions, and this is what makes him an allegorical figure rather than a "character."

THE CRITICAL RESPONSE

Nothing better illustrates the centrality of Grimes's character in the plot than the speed with which ambivalence about him emerged, especially around issues of guilt and sadism. Even before the opera had been performed, Edward Sackville-West, a critic close to Britten, had written for the official introductory booklet an account of the music that includes, in the course of a rather specific programmatic interpretation of the Passacaglia, this surprising statement: "it would not do to shirk the fact that Grimes is guilty of manslaughter."[22] What the Borough court shrank from doing in the Prologue, then, and what Slater had so carefully circumvented in the hut scene, could readily be contemplated by one of the most intelligent and well-connected critics of the period. More extreme is Desmond Shawe-Taylor who, in his articulate review of the original production in *The New Statesman*, declared that "what neither composer nor librettist seems to realize is that, after all, the sympathetic schoolmarm was wrong (and therefore, in effect, an accessory in the second boy's death), whereas poor Mrs. Sedley was dead right." Drawing a moral, he found "something shocking in the attempt to win our sympathies for a character *simply because* he is an outlaw and an enemy of society" and called it "an adolescent conception of man and society."[23] This conclusion alerts us to a specific phenomenon in Britten reception. "Adolescent" (like the more hostile labels "immature" and "clever" also often leveled at the composer) is a code word referring to a particular view of homosexuality during the period as a matter of arrested development leading to a failure to "adjust." Possibly what lies at the root of these and many similar rejections of the surface of the plot is the trace of something deliberately expunged from the plot that nevertheless made critics extremely uncomfortable, but that could not be articulated at the time. Tippett put his finger on it while talking much later to Humphrey Carpenter: "I don't think [Britten] seemed to understand that a problem would come over the question of Peter Grimes's relation to the boys."[24]

Of course this could only have been true among the many who knew the "open secret" of Britten's homosexuality. Edmund Wilson, who caught one of the early performances on a visit to London, contextualized the problem of sadism in terms of the European war, which he considered to have degraded the victors as much as the vanquished. He saw Grimes as a symbol for "the whole of bombing, machine-gunning, mining, torpedoing, ambushing humanity, which talks about a guaranteed standard of living but does nothing but wreck its own works, degrade or pervert its own moral life and reduce itself to starvation" and observed that "the indignant shouting trampling mob which comes to punish Peter Grimes is just as sadistic as he."[25] Hans Keller, a straight insider, on the other hand, refused to endorse the sadism of Grimes, even in his (rejected but now posthumously published) "psychoanalytic notes." He describes instead the chorus (at the appearance of Peter in Act I, scene 2) as "projecting their own repressed anal sadism on to him," and notes for good measure that "in view of the fact that even competent listeners have shut their ears to 'what the music clearly shows,' a quite important sidelight is here thrown on how musical understanding can be prevented by such mechanisms as projection."[26] Putting Grimes on the couch and impaling him on the twin spikes of anal eroticism and unresolved Oedipal complex, Keller manages almost completely to undo the social work of the libretto. No doubt aware of this, he confined himself in print to two paragraphs on Grimes's character that specifically address the social dimension and rather strikingly take account of the difference the music makes.[27]

In spite of Keller, and the statements of Peter Pears that he endorses, the views of Grimes as sadist and of *Peter Grimes* as a "problem opera" on that account do not go away. They surfaced most recently in Humphrey Carpenter's biography, where the materials I have discussed are used, without regard for the larger picture they form, to construct meanings for the opera that play down its political import and implicitly contradict its dramatic portrayal of the mechanics of oppression. Carpenter brings up the father image of Slater's early drafts, and draws attention to the word "murder" in the original scenarios of the hut scene drafted by Britten and Pears. Quoting Slater's more sadistic drafts for the hut scene (including the one quoted above), Carpenter asserts that the librettist "tried to show the audience much more of *what was really happening*" (my italics), as though there were a secret "real" text behind the opera linked directly to its composer's psyche, a special penetration of that psyche on the part of the librettist, and no problem at all with the use, in interpreting a work, of material rejected by its authors.[28] To unearth morsels from the sketches and drafts helpful to one's argument while ignoring the general flow of the evidence, is, of course, a danger of their being available. But there is something homophobic, too, in the tendency to confine a reading of Britten's operas, as opposed to those of, say, Berg, Janáček or Stravinsky, to the expression of the particularity of the composer's own psychology and inner life. It is true that one of the things Britten's operas (as well as his other works) seem to achieve is an exploration of various issues surrounding sexuality that the composer could not discuss in any other public forum (except obliquely through the code of antiphilistinism or the discourse of pacifism). His perseverance in this endeavor is one of the truly remarkable and even noble features of his career. Yet it is particularly ironic that *Peter Grimes* should come to be seen as a drama about Britten's own struggle with sadism in a homosexual or pederastic context when it was the work of so many hands, nearly all of whom (except the straight Marxist Slater) were trying toward its completion to purge it of the particular and present it in terms sufficiently open for it to have significance for a wide range of people.

FURTHER EXPLORATIONS

There is surely an advantage to be gained in looking past the composer himself, however, toward the extraordinary set of events, political and cultural, that took place between the summer holiday in California in 1941 and the première in London in 1945. For, at a deeper level, *Peter Grimes* would seem to have tapped critical issues about modern society for which Britten and his friends were a rather surprising conduit—issues for which the controversy over Grimes's character acts as a kind of symptom. One, as we have seen from Edmund Wilson's account (prompted by World War II), is the nature of aggression and its deleterious effect on "both sides." Another, looking forward anxiously to the aftermath, is the (always unresolved) question of responsibility in the relation of individual and state in modern capitalistic democracies. The "more liberal view" espoused by the authors sees deviance, even criminality, as a symptom of society's failure, and tends to want to deal with it accordingly, by trying either to understand and allow for it, or, in a more problematic strategy, to control it by "medicalizing" it. The opposing view, espoused by conservatives who oppose state interference only when their own interests are threatened, insists on maintaining individual conformity and responsibility, and uses institutionalization as a means of control. *Peter Grimes,* not coincidentally, emerged at the dawn of the welfare state, and it reflects many of the questions that occupied British society at the dawn of that great social experiment.

An even wider issue stems from the ambiguous nature of the plot as an allegory and of the protagonist as a symbol. One feat of the music, one that disturbed Shawe-Taylor, was to create in sensitive listeners a warm sympathy for and even identification with a character who in the unmusical light of day may seem a brutal child abuser. To make matters worse, the ploy that critics so readily embraced in dealing with *Death in Venice*—of turning the protagonist into a symbol (of the artist) in order to avoid the (to them) embarrassing materiality of Aschenbach's declaration of love to a boy at the end of Act I—was simply unavailable in *Grimes*. This strategy was unavailable mainly owing to Britten and Pears's "open secret": as an "ordinary weak person . . . who offends against the conventional code, is classed by society as a criminal, and destroyed as such" (as Pears puts it in the quotation that serves as my epigraph), Grimes would inescapably be read as a symbol for the "homosexual."[29]

Since the trial of Oscar Wilde exactly a half-century earlier, the male homosexual, as a notionally uniform but actually incoherent identity, had been foregrounded in a special way in Anglo-American society and ideology, in a manner analogous to that of the Jew in Fascist countries, as "the embodiment of a certain blockage—of the impossibility which prevents the society from achieving its full identity as a closed, homogeneous totality." Slavoj Žižek, who writes with particular eloquence about this situation, goes on to display the ideological mechanism by reversing the equation: "Society is not prevented from achieving its full identity because of Jews: it is prevented by its own antagonistic nature, by its own immanent blockage, and it 'projects' this internal negativity into the figure of the 'Jew.'"[30] By analogy, one might say that the impossibility, the "immanent blockage," of the institution of compulsory heterosexuality that binds all the institutions of the well-ordered capitalistic democracy without regard to the ethnic or class differences that operate at other levels, is revealed in the return of the homosexual through all levels of that society and in all guises. The immanent failure of the patriarchy is demonstrated by, and projected on, those who exercise its privilege as men but undermine the principles of sexual relation and patterns of domination on which it is founded in the modern world.

Grimes marks the opening of a new stage in the debate over homosexuality, one that was perhaps inevitable as the result of the social changes wrought by the war. It was to emerge, out of hints and innuendos (like "adolescent"), into something closer to a witch hunt than a debate as the result of the defection of Burgess and Maclean from Britain to the U.S.S.R early in the following decade. "Conformity" and "adjustment" began to have special connotations, when even (one might say especially) the gentleman's agreement that had existed between the authorities and homosexuals of the leisured class was abrogated in a horrifying series of arrests and trials. The overplaying of the disciplinary hand stimulated the growth of a movement that, beginning with the ameliorating but in many ways reactionary Wolfenden Report, led eventually to a modest reform of the law.[31] The point is not that *Peter Grimes* initiated or even participated in this debate, but that it stands as a symptom of the conditions of that debate. For one thing, its juxtaposition of the outsider with stereotypical masculinity and working class affiliations preserved resonances of the Wilde scandal (marked as much by the crossing of class boundaries and the revelation of an underworld of lower-class male homosexuals as by the "offense" itself). In the context of theater dominated by Coward and Rattigan plays (and the Lord Chamberlain's embargoes), in which subversion was limited to innuendo and the characters reflected their audience in leisure-class appearance and values, even Peter Pears's aristocrat-manqué fisherman must for many have been disturbing, for it crossed the aesthete/hearty, homosexual/heterosexual binaries that were powerfully present in all kinds of representations.[32]

Fifty years later the story of *Peter Grimes* is still relevant as the broader conditions out of which it grew, the repressive social atmosphere of the thirties, threaten to return—some would say *have* returned—to Anglo–North American life. The situation has been altered, of course, by the success of the gay and other movements in exacting recognition and discovering the efficacy of community and alliance. The protagonist of Suri Krishnamma's film *A Man of No Importance* (British, 1994), a bus conductor in the Dublin of the early sixties, is still surrounded by oppressive figures comparable to those in the opera, but he externalizes his interior life by reciting poetry to his passengers and getting them to collaborate in his project to stage Wilde's *Salome*. Supported by his loyal band—all misfits themselves, we are allowed to realize—he is able almost heroically to defy the mean-spirited bus inspector, his Bob Boles, and retain the friendship (nothing more, mind you) of his bus driver "Bosie." But behind this almost tragic comedy lies the old set of social assumptions that *Grimes* dramatizes in an almost archetypal manner for a modern society policed out of homosexuality and other irregularities by certain myths and fears: the deviant is an ordinary person, not a hero, nor a camp matinee idol; his offense is not what he does but what he represents; and he is "alone, alone, alone . . . "

Notes

Introduction

1. The question was submitted by James McCalla, who kindly reminded me of his wording in a personal communication. The quiz was broadcast in March 1996.

2. McClary, Foreword to *Opera, or the Undoing of Women,* by Clément, trans. Betsy Wing (Minneapolis: University of Minnesota Press, 1988), xii; originally published as *Opéra, ou la défaite des femmes* (Paris, 1979).

3. Clément, 10.

4. The challenge of bringing "ineffable" music down to earth, returning it to its well-concealed origins in social practice, has been a pressing conern of that subdiscipline that we still reluctantly call "new musicology." The three scholars whose writings have made the most difference in this area are certainly Susan McClary, Gary Tomlinson, and Lawrence Kramer. For an overview of these discussions about close reading and music's situatedness in culture, see the exchange between Tomlinson and Kramer initiated by Kramer's article "The Musicology of the Future," *repercussions* 1 (1992): 5–18 and continued in *Current Musicology* 53 (1993): 18–40.

5. Cusick, "Gendering Modern Music: Thoughts on the Monteverdi-Artusi Controversy," *Journal of the American Musicological Society* 46 (spring 1993): 4.

6. Avital Ronell has offered a provocative Derridean critique of the tendency of writers of opera (and of Clément in particular) to reinforce rather than deconstruct (or "divorce") the constitutive "couples" of operatic discourse: man/woman, word/music, poet/composer, voice/orchestra. Ronell complains that feminism is too often channelled through reverse sexism and resentment against men, but her own glorification of the relationship between woman and telephone in Poulenc's *La Voix humaine* seems strangely oblivious to the male power and female pain of that opera's libretto. See Ronell, "Finitude's Score," in *Thinking Bodies,* ed. Juliet Flower McCannell and Laura Zakarin (Stanford: Stanford University Press, 1994), 87–108.

7. McClary, *Feminine Endings* (Minneapolis: University of Minnesota Press, 1991), 59.

8. See, for example, Suzanne G. Cusick, "Of Women, Music, and Power: A Model from Seicento Florence," in *Musicology and Difference: Gender and Sexuality in Music Scholarship,* ed. Ruth Solie (Berkeley and Los Angeles: University of California Press, 1993), 281–304; Wendy Heller, "The Queen as King: Refashioning Semiramide for Seicento Venice," *Cambridge Opera Journal* 5/2 (1993): 93–114; Elizabeth Hudson, "Gilda Seduced," *Cambridge Opera Journal* 4/3 (1992): 229–51; Mary Ann Smart, "The Silencing of Lucia," *Cambridge Opera Journal* 4/2 (1992): 119–41; and Gretchen Wheelock, "*Schwarze Gredel* and the Engendered Minor Mode in Mozart's Operas," *Musicology and Difference,* 201–21.

9. Clément, 49.

10. Since these influential commentaries were published, *Carmen* has remained a focus of scholarly attention, but the most recent writing on the opera focuses on the political background of the story and its exoticism and "otherness," perhaps a sign that feminism is being displaced by this broader, new-musicological approach. See James Parakilas, "The Soldier and the Exotic: Operatic Variations on a Theme of Racial Encounter," *Opera Quarterly* 10, no. 2 and 10, no. 3 (1993–94): 33–56 and 43–69; and H. Marshall Leicester, Jr., "Discourse and the Film Text: Four Readings of *Carmen*," *Cambridge Opera Journal* 6, no. 3 (1994): 245–82. On musical "others," see also Ralph Locke, "Constructing the Oriental 'Other': Saint-Saens's *Samson et Dalila*," *Cambridge Opera Journal* 3, no. 3 (1991): 261–302; and (although not directly concerned with opera) McClary's "Narrative Agendas in 'Absolute Music': Identity and Difference in Brahms' Third Symphony" in *Musicology and Difference*, 326–44.

11. Robinson, "It's Not over until the Soprano Dies," *New York Times*, 1 January 1989. On Clément's "deafness" to female voices, see also Katherine Bergeron, "Clément's Opera, or One Woman's Undoing," *Cambridge Opera Journal* 2, no. 1 (1990): 93–98.

12. Michel Poizat, *The Angel's Cry*, trans. Arthur Denner (Ithaca: Cornell University Press, 1993).

13. Gary Tomlinson, *Metaphysical Song: An Essay on Opera* (Princeton: Princeton University Press, 1999), 85–87.

14. This idea runs through most of Abbate's work, but is expressed with particular force in "The Dangerous Diva," a review of *Embodied Voices: Representing Female Vocality in Western Culture*, ed. Leslie C. Dunn and Nancy A. Jones. *Times Literary Supplement*, 30 June 1995: "When we write about opera, what do we think 'opera' is? The answers vary by profession. For musicologists, it's generally the score; for literary critics, libretti, or fictions about singers; for historians, opera's social contexts; for opera buffs, a particular recording or singer. Yet most of these things are shadows cast by opera at its loudest, in live performance."

15. Abbate, "Opera; or, the Envoicing of Women," *Musicology and Difference*, 228–29.

16. Abbate, "Brünnhilde Walks by Night," *Unsung Voices* (Princeton: Princeton University Press, 1992), 206–49.

17. See Butler, *Gender Trouble: Feminism and the Subversion of Identity* (New York and London: Routledge, 1990) and *Bodies That Matter: On the Discursive Limits of "Sex"* (New York and London: Routledge, 1993).

18. Like Claude Lévi-Strauss's famous recourse to the layout of the musical score as an analogy for the structure of myth, Barthes's metaphorical use of musical notation to represent the relationship among his five codes has inspired attempts to apply its apparatus back to music; see Patrick McCreless, "Roland Barthes's *S/Z* from a Musical Point of View," *In Theory Only* 10, no. 7 (1988): 1–28. For a broader examination of attempts to map language onto music and vice versa, see Harold S. Powers, "Language Models and Musical Analysis," *Ethnomusicology* 24, no. 1 (1980): 16–18.

19. Barthes, *S/Z*, trans. Richard Miller (New York: Hill and Wang, 1974), 110.

20. Barthes, *S/Z*, 66.

21. Peter Brooks notes the Romantic antecedents of this position in his essay in this volume, 125–26. Barbara Engh has also drawn attention to Barthes's contradictory urges to glorify music as the supreme art and to disregard its underlying structures; see "Loving It: Music Criticism and Roland Barthes," *Musicology and Difference,* 66–79.

22. Cixous and Clément, *The Newly Born Woman,* trans. Betsy Wing (Minneapolis: University of Minnesota Press, 1986), 93; quoted in Leslie C. Dunn, "Ophelia's Songs in *Hamlet:* Music, Madness, and the Feminine," in *Embodied Voices,* ed. Dunn and Jones, 55. On the role played by music (or by the idea of music) in the theory of Luce Irigaray and Julia Kristeva, see also Abbate, "Opera; or the Envoicing of Women," *Musicology and Difference,* 232, n. 14.

23. Barthes is by no means always made passive by music; see also the probing analyses of his essays "Rasch," "Loving Schumann," and "The Grain of the Voice"; all in *The Responsibility of Forms: Critical Essays on Music, Art, and Representation,* trans. Richard Howard (Berkeley and Los Angeles: University of California Press, 1991).

24. Another important attempt to integrate the body into opera studies comes from several scholars who have recently studied the castrato and the travesty role, both phenomena in which physical appearance is dramatically severed from vocal manifestation. See Susan McClary, "Gender Ambiguities and Erotic Excess in Seventeenth-Century Venetian Opera," in *Acting on the Past: Historical Performance Across Disciplines,* ed. Mark Franko and Annette Richards (Middletown, Conn.: Wesleyan University Press, 2000); Nina Treadwell, "The Performance of Gender in Cavalieri/Guidiccioni's *Ballo* 'O che nuovo miracolo' (1589)," *Women and Music: A Journal of Gender and Culture* 1 (1997): 55–70; Treadwell, "Female Operatic Cross-Dressing: Bernardo Saddumene's Libretto for Leonardo Vinci's *Li zite 'n galera* (1722)," *Cambridge Opera Journal* 10/2 (1998): 131–56; and Heather Hadlock's forthcoming study of the travesty role in nineteenth-century Italian and French opera, *Pants Parts: Female Travesty in Opera.*

25. See Wayne Koestenbaum, *The Queen's Throat: Opera, Homosexuality, and the Mystery of Desire* (New York: Vintage, 1993); Terry Castle, "In Praise of Brigitte Fassbaender: Reflections on Diva-Worship," in *En Travesti, Women, Gender Subversion, Opera,* ed. Corinne E. Blackmer and Patricia Juliana Smith (New York: Columbia University Press, 1995), 20–58; and Mitchell Morris, "Reading as an Opera Queen," in *Musicology and Difference,* 184–200.

26. Opera's function as a place of escape on various levels comes through clearly in the remarkable parallels between the autobiographical vignettes that begin many of the articles in *En Travesti;* see, for example, Corinne E. Blackmer, introduction to *En Travesti,* 1–19; and Patricia Juliana Smith, "*Gli Enigmi Sono Tre:* The [D]evolution of Turandot, Lesbian Monster," 242–84. See also Sam Abel, *Opera in the Flesh: Sexuality in Operatic Performance* (Boulder, Colo.: Westview Press, 1996).

27. Koestenbaum, 43.

28. Koestenbaum, 17.

29. Koestenbaum, 17.

30. Schor, *Reading in Detail: Aesthetics and the Feminine* (New York and London: Methuen, 1987).

31. Anselm Gerhard, *The Urbanization of Opera: Music Theater in Paris in the Nineteenth Century,* trans. Mary Whittall (Chicago: University of Chicago Press, 1998).

32. The "motherhood" metaphor came originally from Judy Tsou, one of the informal correspondents Solie cites in her article. See Solie, "Defining Feminisms: Conundrums, Contexts, Communities," *Women and Music* 1 (1997): 1–11, here 11.

33. Solie, 10.

34. The first term was perhaps used most contentiously by Carolyn Abbate and Roger Parker in their "Dismembering Mozart," *Cambridge Opera Journal* 2 (1990): 187–95; the second derives from Pierluigi Petrobelli, "Music in the Theater (apropos of *Aida,* Act III)," in his *Music in the Theater: Essays on Verdi and Other Composers,* with translations by Roger Parker (Princeton: Princeton University Press, 1994), 113–26.

Through Voices, History

1. Claude Lévi-Strauss, *Mythologiques* (Paris: Plon, 1964).

2. Vladimir Jankélévitch, *La musique et l'ineffable* (Paris: Editions du Seuil, 1983), 7.

3. Gilles de Van, *Verdi: Un théâtre en musique* (Paris: Fayard, 1992), trans. Gilda Roberts as *Verdi's Theater: Creating Drama through Music* (Chicago: University of Chicago Press, 1998).

The Absent Mother in Opera Seria

1. A useful sketch of the modernist paradigm of spectatorship is given in Kenneth Little, "Masochism, Spectacle, and the 'Broken Mirror' Clown Entrée: A Note on the Anthropology of Performance in Postmodern Culture," *Cultural Anthropology* 8 (1993): 117–29. Little's account is partly based on models of modernist visuality generally, on which see Martin Jay, "Scopic Regimes of Modernity," in *Vision and Visuality,* ed. Hal Foster (Seattle: Bay Press, 1988), 3–23.

2. See "Magic Mirrors and the *Seria* Stage: Thoughts toward a Ritual View," *Journal of the American Musicological Society* 48 (1995): 423–84, parts of which have been adapted for sections 2 through 4 below.

3. I use "king" and "monarch" generically here as structural equivalents for "sovereign," a category that may (in a given situation) pertain to a prince, a duke, and so forth. Indeed, for some analytic purposes, an absolutist ruling body in an oligarchy such as Venice may function in a manner equivalent to the monarch. Elsewhere I develop the notion that such abstract equivalencies, as part of the mythical power of sovereignty in the absolutist imaginary, account in part for the capacity of opera seria to resonate beyond the confines of the absolutist polity *sensu stricto.*

With respect to the relationship between the physical locations of boxes and the social positions of their occupants, I should also note that what I describe here is the most widespread model, on which there were numerous variations. The most common of these was the relegation of the first tier of boxes to a somewhat lower social station so that nobles could keep their distance from *hoi polloi* on the parterre. Also, the monarchical box was sometimes located nearer to the proscenium, on an inner side of the horseshoe curve that characterized the architecture of a typical eighteenth-century theater, in order to provide better viewing of the stage. For instance, the Regio-Ducal Teatro of Parma had a ducal box in such a location during the eighteenth century, while in Naples King Ferdinand IV often sat in the proscenium boxes at the San Carlo (although without ever altering the royal box architecturally).

4. Jürgen Habermas, *The Structural Transformation of the Public Sphere: An Inquiry into a Category of Bourgeois Society,* trans. Thomas Burger with Frederick Lawrence (Cambridge, Mass.: MIT Press, 1989); see especially the introduction and 43–51.

5. A rare exception is Dircea in Metastasio's *Demofoonte,* a woman thought to be a nobleman's daughter who has a son through a secret marriage to the king's heir; but through strange twists of fate she instead turns out to be the king's daughter, and her secret spouse in his turn is revealed to be the nobleman's son. Thus Dircea is put in the lowly place proper to a Metastasian mother by having to yield the throne to another (unmarried and childless) woman who then marries Dircea's brother, the king's real son. More typical of Metastasio is his *Semiramide,* who was evidently a mother everywhere throughout the long literary tradition she inhabited, *except* in Metastasio's 1748 libretto, composed in honor of the empress Maria Teresia, where the fact of her motherhood is suppressed.

6. The foundational text on this concept is Ernst H. Kantorowicz, *The King's Two Bodies: A Study in Medieval Political Thought* (Princeton: Princeton University Press, 1957)—though, as Kantorowicz shows, medieval Europe conceived the king's two bodies as having separate temporalities. On cross-cultural features of kingship and secondary literature thereon, see also Gillian Feeley-Harnik, "Issues in Divine Kingship," *Annual Review of Anthropology* 14 (1984): 273–313, and the introduction to *Rituals of Royalty: Power and Ceremonial in Traditional Societies,* ed. David Cannadine and Simon Price (Cambridge: Cambridge University Press, 1987). For an historical ethnography with strong resonances of the kingship of absolutist Naples see Clifford Geertz, *Negara: The Theatre State in Nineteenth-Century Bali* (Princeton: Princeton University Press, 1980), especially the conclusion.

7. The scene is dense with signs of the king as a divine father surrogate—and designed to be spectacular enough to win the audience's attention. Metastasio's stage directions place Artaserse before the populace for a magnificent coronation scene in which a throne is laid with crown and scepter and a burning altar is adorned with a simulacrum of the sun. Artaserse proclaims: "A voi, popoli, io m'offro / Non men padre, che Re. Siatemi voi / Più figli, che vassalli" [To you people, I offer myself, no less a father than a King. May you be more sons to me than vassals.] After the speech of which this forms a part, an attendant brings him the sacred cup.

8. See Norbert Elias, *The Court Society,* trans. Edmund Jephcott (Oxford: Basil Blackwell, 1983).

9. On this process in cross-cultural perspective see Valerio Valeri, *Enciclopedia Einaudi,* vol. 11, *Prodotti—Ricchezza;* s.v. "Regalità," (Turin: Einaudi, 1980), 764 and passim; forthcoming in translation by Lynn Westwater as s.v. "kingship," in Valerio Valeri, *Rituals and Annals: Between Anthropology and History,* ed. Janet Hoskins (Oxford: Berg). See also Georges Bataille's argument about the relationship between sovereignty and subjectivity in *Sovereignty,* vol. 3 of *The Accursed Share,* trans. Robert Hurley (New York: Zone Books, 1993).

10. Indeed one could say that opera seria in this sense was more necessary to affirming sovereignty when a monarch was absent than when present. For a comparative case see Ward Keeler, *Javanese Shadow Plays, Javanese Selves* (Princeton: Princeton University Press, 1987), chap. 8; see also Clifford Geertz, "Centers, Kings, and Charisma: Reflections on the Symbolics of Power," in his *Local Knowledge: Further Essays in Interpretive Anthropology* (New York: Basic Books, 1983), 121–46.

11. This resembles what Jonathan Z. Smith calls "signal[ing] significance without contributing signification"; *To Take Place: Toward Theory in Ritual* (Chicago and London: University of Chicago Press, 1987), 108.

12. I take the terms from Franco Piperno, who schematizes the actors in eighteenth-century opera as promoters, producers, and addressees; see "Il sistema produttivo fino al 1780," in *Storia dell'opera italiana*, vol. 4, ed. Lorenzo Bianconi and Giorgio Pestelli (Turin: E. D. T., 1987), 1–75.

13. This is a point I develop further in "Magic Mirrors and the *Seria* Stage."

14. The best general account of the institutions of the Italian family in the eighteenth century is that of Marzio Barbagli, *Sotto lo stesso tetto: mutamenti della famiglia in Italia del XV al XX secolo* (Bologna: Il Mulino, 1984).

15. Elisja Schulte van Kessel, "Virgins and Mothers between Heaven and Earth," trans. Clarissa Botsford, in *Renaissance and Enlightenment Paradoxes*, vol. 3 of *A History of Women in the West*, ed. Natalie Zemon Davis and Arlette Farge (Cambridge, Mass. and London: Belknap Press of Harvard University Press, 1993), 132–66, esp. 150.

16. For what follows I have relied (in the near absence of other writings) mostly on a variety of late-nineteenth-century and early-twentieth-century Italian chroniclers who rely in turn on extensive anecdotal accounts in travel literature, diaries, letters, treatises, and fictional sources, including plays, poems, and satires. See Achille Neri, *Costumanze e sollazzi* (Genoa: R. Istituto, 1883), 117–216; Antonio Marenduzzo, "I cicisbei nel Settecento," *Rivista d'Italia* 8 (1905): 271–82; Abd-el-Kader Salza, "I cicisbei nella vita e nella letteratura del Settecento," *Rivista d'Italia* 13 (1910): 184–251; Giulio Natali, *Idee, costumi, uomini del Settecento* (Turin: Società Tipografico-editrice Nazionale, 1916), 133–44; and most especially Luigi Valmaggi, *I cicisbei: contributo alla storia del costume italiano nel secolo XVIII*, post. ed. Luigi Piccioni (Turin: G. Chiantore, 1927). More recent treatments include Barbagli, *Sotto lo stesso tetto*, 360–65, and Luciano Guerci, *La discussione sulla donna nell'Italia del Settecento: aspetti e problemi* (Turin: Tirrenia, 1987), chap. 3, "Le conversazioni e il cicisbeismo," 89–140; and, most recently and provocatively, Roberto Bizzocchi, "Cicisbei: la morale italiana," *Storica* 9 (1997): 63–90, to whom I am grateful for promptly sending me a copy of his article. All in all, very little has been written on *cicisbeismo* in modern times, nor to my knowledge has serious archival work pertinent to it been carried out—work that may be quite onerous if, as Bizzocchi argues convincingly, the phenomenon was more part of informal social arrangements and unwritten practices than it was a juridical "institution" formalized in contracts, as has commonly been claimed (seemingly without evidence) in the past. My conversations with social historians Giulia Calvi and Ottavia Niccoli have persuaded me that such archival evidence as may exist (whether in family letters, court trials, etc.) could turn out to be quite difficult to cull.

17. The verses of the Milanese poet Giuseppe Parini are filled with ironic commentary on the moral relation of the aristocracy to the *cicisbeo*. See especially his famous poem *Il giorno*, part two, "Il meriggio," vv. 39–49, and part 3, "Il vespro," vv. 270–83.

18. Information on Longhi's paintings is given in *L'opera completa di Pietro Longhi*, introduced and coordinated by Terisio Pignatti (Milan: Rizzoli, 1974). For "La dichiarazione" (plate 2) see nos. 281–84. According to Pignatti, the image provided here as plate 2 is most likely a copy of a lost original from 1750, corresponding to catalogue entry no. 284.

19. Barbagli, *Sotto lo stesso tetto,* 363.

20. Cited in Barbagli, 364.

21. The question of how many wives actually slept with their *cicisbei,* on the other hand, can only be—and has nevertheless copiously been—the subject of speculation (see the historical critique of Bizzocchi, "Cicisbei," 65); likewise the question (probably anachronistic in any case) of how many may have been homosexual or bisexual. De Brosses reports having been told by the Venetian ambassador that only about fifty of those he knew of slept with their "wives," but this doubtless says more about what the ambassador believed, or what he wanted de Brosses to think or write, than it does about what actually happened; see Salza, "I cicisbei nella vita e nella letteratura," 189.

22. See Valmaggi, *I cicisbei,* chap. 1, "Letteratura," 1–44. Happily, Roberto Bizzocchi has recently undertaken a large-scale study of *cicisbeismo* within a broader set of questions concerning the Italian character and social practices in the years 1700–1800.

23. The essay is the eleventh of his *Trattenimenti,* added to the *Ritiramenti per le dame* by the French Jesuit François Guilloré, which Maggi translated into Italian and published in Milan in 1687 (see Valmaggi, *I cicisbei,* 7–8). Similar views were held by the anonymous author of *Alcune conversazioni e loro difese esaminate coi principi della Teologia, dai quali facilmente si può dedurre quando sia illecito l'amore tra la gioventù* (Ferrara, 1711), an extremist in the Madre di Dio order who bristled that the world pretended the *cicisbeo* was a "noble servant."

24. Barile, *Alcune conversazioni,* 80; cited in Valmaggi, *I cicisbei,* 10–11.

25. See, for example, Valmaggi's discussion (11) of Costantino Roncaglia's *Moderne conversazioni volgarmente dette dei cicisbei* (1720; reprint, Lucca: Venturini, 1736).

26. *Dialogo nel quale esaminandosi la cagione per la quale le donne danzando non si stancano mai, si fa il ritratto d'un Petit Maître italiano affettato laudatore delle massime, e dei costumi dei Petits Maîtres oltramontani e cicisbei,* in vol. 2, pt. 1 of *Lettere e ragionamenti vari* (Perugia, 1741), 331 ff.; as cited in Valmaggi, *I cicisbei,* 11.

27. Valmaggi, *I cicisbei,* 11–12. Still more progressive was the Venetian lawyer Antonio Costantini, who published letters on the subject between 1751 and 1756 (see Valmaggi, 12–13).

28. Cited in Valmaggi, *I cicisbei,* 45–46 and 46 n.1.

29. From Baretti's "Gli Italiani," 234 ff.; cited in Valmaggi, *I cicisbei,* 69.

30. The woman in Goldoni's *La dama prudente,* for example, had several *cicisbei* "per prudenza," so that she wouldn't be left high and dry whenever her "cav-

alier di fiducia" could not be at her side. On taboos against husbands performing services for their wives, see Valmaggi, *I cicisbei*, 65.

31. Namely monsignor Nicolò Forteguerri; cited in Valmaggi, *I cicisbei*, 21 (emphasis mine).

32. My notion of a spectacle of normativity was inspired by my colleague Martin Stokes's analysis of Turkish pop stars in the context of the Turkish nation-state, as presented in a paper entitled "Mediterraneanism, Hypergender, and Realism," read to the study group on "The Anthropology of Music in Mediterranean Cultures" (meeting on Music as Representation of Gender in Mediterranean Cultures, Venice, Fondazione Levi, 9–11 June 1998).

33. Note here the linguistic continuity of *palco* and *palcoscenico:* the former refers to a box, the latter to the stage, but literally to a stage-box. It thus underscores the way in which the proscenium framed and boxed the stage, much as decorative architectural motifs in the hall did for the boxes of individual groups of spectators.

34. Amid the abundant literature cited by Salza are numerous treatises on the vanities of women ("I cicisbei nella vita e nella letteratura," 235 ff.). For one foreigner's explanation of how the practice of *cicisbeismo* related to masking see John Moore, *A View of Society and Manners in Italy,* 4th ed., 2 vols. (London, 1781), 1:240–48.

35. See Marenduzzo, "I cicisbei nel Settecento," 282, who cites Alfieri's play *La famiglia antiquariato,* 3.6.

36. I borrow the term from Lynn Hunt, *The Family Romance of the French Revolution* (Berkeley and Los Angeles: University of California Press, 1992), xiv. On the corruption of the nation by *cicisbeismo* from an eighteenth-century Italian perspective, see *Amore disarmato:* "The Nation in vain defends itself . . . yet still languishes with its sons" (cited by Salza, "I cisisbei nella vita e nella letteratura," 224). As pointed out by Bizzocchi ("Cicisbei," 63), the anxieties that linked the phenomenon with the decay of the nation were rearticulated in the early nineteenth century by Jean-Charles-Léonard Simonde de Sismondi, who viewed it as a form of decadence inseparable from Italy's loss of political and religious freedoms and dating from the sixteenth century (i.e., the foreign invasions and the Counter-Reformation).

37. See Salza, "I cicisbei nella vita e nella letteratura," 234 ff., esp. the views of Roncaglia, *Moderne conversazioni,* 239. As Salza points out, this impulse is part of an emergent work ethic voiced by noble literati who reject the premise that aristocrats should be people of leisure while the plebians are those who work. Of course many nobles had long since, of necessity, joined the work force, husbands included—a fact of life that was relevant both to the advent of *cicisbeismo* and the rejection of the nobility as a leisure class.

38. The language of father-son relations was pervasive in French parliamentary discourse, as shown by Jeffrey Merrick, "Patriarchalism and Constitutionalism in Eighteenth-Century Parliamentary Discourse," *Studies in Eighteenth-Century Culture* 20 (1990): 317–30. The family metaphor of course presupposes a body metaphor, applicable to the state as well as its individual members. See Antoine de Baecque, *The Body Politic: Corporeal Metaphor in Revolutionary France, 1770–1800,* trans. Charlotte Mandell (Stanford: Stanford University Press, 1997), esp. chaps. 1 and 4.

39. See also Marthe Robert, *Origins of the Novel,* trans. Sacha Rabinovitch (Bloomington: Indiana University Press, 1980).

40. Hunt, *The Family Romance of the French Revolution,* 53.

41. *Moniteur universel,* no. 266, 22 September 1792 (cited in Hunt, 53 n. 1).

42. Quoted in Hunt, 10. Hunt reads the specific form of ritual sacrifice enacted in revolutionary France through the sacrificial theories of René Girard, *Violence and the Sacred,* trans. Patrick Gregory (Baltimore: University of Maryland Press, 1977).

43. Quoted in David P. Jordan, *The King's Trial: Louis XVI versus the French Revolution* (Berkeley and Los Angeles: University of California Press, 1979), 222.

44. Hunt, 93.

45. A sobering comparison of eighteenth-century representations of Marie Antoinette with twentieth-century representations of Hillary Clinton in leather magazines is offered by Pierre Saint-Amand in "Terrorizing Marie Antoinette," trans. Jennifer Curtis-Gage, *Critical Inquiry* 20 (1994): 379–400.

46. On *opera semiseria* and sentimental literature in Italy and France, see Stefano Castelvecchi, "Sentimental Opera: The Emergence of a Genre, 1760–1790" (Ph.D. diss., University of Chicago, 1996); and his "From *Nina* to *Nina:* Pyschodrama, Absorption and Sentiment in the 1780s," *Cambridge Opera Journal* 8 (1996): 91–112.

47. Indeed the production given at Venice on 21 May 1797, nine days after the Republic fell to Napoleon's forces, added liberty choruses at the end as the chorus rejoices at Mitridate's demise. See my "Opera, Festivity, and Spectacle in 'Revolutionary' Venice: Phantasms of Time and History," in V*enice Reconsidered: Venetian History and Civilization, 1297–1797,* ed. John Martin and Dennis Romano (Baltimore: John Hopkins University Press, in press).

48. For a history of these versions see Marita P. McClymonds, "'La morte di Semiramide ossia La vendetta di Nino' and the Restoration of Death and Tragedy to the Italian Operatic Stage in the 1780s and 90s," in Angelo Pompilio et al., eds., *Report of the 14th Congress of the International Musicological Society,* Bologna 1987 (Bologna: International Musicological Society, 1990), 285–92.

Insofar as neoclassical opera seria survived into the nineteenth century, this was no longer true by that time. As Philip Gossett has kindly pointed out to me, Rossini's neoclassical operas of 1818 to 1822 do have mothers and in some cases children too, including: *Mosè in Egitto* (1818; the character of Amaltea); *Ermione* (1819; Andromaca); and *Zelmira* (1822; the title character). More ambiguously, in *Maometto II* (1820) a mother's tomb is present onstage throughout the opera.

Staging Mozart's Women

Konstanze Performs Constancy

1. Edward J. Dent, who had no fondness for the opera as a whole, was most dismissive of "Martern aller Arten," regarding it as a mistake all around. As a concert aria, it was "simply impossible" to stage and "out of place in any opera on any subject" (*Mozart's Operas,* 2nd ed. [London: Oxford University Press, 1947], 77). William Mann notes that the extended passages for concertante soloists in the open-

ing ritornello "would tax the casting powers of even Boris Goldovsky" (*The Operas of Mozart* [New York: Oxford University Press, 1977], 307).

2. In *W. A. Mozart: "Die Entführung aus dem Serail"* (Cambridge: Cambridge University Press, 1987), 119, Thomas Bauman recounts various directorial struggles with "Martern aller Arten." In Carl Ebert's version, the Pasha Selim exits the stage during the opening ritornello. Giorgio Strehler had the Pasha signal a curtain drop for this same extended orchestral introduction. At Covent Garden, Sir Thomas Beecham unaccountably relocated the entire number to Act III, where Konstanze sings alone on stage just after the attempted escape and before the Selim has been informed of it.

3. Mozart's reference to Cavalieri relates to the vocal demands of Konstanze's Act I aria, "Ach, ich liebte," and is found in a letter written from Vienna to his father on 26 September 1781. See letter 426 in Emily Anderson, ed. and trans., *The Letters of Mozart and His Family,* 2nd ed., 3 vols. (London: Macmillan, 1966), 2:769.

4. Bayerischen Staatsoper, conducted by Karl Böhm; stage direction by August Everding; directed for television by Karlheinz Hundorf; Konstanze: Edita Gruberova; Pasha Selim: Thomas Holtzmann (Munich: Unitel, 1980): Deutsche Grammophon Video 072-508-3.

5. In additon to the Everding production, the following videotape versions of *Die Entführung* were compared:

Glyndebourne, 1975 production, conducted by Gustav Kuhn, directed by Peter Wood, with Valerie Masterson as Konstanze and Joachim Bissmeier as Selim (New York: Video Arts International, 1985).

Dresden Staatsoper, 1980 production, conducted by Peter Gålke, staged and directed by Harry Kupfer, with Carolyn Smith-Meyer as Konstanze and Werner Haseleu as Selim (New York: VIEW Video, 1986).

Royal Opera, 1987 production, conducted by Sir Georg Solti, directed by Humphrey Burton, with Inge Nielsen as Konstanze and Oliver Tobias as Selim (London: National Video Corp, 1988).

6. See Jean and Brigitte Massin, *Wolfgang Amadeus Mozart,* 2nd ed. (Paris: Fayard, 1990), 906-8.

7. Michel Poizat, *The Angel's Cry: Beyond the Pleasure Principle in Opera,* trans. Arthur Denner (Ithaca: Cornell University Press, 1992), 64.

8. For a discussion of the *alla turca* elements in Konstanze's aria, see Bauman, *Die Entführung,* 81-82.

9. In Mozart's original version, a passage of 12 measures extended the coloratura on "Segen" in the B section (between mm. 108-9), and another of 15 measures extended the final C section (between mm. 264-65). This version can be heard in John Eliot Gardiner's recording of the opera (see note 16 below).

10. Bauman, *Die Entführung,* 77-78.

11. Maynard Solomon, *Mozart: A Life* (New York: HarperCollins, 1995), 259. Dent, *Mozart's Operas* (69) also makes note of this letter.

12. *The Present State of Matrimony, or: The Real Cause of Conjugal Infidelity and Unhappy Marriages* (London, 1739), in *Women in the Eighteenth Century: Constructions of Femininity,* ed. Vivien Jones (New York and London: Routledge, 1990), 78. Jones notes that midcentury debate concerning conjugal fidelity was

aimed not only at women who were actually married, but also at those betrothed. Before the Hardwicke Marriage Act of 1753 in England, for instance, which institutionalized published banns and church weddings, betrothal was regarded as binding and also as permission for premarital sexual relations.

13. Jones, ed., *Women in the Eighteenth Century,* 79–80.

14. When we originally presented these papers at the Stony Brook conference, a videotape of the Everding production of "Martern aller Arten" was shown at this point.

15. Bauman (117) notes a political resonance with events in Iran during the hostage crisis contemporary with this 1980 production at the Munich National Opera. He points in particular to the resemblance of the Pasha's Act II costume and appearance to that of the Ayatollah Khomeni.

16. One possibility for a resisting reading of this number lies in the singer's autonomy—namely, in freely improvised elaborations. This aspect of virtuosity is rarely undertaken in modern productions of Mozart's operas but was certainly part of performance practice in his day, never more so than in concertos, to which this aria's textures and structure are audibly related. Whether in extending fermatas with cadenza-like embellishments or simply in varying repetitions, the singer makes a final gesture toward freedom from "fidelity" to the written text (albeit, not from performance conventions of Mozart's day). In John Eliot Gardiner's recording of *Die Entführung,* for example, Luba Orgonasova briefly embellishes the fermata at m. 91, and the solo winds ornament their repeated melody at m. 191. (The Monteverdi Choir and the English Baroque Soloists, conducted by John Eliot Gardiner; recorded London 1991 [Hamburg: Deutsche Grammophon GmbH, 1992], Archiv Produktion 435 857-2. As written, the aria features its most extended passage in the imploring second section of mm. 93–141 (uncut version), but it is in the repetition of this and the third "C" section especially that varied elaboration can underscore the freedom of the soloist relative to the orchestra. In providing opportunities for the singer's release from notational "constraints" in performance, these moments can point to the possibility of Konstanze's escape from performing constancy.

"The Gaze" and Power in "Martern aller Arten" and "Batti, batti"

17. See, for example, Mary Ann Smart, "The Lost Voice of Rosine Stolz," *Cambridge Opera Journal* 6 (1994): 31–50; Heather Hadlock, "Return of the Repressed: The Prima Donna from Hoffmann's Tales to Offenbach's *Contes,*" *Cambridge Opera Journal* 6 (1994): 221–44; Carolyn Abbate, "Opera; or, the Envoicing of Women," in *Musicology and Difference: Gender and Sexuality in Music Scholarship,* ed. Ruth A. Solie (Berkeley and Los Angeles: University of California Press, 1993), 225–58.

18. Elin Diamond, "Brechtian Theory/Feminist Theory: Toward a Gestic Feminist Criticism," *The Drama Review* 32 (1988): 82–94.

19. *Die Entführung aus dem Serail,* directed by Humphrey Burton, Royal Opera House, Covent Garden (New York: Video Arts International, 1988); see note 5 above for full details.

20. The two laserdisc sources for these productions are *Wolfgang Amadeus Mozart: Don Giovanni,* directed by Peter Sellars, conducted by Craig Smith (Lon-

don: London, 1991), Decca 071511-1; and *Mozart: Don Giovanni,* directed by Göran Järvefelt, conducted by Arnold Östman (New York: Polygram, 1987), Philips 440070519-1.

21. One could argue that presenting Zerlina as a sort of stereotypical wench is in fact "authentic"—that this is likely how Mozart's audiences would have viewed her. And indeed, the apparatus of Drottningholm productions, which take place in a genuine eighteenth-century theater, with original machinery, certainly lends an aura of historical veracity. For me, however, (and maybe this is an effect of video production, where the historical aspect of the theater itself is lost every time the camera focuses on the characters) the "Drottningholm frame" is insufficient to make Zerlina's bottom-waggling seem historically contextualized.

Zerlina's "Batti, batti": A Case Study?

22. *Rhythmic Gesture in Mozart: "Le nozze di Figaro" and "Don Giovanni"* (Chicago: University of Chicago Press, 1983), 269.

The Career of Cherubino, or the Trouser Role Grows Up

1. Dorothy Sayers, *Whose Body?* (1923; reprint, New York: Harper and Row, 1987), 100.

2. The practice was more widespread than the rather short list of trousered heroes familiar to opera-goers today (for example, Rossini's Tancredi and Arsace; Bellini's Romeo) would suggest. I have discussed the use of female *musico* singers in "A Voice for the Hero: The Italian *Musico* Tradition, 1800–1840," presented at the national meeting of the American Musicological Society, Phoenix, Ariz., 1 November 1997. On the musical and erotic implications of modern female singers singing castrato roles, see Joke Dame, "Unveiled Voices: Sexual Difference and the Castrato," in *Queering the Pitch: The New Gay and Lesbian Musicology,* ed. Philip Brett, Elizabeth Wood, and Gary C. Thomas (New York and London: Routledge, 1994), 139–53.

3. Théophile Gautier, *Emaux et camées,* ed. Claudine Gothot-Mersch (Paris: Gallimard, 1981). See the editor's notes on this poem, and also the discussion in Felicia Miller Frank's *The Mechanical Song: Women, Voice, and the Artificial in Nineteenth-Century French Narrative* (Stanford: Stanford University Press, 1995), 105–10. I quote Miller Frank's translation.

4. It is clear that in the Italian serious repertoire, at least, voice, performer, and role were bound together according to parameters other than gender. Roger Covell argues that a character's age, not gender, determined vocal *gravitas;* see "Voice Register as an Index of Age and Status in Opera Seria," in *Opera and Vivaldi,* ed. Michael Collins and Elise C. Kirk (Austin: University of Texas Press, 1984), 193–210. Marie-France Castarède suggests that "composers who entrusted the roles of Caesar, Achilles, Alexander, and Hercules to castrati knew well that true heroes participate in divinity, and that divinity knows no distinction of age or of sex," see her *La Voix et ses sortilèges* (Paris: Société d'édition "Les Belles Lettres," 1987), 171. See Stephen LaRue, *Handel and His Singers* (Oxford: Oxford University Press, 1993) for a discussion of Margherita Durastanti, a female exponent of heroic male parts in Handel's Italian operas.

5. Wye Jamison Allanbrook calls Cherubino "neither . . . male nor female," arguing that the travesty casting "keeps Cherubino from being particularized and 'embodied,' located in a real place and time like the other characters in the opera." See her *Rhythmic Gesture in Mozart* (Chicago: University of Chicago Press, 1983), 96.

6. Beaumarchais, *Le Mariage de Figaro,* ed. Jean Goldzink (Paris: Classiques Larousse, 1992), Act I, scene 7. All subsequent citations will be from this edition.

7. Beaumarchais, preface to *Le Mariage de Figaro.*

8. Beaumarchais, "Les personnages," 72. Louis Forestier identifies the first male actor to play the role at the Comédie-Française as "Carette," in 1921; see *Le Mariage de Figaro,* ed. Louis Forestier (Larousse, Paris: 1971), 57 n. 6.

9. *Le Mariage de Figaro,* Act II, sc. 6.

10. For a historical examination of "anandryne" cults in the ancien régime, see Marie-Jo Bonnet, *Un Choix sans équivoque: recherches historiques sur les relations amoureuses entre les femmes, XVIe–XXe siècle* (Paris: Denoël, 1981). On pornographic representations of Marie Antoinette, see Lynn Hunt, "The Many Bodies of Marie Antoinette," in *Eroticism and the Body Politic,* ed. Lynn Hunt (Baltimore: Johns Hopkins University Press, 1991), 103–30; Robert Darnton's *The Forbidden Best-Sellers of Pre-Revolutionary France* (New York: Norton, 1995) explores the relationship of pornography, philosophy, and politics in that era. On postrevolutionary lesbian fantasies attached to Marie Antoinette, see Terry Castle, "The Marie Antoinette Obsession," in her *The Apparitional Lesbian* (New York: Columbia University Press, 1994), 107–49.

11. In the final trio of Rossini's *Le Comte Ory,* where the page Isolier's attentions to the Countess are allowed to proceed much further than Cherubino's had been, the interruption by the male order is correspondingly more emphatic. The increasingly chromatic vocal lines and disoriented harmonies at the trio's climax, musical representations of the fervent and misdirected seduction(s) taking place on stage, are not so much resolved as they are cut short by the unison martial blast that announces the return of the castle's crusading menfolk. Twenty-eight bars of dominant arrival (which we might as well call "imposition") are required to disperse both harmonic tension and erotic confusion.

12. Allanbrook, *Rhythmic Gesture in Mozart,* 148.

13. Hector Berlioz, "Romeo and Juliet, Opera in Four Acts by Bellini," feuilleton of 13 September 1859, reprinted in *A Travers Chants,* trans. Elisabeth Csicsery-Rónay (Bloomington: Indiana University Press, 1994), 223.

14. Eugène Scribe, *Les Huguenots,* Act II. Illustration from "Les Beautés de l'Opéra," reproduced in liner notes to *Les Huguenots,* cond. Richard Bonynge (London OSA 1437, 1970), 13.

15. Lynn Garafola, "The Travesty Dancer in Nineteenth-Century Ballet," *Dance Research Journal 7,* no. 2 (1985): 35–40. On related practices in English light opera of the early nineteenth century, see Alicia Finkel, "Madame Vestris, the English Adonis," *Dress* 18 (1991): 4–13.

16. Offenbach's operettas and opéra-comiques provide a catalog of "light" travesty types. Only one is literally a pageboy (Amoroso, in *Le Pont des soupirs* [1861/1868]), but in two cases young men disguise themselves as pages in order to be near their sweethearts (the baker Drogan, in *Geneviève de Brabant,* [rev. 1867]; and the chocolatier Fragoletto, in *Les Brigands,* [1871]). Cupidon, in *Orphée aux Enfers*

(1858/1874), embodies the playful spirit of the pageboy, while Vendredi, in *Robinson Crusoe* (1872) and Prince Caprice in *Le Voyage dans la lune* (1875) have his quality of yearning for the unattainable. Oreste, in *La Belle Hélène* (1864), is a dandy; the jaded Prince Orlofsky, of Johann Strauss's *Die Fledermaus,* also has a French ancestry, for that operetta originated as a French libretto entitled *La Tzigane* (1877).

17. Carl Dahlhaus, *Nineteenth-Century Music,* trans. J. Bradford Robinson (Berkeley and Los Angeles: University of California Press, 1989), 282.

18. See Claudine Brécourt-Villars, *Petit Glossaire raisonné de l'érotisme saphique, 1880–1930* (Paris: J.-J. Pauvert, 1980).

19. Karla Jay, *The Amazon and the Page* (Bloomington: Indiana University Press, 1988).

20. See Esther Newton, "The Mythic Mannish Lesbian: Radclyffe Hall and the New Woman," *Signs* 9, no.4 (1984): 557–75.

21. "Le génie féminin revient sur lui-même et se met en formules, afin de se connaître et de se décrire. Il n'aime plus. Au lieu d'aimer, il pense l'amour et se pense" (emphasis mine). Charles Maurras, *L'Avenir de l'intelligence* (Paris, 1905), quoted in Jacques Robichez, *Précis de littérature française du XXe Siécle* (Paris: Presses universitaires de France, 1985), 149.

22. Gillian Rodger points out that developments in sexology complicated the reception of male impersonators in American popular musical theater: "[the medical profession's] 'discovery' of the 'mannish' or masculine woman . . . would eventually affect all women, and particularly those women who chose to portray men on the stage. . . . The social anxieties that surrounded the mannish woman eventually proved to be the death of male impersonation in this country." Rodger, "Cross-Dressed Women on the American Popular Musical Stage, 1868–1890: Negotiating the Boundaries of Decency," *MACSEM Newsletter* 14, no. 2 (1995): 3–6.

23. Interview with Mary Garden, *La Liberté,* 24 May 1905.

24. Louis Schneider, "Chérubin," *Le Théâtre* 149 (1 March 1905): 22.

25. I have based my synopsis and interpretation of the stage action on the detailed directions that appear in Massenet's autograph score, *F-Po,* Rés. 550, vol. 2.

26. It must be admitted that Chérubin has not yet attained L'Ensoleillad's poetic sophistication: although his first line for the second strophe elegantly parallels her opening, his next contribution (line 3) breaks the ABBA rhyme scheme that she had originally established, forcing the second strophe into the more banal ABAB pattern.

27. Castle, *The Apparitional Lesbian.*

28. This passage, with a unison melody for two sopranos and counter-melody for baritone, was originally the *cabaletta* for the Act I trio in *Zaira* (1829), the source of much of the music in *I Capuleti e i Montecchi.* The key textual line, "Quest' addio non sia l'estremo / ci vedremo almeno in ciel" is unchanged, as is the dramatic situation of declaring unity in the face of separation.

29. For a discussion of the "meta-chiastic relationship between [Tristan and Isolde] in which, by denying *self*-consciousness, they become *one*-conscious, 'einbewußt,'" see Arthur Groos, "Appropriation in Wagner's *Tristan* Libretto," in *Reading Opera,* ed. Arthur Groos and Roger Parker (Princeton: Princeton University Press, 1988), especially 18–25.

Thanks to Wagner's "decadent" and "narcotic" musical style, together with his representations of Amazonian heroines, irrepressible taboo desire, and self-obliterating passion, his works exercised a powerful fascination on fin-de-siècle lesbian imaginations. The same Parisian *coterie* that impersonated ladies and pages for their own pleasure were also ardent Wagnerians, as is evidenced by their memoirs of intrigues at Bayreuth. Satirical images also abound of French and German "Wagneriennes," analogous to the male Wagner cults discussed by Mitchell Morris in "Tristan's Wounds," presented at this conference. On female Wagnerites, see Elizabeth Wood, "Sapphonics," in *Queering the Pitch*, 27–66, and Terry Castle, "In Praise of Brigitte Fassbaender," in *The Apparitional Lesbian*.

30. *Le Mariage de Figaro*, Act II, sc. 6.

31. Schneider, "Chérubin."

32. See, for example, Wayne Koestenbaum, *The Queen's Throat: Opera, Homosexuality, and the Mystery of Desire* (New York: Poseidon Press, 1993); Corinne Blackmer and Patricia Juliana Smith, eds., *En Travesti: Women, Gender Subversion, Opera,* (New York: Columbia University Press, 1995); Sam Abel, *Opera in the Flesh* (Boulder: Westview Press, 1996); Rebecca Pope and Susan J. Leonardi, *The Diva's Mouth* (New Brunswick: Rutgers University Press, 1996).

33. Gary Le Tourneau, "Kitsch, Camp, and Opera: *Der Rosenkavalier*," *Canadian University Music Review* 14 (1994): 77–97.

34. This is not, however, to deny that Octavian and the Marschallin have become lesbian icons precisely because of the exceptional shamelessness with which their affair is presented. Terry Castle's praise for Fassbaender and her "gynophilic" stage persona is the most elegant celebration of the empowering quality of this shamelessness; see Castle, *The Apparitional Lesbian*, 229–38.

35. See for example the introduction to *En Travesti*, together with Margaret Reynolds's "Ruggiero's Deceptions, Cherubino's Distractions" and Wendy Bashant's "Singing in Greek Drag: Gluck, Berlioz, and George Eliot," in that volume. See also the chapters on female cross-dressing in Pope and Leonardi, *The Diva's Mouth* and in Abel, *Opera in the Flesh*.

Elisabeth's Last Act

1. Michel Foucault, "Nietzsche, Genealogy, History," first written in 1971 and reprinted in English translation more than once, perhaps most accessibly in Paul Rabinow, ed., *The Foucault Reader* (New York: Pantheon, 1984).

2. Bernhard Schlink, *The Reader* (New York: Pantheon, 1997).

3. As always, the complicated history is ably summed up by Julian Budden's chapter on the opera in *The Operas of Verdi: Don Carlos to Falstaff* (London: Cassell, 1981). Many of the documents are reproduced in Ursula Günther, "La genèse de *Don Carlos*," *Revue de musicologie* 58 (1972): 16–64; 60 (1974): 87–158; and in Günther and Gabriella Carrara-Verdi, "Der Briefwechsel Verdi-Nuitter-Du Locle zur Revision des *Don Carlos*," *Analecta musicologica* 14 (1974): 1–13; 15 (1975): 334–401.

4. For a lengthy anthology of the critical reception of the opera's première in Paris, see Hervé Gartioux, ed., *Giuseppe Verdi: Don Carlos: Dossier de presse parisienne (1867)* (Heilbronn: L. Galland, 1997).

5. Quoted in Budden, 19.

6. These and subsequent references to the score are to Ursula Günther's composite vocal score of the opera's various versions, published by Ricordi in 1974.

7. Letter to Nuitter, 14 June 1882, in Günther, "Der Briefwechsel," 349–50.

8. Günther, "Der Briefwechsel," 350–52.

9. Letter to Giulio Ricordi, 19 February 1883, in Günther, "Der Briefwechsel," 340; English from Budden, 37.

10. Originally published in 1992 as *Die Verstädterung der Oper: Paris und das Musiktheater des 19. Jahrhunderts* (Stuttgart: Metzler, 1992); English translation as *The Urbanization of Opera: Music Theater in Paris in the Nineteenth Century* (Chicago: University of Chicago Press, 1998).

11. Richard Sennett, *The Fall of Public Man* (New York: Knopf, 1977).

12. Gerhard, 440; cf. Carl Dahlhaus, *Nineteenth-Century Music,* trans. J. Bradford Robinson (Berkeley and Los Angeles: University of California Press, 1989), 277, where *drame lyrique* is described as "a genre that withdrew from the staged world history of Meyerbeer to interior tragedies."

13. Gerhard, 440–41.

14. Gerhard, 256.

15. The contemporary production book specifies: four valets with torches; the Count of Lerma escorting the Countess of Aremberg; two ladies of the court; four French lords; four Spanish lords; a litter carried by eight valets; seven royal French bodyguards. See *Disposizione scenica per l'opera Don Carlo di G. Verdi compilata e regolata secondo la mise en scène del Teatro Imperiale dell'Opera di Parigi* (Milan, n.d), 8; quoted in Budden, 53.

16. Gerhard, 439.

17. I should mention here a debt to John Deathridge, whose discussion of this motive and its vision of history—in a paper focusing on Walter Benjamin's idea of the *Trauerspiel* given at the Nottingham Conference on Nineteenth-Century Music, July 1996—first set me thinking about this aspect of *Don Carlos.*

18. See in particular Frits Noske, "*Don Carlos:* The Signifier and the Signified," in his *The Signifier and the Signified: Studies in the Operas of Mozart and Verdi* (The Hague: Nijhoff, 1977), 294–308.

19. Gerhard, 370.

20. See my *Leonora's Last Act* (Princeton: Princeton University Press, 1997), 9–19. I might as well admit that the present essay feels like a key chapter of the book that remained unwritten. These days such a circumstance might seem satisfyingly postmodern, a consummation if not to be wished, then at least to be tolerated with some patience. Initially I had thought this phantom chapter would address a relationship flowering very much on the periphery of the plot of *Don Carlos:* between two characters—Elisabeth and Posa—who, if they touch, do so only mysteriously, in ways difficult to discuss. I was attracted to the notion that operatic characters might under certain pressures (exegetical rather than internal) become unruly in their elective affinities, in the process developing relationships that largely unfold in the musical domain—ones that might challenge and then perhaps stimulate our discursive capabilities. That idea, though it still attracts me, largely got shouldered aside by other matters. The notion of voices touching (us and each other) is now buried, as is that of "musical" relationships; but some small resonances remain.

21. Gerhard, 180.

22. This quotation, and the ensuing discussion of the Carlos aria, is based on Andrew Porter, "A Sketch for *Don Carlos*," *The Musical Times* 111 (1970): 882–85, which also provides a transcription of the sketch material that survives from the start of Act V.

23. Letter to Emile Perrin, director of the Opéra, 21 June 1866, quoted in Porter, 883.

24. See Budden, 211, and Porter, 883, the second of whom offers further possible reasons for Verdi's change of plan. A letter from Verdi to Camille du Locle dated 11 September 1866, quoted in Franco Abbiati, *Verdi* (Milan: Ricordi, 1959), 3:102, further confirms doubts about the tenor and also invites the librettist to suggest changes to the start of the act: "Your last letter has made me worry a bit about the role of Morère (Don Carlos). I knew that the role was dangerous [*grave*], and you'll remember what I said at the first rehearsal: "*nous jouons hors jeu!*" But there's no way round it—it's the plot that required such a role. In the fifth act I've tried to rely on Elisabeth . . . from the moment she comes onstage, she has more prominence.

What do you want to do in the first scene? Tell me your ideas and if it's possible I'll do what you want, even though this scene is already done and prepares well for what follows."

25. The comparison with Verdi's treatment of Leonora at the start of the final act of *Il trovatore* is perhaps significant: she also was entrusted with a substantial aria very late in the compositional day, almost as an afterthought. For a discussion of this scene, see the final chapter of my *Leonora's Last Act*, 168–87.

26. See Carolyn Abbate, *Unsung Voices* (Princeton: Princeton University Press, 1991), and her "Opera; or the Envoicing of Women," in *Musicology and Difference: Gender and Sexuality in Musical Scholarship*, ed. Ruth A. Solie (Berkeley and Los Angeles: University of California Press, 1993), 225–58.

27. Were I to do so, I would of course want to relate Elisabeth's transformations here to those made by Posa in the previous act, though his are by comparison understated and truncated, buried under plot exigencies. These two characters do, nevertheless, touch curiously in the opera's musical world; in my version of *Don Carlos 2*, the bullet that fells Posa would, passing dangerously close to his heart, exit to wound Carlos fatally. Posa and Elisabeth would then console each other, gradually fall in love, and finally elope to Flanders where they become national heroes and appear on postage stamps to this very day.

28. On the origins of Schiller's "history," see M. J. Rodríguez-Salgado's "The Reality behind the Myth," in the Royal Opera House, Covent Garden program book for their June-July 1996 series of performances of *Don Carlos*. For an acute critique of the contemporary reception, see Karen Henson's review of Gartioux's collection, in *Music & Letters* 79 (1998): 616–17.

29. Letter to Clara Maffei, 20 October 1876, in *I copialettere di Giuseppe Verdi* (Milan, 1913), 624.

30. Günther, "Der Briefwechsel," 340.

Body and Voice in Melodrama and Opera

1. On these points, see my *The Melodramatic Imagination* (New Haven and London: Yale University Press, 1995); and "Melodrama, Body, Revolution," in

Melodrama: Stage, Picture, Screen, ed. Jacky Bratton, Jim Cook, and Christine Gledhill (London : British Film Institute, 1994), 11-24.

2. Henry James, "Notes on the Theatres: New York," in *The Scenic Art,* ed. Allan Wade (New Brunswick: Rutgers University Press, 1948), 24.

3. Sigmund Freud, "Fragment of an Analysis of a Case of Hysteria," in *Standard Edition of the Complete Psychological Writings,* ed. Lytton Strachey (London: Hogarth Press, 1953-74), 7:77-78.

4. Roland Barthes, *S/Z* (Paris: Editions du Seuil, 1970), 116 (my translation).

Ulterior Motives

1. Edward Said, "The Empire at Work: Verdi's *Aida,*" in his *Culture and Imperialism* (New York: Knopf, 1993), 111-32. Verdi studied descriptions and drawings of ancient Egypt sent to him by French Egyptologist Auguste Mariette, as well as finding out as much as he could about Egyptian music. At one point he even considered having special "Egyptian trumpets" constructed to give an authentic tint to the ceremonial scenes. On Verdi's inquiries into Egyptology, see Jean Humbert, "A propos de l'egyptomanie dans l'oeuvre de Verdi: Attribution à Auguste Mariette d'un scénario anonyme de l'opéra *Aida,*" *Revue de musicologie* 62:2 (1976): 229-55.

2. Said, 114.

3. As Said puts it, "I believe Verdi fatally confused this complex and in the end collaborative capacity to bring a distant operatic fable to life [through concern for authentic representation] with the Romantic ideal of an organically integrated, seamless work of art, informed only by the aesthetic intention of a single creator. Thus an imperial notion of the artist dovetailed conveniently with an imperial notion of a non-European world whose claims on the European composer were either minimal or non-existent" ("The Empire at Work," 116-17).

4. Both the 1871 Cairo première and the Italian première the following year were in fact popular successes, but met with a mixed reception among journalists, who complained both that the opera was too old-fashioned and that it was too daring. Partly in response to these criticisms, Verdi wrote to his friend Clara Maffei of the 1873 Naples production that: "The success of *Aida,* as you know, was outspoken and decisive, untainted by *ifs* and *buts.* . . . The audience surrendered to its feelings and applauded. That's all. It applauded and even gave way to a hysteria that I don't approve of, but after all, it expressed its sentiments without inhibitions and without *arrière-pensée.*" Letter to Clara Maffei, 9 April 1873, *Verdi's "Aida": The History of an Opera in Letters and Documents,* coll. and trans. Hans Busch (Minneapolis: University of Minnesota Press, 1978), 339. On the opera's early reception, see Julian Budden, *The Operas of Verdi,* vol.3 (London: Cassell, 1981), 187-97.
One might also question Said's assumption that the *"risorgimento"* operas of the 1840s provoked quite such unequivocal displays of audience participation and engagement. As Roger Parker has shown, many of the oft-repeated stories about spontaneous outbursts of patriotic feeling at Verdi performances were invented or enhanced later in the century. See his "'Va pensiero' and the Insidious Mastery of Song," in his *Leonora's Last Act: Essays in Verdian Discourse* (Princeton: Princeton University Press, 1997), 20-41; and *"Arpa d'or dei fatidici vati": The*

Verdian Patriotic Chorus in the 1840s (Parma: Istituto Nazionale di Studi Verdiani, 1997).

5. I should perhaps point out that I have no quarrel with Said's conclusion, which seems both important and well-argued: that works such as *Aida* that "stage" orientalist images of colonized nations work to naturalize the violence of colonial domination, elevating it, as he puts it, into a kind of theory ("The Empire at Work," 131).

6. Said, 124–25.

7. In other words, critics have complained about Verdi's identifying themes both as too loose (not signifying as clearly and specifically as Wagner's) and as too rigidly tied to verbal meaning. It is interesting that one of Verdi's earliest critics, Abramo Basevi, found no fault with *I due Foscari*'s identifying themes, noting only that this was not a new practice, having been used previously by Meyerbeer before being carried to exaggerated ends by Wagner. Basevi conserved his ire instead for another variety of literalness, Verdi's musical imitation of the breeze in the introduction to Jacopo Foscari's cavatina, "Brezza del mar natio." (Basevi, *Studio sulle opere di Giuseppe Verdi* [Florence, 1859], 63–64.) Gabriele Baldini, on the other hand, is fairly typical of twentieth-century critics when he labels the motives in *Foscari* as mechanical "visiting cards" and connects the practice to Wagner's systematic (but, in Baldini's view, wooden) use of leitmotives in the *Ring of the Nibelungen* (see Baldini, *The Story of Giuseppe Verdi*, trans. Roger Parker [Cambridge: Cambridge University Press, 1970], 92–93).

For a thorough discussion of the presence and influence of Wagner's music in Italy in the last third of the century, see Budden, *The Operas of Verdi*, 3:271–74; for an overview of the links drawn by contemporary critics between *Aida* and Wagner's style, see Budden, 3:192. And for a perceptive assessment of the power Wagnerian analytical models have exerted on the study of Verdi's operas in this century, see Carolyn Abbate and Roger Parker, introduction to *Analyzing Opera: Verdi and Wagner*, ed. Abbate and Parker (Princeton: Princeton University Press, 1988), 11–13.

8. By this point the audience has already heard the Aida theme once before, in the prelude, but this is the first time the melody is presented with an explicit association to the character.

9. Kerman, "Verdi's Use of Recurring Themes," in *Studies in Music History: Essays for Oliver Strunk*, ed. Harold Powers (Princeton: Princeton University Press, 1968), 495–510; here 496.

10. Kerman, *Opera as Drama*, (1956; rev. ed., Berkeley and Los Angeles: University of California Press, 1988).

11. Brooks, *The Melodramatic Imagination: Balzac, Henry James, and the Mode of Excess* (1976; reprint, New Haven: Yale University Press, 1995). On Verdi's exposure to Parisian melodrama and its influence on him, see Emilio Sala, "Verdi and the Parisian Boulevard Theatre, 1847–9," *Cambridge Opera Journal* 7, no. 3 (1995): 185–205.

12. Although *Aida* and *I due Foscari* are Verdi's only experiments with assigning recurring themes to characters on a one-to-one basis, he frequently used recurring melodies to represent dramatic ideas. Examples of the latter include the curse motive in *Rigoletto*, Azucena's "Stride la vampa" in *Il trovatore* (representing her obsessive memory of her mother's death), the love themes in *La traviata* ("Di

quell'amor") and *Un ballo in maschera* ("La rivedrà nell'estasi"), and the "Bacio" theme in *Otello*. All except the first of these is first heard as part of a set piece, but when they recur it is always as clearly marked interruptions of an ongoing lyrical discourse, never as fully integrated into the vocal world of the principal characters the way the Aida motive is.

13. The other identifying themes in *Aida* are less clearly gestural than is Aida's. Aida's rival Amneris is represented by a descending triplet pattern that seems more closely tied to speech than to movement, but the melody assigned to the Egyptian high priests is unequivocally processional in nature. Strangely (or perhaps not so strangely, if the motivic impulse *is* closely related to depicting the body), neither Radames nor Aida's father, the Ethiopian king Amonasro, have identifying themes.

14. Roger Parker has suggested that "the theme represents Aida by reference to just one aspect of her character: her timorous, uncertain love for Radames"; see Parker, "Motives and Recurring Themes in *Aida*," in *Analyzing Opera*, ed. Abbate and Parker, 229.

15. Carolyn Abbate, *Unsung Voices: Opera and Musical Narrative in the Nineteenth Century* (Princeton: Princeton University Press, 1991); and her "Opera; or, the Envoicing of Women," in *Musicology and Difference: Gender and Sexuality in Music Scholarship*, ed. Ruth Solie (Berkeley and Los Angeles: University of California Press, 1993), 225–58. Film theory that has been particularly influential on opera studies includes Kaja Silverman, *The Acoustic Mirror: The Female Voice in Psychoanalysis and Cinema* (Bloomington: Indiana University Press, 1988); Laura Mulvey, "Visual Pleasure and Narrative Cinema," in her *Visual and Other Pleasures* (Bloomington: University of Indiana Press, 1989), 14–26; and Mary Ann Doane, "The Voice in Cinema: The Articulation of Body and Space," *Yale French Studies* 60 (1980): 33–50.

16. The idea of female characters using vocal pyrotechnics to counter the objectifying force of the gaze has been articulated most forcefully by Susan McClary in her analysis of the mad scene in Donizetti's *Lucia di Lammermoor;* see her "Excess and Frame: The Musical Representation of Madwomen," in her *Feminine Endings: Music, Gender, Sexuality* (Minneapolis: University of Minnesota Press, 1991), 80–111. For another approach to the politics of voice and body in the *Lucia* mad scene, see my "The Silencing of *Lucia*," *Cambridge Opera Journal* 4, no. 2 (1992): 119–41.

17. Abbate, "Opera; or, the Envoicing of Women," 239.

18. An example of the first is the string section's passionate quotation at the end of *Götterdämmerung* of the motive Wagner labeled as "Die Verherrlichung Brünnhildes." See Abbate, "Why Do They Burn Brünnhilde?," program book for Wagner's *Ring of the Nibelungen*, Royal Opera House, Covent Garden; and her "Mythische Stimmen, Sterbliche Körper," in *Richard Wagner, "Der Ring des Nibelungen": Ansichten des Mythos*, ed. Udo Bermbach and Dieter Borchmeyer (Stuttgart: J. B. Metzler, 1995), 75–86.

19. Abbate, *Unsung Voices*, 19–27.

20. The music connected with the third principal character, Francesco Foscari, is more consistent, his orchestral theme and his vocal style conveying fairly similar moods of gravity and wisdom.

21. As Roger Parker puts it, "occasionally a key centre or motif may briefly shoul-

der the burden of semantic weight . . . , but—as [Verdi] had learnt much earlier, in the experiment of *I due Foscari*—the continuing formal fixity of Verdi's musical language militates against the sustained use of such techniques, and they never approach a level of 'structural' significance"; see s.v. "Verdi, Giuseppe (Francesco Fortunio)," *Grove Dictionary of Opera* (London: Macmillan, 1992).

22. To treat the implications of Aida's identity as a dark-skinned Ethiopian as set off against Amneris as a "white" Egpytian woman would require another article. For the purposes of my argument here, I am (no doubt sloppily and irresponsibly) assuming that the musical representation of Aida's race is largely subsumed into, or synonymous with, that of her femininity. The moment in the opera where race becomes important separate from gender is the third act, especially its opening scene, Aida's evocation of her distant homeland in the aria "O patria mia," where her voice and body are equated with and submerged in the numerous pictorial orchestral effects used to evoke nature and landscape. In a longer version of this article, I plan to discuss the depiction of landscape in Act III as a technique of musical imitation continuous with the mimesis of Aida's gesture in her identifying theme.

23. On the vestiges of traditional number opera in *Aida,* see Philip Gossett, "Verdi, Ghislanzoni, and *Aida:* the 'Uses of Convention,'" *Critical Inquiry* 1, no. 1 (1974): 291–334.

24. This speech by Amneris ("Trema, vil schiava!") is the only passage where she cites Aida's motive literally, but it is interesting that Amneris here takes up Aida's theme only with its second phrase of Aida's theme, whose triplet motion bears a strong resemblance to the defining rhythm of Amneris's own identifying theme.

25. The identity of "Numi, pietà" as a variation on the stock melodramatic gesture seems especially clear when the prayer is heard in relation to two other Verdian perorations, both of which call for almost identical gestures: the refrain of Amelia's Act II aria "Dell'arido stelo divulsa" (where Amelia is directed to fall to her knees at the words "Deh! mi reggi, m'aita, signor") in *Un ballo in maschera* (1859) and the closing measures of the duet for Elisabeth and Don Carlos in Act II of *Don Carlos* (1867), where, like Aida, Elisabeth is left alone on stage to utter her prayer.

26. "Production Book by Giulio Ricordi," in *Verdi's "Aida": The History of an Opera in Letters and Documents,* coll. and trans. Hans Busch, 558–618. The *disposizione* is much less informative about the desired staging for the two scenes discussed above. About Aida's first entrance, and the first occurrence of her identifying motive, it tells us only: "Aida enters from the left rear" (561). For her entrance before the Act II duet with Amneris, the *disposizione* specifies that Amneris should notice Aida in the wings before she becomes visible to the audience, and should then motion her attendants to withdraw, at which point "Aida enters upstage right, holding Amneris' crown, which she places on the table" (575).

27. "Production Book," 565.

28. Letter to Giovanni Bottesini, 7 December 1871; in Gaetano Cesari and Alessandro Luzio, *I copialettere di Giuseppe Verdi* (1913; Bologna: A. Forni, 1987). The staging specified in the *disposizione* itself closely echoes the instructions for the first occurrence of the prayer, directing: "Aida, in deepest sorrow, has almost no strength left to follow Amneris; after having said *Numi pietà del mio martir,* she

walks with great effort in the direction of Amneris, so that she has disappeared by the last note of *pietà*" (576).

29. Elin Diamond, "The Shudder of Catharsis in Twentieth-Century Performance," in *Performativity and Performance*, ed. Andrew Parker and Eve Kosofsky Sedgwick (New York and London: Routledge, 1995), 152–72.

30. In her book *Unmaking Mimesis,* Diamond uses a variety of interpretive strategies to discover ways women's theater and women represented on stage can speak past the one-dimensional (usually male-authored) mimetic perspective of conventional theater. Her aim is to move beyond the feminist theater theory of the 1970s and 80s, for which "the 'scene of representation' was generally understood as a narrativization of male desire. Representation, we tended to say, *inevitably* transforms female subjects into fetishized objects whose referent is ideologically bound to dominant—heterosexual—models of femininity and masculinity." Diamond, *Unmaking Mimesis: Essays on Feminism and Theater* (New York and London: Routledge, 1997), xii. Although the strategies are different, the interpretive result is strikingly similar to that of Abbate's quest for autonomous voices emanating from female characters in opera.

Mélisande's Hair, or the Trouble in Allemonde

1. François Lesure and Roger Nichols, eds., *Debussy Letters,* trans. Roger Nichols (London: Faber and Faber, 1987), 62.

2. Roger Nichols and Richard Langham Smith, *Claude Debussy: Pelléas et Mélisande* (Cambridge: Cambridge University Press, 1989).

3. See Catherine Clément, *Opera, or the Undoing of Women,* trans. Betsy Wing (Minneapolis, University of Minneapolis Press, 1988), 111–15.

4. Joseph Kerman, *Opera as Drama,* rev. ed. (Berkeley and Los Angeles: University of California Press, 1988), 144.

5. René Terrasson, *Pelléas et Mélisande, ou l'initiation* (Paris: Editions EDI-MAF, 1982).

6. Maurice Maeterlinck, "Mystic Morality," in his *The Treasure of the Humble,* trans. Alfred Sutro (New York: Dodd, Mead, 1900), 61.

7. This production marked the fifth time since 1962 that Pierre Médecin, former protégé of Wieland Wagner, who today acts as artistic director of the Opéra-Comique, had put Debussy's *Pelléas* on stage. His new concept was realized together with Georges Prêtre directing the Orchestre national de France and the chorus of the Opéra-Comique. The role of Pelléas was played by William Dazelay, Golaud by François Le Roux, Arkël by Christian Tréguier, Mélisande by Anne-Marguerite Werster, Geneviève by Brigitte Balleys, the doctor by François Harismendy, and Yniold by Romain Levêque.

8. "The Tragical in Daily Life," in Maeterlinck, *The Treasure of the Humble,* 105.

9. Nor should we forget the important studies of mental disturbances that were taking place in France right around the time of Debussy's *Pelléas.* Both the work of Théodule Ribot (*Les Maladies de la personnalité,* 1885), and especially Jean-Martin Charcot (*L'Hystérie chez l'homme,* 1887) offer suggestive possibilities for understanding, in contemporaneous terms, the disturbed psychology of Golaud.

10. On the subject of *Pelléas,* Edward Lockspeiser, to choose just one critic

among many, has written: "Pour l'essentiel, l'intrigue de ce drame symbolique présente une affinité avec la légende de *Tristan*." See his *Claude Debussy,* trans. Léo Dilé (Paris: Fayard, 1980).

11. Lesure and Nichols, *Debussy Letters,* 40.

12. Catherine Clément, "Mélisande à la question, ou le secret des hommes," in *Debussy: Pelléas et Mélisande, L'Avant-scène Opéra* 9 (1977): 15–19.

13. In a scientific study on hair published in 1910 by Marcelle Lambert and Victor Balthazard, we find a proposition that oddly corroborates the equation between hair, woman, and sexuality suggested by the symbolism of *Pelléas*. The authors observe that "among animals that live in the wild, the hair of which has never been cut, the tip retains its primitive form. We find the same condition in . . . the hair of women, as well as the pubic hair of both sexes." See *Le Poil de l'homme et des animaux* (Paris: G. Steinheil, 1910), 5.

14. Sigmund Freud, *Civilization and Its Discontents,* trans. and ed. James Strachey (New York: Norton, 1961).

15. Freud, *Essays on Sexuality,* in *The Standard Edition of the Complete Psychological Works of Sigmund Freud,* ed. James Strachey (New York: Norton, 1961), 7:155.

16. Elizabeth Gitter has treated these representations in her impressive survey, "The Power of Women's Hair in the Victorian Imagination," *Publications of the Modern Language Association* 99 (1984): 936–54.

17. Leo Bersani, *Baudelaire and Freud* (Berkeley and Los Angeles: University of California Press, 1977), 45.

18. Bersani is referring specifically to the concept of *Wunsch* in Freud's *Interpretation of Dreams*. See *Baudelaire and Freud,* 38.

19. Freud, *Civilization and Its Discontents,* 88.

Two or Three Things I Know

1. For a best-case account of opera's association with extravagance, see Herbert Lindenberger, *Opera: The Extravagant Art* (Ithaca: Cornell University Press, 1984). For suggestive readings of operatic extravagance in relation to social and sexual resistance, see the essays collected in *En Travesti: Women, Gender Subversion, Opera,* ed. Corinne E. Blackmer and Patricia Juliana Smith (New York: Columbia University Press, 1995). Carolyn Abbate's "Opera; or, the Envoicing of Women," in *Musicology and Difference,* ed. Ruth Solie (Berkeley and Los Angeles: University of California Press, 1993), 225–58, requires special comment and receives it in note 9, below.

2. Michel Foucault, *Discipline and Punish: The Birth of the Prison,* trans. Alan Sheridan (New York: Random House, 1979), 170–94.

3. Jacques Derrida, *Positions,* trans. Alan Bass (Chicago: University of Chicago Press, 1981), 41–42. Subsequent citations in text.

4. Derrida, "Différance," in his *Margins of Philosophy,* trans. Alan Bass (Chicago: University of Chicago Press, 1972), 17.

5. Avital Ronell, "Finitude's Score," in *Thinking Bodies,* ed. Juliet Flower McCannell and Laura Zakarin (Stanford: Stanford University Press, 1994), 87–108; quotation from 90–91.

6. Catherine Clément, *Opera, or the Undoing of Women,* trans. Betsy Wing (Minneapolis: University of Minnesota Press, 1988); Susan McClary, *Feminine Endings: Music, Gender, and Sexuality* (Minneapolis: University of Minnesota Press, 1991), 80–111.

7. Wayne Koestenbaum, *The Queen's Throat: Opera, Homosexuality, and the Mystery of Desire* (New York: Random House, 1993); Mitchell Morris, "Reading as an Opera Queen," in *Musicology and Difference,* ed. Solie, 184–200; idem, "On Gaily Reading Music," *repercussions* 1, no. 1 (1992): 48–64; Philip Brett, "Eros and Orientalism in Britten's Operas," in Brett, Elizabeth Wood, and Gary C. Thomas, eds., *Queering the Pitch: The New Gay and Lesbian Musicology* (New York: Routledge, 1994), 235–56; idem, "Britten's Dream," in *Musicology and Difference,* 259–80; idem, "Britten's Bad Boys: Male Relations in *The Turn of the Screw,*" *repercussions* 1, no. 2 (1992): 5–25; Elizabeth Wood, "Sapphonics," in *Queering the Pitch,* 27–66; idem, "Lesbian Fugue: Ethel Smyth's Contrapuntal Arts," in *Musicology and Difference,* 164–83.

8. Ralph Locke, "Constructing the Oriental 'Other': Saint-Saens's *Samson et Dalila,*" *Cambridge Opera Journal* 3 (1991): 261–302; McClary, *Georges Bizet: Carmen* (Cambridge: Cambridge University Press, 1992); Kramer, "Music and Cultural Hermeneutics: The Salome Complex," *Cambridge Opera Journal* 2 (1990): 269–94, reprinted, in revised and expanded form, in *Queen of Decadence: Salome and Modern Culture,* ed. Charles Bernheimer and Richard Kaye (Chicago: University of Chicago Press, forthcoming); idem, "*Fin-de-Siècle* Fantasies: *Elektra,* Degeneration, and Sexual Science," *Cambridge Opera Journal* 5 (1993): 141–66.

9. Abbate falsifies my argument about *Salome* in order to set it up as the binary opposite of her own, which she then asserts in unqualified form: "Strauss *rejects* the notion of operatic music as an objectifying gaze" (247, italics in original; this insistence on the simple truth, however complex its argumentative setting, is not what one would expect from a writer who claims to have "extensively used literary theory and postmodern philosophical and critical orientations in her work" [345]). It is worth noting that Abbate's most drastic falsification of my argument concerns, precisely, the decapitation scene that she takes as the crux of hers (248–52). Distortion aside, the problems with Abbate's argument are, first, its casual refusal to give any weight to the role of cultural codes and contexts in the production of meaning, and, second—again something unexpected in the framework of postmodern theory—its investment of such sovereignty in Strauss as a subject.

10. Foucault, *The History of Sexuality, Volume 1: An Introduction,* trans. Robert Hurley (New York: Random House, 1978), 95.

11. Walt Whitman, *Leaves of Grass,* ed. Sculley Bradley and Harold W. Blodgett (New York: Norton, 1973).

12. For more on the interrelations of opera and sexuality in Whitman, including further exploration of some of the themes and passages addressed in the present essay, see the sheaf of discussions in my *After the Lovedeath: Sexual Violence and the Making of Culture* (Berkeley and Los Angeles: University of California Press, 1997).

13. The role of the cornet in mediating between this scene and the orbic mouth of the primal tenor (large as creation) is intriguing enough to permit some speculation. The cornet assumes a virile character through its popularity as a military

band instrument, despite its "soprano" voice—which, in relation to Edgardo's cello, may almost have a visionary-transgressive value here resembling that of Lucia's flute. At the same time, the cornet's size and shape are such that, of all brass instruments, it brings the player's mouth, the "keys" (valves), and the bell into closest proximity. Its voice is thus literally closer than any other to the player's, which, correspondingly, comes closer than any other to singing through its "key'd" instrument.

14. Peter Rabinowitz, "'With Our Own Dominant Passions': Gottschalk, Gender, and the Power of Listening," *19th-Century Music* 16 (1993): 242–52.

15. On masochism and coldness, see Gilles Deleuze, *Coldness and Cruelty* (New York: Zone Books, 1989), 47–55, 69–80.

16. Jacques Lacan, *Four Fundamental Concepts of Psychoanalysis,* trans. Alan Sheridan (New York: Norton, 1978), 174–81, 263–76.

17. It is worth noting that, in the first edition of *Leaves of Grass* (1855), this passage lacked many of its most suggestive features: the blurred boundary between the soprano voice and the orchestra, the "breath"-"death" rhyme, and the key word "throttled." Although Whitman did sacrifice an image of being made to "gulp" by the throbbing of the music, his changes tend to expose rather than evade the oral impetus. For the original version, see *Walt Whitman's Leaves of Grass: His Original Edition,* ed. Malcolm Cowley (New York: Viking Press, 1959), 52.

18. Slavoj Žižek, *Looking Awry: An Introduction to Jacques Lacan Through Popular Culture* (Cambridge, Mass.: MIT Press, 1993), 88–96.

19. On magnetism and mesmerism in Whitman, see David S. Reynolds, *Walt Whitman's America: A Cultural Biography* (New York: Alfred A. Knopf, 1995), 259–62.

20. Sigmund Freud, *The Interpretation of Dreams,* trans. James Strachey (New York: Avon Books, 1965), 421.

21. Freud's construction of this chain of associations exemplifies the kind of reasoning that often infuriates empirically minded readers. The chain is not constructed by linking each well-grounded association to the next, but by filling in the gaps between the best-grounded associations. Evidential value is invested more in the associative pattern as a whole than in any of its components. This is hardly the place to present a rationale for this practice. Suffice it to say that the primary resources for filling associative gaps are language habits and practices, which are understood to inform all speech acts continuously. At issue in this case is the influence of a text so familiar in the milieu of Freud and his patient that Freud's expository paragraph does not bother to identify it; that everyone has it by heart goes without saying. I do not find this much of a stretch. From a latter-day perspective, however, one might also suggest that the resemblance between Schiller's phrase and the central dream image is indicative of the discursive positioning of homosexual desire in culture. Such desire, one might say, is always a gamble; and in the passage from the homosocial in Schiller to the homosexual in Freud's patient, the throw of the dice becomes something more violent, a throw of the body. This troping on the throw, implicit in the meaning of *Wurf,* also points to the pervasive theme of violence in the dream, which always positions the dreamer as victim.

22. Lacan, *Four Fundamental Concepts,* 197–99.

23. From Lacan, "Position de l'inconscient," in his *Ecrits* (Paris: Editions du

Seuil, 1966), 845; translation here from John Brenkman, "The Other and the One: Psychoanalysis, Reading, *The Symposium*," *Yale French Studies* 55–56 (1977): 420.

24. Ernst Kurth, *Selected Writings,* trans. Lee Rothfarb (Cambridge: Cambridge University Press, 1991), 104.

25. *Sigismund* was a generic derogatory term for a male Jew; it was, incidentally, Freud's original first name. On Wagner's anti-Semitism, see Marc A. Weiner, *Richard Wagner and the Anti-Semitic Imagination* (Lincoln: University of Nebraska Press, 1995); Paul Lawrence Rose, *Wagner: Race and Revolution* (New Haven: Yale University Press, 1993); Jean-Jacques Nattiez, *Wagner Androgyne: A Study in Interpretation,* trans. Stewart Spencer (Princeton: Princeton University Press, 1993). For more on the relationship of sexuality and anti-Semitism in the Ring, see my "The Waters of Prometheus: Nationalism and Sexuality in Wagner's *Ring*," in *The Work of Opera: Genre, Nationhood, and Sexual Difference,* ed. Richard Dellamora and Daniel Fischlin (New York: Columbia University Press, 1997); this essay also goes further into several of the topics touched on by the present essay, especially the nature of the desires binding Siegfried and Hagen and Brünnhilde and Siegfried.

26. Gutrune, however, is by no means the only object of desire that Siegfried addresses through the sexualized abuse of Brünnhilde; for more on the subject, see my "The Waters of Prometheus."

27. Freud, "The Relation of the Poet to Day-Dreaming," trans. I. F. Grant Duff, in Freud, *Character and Culture,* ed. Philip Rieff (New York: Macmillan, 1963), 43.

28. Philippe Lacoue-Labarthe, *Musica Ficta: Figures of Wagner,* trans. Felicia McCarren (Stanford: Stanford University Press, 1994), xv–xxii; Žižek, "'The Wound Is Healed Only by the Spear That Smote You . . . '" in his *Tarrying with the Negative: Kant, Hegel, and the Critique of Ideology* (Durham: Duke University Press, 1993), 165–99; Ronell, "Finitude's Score."

Staging the Female Body

1. Carolyn Abbate, *Unsung Voices: Opera and Musical Narrative in the Nineteenth Century* (Princeton: Princeton University Press, 1991), 119; Edward T. Cone, *Music; A View From Delft: Selected Essays,* ed. Robert P. Morgan (Chicago: University of Chicago Press, 1989), 125.

2. On modern dance, see Felicia McCarren, "The 'Symptomatic Act' circa 1900: Hysteria, Hypnosis, Electricity, Dance," *Critical Inquiry* 21 (1995): 748.

3. Mark 6: 14–29 and Matthew 14: 1–12. For a sense of the complexity of biblical and historical accounts of Herod Antipas, Herodias, Salome, and John the Baptist, see Françoise Meltzer, *Salome and the Dance of Writing: Portraits of Mimesis in Literature* (Chicago: University of Chicago Press, 1987), 29–41; see also René Girard, "Scandal and the Dance: Salome in the Gospel of Mark," *New Literary History* 15 (1984): 311–24. For Meltzer's response, see 325–32.

4. See Charles Michael Carroll, "Eros on the Operatic Stage: Problems in Manners and Morals," *Opera Quarterly* 1 (1983): 43.

5. For an extensive discussion of the first reviews, see Franzpeter Messmer, ed., *Kritiken zu den Uraufführungen der Bühnenwerke von Richard Strauss* (Pfaffenhofen: W. Ludwig, 1989), 30–68; Bryan Gilliam, ed., *Richard Strauss and His*

World (Princeton: Princeton University Press, 1992), 333–47; John Williamson, "Critical Reception," in *Richard Strauss: "Salome,"* ed. Derrick Puffett (Cambridge: Cambridge University Press, 1989), 131–44. Julius Korngold suggested in Vienna in 1907 that the popular success of the opera was proof of its inferior musical quality: great art "that is truly original and profound generally requires a longer period to put down roots" (cited in the Gilliam collection, 343). Strauss's personality was also at issue in the responses to the opera: he was no late romantic interested in "angst and introspection" (Robin Holloway, "*Salome:* Art or Kitsch?" in Puffett, *Richard Strauss: "Salome,"* 152). A craftsman, occupied with the business of music, and perhaps a worldly wise opportunist (when it came to audience response), Strauss had his defenders, however: "Strauss was not just a scat playing, money grubbing, haute bourgeois opportunist," wrote Kurt Wilhelm (*Richard Strauss: An Intimate Portrait,* trans. Mary Whittall [New York: Rizzoli International, 1989], 199). But the combination of his personality and his taste for writing mimetic music made those of other musical tastes recoil: Joseph Kerman calls the opera "insincere in every gesture, meretricious" (in *Opera as Drama* [1956; rev. ed., Berkeley and Los Angeles: University of California Press, 1988], 212).

6. On Beardsley's decadent attraction and "Japanese grotesque" response to the shocking nature of the play, see Chris Snodgrass, *Aubrey Beardsley: Dandy of the Grotesque* (Oxford: Oxford University Press, 1995), 52–54, 87, 276.

7. Cited in Derrick Puffett, introduction to *Richard Strauss: "Salome,"* 4.

8. Cited in Alan Jefferson, *The Operas of Richard Strauss in Britain, 1910–1963* (London: Putnam, 1963), 46.

9. See John Fludras, "Fatal Women: Exploring the Eternal Mystique of the Femme Fatale," *Opera News,* 12 February 1977, 15.

10. See Marie-Claire Hamard, "La Femme fatale: *Salome* et le *Yellow Book,*" *Cahiers Victoriens et Edouardiens* 36 (1992): 40.

11. Terry Eagleton, *The Illusions of Postmodernism* (Oxford: Blackwell, 1996), 25.

12. Elizabeth Grosz, *Volatile Bodies* (New York: Routledge, 1994), 5. For others, see Andreas Huyssen, *Twilight Memories: Marking Time in a Culture of Amnesia* (New York: Routledge, 1995), 165, especially the discussion of Peter Sloterdijk's *Critique of Cynical Reason* and his assertion that the Enlightenment had not been able to include the body and the senses in its emancipatory project.

13. See Joseph R. Roach, *The Player's Passion* (Cranbury, N.J.: Associated University Presses, 1985) on the theatricalization of the human body and its relation to medical, physiological discourses.

14. Puffett, introduction, 8.

15. Carolyn Abbate, "Opera; or, the Envoicing of Women," in *Musicology and Difference: Gender and Sexuality in Music Scholarship,* ed. Ruth A. Solie (Berkeley and Los Angeles: University of California Press, 1993), 234.

16. See Joseph R. Roach, "Power's Body: The Inscription of Morality as Style," in *Interpreting the Theatrical Past,* ed. Thomas Postlewait and Bruce McConachie (Iowa City: University of Iowa Press, 1989), 101: "Self-evidently, the signifying body is central to theatrical representation in any form. The techniques whereby the body is prepared for performance, the particular bodily expressions whereby the public accepts the truth of performance, and the imagery whereby the body is

eroticized in performance illuminate at any given cultural moment the relationships between sexuality and power."

17. Compare one musical commentator's "pudeur" about the body in Salome's famous dance: "Une voix nue, non un corps 'strip-teasé,' chante l'absence, hurle le silence, déroule l'écheveau du mystère" (Marie-Françoise Vieuille, "La Voix de Salomé ou la Danseuse," *Strauss: "Salome," L'Avant-scène Opéra* 47/48 [1983]: 140). The body is referred to as a "corps/voix" when it is significant; the body's voiceless dance is called a pseudo-dance (146).

18. Anthony Pym, "The Importance of Salomé: Approaches to a Fin-de-siècle Theme," *French Forum* 14 (1989): 312–13 offers statistical proof of this: 82 percent of the Salome images (in various art forms) appeared between 1860 and 1920, and Paris was the center of activity. The height was at the turn of the century. See also Meltzer (15–16) on how Salome has tended to rise into cultural consciousness at "decadent" moments.

19. "Elle dansa comme les prêtresses des Indes, comme les Nubiennes des cataractes, comme les bacchantes de Lydie." Flaubert, *Trois Contes* (Paris: Gallimard, 1966), 130.

20. Jules Massenet's 1881 opera, *Hérodiade,* is based on this story as scripted by Paul Milliet and Henri Grémont, but it eroticizes (by increasing Herod's lust for Salome) and sentimentalizes the plot considerably, making Salome into a daughter seeking the mother who has abandoned her and falling in (chaste) love with John the Baptist—who persuades her to love him "comme on aime en songe." He does eventually confess his love for her just before his execution, forbidding her to follow him in death. This Salome dances, but does so in order to beg for mercy for a John the Baptist sentenced to death. When the execution does take place nonetheless, Salome attacks Hérodias with a dagger, but turns it on herself when she learns that Hérodias is the mother she has been seeking. An opera about lust and religion, about erotic obsession and spirituality, it has some of the paradoxes we shall see in Strauss's opera, but Salome's relation to John here is chaste, spiritual, and sentimental—in short, a far cry from the later version. It has been argued by Richard Bizot ("The Turn-of-the-Century Salome Era: High and Pop-Cultural Variations on the Dance of the Seven Veils," *Choreography and Dance* 2 [1992]: 85), that Salome's "prominence at the outset of the century was symptomatic of two major strains of cultural influence just then intersecting: orientalism, with its overtures of 1890s decadence, and feminism."

21. See Julius Kaplan, *The Art of Gustave Moreau: Theory, Style, and Content* (Ann Arbor: UMI, 1982), 58–67.

22. See Pierre-Louis Mathieu, *Gustave Moreau: sa vie, son oeuvre* (Paris: Bibliothèque des arts, 1976), 16, 250 and "La religion dans la vie et l'oeuvre de Gustave Moreau," *Gustave Moreau et la Bible,* catalog for exhibit (Nice: Musée Nationale Message Biblique Marc Chagall, 1991), 16–17. In the reverse direction of literary/artistic influence, see Meltzer, 17–18, on how Flaubert's *Salammbô* had influenced Moreau's depiction of Salome. Moreau did 120 drawings of this work, 70 of them of Salome's body alone. See Mathieu, *Gustave Moreau,* 122.

23. J.-K. Huysmans, *Against Nature,* trans. Robert Baldick (London: Penguin, 1959), 64. "Elle commence la lubrique danse qui doit réveiller les sens assoupis du vieil Hérode; ses seins ondulent et, au frottement de ses colliers qui tourbillonnent,

leurs bouts se dressent; sur la moiteur de sa peau les diamants, attachés, scintillent" (*A Rebours* [Paris: Gallimard, 1977], 143). Inverting this process from image to dance, Peter Conrad, in *Romantic Opera and Literary Form* (Berkeley and Los Angeles: University of California Press, 1977), sees Strauss's dancing Salome as freezing into an "image"—in the sense that she is both narcissistic and self-absorbed (155) and a cult figure for later generations (173).

24. *Against Nature*, 65. "L'inquiétante exaltation de la danseuse, la grandeur raffinée de l'assassine" (*A Rebours*, 144).

25. *Against Nature*, 66. "Elle devenait, en quelque sorte, la déité symbolique de l'indestructible Luxure, la déesse de l'immortelle Hystérie, la Beauté maudite, élue entre toutes par la catalepsie qui lui raidit les chairs et lui durcit les muscles; la Bête monstrueuse, indifférente, irresponsable, insensible, empoisonnant, de même que l'Hélène antique, tout ce qui l'approche, tout ce qui la voit, tout ce qu'elle touche" (*A Rebours*, 144–45).

26. *Against Nature*, 66. "la danseuse . . . la femme mortelle . . . [le] Vase souillé, cause de tous les péchés et de tous les crimes" (*A Rebours*, 146).

27. *Against Nature*, 67. "repousse la terrifiante vision qui la cloue, immobile, sur les pointes" (*A Rebours*, 147).

28. *Against Nature*, 68. "Ici, elle était vraiment fille; elle obéissait à son tempérament de femme ardente et cruelle . . . ; elle réveillait plus énergiquement les sens en léthargie de l'homme, ensorcelait, domptait plus sûrement ses volontés, avec son charme de grande fleur vénérienne, poussée dans des couches sacrilèges, élevée dans des serres impies" (*A Rebours*, 148).

29. See Oscar Wilde, *The Picture of Dorian Gray* (London: Penguin, 1992), 147: "For years Dorian Gray could not free himself from the influence of this book. Or perhaps it would be more accurate to say that he never sought to free himself from it. . . . The hero, the wonderful young Parisian, in whom the romantic and the scientific temperaments were so strangely blended, became to him a kind of prefiguring type of himself. And, indeed, the whole book seemed to him to contain the story of his own life, written before he had lived it." For more on the impact of Huysmans's descriptions of Salome, see Megan Becker-Leckrone, "Salome ©: The Fetishization of a Textual Corpus," *New Literary History* 26 (1995): 239–40.

30. Richard Ellmann, *Oscar Wilde* (London: Hamish Hamilton, 1987), 321. His acquaintance with Mallarmé, who was writing his "Hérodiade" at the time, was another factor, as was his reading of J. C. Heywood's dramatic poem, published in England in 1888, which retold Heine's *Atta Troll* (where the phantom Herodias kisses the head of John the Baptist). He also studied many other visual representations of Salome (321–23).

31. *Against Nature*, 69. "Ses hiératiques et sinistres allégories aiguisées par les inquiètes perspicuités d'un nervosisme tout moderne" (*A Rebours*, 149). Not surprisingly, perhaps, others have been attracted to other allegorical readings. In *Salome and the Dance of Writing*, Meltzer reads Huysmans's descriptions of these two works as an allegory of the ontology of writing: "The Salome of Moreau and her verbal rendition by Huysmans, then, is a mimetic elaboration, both ideological and figural, of the logocentrism informing the writings of the Gospels" (43).

32. Geneviève Lacambre, *Gustave Moreau: Maître sorcier* (Paris: Gallimard/ Réunion des musées nationaux, 1997), 34; Mathieu, *Gustave Moreau*, 200.

33. Mathieu, *Gustave Moreau,* 202.

34. Gary Schmidgall, *Literature as Opera* (Oxford: Oxford University Press, 1977), 250–51; Patricia Kellogg-Dennis, in *Rediscovering Wilde,* ed. C. George Sandulescu (Gerrards Cross, U.K.: Colin Smythe, 1994), 225, suggests that Strauss may actually have been doing a "brilliant pastiche of turn of the century Decadent art."

35. For instance, Lawrence Kramer, in "Culture and Musical Hermeneutics: The Salome Complex," *Cambridge Opera Journal* 2 (1990): 284, sees Wilde as stagey and Strauss as sensationalist. Robin Holloway, in "Art or Kitsch?" sees the music as fleshing out Wilde's "flashy insubstantiality" (155). Writing in 1907, Robert Hirschfeldt (cited in Gilliam, *Richard Strauss and His World*) says: "Oscar Wilde's poetry is moonlight. In this airy magic, Richard Strauss installs the spotlights of his leitmotifs" (334).

36. Holloway, "Art or Kitsch?" 150.

37. See Hanna B. Lewis, "Salome and Elektra: Sisters or Strangers," *Orbis Litterarum* 31 (1976): 127 on the play as an "extended lyric"; Wilde himself thought of it as a ballad (see the letter to Lord Alfred Douglas from 2 June 1897 where he discusses his aim to make drama as personal as lyric poetry), as have critics since. See Richard Specht, *Richard Strauss und sein Werk,* vol. 2 (Leipzig: E. P. Tal, 1921), who opens his discussion of the piece with "Eine Ballade. Kein Drama."

38. This has frequently been commented upon: for example, throughout Stéphane Goldet's "Commentaire littéraire et musicale," in *Strauss, Salome. Quatres derniers Lieder, L'Avant-scène Opéra* 47–48 (1987): 55, 75, 102. Also to be considered in the impact, of course, would be the cuts Strauss made in Wilde's text (or rather to Lachmann's German translation of it), reducing the subplots, repetitions, political maneuverings in the name of structural symmetries and formal groupings of events. See Roland Tenschert, "Strauss as Librettist," in *Richard Strauss: "Salome",* and Tethys Carpenter, "Tonal and Dramatic Structure," in the same volume, 89–93.

39. On the disquieting erotic appeal of Salome as young girl, see Arthur Ganz, "Transformations of the Child Temptress: Mélisande, Salomé, Lulu," *Opera Quarterly* 5 (1987/1988): 13.

40. See Ellmann, *Oscar Wilde,* 232, 255.

41. See Puffett's "Postlude: Images of Salome," *Richard Strauss: "Salome"* 161–63.

42. The biblical Salome was not always portrayed this way, of course, and the history of these representations illuminates the choices made by Wilde. In the New Testament accounts, the dancer is simply referred to as the (unnamed) daughter of Herodias; her function is simply to be the tool of her mother's desire to have John the Baptist executed. There is no mention of the play's incestuous attraction of Herod to Salome or of her violent desire for John the Baptist. But the biblical Salome takes on more character, so to speak, over the centuries, with the increased veneration of John. By the fourth century, she had become a symbol of evil for her role in his martyrdom, though the major focus in both the literary and visual arts is on the death of the Baptist, of which she is simply the agent. The Church fathers used her story to underline the evils of dancing, as explained by Kerstin Merkel, *Salome: Ikonographie im Wandel* (Frankfurt am Main: Peter Lang, 1990), 2–3; and

Helen Grace Zagona, *The Legend of Salome and the Principle of Art for Art's Sake* (Geneva: Droz; Paris: Minard, 1960), 20. By the Middle Ages, the dancing scene was inspiring religious artists who used it as a moral warning; by the Renaissance, however, Salome had simply become the image of the graceful young dancer. It was not, in fact, until the late nineteenth century that Salome took on her femme fatale identity, thanks to that postromantic French obsession with her and her body.

43. See Hamard, "La Femme fatale," 29. On Salome's appeal, see also Patrick Bade, *Femme Fatale: Images of Evil and Fascinating Women* (London: Ash and Grant, 1979), 6: "This preoccupation with evil and destructive women is one of the most striking features of late nineteenth-century culture. The theme was all pervasive, appealing to men of opposing artistic creeds, symbolists and realists, rebels and reactionaries, and penetrating deeply into the popular consciousness." On the danger element, see Rebecca Stott, *The Fabrication of the Late-Victorian Femme Fatale: The Kiss of Death* (London: Macmillan, 1992).

44. Fludras, "Fatal Women," 15.

45. See Paul Kluckhohn, *Die Auffassung der Liebe in der Literatur des 18. Jahrhunderts und in der deutschen Romantik* (1922; reprint, Tübingen: Max Niemeyer, 1966), 213–14 on the German Sturm und Drang construction of woman as either "das einfache natürliche Weib" or "das Machtweib" or femme fatale.

46. Fludras, "Fatal Women," 15; see also Hamard, "La Femme fatale," 46.

47. Kramer, "Culture," 271. Bade, in fact, calls her "the paedophile's femme fatale" (16). See also Tim McCracken, "Redeeming Salome: The Face in the Figure," unpublished manuscript, on the links between the nineteenth-century notions of children and the twentieth-century Lolita figure. For him, Salome is the "Ur-nymphet."

48. See J. E. Chamberlin, *Ripe Was the Drowsy Hour: The Age of Oscar Wilde* (New York: Seabury Press, 1977) on both the narcissism of Wilde's Salomé (105, 175–76, 178) and her contradictions: "the confusion of evil and pride and beauty and horror" (179).

49. See Goldet, "Commentaire littéraire et musicale," 64–65.

50. William Mann, *Richard Strauss: A Critical Study of the Operas* (London: Cassell, 1974), 54.

51. Paul Banks, "Richard Strauss and the Unveiling of *Salomé*," in *Salome/Elektra*, ed. Nicholas John (New York: Riverrun Press, 1988), 11.

52. See Moreau, *L'Assembleur de rêves: Ecrits complets de Gustave Moreau* (Fontfroide: Bibliothèque Artistique et Littéraire, Fata Morgana, 1984), on "Salome dansant devant Hérode": "Cette femme que représente la femmet éternelle . . . à la recherche de son idéal vague, souvent terrible. . . . C'est l'emblème de cet avenir terrible, réservé aux chercheurs d'idéal sans nom, de sensualité et de curiosité malsaine" (78). Modern French commentators on the opera use similar language, interestingly. See Martial Petitjean, "Symbolisme et sacrifice," *L'Avant-scène Opéra*, 132: "Définir Salomé par la banale perversion d'une cruauté capricieuse serait n'en rien saisir. Salomé représente au vrai l'idéal féminin, porté à sa dimension métaphysique la plus effroyable . . . [E]lle crée l'angoisse totale."

53. See Bram Dijkstra, *Idols of Perversity: Fantasies of Feminine Evil in Fin-de-Siècle Culture* (Oxford: Oxford University Press, 1986), 283. For a very different

view of Wilde's Salome as related to the androgyn in fin-de-siècle associations of both virginity (and sterility) and lechery, see Chamberlin, *Ripe Was the Drowsy Hour,* 173, 175–76. We feel that the operatic Salome is definitely coded as *female* and also as young (rather than androgynous), given the resonance with contemporary medical discourses.

54. Cesare Lombroso and William Ferrero, *Female Offender* (New York: Philosophical Library, 1958), 151. On the importance of Lombroso and the Italian school of criminal anthropology to this view of women in general, see Ruth Harris, "Melodrama, Hysteria, and Feminine Crimes of Passion in the Fin-de-Siècle," *History Workshop* 25 (1988): 32.

55. Roy Porter, "The Body and the Mind, the Doctor and the Patient: Negotiating Hysteria," in *Hysteria beyond Freud,* ed. Sander L. Gilman et al. (Berkeley and Los Angeles: University of California Press, 1993), 251.

56. For more on this, see Harris, "Melodrama, Hysteria," 32, 52.

57. Havelock Ellis, *Man and Woman: A Study of Human Secondary Sexual Characters* (London: Walter Scott, 1899), 307, paraphrasing Clouston's "Developmental Insanities."

58. See Ellis: "Whenever a woman commits a deed of criminal violence, it is extremely probable that she is at her monthly period" (255).

59. Ellis, 256.

60. Henry Maudsley, *The Physiology and Pathology of Mind,* 2nd ed. (London: Macmillan, 1868), 341. See also John Haslam, *Considerations on the Moral Management of Insane Persons* (London: R. Hunter, 1817), 4–5; George Man Burrows, *Commentaries on Insanity* (London: Underwood, 1828), 146. In addition to these, Porter cites German psychiatrist Wilhelm Griesinger (254–55) on the linking of the erotic and menstrual to hysteria.

61. "The Decadent movement was nocturnal and avoided the harsh light of conscience. Its unspeakable acts and intoxicating dreams required the cover of dark. What light the Decadents needed the moon could supply," according to Schmidgall, *Literature as Opera,* 254.

62. His eyes are said to be like lakes upon which mad moonlight flickers ("irres Mondlicht flackert"); his black hair is like the dark nights when the moon is hidden.

63. August Forel, *The Sexual Question,* trans. C. F. Marshall (London: Rebman, 1908), 225–26. For further discussion, see Harry Campbell, *Differences in the Nervous Organization of Man and Woman: Physiological and Pathological* (London: H. K. Lewis, 1891), 200; and Ellis, *Man and Woman,* 254 on erotomania. The Mosher survey in the United States also looked at this conjunction at this time. See Clelia Duel Mosher, *The Mosher Survey: Sexual Attitudes of Forty-Five Victorian Women,* ed. James MaHood and Kristine Wenburg (New York: Arno Press, 1980).

64. See Ernest Newman, *More Opera Nights* (London: Putnam, 1954): "In a final ecstasy of perversion her mind cracks" (36); Michael Kennedy, *Richard Strauss* (Oxford: Oxford University Press, 1976), 143–44, sees the opera as "a study in obsession." See also François-René Tranchefort, "Le mythe subverti," in *L'Avant-scène Opéra,* 127 on her "psychose délirante."

65. Charcot's private belief, however, that hysteria was "toujours la chose géni-

tale" was never really publically admitted. See Marth Noel Evans, *Fits and Starts: A Genealogy of Hysteria in Modern France* (Ithaca: Cornell University Press, 1991), 26–28.

66. Ellis, referring to Conolly Norman and Charcot, 281. Cf. Pierre Janet's somewhat different linking (in 1907) of hysteria to a variety of psychic symptoms, from somnambulism to suggestion, in *The Major Symptoms of Hysteria* (2nd ed. New York: Macmillan, 1929). For a full history of the meanings of hysteria from ancient times to Freud, see Gilman et al., eds., *Hysteria beyond Freud*.

67. Maudsley, *Physiology,* 287.

68. Banks, "Richard Strauss," 11. The music itself has been called nervous and even neurotic. See Theodor W. Adorno, "Richard Strauss, Part Two," *Perspectives of New Music* 4 (1966) on Strauss's "artistic morality of nervousness": "'Nervous' was a catchword of the modern style. It covers what since Freud has been called 'neurotic,' pathogenic disturbances resulting from repression, as well as Ibsen's doomed utopia of hysterical women who, foreign to the reality principle and powerless, protest against the *contrainte sociale.* Nervousness becomes a sign of prestige, denoting the greatly intensified and differentiated reactive capacity of the person who becomes his own precision instrument, who is defenselessly abandoned to the world of sensation and who, through this defenselessness, accuses the gross way of the world" (115).

69. Grosz, *Volatile Bodies,* 157–58, in response to Foucault's interpretation of the "hystericization of women's bodies."

70. See Elaine Showalter, *The Female Malady: Women, Madness, and English Culture, 1830–1980* (New York: Pantheon, 1985). Susan McClary, in *Feminine Endings: Music, Gender, and Sexuality* (Minneapolis: University of Minnesota Press, 1991), 99, uses Showalter's thesis of nineteenth-century madness as a "female malady" to read Salome's mental state as explicitly linked to excessive female sexuality. In "Hysteria, Feminism, and Gender," in *Hysteria beyond Freud,* ed. Gilman et al., 286–344, Showalter shows how both the treatment and historical accounts of hysteria as the potential condition of all women have been informed by traditional gender roles in which the male is the therapist and the female, the patient. See also Mark S. Micale, "Hysteria Male/Hysteria Female: Reflections on Comparative Gender Construction in Nineteenth-Century France and Britain," in *Science and Sensibility: Gender and Scientific Inquiry,* ed. Marina Benjamin (Oxford: Blackwell, 1991), 200–39; see also Evans, *Fits and Starts,* esp. 2–3.

71. "The sexual instinct is very much less intense in woman than in man," claims Campbell (210). Krafft-Ebing adds: "Woman, however, if physically and mentally normal, and properly educated, has but little sensual desire" (14); Eric Trudgill, in *Madonnas and Magdalens: The Origins and Development of Victorian Sexual Attitudes* (London: Heinemann, 1976), explains the medical profession's role in promoting anxiety about sex in the nineteenth century, in part by assuming women to be asexual and willing to submit to their husband's sexual needs only to please them and to procreate (50–63).

72. See Thomas Szasz, *Sex: Facts, Frauds, and Follies* (Oxford: Blackwell, 1980), 16.

73. Forel, *The Sexual Question,* 97.

74. Dijkstra, *Idols,* 249; Krafft-Ebing, 483; Forel, 227.

75. As recounted by Strauss himself in "Reminiscences of the First Performance of My Operas," in *Recollections and Reflections,* ed. Willi Schuh, trans. L. J. Laurence (London: Boosey and Hawkes, 1953), 151.

76. Cited in Williamson, "Critical Reception," 131–32.

77. For an acute and pointed analysis of Wilde's reception, especially in Germany and Austria, and on the links between Wilde's homosexuality and the Jewish theme of the play and opera, see Sander L. Gilman, "Opera, Homosexuality, and Models of Disease: Richard Strauss's *Salome* in the Context of Images of Disease in the Fin-de-Siècle," in his *Disease and Representation: Images of Illness from Madness to AIDS* (Ithaca, N.Y.: Cornell University Press, 1988), esp. 156–62.

78. See Elgna Adam and Laurent Worms, "Salomé au pays des hommes," in *L'Avant-scène Opéra,* 156 on the fear of symbolic castration that Salome represents.

79. Ronald Pearsall, *The Worm in the Bud* (London: Pimlico-Random House, 1969), 85.

80. Gary Schmidgall, "Imp of Perversity," *Opera News,* 12 February 1977, 13. David Murray, in s.v. "Salome," (*The New Grove Dictionary of Opera*), describes the orchestra here as adding "one gross dissonance like an obscene jeer."

81. Craig Ayrey, "Salome's Final Monologue," in *Richard Strauss: "Salome,"* 117. See also one of the few vaguely complimentary things Adorno ever said about Strauss: "His ability to compress the plenitude of emotions, including those which are incompatible, into isolated complexes, to fit the up and down oscillation of feeling into a single instant, has no prototype" ("Richard Strauss," 117).

82. Ayrey, "Salome's Final Monologue," 118–19 quite bizarrely connects these keys with the "moralistic and repressive world of orthodoxy" (which he strangely associates with the decadent court of Herod) and "sincerity and innocence."

83. See Catherine Clément, "Désir de sainte," in *L'Avant-scène Opéra,* 124, on the chaste but desirous Salome.

84. The dance is named by Wilde, but takes its name from the Babylonian myth of Ishtar, claims Becker-Leckrone, "Salome ©," 254–55.

85. Marjorie Garber, *Vested Interests: Cross-Dressing and Cultural Anxiety* (New York: HarperPerennial, 1993), 341. While the literary tradition had been silent about the details of the dance, the visual arts had filled in the blanks admirably. Salome's dance had changed with the changing conventions of the times—from medieval maenadic frenzy to Renaissance innocent elegance. Moreau and other nineteenth-century artists took the unnamed biblical dancer and made her into the demonic femme fatale we know today. See Torsten Hausamann, *Die tanzende Salome in der Kunst vor der christlichen Frühzeit bis um 1500* (Zürich: Juris Druck, 1980); Danièle Devynck, "'La Saulterelle déshonnête'" in *Salomé dans les collections françaises,* 18; Merkel, *Salome,* 13. On the entry of the sexual into the representations in the nineteenth century, see Bruno Serrou, "Mille et un regards sur Salomé," program of Opéra de Paris Bastille's 1994 *Salome,* 18.

86. Murray, "Salome," 147. On the Hollywood aspects and what is seen as failed exoticism, see Goldet, "Commentaire littéraire et musicale," 88–89.

87. See appendix to Puffett, *Richard Strauss: "Salome,"* 165–66.

88. Abbate, "Opera; or, the Envoicing of Women," 241.

89. Strauss, "Reminiscences," 151.

90. Kramer, "Culture," 281.

91. For the most interesting description of the music as vulgar, mediocre, and frankly bad, as "bargain-basement orientalism" that works dramatically nonetheless, see Holloway, "Art or Kitsch?" where it is argued that by "sheer genius" Strauss raises "[s]ustained, masterly, deeply-thrilling" (149) "kitsch to *Kunst*" (157).

92. Admittedly, many directors do come closer to Strauss's wishes, preferring a dance of almost static swaying that leaves most to the imagination. It may depend on the skill (and appearance) of the singer, of course.

93. On gender and dance, see Elizabeth Dempster, "Women Writing the Body: Let's Watch a Little How She Dances," in *Bodies of the Text: Dance as Theory, Literature as Dance,* ed. Ellen W. Goellner and Jacqueline Shea Murphy (New Brunswick: Rutgers University Press, 1995), 21–38.

94. Banks, "Richard Strauss," 15.

95. For an extended discussion of this tension, see Peter W. Schatt, *Exotik in der Musik des 20. Jahrhunderts: Historische-systematische Untersuchungen zur Metamorphosen einer aesthetischen Fiktion* (Munich: Musikverlag Emil Katzbichler, 1986), esp. 18–22. Of course, luxury and cruelty are not the only associations with the East at this or any other time in history: spirituality was another, and very different, connection.

96. See Chamberlin, *Ripe Was the Drowsy Hour,* 177, on the associations in nineteenth-century Europe with dance as "pessimistic and diseased."

97. Kramer, "Culture," 279.

98. On Charcot and Richer's representations, see Sander L. Gilman, "The Image of the Hysteric, " in *Hysteria beyond Freud,* esp. 359–74.

99. See Christoph-Hellmut Mahling, "'Schweig' und tanze!' Zum 'tönenden Schweigen' bei Richard Strauss," in *Die Sprache der Musik: Festschrift Klaus Wolfgang Niemöller,* ed. Jobst Peter Fricke (Regensburg: Gustav Bosse, 1989) for more on Loïe Fuller's 1895 "Salome" dance to Gabriel Pierné's music; in 1907 Florent Schmitt (on a libretto by Robert d'Humières) wrote a ballet for Fuller's troupe called "La Tragédie de Salomé" in two acts with seven tableaux; Maud Allan's "Die Vision Salome" was performed in Vienna in 1906—the year before Strauss's opera first played there.

100. See McCarren, "Symptomatic Act," 752.

101. Dempster, "Women Writing the Body," 27–28.

102. In the 1907 Metropolitan Opera production, the dancing Salome was portrayed by a diminutive dancer (Bianca Froelich), while the singing Olive Fremstad weighed in at about 250 pounds. As one unkind critic noted, it was as if "some antifat remedy had worked wonders for a few minutes and then suddenly lost its potency." Cited in Bizot, "Turn of the Century Salome Era," 73.

103. Conrad, *Romantic Opera and Literary Form,* 156.

104. Of course, a completely different interpretation is offered by Joseph Kerman, in *Opera as Drama,* who finds it a "*gemütlich* bellydance" at which he does not know "whether to laugh or cry" (211). Others see it as prefiguring the end of the opera, like a dance before human sacrifice: "la dance, comme exhibition déréglée, dislocation du corps, porte en soi le démembrement, et annonce la décapitation de Jean-Baptiste" (Petitjean, "Symbolisme et sacrifice," 134).

105. Amy Koritz, *Gendering Bodies/Performing Art: Dance and Literature in*

Early Twentieth-Century British Culture (Ann Arbor: University of Michigan Press, 1995), 81.

106. See Jeffrey Wallen, "Illustrating *Salomé:* Perverting the Text?" *Word and Image* 8 (1992): 124 on how the dramatic action of the play "aligns the field of vision with the body and with sexual desire, in contrast with the verbal field, which is aligned with the immaterial and the supersensual."

107. See Garber, *Vested Interests,* on the "binary myth of Salome": "the male gazer (Herod), the female object of the gaze (Salome); the Western male subject as spectator (Flaubert, Huysmans, Moreau, Wilde himself) and the exotic, feminized Eastern other" (340). That the myth is far from this simple will be clear shortly, we hope.

108. Petitjean, "Symbolisme et sacrifice," 132. See also Bradley Bucknell, "On 'Seeing' Salome," *ELH* 60 (1993): 515 on the "complex interplay between the eye and the object of vision." For others on the gaze, see Clément, "Désir de sainte," 125–26; Philippe Godefroid, "Le regard interdit," in *L'Avant-scène Opéra,* 146–49.

109. See especially chapter 1, "The Noblest of the Senses: Vision from Plato to Descartes," in Jay's *Downcast Eyes: The Denigration of Vision in Twentieth-Century French Thought* (Berkeley and Los Angeles: University of California Press, 1993), 21–82.

110. For a full discussion of this theme, see John Berger, *Ways of Seeing* (Harmondsworth: Penguin, 1972); Norman Bryson, *Vision and Painting: The Logic of the Gaze* (New Haven: Yale University Press, 1983).

111. Craig Owens, "The Discourse of Others: Feminism and Postmodernism," in *The Anti-Aesthetic: Essays on Postmodern Culture,* ed. Hal Foster (Seattle: Bay Press, 1983), 58.

112. Laura Mulvey, "Visual Pleasure and Narrative Cinema," *Screen* 16 (1975): 11.

113. See Jay for extended analyses of postmodern discourses on the negativity of the gaze, including a cogent treatment of Foucault's critique of ocularcentrism (384–416) and on the film theory debate over gender and the gaze of the camera (489–91, 588–89, 591–92).

114. Wilde's less innocent Salomé says she knows why, but Strauss cut this line. The importance of it for Wilde's text has been argued in Tres Pyle, "Extravagance, or Salomé's Kiss," guest lecture at University of Toronto, 22 October 1997.

115. It isn't surprising that, when the unseen Jochanaan first speaks from the cistern, his words concern vision—as well as hearing: the two senses crucial to the staged operatic form. He speaks of Christ who will come and will make the eyes of the blind see the day and will open the ears of the deaf ("die Augen der Blinden den Tag sehn . . . die Ohren der Tauben geöffnet").

116. His first condemnation of Herodias is because she gave in to the lust of her eyes and looked upon painted images of men ("die sich hingab der Lust ihrer Augen, die gestanden hat vor buntgemalten Männerbildern"). Whether she looked at erotic images or simply at images women should not have seen, the link between the erotic and the visual is reinforced.

117. Ayrey, "Salome's Final Monologue," 109, 113.

118. This power is aural as well as visual. It is not (as Kramer, "Culture," 280,

has argued) at the end when she kisses Jochanaan's mouth that Salome is permitted a "triumphant incorporation of the male power of speech," for which she must die. She has that power earlier and she attains it specifically through being looked at. After the dance Herod loses his verbal power and is reduced to echoing Salome's words and music ("In einer Silberschüssel"; "einen Eid geschworen"); so too does Herodias ("Du has einen Eid geschworen"). As Salome insists on her reward in the form of Jochanaan's head, Herod repeatedly protests that she isn't listening to him ("Du hörst nich zu, du hörst nicht zu") and indeed she isn't, for he has lost the power to command her listening.

119. John Paul Riquelme, "Shalom/Solomon/Salomé: Modernism and Wilde's Aesthetic Politics," *The Centennial Review* 39 (1995): 596.

120. Kramer, "Culture," 277–78; Abbate, "Opera; or, the Envoicing of Women," 254.

121. While the visual dominates the text and the aural takes over our ears, all the senses contribute to the representation of Salome's staged physicality: "Salome . . . illustrates desire in so far as desire is figured as bodily, sensual, unmediated, and visible, rather than as hidden, veiled, mediated" (Wallen, "Illustrating *Salomé*, 129–30). This is a world "where religious order merges into sexual desire and all the senses are synaesthetically exploited and deranged" (Conrad, *Romantic Opera*, 159). Salome is seen before being heard; Jochanaan is heard before being seen (Koritz, *Gendering Bodies*, 79). But other senses are invoked as well: Salome goes from wanting to speak to Jochanaan to wanting to see him to wanting to touch his body and hair and kiss his lips. After getting her lethal wish, she addresses the head in terms that mix the senses: his voice is associated with incense ("Deine Stimme war ein Weihauchgefäss"), his physical image with music. She describes her desire for him in terms of thirst and hunger—that neither rivers nor lakes can relieve ("Nicht die Fluten, noch die grossen Wasser können dieses brünstige Begehren löschen").

122. Notice the strange conflation there: the public is said to stare at the music. Hirschfelt (in 1907) cited by Gilliam, *Richard Strauss and His World*, 334.

123. Schmidgall, "Imp," 13. On an early attack on the musical decadence of Strauss's tonal practice, see Walter Klein, "Die Harmonisation in *Elektra* von Richard Strauss," *Der Merker* 2 (1911): 512–14.

124. McClary, *Feminine Endings*, 100.

125. Schmidgall, *Literature as Opera*, 281; Murray, "Richard Strauss," 569.

126. Chamberlin suggests that this ambivalent response characterizes the audience's reaction to the play's dance scene too: "we watch Salome's dance with appropriately perverse fascination, unable to avoid a shivery sense that *Salome* embodies something to which we are mysteriously vulnerable, something like the inseparability of Beauty from Decay and Death. And we develop a set of strategies for maintaining ourselves in a kind of delicious moral and rational suspension in the face of this mystery." "From High Decadence to High Modernism," *Queen's Quarterly* 87 (1980): 606.

127. Holloway, "Art or Kitsch?" 149.

128. *Against Nature*, 68. In the French: "Tel que le vieux roi, des Esseintes demeurait écrasé, anéanti, pris de vertige, devant cette danseuse" (*A Rebours*, 148).

129. Mireille Dottin, "Le développement du 'Mythe de Salome," in *Salome dans les collections françaises*, 14. Klimt's 1907 painting called *Judith* has also been

named after Salome. See Eva di Stefano, *Il complesso di Salomé: la donna, l'amore e la morta nella pittura di Klimt* (Palermo: Sellerio, 1985). Strauss himself said that, in the world of Klimt, he saw much of his own music, "especially Salome." As cited in Schmidgall, *Literature as Opera*, 286.

130. Abbate, "Opera; or, the Envoicing of Women," 254.

131. For a different, psychoanalytic reading that, in blunt terms, argues that to decapitate equals to castrate, see Sigmund Freud's brief essay, "Medusa's Head" in *The Standard Edition of the Complete Psychological Works of Sigmund Freud,* ed. James Strachey (London: Hogarth Press and the Institute of Psycho-Analysis, 1955), 18:273–74.

132. Salome's death has been seen as both a "misogynist anxiety dream" and a "patriarchal wish-fulfilment" by Kramer, "Culture," 279. See Chamberlin, "From High Decadence," 604: "Decadent art went to the limit . . . and created conditions in which we might enjoy images of the most harrowing and depraved of human experiences. In going to this limit, it deliberately tested the character and conditions of aesthetic appeal."

"Souless Machines" and Steppenwolves

1. Hermann Hesse, *Steppenwolf,* trans. Basil Creighton, Joseph Mileck, and Horst Frenz (New York: Henry Holt and Company, 1990), 30. My reading of *Steppenwolf* is based in part on the discussion in Marc A. Weiner, *Undertones of Insurrection: Music, Politics, and the Social Sphere in the Modern German Narrative* (Lincoln and London: University of Nebraska Press, 1993), 101–50.

2. Hesse, 135–36.

3. Hesse, 31.

4. Hesse, 62–64. The entanglement between Haller's interactions with music and women is evident in his remarks about Maria: "I had always wanted mind and culture in the women I had loved, and I had never remarked that even the most intellectual and, comparatively speaking, educated women never gave any response to the Logos in me, but rather constantly opposed it. I took my problems and my thoughts with me to the company of women, and it would have seemed utterly impossible to love a girl for more than an hour who had scarcely read a book, scarcely knew what reading was, and could not have distinguished Tchaikovsky from Beethoven. Maria had no education. She had no need of these circuitous substitutes. Her problems all sprang directly from the senses. . . . The first shy dance I had had with her had already told me this much" (142–43).

5. Richard Taruskin, "The Golden Age of Kitsch," *The New Republic,* 21 March 1994, 36. For an excellent introduction to *Jonny spielt auf,* along with an account of its origins and reception, see Susan C. Cook, *Opera for a New Republic: The Zeitopern of Krenek, Weill, and Hindemith* (Ann Arbor: UMI, 1988), 76–114. For more general background on the period, see Stephen Hinton, *The Idea of Gebrauchsmusik: A Study of Musical Aesthetics in the Weimar Republic (1919–1933) with Particular Reference to the Works of Paul Hindemith* (New York: Garland Press, 1989), and Bryan Gilliam, ed., *Music and Performance during the Weimar Republic* (Cambridge: Cambridge University Press, 1994).

6. Hesse, 37. For the purposes of this essay, I will retain the free contemporary

usage of the term "jazz" to characterize a broad range of imported and homegrown styles and mannerisms associated with American dance musics. See J. Bradford Robinson: "Jazz Reception in Weimar Germany: In Search of a Shimmy Figure," *Music and Performance during the Weimar Republic,* ed. Gilliam, 107–34; and his "The Jazz Essays of Theodor Adorno: Some Thoughts on Jazz Reception in Weimar Germany," *Popular Music* 13, no. 1 (1994): 1–25.

7. Andreas Huyssen, *After the Great Divide: Modernism, Mass Culture, Post-modernism* (Bloomington and Indianapolis: Indiana University Press, 1986), 44–62. Some recent studies of Ives, Futurism, and the "anxiety of influence" have further explored the relevance for musical modernism of this gendered notion of the authentic art work, marked by its autonomy and by its resistance to the "seductive lure" of the masses. See Susan McClary, *Feminine Endings: Music, Gender, and Sexuality* (Minnesota: University of Minnesota Press, 1991), 17–18; Catherine Parsons Smith, "'A Distinguishing Virility': Feminism and Modernism in American Art Music," in *Cecilia Reclaimed: Feminist Perspectives on Gender and Music,* ed. Susan C. Cook and Judy S. Tsou (Urbana: University of Illinois, 1994), 90–106; Judith Tick, "Charles Ives and Gender Ideology," in *Musicology and Difference: Gender and Sexuality in Music Scholarship,* ed. Ruth A. Solie (Berkeley and Los Angeles: University of California Press, 1993), 83–106; and Lloyd Whitesell, "Men with a Past: Music and the 'Anxiety of Influence,'" *Nineteenth-Century Music* 18, no. 2 (1994): 152–67.

8. On foreign violinists in Weimar popular-music circles, see Robinson, "The Jazz Essays of Theodor Adorno," 5. Quotations from the libretto are taken from the translation in the program booklet by Gerry Bramall, from Ernst Krenek, *Jonny spielt auf,* Gewandhausorchester Leipzig/Lothar Zagrosek (London [Decca Record Company] 436 631–2, 1993). Subsequent references to the libretto will be given in the text.

9. Huyssen, *After the Great Divide,* 48–50.

10. Ernst Krenek, *Exploring Music,* trans. Margaret Shenfield and Geoffrey Skelton (London: Calder and Boyars, 1966), 23–24; translation modified.

11. Cornelius Partsch, "Hannibal Ante Portas: Jazz in Weimar," in *Dancing on the Volcano,* ed. Thomas W. Kniesche and Stephen Brockmann (Columbia, S.C.: Camden House, 1994), 108.

12. For a useful introduction to the large literature on these topics, see Kniesche and Brockmann, eds., *Dancing on the Volcano.* My discussion is indebted in particular to the essays by Beeke Sell Tower ("'Ultramodern and Ultraprimitive': Shifting Meanings in the Imagery of Americanism in the Art of Weimar Germany," 85–104), Mary Nolan ("Imagining America, Modernizing Germany," 71–84), and Jost Hermand ("*Neue Sachlichkeit:* Ideology, Lifestyle, or Artistic Movement?" 57–67). See also Detlev J. K. Peukert, *The Weimar Republic: The Crisis of Classical Modernity,* trans. Richard Daveson (New York: Hill and Wang, 1987), 178–90.

13. The question of modern performances of the opera is still a subject of debate. Critics such as Susan Cook have suggested that the portrayal of Jonny "would probably prohibit the work's performance today in the United States" (*Opera for a New Republic,* 86). However, Glenn Watkins has suggested that "a review of the terms which marked the original productions of *Four Saints* and *Jonny* should assist in removing the taint of a racist manifesto that has been periodically charged to

both and perhaps encourage a return of *Jonny* in particular to the stage today"; Watkins, *Pyramids at the Louvre: Music, Culture, and Collage from Stravinsky to the Postmodernists* (Cambridge and London: The Belknap Press of Harvard University, 1994), 160.

14. See Cook, *Opera for a New Republic*, 92.

15. Ernst Krenek, *Horizons Circled: Reflections on My Life in Music* (Berkeley: University of California Press, 1974), 38–39.

16. For a further discussion of this exchange, see Cook, *Opera for a New Republic*, 85. See also Krenek, "Musik in der Gegenwart," in *25 Jahre neue Musik* (Vienna: Universal Edition, 1925), 43–58, and Schoenberg's response in Arnold Schoenberg, "Krenek für leichte Musik: zu Artikel Kreneks im Jahrbuch Musik in der Gegenwart," dated 26 February 1926; Archives of the Arnold Schoenberg Center, Vienna.

17. John L. Stewart, *Ernst Krenek: The Man and His Music* (Berkeley and Los Angeles: University of California Press, 1991), 11–12.

18. Krenek, *Exploring Music*, 116–17.

19. See McClary, *Feminine Endings*, 107–9.

20. Huyssen, *After the Great Divide*, 54; see also Judith Butler, *Gender Trouble: Feminism and the Subversion of Identity* (New York and London: Routledge, 1990), 57–78.

21. Max Brod, "Women and the New Objectivity," orig. pub. 1929; reprinted in *The Weimar Republic Sourcebook*, ed. Anton Kaes, Martin Jay, and Edward Dimendberg (Berkeley and Los Angeles: University of California Press, 1994), 205–6.

22. Krenek, *Exploring Music*, 118–19.

23. Arnold Schoenberg, *Theory of Harmony*, trans. Roy E. Carter (Berkeley and Los Angeles: University of California Press, 1978), 96. See McClary, *Feminine Endings*, 11–12; and Jennifer Shaw, "Androgyny and the Eternal Feminine in Schoenberg's Oratorio *Die Jakobsleiter*," in *Political and Religious Ideas in the Works of Arnold Schoenberg*, ed. Charlotte Cross (New York: Garland Press, 2000).

24. "Ernst Kreneks Jazz-Oper: Jonny spielt auf," *Neue Zeitschrift für Musik* 94 (1927): 169.

25. Beyond this one aria, the libretto says little directly about what sort of opera Max has written. Yet the fact that Anita needs a banjo for her part—also necessitating the banjo case that will serve an important dramatic function—and indications that the opera turns out to be a "huge success" hint that Max's opera and Krenek's might sound quite similar.

26. Cook points out the Schoenberg reference in *Opera for a New Republic*, 85.

27. Cook, *Opera for a New Republic*, 85, 101.

28. David Lewin, "Women's Voices and the Fundamental Bass," *Journal of Musicology* 10, no. 4 (1992): 469.

29. Ernst Krenek, *Music Here and Now* (1939; reprint, New York: Russell and Russell, 1967), 86.

30. Ivan Goll, "The Negroes Are Conquering Europe" (orig. pub. 1926), in *The Weimar Sourcebook*, 560; and Kurt Pinthus, "Masculine Literature" (1929), in *The Weimar Sourcebook*, 518–19.

31. See Susan Cook, "Jazz as Deliverance: The Reception and Institution of

American Jazz during the Weimar Republic," *American Music* 7 (1989): 40, and see Weiner, *Undertones of Insurrection,* 101–50.

32. Cook, *Opera for New Republic,* 86–88, 105. For a discussion of Lawrence Tibbett's portrayal of black characters, including Jonny, on American stages, see David Metzer, "'A Wall of Darkness Dividing the World': Blackness and Whiteness in Louis Gruenberg's *The Emperor Jones*," *Cambridge Opera Journal* 7, no. 1 (1995): 55–72.

33. Krenek, *Horizons Circled,* 38; and Stewart, *Ernst Krenek,* 82. An extensive essay on *Jonny spielt auf* from 1928 discusses the figure of Jonny in the context of a wide range of nineteenth- and twentieth-century literary works, including *Steppenwolf:* see Rudolf Majut, "Kreneks Jonny-Dichtung im geistesgeschichtlichtlichen Zusammenhang des Weltschmerzes und des Rousseauismus," *Germanisch-Romanische Monatsschrift* 16 (1928), 437–58.

34. Herbert Peyser, "Jonny over There," *Modern Music* 6, no. 29 (1928): 34.

35. Cited in Sell Tower, "'Ultramodern and Ultraprimitive,'" 93–94.

36. That such links were made is evident in Herbert Peyser's essay on the coming American première of *Jonny:* "*Jonny spielt auf* (and I say this with no reference whatever to its sleazy musical qualities) is a good, home-grown European's assurance of his own jazzification. The people who believe it a veracious representation of influences from the general direction of Sandy Hook are, after all, just sons and daughters of the generation which was easily persuaded that red Indians roamed Broadway and that lions mingled with the shoppers on Twenty-Third street. They get out of it some of the same vicarious thrill that part of our best domesticated ladyhood derives from the topographical tea-shops of Alice Macdougall, where flappers and matrons can take nourishment amid tailor-made illusions of Italy and Spain." Peyser, "Jonny over There," (1928), 33.

37. Stephen Brockmann argues that the "rejection of all forms of romantic ideology" following World War I, "went along with the rejection of women themselves, since for male avant-gardists the ideology of love was specifically female and effeminate." See Brockmann, "Weimar Sexual Cynicism," in *Dancing on the Volcano,* 170.

38. Hesse, *Steppenwolf,* 37–38.

39. Hesse, 61. And see Weiner, *Undertones of Insurrection,* 140–49.

40. Krenek, *Exploring Music,* 24. Compare also Krenek's remark that Jonny was "the fulfillment of a wish dream, for I felt that all these elements, which I admired so greatly and passionately desired to acquire for myself, were really foreign to my nature"; cited in Stewart, *Ernst Krenek,* 82.

41. Cited in Stewart, *Ernst Krenek,* 87.

42. Ernst Krenek, *Horizons Circled,* 26.

43. Taruskin, "The Golden Age of Kitsch," 37.

44. See Cook, *Opera for New Republic,* 90–101.

45. Carolyn Abbate has defined phenomenal music as "singing that is heard by its singer, the auditors on stage, and understood as 'music that they (too) hear' by us, the theater audience"; *Unsung Voices: Opera and Musical Narrative in the Nineteenth Century* (Princeton: Princeton University Press, 1991), 5.

46. Krenek, *Horizons Circled,* 26. A commentary by Adolph Weissmann indicates that some critics also heard the work this way, "he gives us romanticism of the

old style, which has been interpreted by some of his most faithful followers as parody but which he, however, means literally." Weissmann, "Germany's Latest Music Dramas," *Modern Music* 4 (1926–1927): 24.

47. Abbate, *Unsung Voices,* 134.

48. Compare to Eric Lott's discussion of blackface minstrelsy: "the spectator may intermittently have identified with black characters—he had to if the minstrel show was to have its impact—but he always knew what he was not: a slave, whether of wages or of the plantation; *he* was no feminized (proletarian) subaltern. Here was a convenient fiction born in part of male panic, a gendered fantasy of renewed mastery over inferiors whose blandishment the mechanic enjoyed and whose pleasure he commanded." Lott, *Love and Theft: Blackface Minstrelsy and the American Working Class* (New York and Oxford: Oxford University Press, 1993), 197.

49. See Krenek, *Music Here and Now,* 85–86. For more on the autobiographical aspects of the work, see Cook, *Opera for a New Republic,* 77–90; and Stewart, *Ernst Krenek,* 80–89.

"Grimes Is at His Exercise"

1. "Neither a Hero nor a Villain," *Radio Times,* 8 March 1946, 3; reprinted in Brett, ed., *Benjamin Britten: "Peter Grimes"* (Cambridge: Cambridge University Press, 1983), 152 (subsequently referred to as *PBPG*).

2. Joseph Kerman, *Opera as Drama* (New York: Knopf, 1956), 13. Kerman preserves this credo word for word in a recent revised edition (Berkeley and Los Angeles: University of California Press, 1988), 10; but in a new epilogue he significantly modifies the verbal constructions, e.g., "There seem to me to be three principal means [defining character, generating action, and establishing atmosphere] by which music can *contribute* to drama" (215, my italics).

3. Philip Reed, "Finding the Right Notes," in *MPG,* 79.

4. See Philip Reed's "A *Peter Grimes* Chronology, 1941–1945," in *MPG,* 21ff; the idea of making an opera out of Crabbe's poetry existed by 29 July 1941; the first mention of the title is in a letter from Isherwood to Britten (18 February 1942) about the novelist's not seeing "any possibility of collaborating with you and Peter on the PETER GRIMES libretto."

5. Britten as quoted in R. Murray Schafer, *British Composers in Interview* (London: Faber and Faber, 1963), 116–17.

6. See, for example, Michael Kennedy, *Britten* (London: Dent, 1981), 123–24. For a general essay on the complicity of pacifism and homosexuality in Britten, see Robin Holloway, "The Church Parables (II): Limits and Renewals," in *The Britten Companion,* ed. Christopher Palmer (London: Faber and Faber, 1984), 215–26.

7. For the most recent and detailed account, see Humphrey Carpenter, *Benjamin Britten: A Biography* (London: Faber and Faber, 1992), 152–58.

8. E. M. Forster, "George Crabbe: The Poet and the Man," *The Listener,* 29 May 1941; reprinted in *PGPB,* 4. The copy of Crabbe's works that Peter Pears bought that summer, most likely on a trip to Los Angeles, and that he and Britten marked up, is preserved in the Britten-Pears Library.

9. See Mitchell in *PBPG,* 34–36, and in Donald Mitchell and Philip Reed, eds., *Letters from a Life: Selected Letters and Diaries of Benjamin Britten* (London: Faber

and Faber, 1991), 979–80 (henceforth *LFAL*). In his letter to Britten, Isherwood went so far as to say "and frankly, the subject doesn't excite me so much that I want to *make* time for it"; in a letter to Donald Mitchell in 1981 he wrote, "I was absolutely convinced it wouldn't work"; and in conversation with me at his home in Santa Monica in 1977 he admitted that he had found the story homophobic.

10. "George Crabbe and Peter Grimes," a lecture given at the Aldeburgh Festival, 1948; reprinted in *Two Cheers for Democracy* (London: Edward Arnold and Company, 1951), 186; also in *PBPG*, 16.

11. *The Borough*, Letter XXII, lines 69–78.

12. Ronald B. Hatch, *Crabbe's Arabesque: Social Drama in the Poetry of George Crabbe* (Montreal: McGill-Queen's University Press, 1976), 108.

13. *Time*, 16 February 1948.

14. For a more detailed account, including the music as well as the libretto, see my "'Fiery Visions' (and Revisions): *Peter Grimes* in Progress," in *PBPG*, 47–87.

15. An early scenario in Pears's hand, designated L5 in *MPG*, 173–75; also printed in *PBPG*, 50.

16. *LFAL*, 1189.

17. This is the final version, only slightly revised (largely by the interpolation of that particular chorus stanza) from the original draft.

18. Stage directors, who are often unaware of the social implications of the opera, frequently omit the crucial "knocking at the other door": for example, Elijah Moshinsky in the 1981 Covent Garden peformance available on laser disc (Montvale, N.J.: Pioneer Artists, 1982), as well as John Copley in the 1998 revival of an old San Francisco Opera production—otherwise very realistic—that prompted my ideas about the opera when I first saw it in 1973 while reading Denis Altman's *Homosexual: Oppression and Liberation* (New York: Avon Books, 1971).

19. See *MPR*, 65–66, for the source citations for these quotations.

20. Montagu Slater, *Peter Grimes and Other Poems* (London: John Lane, 1946), 43. This publication, undertaken perhaps to reclaim something of what Slater felt he had lost in revision, acts as a control on what he sanctioned in that process. At the beginning of the hut scene (Act II, scene 2), however, he included a two-stanza aria with refrain, amounting to an extra twenty lines, which is not to be found in *any* of the documents at Aldeburgh. It must therefore have been written expressly for the publication, in contradiction of the prefatory remark that "the present text is to all intents and purposes the one to which the music was composed." In his "The Story of the Opera" for the Sadler's Wells booklet on the work, Slater uses his own version in quoting Peter's entire existing aria, even though he must have agreed to many of the changes in the vocal score: see Eric Crozier, ed., *Benjamin Britten: "Peter Grimes,"* Sadler's Wells Opera Books, no. 3 (London: Sadler's Wells, 1945), 23–24. Crozier informs us that Slater's book was on sale side by side with the libretto at Sadler's Wells during the first run of performances (in *Opera Quarterly* 10 [1994]: 16).

21. This was in 1981, I believe, as I was completing my earlier study of the sources. I did not fully understand the remark at the time, and could not bring myself to ask Pears to elaborate—his statement sounded so final and perfect and unassailable.

22. Edward Sackville-West, "The Musical and Dramatic Structure," in *Benjamin Britten: "Peter Grimes,"* ed. Eric Crozier, 44.

23. *The New Statesman,* 9 and 16 June 1945; reprinted in *PGPB,* 155.

24. Tippett in interview with Humphrey Carpenter, *Benjamin Britten: A Biography,* 200.

25. *Europe without Baedeker* (New York: Farrar, Straus and Giroux, 1947); reprinted in *PGPB,* 162.

26. *Three Psychoanalytic Notes on "Peter Grimes,"* ed. Christopher Wintle (London: King's College Institute of Advanced Musical Studies), 13, 43; "what the music clearly shows" is derived from Pears's statement, which Keller quotes, that "[Grimes] is not a sadist nor a demonic character, and the music quite clearly shows that" (*Radio Times,* 8 March 1946). One of the most interesting aspects of Keller's document is its open letter to the (plural) "Authors of *Peter Grimes*" (34), and the care with which Keller acknowledges Pears's contribution here and in his published writings on the opera.

27. The "two paragraphs" occur at the beginning of his "*Peter Grimes:* The Story, the Music not Excluded," in *Benjamin Britten: A Commentary on His Works from a Group of Specialists,* ed. Mitchell and Keller (London: Rockcliff, 1952); reprinted in *PGPB,* 105.

28. *Benjamin Britten: A Biography,* 210. To be fair, Keller falls into a similar trap. His scholarly instincts alerted him to the fact that the quotations in Slater's essay in the Sadler's Wells booklet represented an earlier stage: "The best means of immediately showing now that when we associate, in Peter's mind, his apprentices (children substitutes) with his father we are not forcing our ideas upon the drama, is to inspect a passage which occurs in a former version" (*Three Psychoanalytic Notes,* 30). On the next page he even allows himself to say that a psychoanalytic observer would have guessed as much anyway, but "would have been reproached with giving free reign to his phantasies." The use of the child-as-father-of-the-man ploy to evade pederasty and pin aggression on the unresolved Oedipal complex is of course a breathtaking move.

29. The writer Colin MacInnes, who at the time had sex with men without considering himself homosexual, confided to his private notebook in the late 1940s: "The theme and tragedy of P. Grimes is homosexuality and, as such, the treatment is quite moving, if a bit watery. Grimes is the homosexual hero. The melancholy of the opera is the melancholy of homosexuality." See Tony Gould, *Inside Outsider: The Life and Times of Colin MacInnes* (London: Chatto and Windus, 1983), 82.

30. Žižek, *The Sublime Object of Ideology* (London: Verso, 1989), 127; in the more Lacanian terms Žižek he tends to use "what is excluded from the Symbolic (from the frame of the corporatist socio-symbolic order) returns in the Real as a paranoid construction of the 'Jew.'"

31. For an account, see H. Montgomery-Hyde, *The Love that Dared not Speak Its Name: A Candid History of Homosexuality in Britain* (Boston: Little, Brown and Company, 1970).

32. See Alan Sinfield, "Private Lives/Public Theater: Noel Coward and the Politics of Homosexual Representation," *Representations* 36 (fall 1991): 43–63; and also his *Literature, Politics, and Culture in Postwar Britain* (Berkeley and Los Angeles: University of California Press, 1989), especially chapters 5 and 13.

Index